# CRITICAL SURVEY OF POETRY

# British
# Renaissance
# Poets

*Editor*

**Rosemary M. Canfield Reisman**
*Charleston Southern University*

SALEM PRESS
A Division of EBSCO Publishing, Ipswich, Massachusetts

Cover photo:
*Sir Walter Ralegh* (© PoodlesRock/Corbis)

ISBN: 978-1-42983-657-9

# CONTENTS

# CONTRIBUTORS

Rosemary Ascherl
*Colchester, Connecticut*

Elizabeth J. Bellamy
*Winthrop College*

Robert E. Boenig
*Texas A&M University*

Mary De Jong
*Pennsylvania State
University*

Desiree Dreeuws
*Sunland, California*

Robert P. Ellis
*Worcester State College*

Kenneth Friedenreich
*Dana Point, California*

C. Herbert Gilliland
*United States Naval
Academy*

Sidney Gottlieb
*Sacred Heart University*

Katherine Hanley
*St. Bernard's Institute*

B. G. Knepper
*Sioux City, Iowa*

Rebecca Kuzins
*Pasadena, California*

John F. McDiarmid
*New College of Florida*

Edmund Miller
*Long Island University*

Gerald W. Morton
*Auburn University-
Montgomery*

Elizabeth Spalding Otten
*Manchester, New Hampshire*

Robert M. Otten
*Marymount University*

Samuel J. Rogal
*Illinois State University*

Charlotte Spivack
*University of Massachusetts,
Amherst*

Gary F. Waller
*Wilfrid Laurier University*

Marie Michelle Walsh
*College of Notre Dame of
Maryland*

Eugene P. Wright
*North Texas State University*

# ENGLISH POETRY
# IN THE SIXTEENTH CENTURY

The poetry of the sixteenth century defies facile generalizations. Although the same can obviously be said for the poetry of other periods as well, this elusiveness of categorization is particularly characteristic of the sixteenth century. It is difficult to pinpoint a century encompassing both the growling meter of John Skelton and the polished prosody of Sir Philip Sidney, and consequently, past efforts to provide overviews of the period have proven unhelpful. Most notably, C. S. Lewis in his *English Literature in the Sixteenth Century Excluding Drama* (1954) contrived an unfortunate division between what he called "drab" poetry and "Golden" poetry. What he means by this distinction is never entirely clear, and Lewis himself further confuses the dichotomy by occasionally suggesting that his own term "drab" need not have a pejorative connotation, although when he applies it to specific poets, it is clear that he intends it to be damaging. Furthermore, his distinction leads him into oversimplifications. As Lewis would have it, George Gascoigne is mostly drab (a condition that he sees as befitting a poet of the "drab" mid-century) though blessed with occasional "Golden" tendencies, while Robert Southwell, squarely placed in the "Golden" period, is really a mediocre throwback to earlier "drab" poetry. Such distinctions are hazy and not helpful to the reader, who suspects that Lewis defines "drab" and "Golden" simply as what he himself dislikes or prefers in poetry.

The muddle created by Lewis's terminology has led to inadequate treatments of the sixteenth century in the classroom. Perhaps reinforced by the simplicity of his dichotomy, teachers have traditionally depicted the fruits of the century as not blossoming until the 1580's, with the sonneteers finally possessing the talent and good sense to perfect the experiments with the Petrarchan sonnet form first begun by Sir Thomas Wyatt early in the century. Students have been inevitably taught that between Wyatt and Sidney stretched a wasteland of mediocre poetry, disappointing primarily because so many poets failed to apply their talents to continuing the Petrarchan experiments begun by Wyatt. Thus, indoctrinated in the axiom that, as concerns the sixteenth century, "good" poetry is Petrarchan and "bad" poetry is that which fails to work with Petrarchan conceits, teachers deal in the classroom mostly with the poets of the 1580's and later, ignoring the other poetic currents of the early and mid-century. It has been difficult indeed to overcome Lewis's dichotomy of "drab" and "Golden."

Fortunately, there have been studies of sixteenth century poetry that are sensitive to non-Petrarchan efforts, and these studies deserve recognition as providing a better perspective for viewing the sixteenth century. In 1939, Yvor Winters's essay "The Sixteenth Century Lyric in England: A Critical and Historical Reinterpretation" focused on some of the less notable poets of the period, such as Barnabe Googe, George Turberville, and

Gascoigne, who, until Winters's essay, had been dismissed simply because they were not Petrarchan in sentiment, and the essay also helped to dispel the notion that the aphoristic, proverbial content of their poetry was symptomatic of their simple-mindedness and lack of talent. By pointing out how their sparse style contributes to, rather than detracts from, the moral content of their poetry, Winters's essay is instrumental in helping the reader develop a sense of appreciation for these often overlooked poets. In addition to Winters's essay, Douglas L. Peterson's book *The English Lyric from Wyatt to Donne: A History of the Plain and Eloquent Styles* (1967), taking up where Winters left off, identified two major poetic currents in the sixteenth century: the plain style and the eloquent style. Peterson provided a more realistic and less judgmental assessment of the non-Petrarchans as practitioners of the "plain" rhetorical style, a term that was a welcome relief from Lewis's "drab." Thus, Winters's and Peterson's efforts were helpful in destroying the damaging stereotypes about the "bad" poets of the mid-century.

### POETRY AS CRAFT

Despite the difficulties inherent in summarizing a century as diverse as the sixteenth, it is possible to discern a unifying thread running through the poetry of the period. The unity stems from the fact that, perhaps more than any other time, the sixteenth century was consistently "poetic"; that is, the poets were constantly aware of themselves as poetic craftsmen. From Skelton to Edmund Spenser, poets were self-conscious of their pursuits, regardless of theme. This poetic self-consciousness was manifested primarily in the dazzling display of metrical, stanzaic, and prosodic experimentation that characterized the efforts of all the poets, from the most talented to the most mediocre. In particular, the century experienced the development of, or refinement upon, for example, the poulter's measure (alternate twelve-and fourteen-syllable lines), blank verse, heroic couplets, rime royal, ottava rima, terza rima, Spenserian stanza, douzains, fourteeners—all appearing in a variety of genres. Characteristic of the century was the poet watching himself be a poet, and every poet of the century would have found himself in agreement with Sidney's assessment of the poet in his *Defence of Poesie* (1595) as prophet or seer, whose craft is suffused with divine inspiration.

### SOCIAL CONTEXT

This process of conscious invention and self-monitoring is one key to understanding the poetry of the sixteenth century. It is a curious fact that whereas in other periods, historical and social factors play a large role in shaping poetic themes, in the sixteenth century, such extraliterary influences did little to dictate the nature of the poetry. Surprisingly, even though Copernicus's theory of a heliocentric universe was known by mid-century, the poetry barely nodded to the New Science or to the new geographical discoveries. Certainly, the century experienced almost constant political and religious turbulence, providing abundant fare for topical themes; a less apolitical period one can hardly imagine. It was the prose, however, more than the poetry, that sought to record the buffetings created by the fact that the official religion in England changed four times between 1530 and 1560.

It seems that the instability created by this uneasiness had the effect of turning the poets inward, rather than outward to political, social, and religious commentary (with the exceptions of the broadside ballads, pseudojournalistic poems intended for the uncultivated, and the verse chronicle history so popular at the close of the century), bearing out the hypothesis that good satire can flourish only in periods of relative stability. For example, despite the number of obvious targets, the genre of political satire did not flourish in the sixteenth century, and its sporadic representatives, in particular anticlerical satire, a warhorse left over from the Middle Ages, are barely noteworthy. A major figure in Spenser's *The Faerie Queene* (1590, 1596) is Gloriana, a figure depicting Queen Elizabeth, but she is an idealized rendering, only one of many such celebrations in poetry of Queen Elizabeth, not intended to provide a realistic insight into her character.

### RISE OF VERNACULAR LANGUAGES

Thus, to the poet of the sixteenth century, the primary consideration of the poetic pursuit was not who or what to write about, but rather how to write. The reason for this emphasis on style over content is simple enough to isolate. By the middle of the sixteenth century, the English language was experiencing severe growing pains. In fact, throughout Europe the vernacular was struggling to overthrow the tyranny of Latin and to discover its essential identity. Nationalism was a phenomenon taking root everywhere, and inevitably, the cultivation of native languages was seen as the logical instrument of expediting the development of national identity. Italy and France were undergoing revolts against Latin, and Joachim du Bellay's *La Défense et illustration de la langue française* (1549; *The Defence and Illustration of the French Language*, 1939) proclaimed explicitly that great works can be written in the vernacular. In England, the invention of new words was encouraged, and war was waged on "inkhornisms," terms of affectation usually held over from the old Latin or French, used liberally by Skelton. Thus, George Puttenham, an influential critical theorist of the period, discusses the question of whether a poet would be better advised to use "pierce" rather than "penetrate," and Richard Mulcaster, Spenser's old headmaster, was moved to announce, "I honor the Latin, but I worship English."

It was no easy task, however, to legislate prescribed changes in something as malleable as language, and the grandeur of the effort nevertheless often produced comic results. Sixteenth century English vernacular, trying to weed out both Latin and French influences, produced such inelegant and uneasy bastardizations as "mannerlier," "newelties," "hable" (a hangover from Latin *habilis*), and "semblably," leading William Webbe in his *Discourse of English Poetry* (1586) to rail in a sneering pun about "this brutish poetry," with "brutish" looming as a veiled reference to "British." Although the sixteenth century was constantly discovering that the subtleties of perfecting a new language could not be mastered overnight, the effort was nevertheless sustained and paved the way for a future confidence in what the vernacular could achieve. Words that often strike the modern reader as outdated, stodgy pedantry are, in fact, the uncertain by-products of innovative experimentation.

Thus, to understand sixteenth century poetry is to ignore the stability of language, which is taken for granted in later centuries, and to understand the challenge that the poets experienced in shaping the new language to fit their poetry. Working with new words meant changes in the old classical syntax, and, in turn, changes in the syntax meant changes in the old classical versifications. These changes often resulted in frustration for the poet (and for the reader), but, depending on the skills of the poet, the result of all this experimentation could mean new rhyme schemes, new meters, and new stanzaic structures. In the wake of all the excitement generated by this constant experimentation, the poets cannot be blamed for often judging innovations in content as secondary to the new prosody. The volatility and flux of the language siphoned all energies into perfecting new styles not into content.

### TRANSLATIONS

The zeal for metrical experimentation that characterized the sixteenth century is manifested not only in the original poetry of the period but also in the numerous translations that were being turned out. The primary purpose of the translations was to record the works of the venerable authorities in the new vernacular, and it is significant that Webbe refers to these works not as being "translated" but as being "Englished." Vergil's *Aeneid* (c. 29-19 B.C.E.; English translation, 1553) was a favorite target for the translators, with Henry Howard, the earl of Surrey, publishing a translation in 1553, Thomas Phaer in 1558, and Richard Stanyhurst in 1582. Stanyhurst translated only the first four books, and he achieved a metrical monstrosity by attempting to translate Vergil in English hexameters, reflecting the tensions of cramming old subject matter into new forms. Ovid was another favorite of the translators. Arthur Golding translated the *Metamorphoses* (c. 8 C.E.; English translation, 1567) in 1567, and also in that year, Turberville translated the *Heroides* (before 8 C.E.; English translation, 1567), featuring elaborate experiments with the poulter's measure, fourteeners, and blank verse. Most of the translations of the period may be dismissed as the works of versifiers, not poets (with the exception of George Chapman's Homer, which has the power of an original poem), but they are valuable reflections of the constant metrical experimentations taking place and, subsequently, of the ongoing process of shaping the new vernacular.

### LITERARY THEORY

An overview of the poetry of the 1500's would be incomplete without an introduction to the critical theory of the period and the ways in which it recorded the successes and failures of the new vernacular experimentations. Not surprisingly, critical theory of the age was abundant. An obvious representative is Sidney's *Defence of Poesie*. The elegance and polish of this argument for the superiority of poetry over any other aesthetic pursuit has made it the most outstanding example of Renaissance critical theory. The easy grace of the work, however, tends to obscure the fact that the new experiments in prosody had created a lively, often nasty debate in critical theory between the guardians of the old and the spokespersons for the new. There were many other works of critical theory closer than the *Defense of Poesie* to the pulse rate of the arguments.

The turbulent nature of the critical theory of the period (and, by implications, the turbulence of the poetry itself) is reflected by Gascoigne, who in his "Certayne Notes of Instruction Concerning the Making of Verse" (1575) serves as a hearty spokesperson for the new vernacular, advocating a more widespread use of monosyllables in poetry and a rejection of words derived from foreign vocabularies so that "the truer Englishman you shall seem and the less you shall smell of the inkhorn," and decrying poets who cling to the old Latin syntax by placing their adjectives after the noun. In his *Art of English Poesy* (1589), Puttenham scolds those poets who "wrench" their words to fit the rhyme, "for it is a sign that such a maker is not copious in his own language." Not every critic, however, was so enchanted with the new experimentation. In his *Art of Rhetorique* (1553), Thomas Wilson called for continued practice of the old classical forms, and he sought to remind poets that words of Latin and Greek derivation are useful in composition. Contempt for new techniques in versification pervades Roger Ascham's *The Schoolmaster* (1570). He condemns innovations in rhyming, which he dismisses as derived from the "Gothes and Hunnes," and calls for renewed imitation of classical forms. In his *Discourse of English Poetry* (1586), William Webbe is even less charitable. He scorns the new experiments in prosody as "this tinkerly verse," and he campaigns for keeping alive the old, classical quantitative verse, in which the meter is governed by the time required to pronounce a syllable, not by accentuation. Clearly the severity of the critical debate needs to be kept in the forefront as one begins consideration of the poetry of the period; to fail to do so is to overlook what the poets were trying to accomplish.

### ALLEGORIES AND DREAM VISIONS

The opening of the sixteenth century, however, was anything but a harbinger of new developments to come. Like most centuries, the sixteenth began on a conservative, even reactionary note, looking backward to medieval literature, rather than forward to the new century. Allegories and dream visions written in seven-line stanzas, favorite vehicles of the medieval poets, dominated the opening years of the sixteenth century. Under Henry VII the best poets were Scottish—William Dunbar, Gavin Douglas, and Sir David Lyndsay—and they were devoted imitators of Geoffrey Chaucer. The first English poet to assert himself in the new century was Stephen Hawes, who published *The Pastime of Pleasure* in 1509 which represented uninspired medievalism at its worst. The work is constructed as a dream-vision allegory. An almost direct imitation of John Lydgate's work, *The Pastime of Pleasure* narrates the hero Grand Amour's instruction in the Tower of Doctrine, employing a profusion of stock, allegorical characters reminiscent of the morality plays. The old medieval forms, especially those combining allegory and church satire, were hard to die. In 1536, Robert Shyngleton wrote *The Pilgrim's Tale*, a vulgar, anticlerical satire directly evocative of Chaucer, and as late as 1556, John Heywood wrote *The Spider and the Fly*, a lengthy allegory depicting the Roman Catholics as flies, the Protestants as spiders, and Queen Mary as wielding a cleanig broom.

## JOHN SKELTON

Another heavy practitioner of the dream allegory was John Skelton (c. 1460-1529), one of the most puzzling figures of the century. Skelton has long been an object of negative fascination for literary historians—and with good reason. He deserves a close look, however, because, despite his reactionary themes, he was the first metrical experimenter of the century. His paradoxical undertaking of being both metrical innovator and medieval reactionary has produced some of the oddest, even comic, poetry in the English language. His infamous Skeltonic meter, a bewildering mixture of short, irregular lines and an array of varying rhyme schemes, relies on stress, alliteration, and rhyme, rather than on syllabic count, and as a result, the reader is left either outraged or amused. His subject matter was inevitably a throwback to earlier medieval themes. He wrote two dream-vision allegories, *The Bowge of Court* (1499), a court satire, and *The Garlande of Laurell* (1523). Skelton is still read today, however, because of his fractured meter. The theme of his *Collyn Clout* (1522), a savage satire on the corruption of the English clergy (whose title, incidentally, was the inspiration for Spenser's *Colin Clouts Come Home Againe*, 1591), is of interest to the modern reader not so much for its content as for its versification. In the work, Skelton describes his own rhyme as being "Tatterèd and jaggèd/ Rudely rain-beaten/ Rusty and moth-eaten." Skelton's rhyme arrives fast and furious, and it is possible to conclude that he may have been the object of Puttenhm's attack on poets who "wrench" their words to fit the rhyme.

### CONTINENTAL INFLUENCES

Despite his original metrical experimentation, Skelton was still entrenched in inkhornisms and looked backward for his themes. Paradoxically, as is often the case, it can be the poet with the least talent who nevertheless injects into his poetry vague hints of things to come. Alexander Barclay wrote no poetry of the slightest worth, but embedded in the mediocrity lay the beginnings of a new respect for the vernacular. To the literary historian, Barclay is of interest for two reasons. First, he was the sixteenth century's first borrower from the Continent. Specifically, in his *Certayn Egloges* (1570), he was the first to imitate the eclogues of Mantuan, which were first printed in 1498 and which revolutionized the genre of the pastoral eclogue by making it a vehicle for anticlerical satire, although such satire was of course nothing new in England at that time. Barclay's second importance, however (and perhaps the more significant), lies in the fact that he was the first to use the vernacular for the pastoral.

## TOTTEL'S MISCELLANY

It was not until mid-century that English borrowings from the Continent were put on full display. In 1557, a collection of lyrics known as *Tottel's Miscellany* was published, and the importance of this work cannot be overemphasized. It was innovative not only in its function as a collection of poems by various authors, some of them anonymous, but also in the profusion of prosodic experimentation that it offered. *Tottel's Miscellany* represented nothing less than England's many-faceted response to the Continental Renaissance. In this collection, every conceivable metrical style (including some strange and not wholly successful experiments with structural alliteration) was attempted in an array of genres, including sonnets, epigrams, elegies, eulogies, and poems of praise and Christian consolation, often resulting in changes in the older Continental forms. Truly there is no better representation of poets self-consciously watching themselves be poets.

Nevertheless, unfair stereotypes about the collection abound. Perhaps because of Lewis's distinction between "drab" age and "Golden" age poetry, students are often taught that the sole merit of *Tottel's Miscellany* is its inclusion of the lyrics of Wyatt and Surrey (which had been composed years earlier)—in particular, their imitations of the amatory verse of Petrarch. The standard classroom presentation lauds Wyatt and Surrey for introducing Petrarch and his sonnet form into England. Students are further taught that the long-range effects of *Tottel's Miscellany* proved to be disappointing since no poet was motivated to continue Wyatt's and Surrey's experiments with Petrarch for decades thereafter. Thus, *Tottel's Miscellany* is blamed for being essentially a flash-in-the-pan work lacking in any significant, literary influence. Such disappointment is absurdly unjustified, however, in view of what the publisher Richard Tottel and Wyatt and Surrey were trying to accomplish. Tottel published his collection "to the honor of the English tong," and in that sense the work was a success, as the conscious goal of all its contributors was to improve the vernacular. Furthermore, its most talented contributors, Wyatt and Surrey, accomplished what they set out to do: to investigate fully the possibilities of the short lyric, something that had never before been attempted in England, and, in Surrey's case, to experiment further with blank verse and the poulter's measure.

By no stretch of the imagination did Wyatt view himself as the precursor of a Petrarchan movement in England, and he made no attempt to cultivate followers. In fact, despite the superficial similarity of subject matter, Wyatt's poetry has little in common with the Petrarchan sonneteers of the close of the century, and he most assuredly would have resented any implication that his poetry was merely an unpolished harbinger of grander efforts to come. As Douglas L. Peterson has pointed out, Wyatt used

Petrarch to suit his own purposes, mainly to perfect his "plain" style; and Yvor Winters maintains that Wyatt is closer to Gascoigne than Sidney. Whereas the sonneteers of the close of the century composed decidedly in the "eloquent" style, Wyatt expressed contempt for trussed-up images and pursued the virtues of a simple, unadorned style.

### PLAIN STYLE

Thus, far from attempting to initiate a new "movement" of Petrarchan eloquence, many of the poems in *Tottel's Miscellany* sought to refine the possibilities of the plain style. As Peterson defines it, the plain style is characterized by plain, proverbial, aphoristic sentiments. It is a style often unappreciated by modern readers because its obvious simplicity is often mistaken for simplemindedness. The practitioners of the plain style, however, were very skilled in tailoring their verse to fit the needs of the poem's message, the pursuit of simplicity becoming a challenge, not a symptom of flagging inspiration. Skelton unwittingly summarizes the philosophy of the plain style when, commenting on his rhyme in *Collyn Clout*, he instructs the reader: "If ye take well therewith/ It hath in it some pith."

Thus, a plain-style poet expressing disillusionment with the excesses of love or extolling the virtues of frugality, rather than adorning his poem with an abundance of extravagant images, he instead pared his sentiments down to the minimum, with the intense restraint itself illuminating the poet's true feelings about love or money. The desiderata of the plain style were tightness and disciplined restraint. In the hands of an untalented poet, such as Heywood, who wrote *A Dialogue of Proverbs* (1546, 1963), the aphoristic messages could easily become stultifying; but as practiced by a poet with the skill of Wyatt, the economy of rendering a truth simply could produce a pleasurable effect. Interestingly, near the close of the century, when the eloquent style was all the rage, Sir Walter Ralegh, Thomas Nashe, and Fulke Greville often employed the techniques of the plain style.

### FURTHER ANTHOLOGIES

The three decades following the publication of *Tottel's Miscellany* have been stereotyped as a wasteland when poetry languished desultorily until the advent of the sonneteers in the 1580's. Nothing could be more unfair to the poetry of the period than to view it as struggling in an inspirational darkness. Amazingly, such a stereotype manages to overlook the profusion of poetry collections that *Tottel's Miscellany* spawned. Though admittedly the poetry of some of these collections is forgettable, nevertheless the continual appearance of these collections for the next fifty years is an impressive indication of the extent to which Tottel's philosophy of prosodic experimentation continued to exert an influence.

The first imitation of Tottel to be published was *The Paradise of Dainty Devices* (1576), the most popular of the imitations. As its title would indicate, a number of amatory poems were included, but the predominant poems had didactic, often pious themes, which offered ample opportunity for further experimentation in the plain style. A number of reasonably accomplished poets contributed to the collection, including Sir Richard Grenville, Jaspar Heywood, Thomas Churchyard, and Barnabe Rich. Another successful collection was *Brittons Bowre of Delights* (1591), interesting for its wide range of metrical experimentation, especially involving poulter's measure and the six-line iambic pentameter stanza.

Imitations of Tottel's works did not always prove successful. In 1577, *A Gorgeous Gallery of Gallant Inventions* appeared, a monotonous collection of poems whose oppressive theme was the vanity of love and pleasure, and it was as plagued with affectations and jargon as *Brittons Bowre of Delights* was blessed with fresh experimentation. Not everyone was pleased, however, with the new direction the lyric was taking after Tottel. In 1565, John Hall published his *Court of Virtue*, an anti-Tottel endeavor designed to preach that literature must be moral. In his work the poet is instructed by Lady Arete to cease pandering to the vulgar tastes of the public and instead to write moral, instructive lyrics, an appeal which results in the poet's moralizing of Wyatt's lyrics.

The experimental spirit of Tottel carried over into the works of individual poets, as well. From such an unlikely source as Thomas Tusser's *A Hundreth Good Points of Husbandry* (1557), an unassuming almanac of farming tips, explodes a variety of metrical experimentation, including Skeltonics, acrostics, and other complicated stanzaic forms. Despite his willingness to experiment, however, Tusser was not an accomplished talent, and thus there are three poets, Googe, Turberville, and Gascoigne, to whom one must turn to refute the stereotype of the mid-century "wasteland." Too often viewed as bungling imitators of Tottel, these poets deserve a closer look as vital talents who were keeping poetry alive during the so-called wasteland years.

## BARNABE GOOGE

In his *Eclogues, Epitaphs, and Sonnets* (1563), Barnabe Googe's explicit poetic mission was to imitate Tottel. Working mostly in the didactic tradition, he wrote some epitaphs and poems in praise of friends, but his eclogues are of primary interest to the literary historian. He revived the Mantuan eclogue, which had been lying dormant in England after Barclay, and his eclogues were good enough to offer anticipations of Spenser's *The Shepheardes Calender* (1579). Another noteworthy work is his *Cupido Conquered* (1563), a dream-vision allegory, which Lewis dismissed as "purely medieval." The dismissal is unfair, however, because, despite the throwback to medieval devices, the plot, in which the languishing, lovesick poet is chided by his muses for his shameful lack of productivity, reveals Googe's self-consciousness of himself as craftsman, a characteristic pose for a poet of the sixteenth century.

## GEORGE TURBERVILLE

George Turberville's dexterity with metrics in his translation of Ovid has already been mentioned. Like Googe, Turberville, in his *Epitaphs, Epigrams, Songs, and Sonnets* (1567), carried on with Tottelian experimentation, primarily in didactic poems employing poulter's measure and fourteeners written in the plain style.

## GEORGE GASCOIGNE

George Gascoigne has been late in receiving the attention that he deserves, his poetry serving as the most impressive evidence disproving the existence of a post-Tottel wasteland. Predictably, Lewis describes him as a precursor of golden age poetry, ignoring Gascoigne's contributions to the plain style. In his *A Hundreth Sundrie Flowres Bounde up in One Small Poesie* (1573, poetry and prose; revised as *The Posies of George Gascoigne Esquire*, 1575), Gascoigne was the first to experiment with Petrarch and the sonnet form since Wyatt and Surrey, but he was no slavish imitator. Gascoigne's poetry is often coarser and more lewd than that of Petrarch, but he never sacrifices a robust wit. In addition, he is an interesting figure for his variations in the sonnet form, featuring the octave-sestet division of the Petrarchan form, but in an English, or *abab* rhyme scheme. Puttenham refers to his "good meter" and "plentiful vein."

### ELIZABETHAN POETRY

Thus, the poetry of the latter part of the century, the great age of the eloquent style, must not be viewed as a semimiraculous phoenix, rising from the ashes between Wyatt's experiments with Petrarch and the advent of Sidney. Nevertheless, it must be noted that the Elizabethan era ranks as one of the outstanding poetic periods of any century, its development of the eloquent style ranking as an outstanding achievement. A valuable representative of what the eloquent style was trying to accomplish is Sir John Davies' *Orchestra: Or, A Poeme of Dauncing* (1596, 1622). In his *Elizabethan World Picture* (1943), E. M. W. Tillyard analyzes the poem at length as a fitting symbol of the Elizabethans' obsession with cosmic order. Though accurate enough, Tillyard's discussion places too much emphasis on the poem's content and does not pay enough attention to the style in which the message is delivered. In the poem, the suitor Antinous launches an elaborate discourse designed to persuade Penelope, waiting for her Odysseus to return, to dance. Through Antinous's lengthy and involved encomium to cosmic order and rhythm, Davies was not attempting a literal plea to Penelope to get up and dance. Rather, he was using Antinous as a vehicle for an ingenious argument, ostentatious in its erudition and profusion of images; in effect, Antinous's argument is the repository of Davies' experiments in the eloquent style. It is the dazzling display of the process of argumentation itself, not the literal effort to persuade Penelope, that is the essence of the poem. The way in which the poem is written is more important than its content, and in that sense (but in that sense only) the goal of the eloquent style is no different from that of the plain style.

### PETRARCHAN AND "ELOQUENT" STYLE

When one thinks of sixteenth century poetry and the eloquent style, however, one almost immediately thinks of the Petrarchan sonnet sequence, and one explanation for the almost fanatic renewal of interest in Petrarch was the inevitable shift of interests in poetic style. The plain style, so dominant for almost half a century, was beginning to play itself out, a primary indication being the decline in use of the epigram, whose pithy wit held little appeal for Elizabethan poets. The more skillful among them were anxious to perfect a new style, specifically the "eloquent" style, almost the total antithesis of the plain style. Not particularly concerned with expressing universal truths, the eloquent style, as practiced by Davies, sought embellishment, rather than pithy restraint, and a profusion of images, rather than minimal, tight expression. The eloquent style effected some interesting changes in the handling of the old Petrarchan themes, as well. It should be noted that in his experiments with Petrarch, Wyatt chafed at the indignities suffered by the courtly lover. By contrast, the sonneteers emphasized with relish the travails of the lover, who almost luxuriates in his state of rejection. In fact, there is no small trace of fin de siècle decadence in the cult of the spurned lover that characterized so many of the sonnets of the period, most notably Sidney's *Astrophel and Stella* (1591), and it decidedly signaled the end of the plain style.

### SONNETS AND SONNET SEQUENCES

The sonnet sequence, a collection of sonnets recording the lover's successes and failures in courting his frequently unsympathetic mistress, was practiced by the brilliant and mediocre alike. Of course, the two most outstanding poets of the century pioneered the form—Sidney in his *Astrophel and Stella*, who in the true spirit of the poetic self-consciousness of the century wrote sonnets about the writing of sonnets and wrote some sonnets entirely in Alexandrines, and Spenser in his *Amoretti* (1595), who, in addition to introducing refinements in the sonnet structure, also intellectualized the cult of the rejected lover by analyzing the causes of rejection.

In the next twenty years the contributions to the genre were dizzying: Greville's *Caelica* (wr. 1577, pb. 1633); Thomas Watson's *Passionate Century of Love* (1582); Samuel Daniel's *Delia* (1592); Henry Constable's *Diana* (1592); Thomas Lodge's *Phillis* (1593); Giles Fletcher's *Licia* (1593); Barnabe Barnes's *Parthenophil and Parthenophe* (1593); Bartholomew Griffin's *Fidessa* (1593); Michael Drayton's *Ideas Mirror* (1594), noteworthy for its experiments with rhyme; *The Phoenix Nest* (1593), a collection of Petrarchan sonnets in a wide variety of meters by George Peele, Nicholas Breton, Thomas Lodge, and others—the list of accomplished poets and tinkering poetasters was almost endless.

By the close of the century, so many mediocre poets had turned out sonnet sequences, and the plight of the rejected lover had reached such lugubrious proportions that the form inevitably decayed. The cult of the masochistic lover was becoming tediously commonplace, and one of the major triumphs of the eloquent style, the Petrarchan paradox (for example, Wyatt's "I burn, and freeze like ice") lost its appeal of surprise and tension as it became overworked, predictable, and trite. The genre had lost all traces of originality, and it is interesting to consider the fact that the modern definition of a sonneteer is an inferior poet. As early as 1577, Greville in his *Caelica* had perceived how easily in the sonnet sequence numbing repetition could replace fresh invention, and to maintain some vitality in his sequence his subject matter evolves from the complaints of the rejected lover to a renunciation of worldly vanity and expressions of disappointment in the disparity between "ideal" love and the imperfect love that exists in reality. (For this reason, of all the sonneteers Greville is the only precursor of the themes so prevalent in seventeenth century devotional poetry.)

The success and subsequent decline of the sonnet sequence left it wide open to parody. Many of the sonnets of William Shakespeare, who himself revolutionized the sonnet structure in England, are veiled satiric statements on the trite excesses of Petrarchan images ("My mistress's eyes are nothing like the sun"), indicating his impatience with the old, worn-out sentiments. Davies' collection of *Gulling Sonnets* (c. 1594) was an explicit parody of Petrarchan absurdities and weary lack of invention, and, following their publication, the genre spun into an irreversible decline.

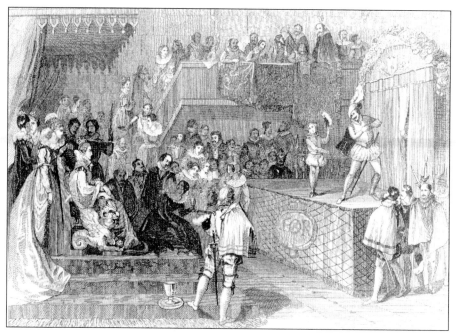

*William Shakespeare performing before Queen Elizabeth and her court.* (Library of Congress)

## MYTHOLOGICAL-EROTIC NARRATIVE

As the sonnet declined, however, another form of amatory verse was being developed: the mythological-erotic narrative. This form chose erotic themes from mythology, embellishing the narrative with sensuous conceits and quasipornographic descriptions. It was a difficult form to master because it required titillation without descending into vulgarity and light touches of sophisticated humor without descending into burlesque. Successful examples of the mythological-erotic narrative are Christopher Marlowe's *Hero and Leander* (1598; completed by Chapman), Shakespeare's *Venus and Adonis* (1593), Chapman's *Ovid's Banquet of Sense* (1595), Drayton's *Endimion and Phoebe* (1595), and Lodge's *Scillaes Metamorphosis* (1589). Like the sonnet, the mythological narrative fell into decline, as evidenced by John Marston's *The Metamorphosis of Pygmalion's Image and Certain Satires* (1598), in which the decadence of the sculptor drooling lustfully over his statue was too absurdly indelicate for the fragile limits of the genre.

## SATIRIC AND RELIGIOUS VERSE

As the mythological narrative and the sonnet declined, both social satire and religious verse experienced a corresponding upswing. The steady growth of a middle-class reading audience precipitated an increased interest in satire, a genre which had not been represented with any distinction since Gascoigne's *The Steele Glas, a Satyre* (1576). Understandably, though inaccurately, Joseph Hall labeled himself the first English satirist. Juvenalian satire flourished in his *Virgidemiarum* (1597), similar to Davies' *Gulling Sonnets*, followed by Everard Guilpin's *Skialetheia: Or, Shadow of Truth in Certain Epigrams and Satyres* (1598), which attacks the "wimpring sonnets" and "puling Elegies" of the love poets, and Marston's *The Scourge of Villainy* (1598).

Perhaps feeling reinforced by the indignation of the satirists, religious verse proliferated at the end of the century. Bedazzled by the great age of the sonnet, the modern reader tends to generalize that the latter decades of the century were a purely secular period for poetry. Such a view, however, overlooks the staggering amount of religious verse that was being turned out, and it should be remembered by the modern reader that to the reader of the sixteenth century, verse was typified not by a Sidney sonnet, but by a versified psalm. Throughout the century, experiments with Petrarch ebbed and flowed, but the reading public was never without religious writings, including enormous numbers of sermons, devotional manuals, collections of prayers and meditations, verse saints' lives, devotional verse, and, of course, an overflow of rhyming psalters. Versifying the psalter had begun as early as the fourteenth century, but its popularity and practice went unsurpassed in the sixteenth. Although many excellent poets tried their hand at the Psalms, including Wyatt, Spenser, and Sidney, who saw them as legitimate sources of poetry, these versifications were led by the Thomas Sternhold and John Hopkins edition of 1549, and it represents a mediocre collection of verse. Nevertheless, the uncultivated reading public hailed it as an inspired work, and people who refused to read any poetry at all devoured the Sternhold and Hopkins edition. Popular collections among the Elizabethans were William Hunnis's *Seven Sobs of a Sorrowfull Soule for Sinne* (1583) and William Byrd's *Psalmes, Sonnets, and Songs of Sadnes and Pietie* (1588).

By the close of the century, attempts at religious verse by more accomplished poets were surpassing the efforts of hack versifiers. While the satirists were ridiculing the atrophied sonnet sequence on aesthetic grounds, other writers were attacking it on moral grounds, and perceptions of what poetry should be and do were shifting as the sonnet lost its influence. Having put a distance of four years between his *Astrophel and Stella* and the publication of his *Defence of Poesie*, Sidney authoritatively proclaimed in the latter work that poetry should celebrate God and Divine Love. Nashe attacks verse in which "lust is the tractate of so many leaves." Physical love was no longer au courant. In his "A Coronet for his Mistress Philosophy," Chapman reflects the new vogue of Neoplatonism by carefully identifying the differences between divine and physical love, also investigated meticulously by Spenser in his *Fowre Hymnes* (1596). Joshua Sylvester's translations between 1590 and 1605 of the works of the French Huguenot poet Guillaume du Bartas helped to reinforce Protestant piety and further counteracted the Petrarchans. The most saintly poet of the period was Southwell, a Jesuit. In his preface to his *Saint Peter's Complaint, with Other Poems* (1595), Southwell laments that the teachings of Christ go unheeded as poets would rather celebrate the glories of Venus. In *Saint Peter's Complaint*, Peter excoriates himself for his denial of Christ, and the fact that the work is oddly adorned with sensuous conceits is an interesting indication that Petrarchan images managed to survive stubbornly, even in works inimical to their spirit. Finally, in 1599, Davies published his *Nosce Teipsum: This Oracle Expounded in Two Elegies*, whose theme was self-knowledge, rather than carnal knowledge of one's mistress, as well as the proper relationship between the soul and the body.

## EDMUND SPENSER

The tug of war between the sonneteers and the religious poets was only one of several noteworthy poetic developments near the close of the century. Edmund Spenser, the most talented poet of the century, contributed to both sides of the battle (the *Amoretti* and *Fowre Hymnes*), but his versatility as a poet enabled him to transcend any one category. Spenser's early poetic career is not without its mysteries. No literary historian would have predicted that at a time when a new poetry was being refined by means of the sonnet form, someone would choose to revive the old medieval forms, but that is what Spenser did. *The Shepheardes Calender* is a throwback to the Mantuan eclogues, at this point almost a century old, and *Colin Clouts Come Home Againe* is reminiscent of Skelton's anticlerical satires. His "Prosopopoia: Or, Mother Hubberd's Tale" is an imitation of a medieval beast fable, and even *The Faerie Queene*, his most famous work, is essentially a compendium of medieval allegory and Italian epic forms derived from

Ludovico Ariosto and Torquato Tasso. Furthermore, many of Spenser's works were written in a deliberately archaic style.

Thus a major contribution to Spenser's fame is not the originality of his themes but the range of his metrical and stanzaic experimentations. In a century characterized by poets self-consciously aware of themselves exercising their craft, Spenser was the apotheosis of the poetic craftsman. Though his archaic diction violated the tenets of many critics who believed that the vernacular must grow, Spenser's experiments in versification furthered the cause of making English more vital. Despite its reactionary themes, *The Shepheardes Calender* explodes with experimentation in poetic forms. The "January" eclogue is written in the six-line ballad or "Venus and Adonis" stanza, "February" is written in Anglo-Saxon accentual verse, "March" is written in the romance stanza of Chaucer's "Sir Topaz," "July" is written in a rough, vulgar ballad meter, and "August" is a contrast of undisciplined folk rhythms and elegant sestinas. Though not Spenser's most famous work, *The Shepheardes Calender* is nevertheless a remarkable symbol and culmination of the poetic self-consciousness of the sixteenth century and a fusion of the experiments in poetic versification that had helped to shape English as a suitable vehicle for poetry.

VERSE CHRONICLES

As the century was drawing to a close, a popular genre flourishing outside the continuing battle between amatory and religious verse was the verse chronicle history. Of all the genres popular in the sixteenth century, the verse chronicle history is probably the most difficult for the modern reader to appreciate, probably because of its excruciating length; but more than any other genre, it serves as a repository for Elizabethan intellectual, historical, and social thought, especially as it reflects the Elizabethan desire for political order, so amply documented by Tillyard in his *Elizabethan World Picture*.

The first treatment of English history in poetry was the landmark publication of *A Mirror for Magistrates* (1555, 1559, 1563). It was a collection of tragedies of famous leaders in the medieval tradition of people brought low by the turning wheel of Fortune and was written in rime royal, the favorite stanzaic vehicle of medieval narrative. The structure of its tragedies was imitated from John Lydgate's *Fall of Princes* (1494), and the constant themes of the tragedies were both the subject's responsibility to his king and the king's responsibility to God; if either the ruler or the subject should fail in his proper allegiance, disorder and tragedy would inevitably ensue. *A Mirror for Magistrates* was extraordinarily popular with a reading public desiring both entertainment and instruction. It went through eight editions in thirty years, with Thomas Sackville's "Induction" being considered at the time the best poem between Chaucer and Spenser.

The major importance of *A Mirror for Magistrates* is the fact that it fulfilled Sidney's mandate in his *Defence of Poesie* that the poet take over the task of the historian, and *A Mirror for Magistrates* exerted a powerful influence on the late Elizabethan poets. Pride in the royal Tudor lineage led not only the prose chroniclers but also the poets of the Elizabethan period to develop a strong sense of Britain's history. Shakespeare's history plays are widely recognized as reflections of England's growing nationalistic fervor, and because of the magnitude of the plays, it is easy to overlook the contributions of the poets to English history, or, perhaps more accurately, pseudohistory. The troublesome murkiness of Britain's origins were efficiently, if somewhat questionably, cleared up by exhaustive embellishments of the legends of Brut and King Arthur, legends that spurred England on to a sharpened sense of patriotism and nationalism. An obvious example is Spenser's chronicle of early British history at the end of book 2 of *The Faerie Queene*. In 1586, William Warner published his *Albion's England*, a long work ambitiously taking as its province all of historical time from Noah's Flood down to the execution of Mary, Queen of Scots.

The following years saw the publication of Daniel's *The First Fowre Bookes of the Civile Warres* (1595, 1599, 1601), whose books represented the apotheosis of all attempts at versified history. Like Shakespeare in his history plays, Daniel focused on a theme common in Elizabethan political theory, the evil that inevitably results from civil and moral disorder—specifically, the overthrow of Richard II. The modern reader has a natural antipathy toward the Elizabethan verse chronicles because of their length and because of the chroniclers' penchant for moral allegorizing, for their tedious accounts of past civil disorder as illustrative of present moral chaos, and for their far-reaching, interweaving parallels among mythological, biblical, and British history (for example, the Titans' defeat of Saturn being contrasted with the victory of Henry V at Agincourt in Heywood's "Troia Britannica," 1609). Nevertheless, these versified histories and their championing of moral order and nationalism constituted much of the most popular poetry of the Elizabethan period, and their impact cannot be overemphasized.

### GROWTH AND TRANSITION

In retrospect, it is indeed astonishing to consider precisely how much the poetry of the sixteenth century grew after Hawes's allegories first limped onto the scene in 1509. The pressing need for most poets at the beginning of the century was to imitate medieval forms as faithfully as possible. There was no question as to the superiority of the classical authorities, and there was no "English" poetry as such. In 1531, Sir Thomas Elyot mentions Ovid and Martial but not English poets, and, as late as 1553, Wilson was defending the rhetoric of the authorities Cicero and Quintilian. Gradually, however, by struggling with the new language and continuing to experiment with verse forms both new and original, poets were starting to shape a new English poetry and were achieving recognition as craftsmen in their own right. By 1586, Webbe respectfully addressed the preface to his *Discourse of English Poetry* to "the Noble Poets of England" and made mention of Skelton, Gascoigne, and Googe, finally recognizing Spenser as "the rightest English poet that ever I read." Thus, by the end of the century the question of whether there could be an English poesy had been replaced by the question of what were the limits of the great English poets.

Because of the struggle to shape the new vernacular, the sixteenth century differs from other centuries in that many innovations were coming from the pens of not particularly gifted poets. Thus, working in a period of volatility and flux in the language, such men as Barclay and Skelton could exert an impact on the shaping of the poetry and earn their place in literary history. The first half of the sixteenth century did not witness the formation of new genres. The old reliables, dream-vision allegories, anticlerical satires, pastorals, ballads, versified psalms, and neomedieval tragedies, were the favorite vehicles of most poets. The extraordinary development of this period was the metrical experimentation, which never stopped, no matter how limited the poet. Perhaps more than any other period, therefore, the first half of the sixteenth century reveals as many noteworthy developments in its bad poets as in its talented ones.

After the publication of *Tottel's Miscellany*, poetry began to settle down somewhat from its pattern of groping experimentation as it gained confidence and stability working with the vernacular. Perhaps the surest indication that poetry had hit its stride in England was the parody of the Petrarchan sonnet. The parody of the first truly great lyric form in England was a significant landmark because only widely popular forms tend to serve as targets for parody. A further indication of the vitality of the poetry was the fact that its poets survived the parody and went on to create new forms. Furthermore, poetic tastes were flexible enough to produce a Spenser who, while forging ahead with prosodic experimentation, looked backward to the archaisms that English poetry had originally used.

As the sixteenth century waned and old genres, such as the sonnet, the pastoral, and the verse chronicle, faded, there were numerous hints of what the poets of the new century would be attempting. In particular, there were several suggestions of the Metaphysicals. The decline in popularity of the Petrarchan sonnet and its subsequent ridicule paved the way for John Donne's satires of the form in many of his secular lyrics. As was seen earlier, Greville's religious themes in his *Caelica* were a precursor of devotional poetry. The sensuous conceits of Southwell heralded the Baroque extravagances of Richard Crashaw. The pastoral, a favorite Elizabethan genre, was fast fading, as indicated by Ralegh's cynical response to Marlowe's "The Passionate Shepherd to His Love," a plea for living a romantic life in pastoral bliss. In his "Nymph's Reply to the Shepherd," Ralegh makes it clear that such idyllic bliss does not exist. The pastoral was being replaced, however, by a less idealized, more rational mode, the theme of self-contained, rural retirement, as embodied at the close of the century in Sir Edward Dyer's "My Mind to Me a Kingdom Is," a theme that became increasingly popular in the new century. Finally, the proliferation of songs and airs, found in such collections as Nicholas Yonge's *Musica Transalpina* (1588), John Dowland's *The First Book of Songs or Airs* (1597), and Thomas Campion's *A Booke of Ayres* (1601), created a vogue that influenced the lyrics of Ben Jonson and his followers.

The true worth of the poetry of the sixteenth century, however, lies not in the legacies that were inherited from it by the next century but rather in the sheer exuberance for the poetic undertaking that characterized the century from beginning to end. Because of the continuing process of shaping the new vernacular, the tools of the poetic craft are evident in every work, and in no other century did the poets better embody the original etymology of the word "poet," which comes from the Greek word for "maker." To use Webbe's term, they "Englished" the old poetry and proved to be untiring "makers" of a new.

BIBLIOGRAPHY

Bell, Ilona. *Elizabethan Women and the Poetry of Courtship.* Illustrated edition. New York: Cambridge University Press, 1999. Argues that women's voices can be heard not only in poems by women writers but also in the implied responses by women to poetry addressed to them. The book bears evidence of extensive research, combined with judicious analysis of the poems mentioned.

Blevins, Jacob. *Catullan Consciousness and the Early Modern Lyric in England: From Wyatt to Donne.* Farnham, Surrey, England: Ashgate, 2004. The purpose of this study is to demonstrate that like Catullus, some English poets departed from convention and used the lyric both to praise and to reject accepted cultural ideals, thus establishing a personal identity. The author is convinced that this process is essential to the creation of good lyric poetry. Bibliography and index.

Braden, Gordon. *Sixteenth-Century Poetry: An Annotated Anthology.* Hoboken, N.J.: Wiley-Blackwell, 2005. Selections from a wide range of poets and from the major genres, including both sacred and political poetry. Fully annotated. Contains both a conventional table of contents and an alternate, thematic listing, as well as a chronology, an index of titles and first lines, a bibliography, and a topical index.

Cheney, Patrick, Andrew Hadfield, and Garrett A. Sullivan, Jr., eds. *Early Modern English Poetry: A Critical Companion.* New York: Oxford University Press, 2006. A collection of twenty-eight essays, three of them dealing with cultural changes and poetic theories, the rest suggesting new approaches to major poems. Contains a list of suggested readings at the end of each chapter and a chronology of Renaissance poetry.

Huntington, John. *Ambition, Rank, and Poetry in 1590's England.* Urbana: University of Illinois Press, 2001. Points out evidence of social protest in the works of writers of relatively humble origins, such as George Chapman, Christopher Marlowe, Ben Jonson, Edmund Spenser, Matthew Roydon, and Aemilia Lanyer. Huntington's close readings indicate that there is a need for reinterpretations of the poetry written during the period.

Kinney, Arthur F., ed. *The Cambridge Companion to English Literature, 1500-1600.*

New York: Cambridge University Press, 2000. Essays about such subjects as Tudor aesthetics, poetry and patronage, lyric forms, romance, the epic, and patriotic works. Bibliographical references and index.

Lewis, C. S. *Poetry and Prose in the Sixteenth Century*. Oxford, England: Clarendon Press, 1990. Originally published as *English Literature in the Sixteenth Century Excluding Drama*, Vol. 3 in *The Oxford History of English Literature*, in 1954. A new version of Lewis's controversial work. Bibliography and index.

Mapstone, Sally, ed. *Older Scots Literature*. Edinburgh: John Donald, 2005. The second section of this volume consists of thirteen essays on sixteenth century writers and their works. One of the essays deals with the "female voice" in the poetry of the period, while others discuss ballads, comic verse, and the elegiac tradition. Writers who flourished both in the late sixteenth century and in the early seventeenth century are discussed in the third part of the volume. Bibliographical references and index.

Morotti, Arthur F. *Manuscript, Print, and the English Renaissance Lyric*. Ithaca, N.Y.: Cornell University Press, 1995. The author of this important study examines the tradition of manuscript transmission of poetic works and explains how the change to print publication was effected. He also notes the ways in which the new process altered not only the creative process but also the cultural milieu. Bibliography and index.

Rivers, Isabel. *Classical and Christian Ideas in English Renaissance Poetry: A Student's Guide*. 2d ed. New York: Routledge, 1994. Contains a number of chapters on classical philosophies and Christian doctrines, as well as one chapter on theories of poetry. Lists of authors, an author index, and a bibliographical appendix.

Vickers, Brian, ed. *English Renaissance Literary Criticism*. 1999. Reprint. Oxford, England: Clarendon Press, 2003. This invaluable work presents thirty-six texts, each preceded by a biographical and textual headnote. Annotations with every selection. Includes suggestions for further reading, a glossary, an index of names, and an index of topics.

Whitney, Isabelle, Mary Sidney, and Amelia Lanyer. *Renaissance Women Poets*. New York: Viking, 2001. Considers the lives and works of three English women poets who wrote during the Renaissance. Though their social and cultural backgrounds were very different, all of them used their poetry to voice their convictions and to establish their identities as women and as talented, intelligent human beings.

*Elizabeth J. Bellamy*

# ENGLISH POETRY
# IN THE SEVENTEENTH CENTURY

A question that can be asked of any century's poetry is whether it owes its character to "forces"—nonliterary developments to which the poets respond more or less sensitively—or whether, on the other hand, the practice of innovative and influential poets mainly determines the poetry of the period. Clearly, great poets do not always shape the literature of their century, as the cases of the twin giants of seventeenth century England, William Shakespeare and John Milton, indicate. What Ben Jonson wrote of Shakespeare is true of both: They are "not of an age, but for all time!" John Donne and John Dryden, however, are poets who seem to have stamped their personalities on much of the poetry of their own and succeeding generations.

## JOHN DONNE AND JOHN DRYDEN

John Donne (1572-1631) turned twenty-nine in the year 1601. John Dryden (1631-1700), busy to the last, died at the end of the century. Thus a century brimming with good poetry may be said to begin with Donne and end with Dryden. On most library shelves, Donne and Dryden are both literally and figuratively neighbors. If not the shaper of poetry in the first half of the century, Donne stands at least as its representative poet, while Dryden, born only a few months after Donne died in 1631, probably has an even more secure claim to the same position in the final decades of the century. They may indeed have determined the poetic climate; certainly they serve as barometers on which modern readers can see that climate registered. The distinctive differences between the writings of the two men testify to the diversity of seventeenth century poetry and to the likelihood that powerful forces for change were at work in the interim.

The differences are apparent even when—perhaps particularly when—roughly similar types of poems (and parallels between the two are inevitably rough) are chosen. Donne wrote two sequences of religious sonnets. One begins:

> Thou hast made me, and shall thy work decay?
> Repair me now, for now mine end doth haste,
> I run to death, and death meets me as fast,
> And all my pleasures are like yesterday.

Dryden is known for two longer religious poems, one of which, *Religio Laici* (1682), begins: "Dim as the borrowed beams of moons and stars/ To lonely, weary, wand'ring travelers,/ Is Reason to the soul. . . ." A long list of contrasts might be drawn up, most of which would hold true of entire poems and, for that matter, of the works of the two poets generally.

Donne addresses God directly, for example, and even ventures to command him, while neither in his opening nor anywhere else in 456 lines does Dryden apostrophize his maker, although several times he refers circumspectly to "God," "Godhead," or "Omnipotence." Donne not only personifies but also personalizes the abstraction *death*, which "runs fast" and "meets" the speaker. Dryden's chief abstraction, *Reason*, is grand but "dim," and another that he introduces soon thereafter, *Religion*, though described as "bright," remains inanimate. Donne's sonnet has an immediate, even urgent, quality; Dryden sets out in a more deliberate and measured way, as if any necessary relationships will be established in due time. Donne achieves that immediacy through a plain, simple vocabulary, thirty-one of his first thirty-five words having only one syllable. Although there are no striking irregularities after the first line, rhetorical stresses govern the rhythm. Dryden's diction is also simple, but there are more polysyllables, and their arrangement, as in "lonely, weary, wand'ring travelers," creates a smoother, more regular cadence.

In other ways, the poems elicit different responses. Donne is paradoxical. The reader senses in his third line that rigorous demands are being made on him. What does "I run to death" mean exactly? How can that be? Why is death said to do the same? Such questions have answers, no doubt, but the reader anticipates that he will have to work for them, that he must stay alert and get involved. Dryden, on the other hand, begins by making a statement that can be accepted without any particular mental activity (which is not necessarily to say that it should be, or is intended to be, so accepted). Whereas the person setting out to read Donne suspects that obscurities may lie ahead, the beginner at Dryden finds nothing to raise such expectations. (The reader will hardly be surprised to find Dryden saying, near the end of the poem: "Thus have I made my own opinions clear.")

Samplers of other poems by the two poets reveal similar contrasts right from the beginning. Frequently, in Donne's poems, a speaker is addressing someone or something—God, a woman, a friend, a rival, the sun—in a tone that is often abrupt, questioning, or imperious. The poems are often dramatic in the sense of implying a situation and a relationship. They make demands, both on the addressee and the reader, who is present in somewhat the same way as an audience in a theater. Dryden was a dramatist, and a highly successful one, but he seems to have reserved drama for his plays. In his poems, he is inclined to begin, as in *Religio Laici*, with statements, often in the form of generalizations: "All human things are subject to decay." "From harmony, from heavenly harmony,/ This universal frame began." "How blest is he who leads a country life." While not condescending to his readers, Dryden is much more likely to go on to tell them something—something clear, measured, plausible.

### THE ELIZABETHAN HERITAGE

The Renaissance came to England late. Sixteenth century Italian poetry is dotted with famous names—Ludovico Ariosto, Pietro Bembo, Michelangelo Buonarroti, Torquato Tasso—and French poets distinguished themselves throughout the century, Pierre de Ronsard and the Pléiade group overshadowing others of whom today's readers would hear much more but for that brilliant constellation of poets. The Elizabethan poets' debt to these older literatures, particularly to that created by their French elders and contemporaries, has been well documented.

After the appearance of *The Shepheardes Calender* (1579) by Edmund Spenser (c. 1552-1599), English poetry came on with a rush, while the post-Renaissance Baroque movement was already rising on the European continent. By 1600, both Spenser and Sir Philip Sidney (1554-1586) were dead, but many of their contemporaries from the 1550's and 1560's worked on, with many of their brightest achievements still ahead. As relief from the earlier but continuing Elizabethan tradition of ponderous, prosaic moralizing exemplified by the incessantly reprinted and expanded *A Mirror for Magistrates* (1555, 1559, 1563), the poets of later Elizabethan decades favored pastorals, love sonnets, mythological narratives, and of course songs and the verse drama.

As part of the last wave of poets to come of age under Elizabeth, Donne and Jonson might have been expected to rebel against their elders. Fifteen years or so of hobnobbing with Hobbinol (poet Gabriel Harvey, c. 1545-1630) and other literary shepherds and of agonizing with woebegone Petrarchan lovers over their unattainable or recalcitrant golden ladies goaded the new generation into staking out new territory. The sweetness and naïveté of much Elizabethan verse cloyed their literary taste buds. The serious side of Elizabethan endeavor ran wearyingly to themes of transience and mutability. There was room for more realism and sophistication, and new forms and conventions.

Donne responded by parodying the ideal Petrarchan mistress in his paean to indiscriminate love, "I can love both fair and brown," meanwhile reserving that standard vehicle for love laments, the sonnet, for religious purposes. Jonson refused to write sonnets at all, coolly praised a goddess named Celia, and claimed, with some exaggeration, that he did not write of love. As mythologizers, Elizabethans were accustomed to plunder from Ovid and the Ovidians, but Donne did not conduct his raids on the *Metamorphoses* (c. 8 C.E.; English translation, 1567), with its wistful accounts of lovers vanished into foliage and feathers; instead, he concentrated on Ovid's saucy prescriptions for both lovemaking and love-breaking in the *Amores* (c. 20 B.C.E.; English translation, c. 1597), *Ars amatoria* (c. 2 B.C.E.; *Art of Love*, 1612), and *Remedia amoris* (before 8 C.E.; *Cure for Love*, 1600). Later (or perhaps just alternatively) he drew on the pre-Petrarchan traditions, including Platonism and Scholasticism, to write of love as a refining and exalting experience. As for Jonson, where the Elizabethans were amply decorous, he tended to be blunt and epigrammatic. More rigorously than Donne, he rejected the medieval trappings that clung to Elizabethan poetry.

Neither man, however, made anything like a clean break with Elizabethan values. In satirizing Petrarchan conventions, Donne was only continuing a tendency implicit in the Petrarchan mode almost from its beginning, Shakespeare already preceding him in English poetry in his sonnet "My mistress's eyes are nothing like the sun." The man most responsible for the English sonnet-writing mania, Sidney, had, in his *Astrophel and Stella* (1591) suggested all sorts of latent possibilities for the deployment of wit that the Elizabethans had barely begun to exploit. Elizabethan moral earnestness awaited poets who could bring fresh resources to its expression. The student of the drama can hardly escape the conclusion that Donne owed something of his penchant for dramatizing love and religious conflict to the fact that he grew up in London at a time of flourishing theatrical activity, when even writers deficient in dramatic talent strove to turn out plays. Jonson must have learned much about friendship from Sidney's *Arcadia* (1590, 1593, 1598), the fourth book of Spenser's *The Faerie Queene* (1590, 1596), and other romances of the sort before turning this subject to account in poetic forms more congenial to him. Again, Jonson's distinctive contribution to songwriting depended on his good fortune in maturing at a time when music was everywhere in the air, as Willa McClung Evans showed in *Ben Jonson and Elizabethan Music* (1929). In short, Elizabethan influences on these Jacobean poets were very far from exclusively negative ones.

## EDMUND SPENSER

Seventeenth century developments originating with Donne and Jonson have absorbed much of the attention of literary students, but the Spenserian tradition must not be underrated. As its master, Edmund Spenser, was a many-faceted poet, the tradition is a rich and diverse one. Michael Drayton carried his adaptations of Spenserian pastoral to the verge of the new century's fourth decade. The greatest English poet after Shakespeare found in *The Faerie Queene* the best model for his own epic. Some poets imitated Spenser's idealism, some his sensuous and even sensual music, some his achievement in romantic narrative, and some his demanding stanza. No one like Spenser wrote in the seventeenth century, but the rays of his genius shone over the century and long afterward. The twentieth century emphasis on Donne and the Metaphysical poets has had the unfortunate effect of obscuring the illumination that Spenser furnished generations of respectful and admiring followers.

### LONDON BROTHERHOOD

In few European countries was there such a concentration of talent and creative energy as in Renaissance London. England had no city to rival it in size or cultural pretensions, and to the city or to the court came all aspiring writers and all ambitious men. Literary associations blossomed easily in its square mile, as did rivalries and jealousies. Although London did not boast a university, many of its creative men came to know one another in school. Beginning in the last quarter of the sixteenth century, for example, and extending over the next seventy years, the roster of poets who attended just one school, Westminster, includes Jonson, Richard Corbett, Giles Fletcher, Henry King, George Herbert, William Strode, Thomas Randolph, William Cartwright, Abraham

Cowley, and Dryden. Half of these men later gravitated to one Cambridge college, Trinity. A similar list of poets who claimed residence at London's Inns of Court might be made. It is likely that the richness of late Elizabethan and seventeenth century English poetry owes much to the cross-fertilization that is almost inevitable when virtually all of the poets of any given time know one another more or less intimately. Although poets have always come together for mutual support and stimulation, in the seventeenth century, the poets who did so were not beleaguered minorities without status in the intellectual world or insulated coteries intent on defending the purity of their theory and practice against one another. Poets constituted something of a brotherhood—although brothers are known to fight—and not a school or club where narrowness can prevail along with good manners.

Realizing the essentially close relationships among poets whose work scholars tend to classify and mark off from one another, modern commentators on seventeenth century poetry have emphasized the common heritage and shared concerns of writers once assumed to be disparate and even antagonistic. It is well to recall this shared heritage and common cause when distinguishing—as criticism must distinguish—among individual achievements and ascertainable poetic movements.

### THE METAPHYSICAL SCHOOL

After Sir Herbert Grierson's edition of Donne's poems in 1912, critics spent some decades attempting to define and delineate "Metaphysical poetry." T. S. Eliot, in a 1921 essay, lent his prestige to the endeavor, and such studies as George Williamson's *The Donne Tradition* (1930), Joan Bennett's *Four Metaphysical Poets* (1934), J. B. Leishman's *Metaphysical Poets* (1934), Helen C. White's *The Metaphysical Poets* (1936), and Rosemond Tuve's *Elizabethan and Metaphysical Imagery* (1947) refined readers' understanding of the movement but created such a vogue that the term "metaphysical" came to acquire a bewildering variety of applications and connotations, with the understandable result that some critics, including Leishman, came to view it with suspicion. Nevertheless, it remains useful for the purpose of designating the kind of poetry written by Donne, Herbert, Richard Crashaw, Henry Vaughan, Thomas Traherne, Andrew Marvell (at least some of the time), and a considerable number of other seventeenth century poets, including the American, Edward Taylor. The earlier tendency to call these poets a "school" has also fallen into disrepute because the term suggests a much more formal and schematic set of relationships than existed among these poets. Douglas Bush, in his valuable contribution to the Oxford History of English Literature series, *English Literature in the Earlier Seventeenth Century, 1600-1660* (1962), refers to the Metaphysicals after Donne as his "successors," while Joseph H. Summers prefers another designation, as the title of his 1970 study, *The Heirs of Donne and Jonson*, indicates.

Because the bulk of English Metaphysical poetry after Donne tends to be religious, it has been studied profitably under extraliterary rubrics, especially by Louis L. Martz as *The Poetry of Meditation* (1954), in which the author demonstrates how many distinctive features of such poetry derive from the Christian art of meditation, especially from such manuals of Catholic devotion as Saint Ignatius of Loyola's *Ejercicios espirituales* (1548; *The Spiritual Exercises*, 1736) and Saint Francis de Sales's *An Introduction to the Devout Life* (c. 1608). More recently, Barbara Kiefer Lewalski has argued for the importance of Protestant devotional literature in her *Protestant Poetics and the Seventeenth Century Religious Lyric* (1979). Donne and some of his followers have been profitably studied as poets of wit, a classification that connects them with Jonson and the Jonsonians, in later books by Leishman (*The Monarch of Wit*, 1951) and Williamson (*The Proper Wit of Poetry*, 1961), as well as in the aforementioned book by Summers.

Students of literature continue to be intrigued by the word "metaphysical," however, and by the challenge of pinpointing its essential denotation. One of the most distinctive traits of this poetry is the Metaphysical conceit, an image that, as its name suggests, is intended to convey an idea rather than a sensory quality. The conceit, as exemplified by Donne's comparison of the quality of two lovers' devotion to the draftsman's compass in "A Valediction: Forbidding Mourning," or the pulley image in Herbert's poem of that title used to express the speaker's sense of the relationship between God and humans, is likely to be ingenious, unexpected, and apparently unpromising; the poet is inclined to develop it at considerable length (Donne uses three stanzas for his compass conceit, while Herbert builds his whole poem on the pulley image) and in a number of particulars; and the result, often arrived at through argumentation, justifies the seeming incongruity of the image. An interesting comparison between Donne's imagery and that of Shakespeare has been made by Cleanth Brooks (in *The Well Wrought Urn*, 1947) with the view of demonstrating the use of similar conceits by Shakespeare, who is never thought of as a Metaphysical.

Describers of Metaphysical poetry have most often cited a cluster of traits, no one of which differentiates this mode from others. Metaphysical poems are often dramatic, colloquial in diction and rhythm, and set forth in intricate and varied forms with respect to line lengths, rhyme schemes, and stanzaic configurations. Whether dealing with sexual or religious love, Metaphysical love poems develop the psychological aspects of loving that are always implicit, sometimes explicit in the Petrarchan tradition. Sexual, Platonic, and religious love are frequently explored in terms seemingly more appropriate to one of the other types. Thus Donne assures God that he will never be "chaste, except you ravish me," and a lady that "all shall approve/ Us canonized for love." Crashaw can refer to a mistress as a "divine idea" in a "shrine of crystal flesh," and, in another poem, to God as a rival lover of Saint Teresa.

The chief trait of Metaphysical poetry in the eyes of Earl Miner (*The Metaphysical Mode from Donne to Cowley*, 1969) is its "private mode." He considers the most distinctive aspect of the love or religious experience in this poetry to be its individual and private character. Either because the poet senses a breakdown of social bonds or because these bonds threaten the integrity of private experience, the Metaphysical poet is in self-conscious retreat from the social realm. Thus Donne's love poems often evoke third parties only to banish them as early as the first line: "For God's sake, hold your tongue, and let me love." The earlier Metaphysicals, however, are familiar with the world that they reject, and its immanence contributes to the dramatic quality in their poetry. In later poets such as Vaughan and Traherne, the interfering world has receded; as a result the dramatic tension largely disappears.

Metaphysical poetry's reputed taste for the obscure and the "far-fetched" has been overemphasized by critics from Dryden to the twentieth century. That it is intellectual and that its allusions are likely to necessitate numerous glosses for modern readers there can be little doubt. The ideal audience for Metaphysical poetry was small and select. To pre-Restoration readers, however, the poems probably did not seem especially difficult. It is simply that Renaissance learning was replaced by a different learning. As the century waned, a gap widened between the old and new learning; as a result Dryden had more difficulty reading Donne than do modern readers, who enjoy the benefit of modern scholars' recovery of much of that older learning. The continuing popularity of Metaphysical poetry demonstrates readers' continuing willingness to absorb glosses without which the richness of the poetry is lost.

*European Metaphysical Poetry* (1961), an anthology by Frank J. Warnke with a long critical introduction, presents French, German, Spanish, Dutch, and Italian texts of selected poems with facing verse translations. The volume includes a number of poems analogous to the works of Donne and his followers and distinguishes between the Metaphysical and Baroque traditions, although clearly they overlap.

### METAPHYSICAL POETS IN THE NEW WORLD

A Mexican nun, Sor Juana Inés de la Cruz (1648-1695), rivals Taylor (c. 1645-1729), who came to America in 1668, as the first Metaphysical poet of the New World. Like Crashaw, Sor Juana writes emotional, sexually charged religious verse, but also like him, she was a keen student of theology and something of an intellectual. In Taylor, the Metaphysical manner and a Puritan religious outlook produced a body of poetry unique in the American colonies or elsewhere. The influence of Richard Baxter's famous book *The Saints' Everlasting Rest* (1692) is heavier on Taylor than on any other Metaphysical poet, and many of his poems are cast as meditations. The language is that of a man who lived and worked on the late seventeenth century American frontier, cut off from the society of the learned and the artistic. Even his conceits, such as the one on which he bases "Huswifery"—"Make me, O Lord, thy spinning wheel complete"—have a homely, rough-hewn air.

### RELIGIOUS POETRY AND OTHER TRENDS

Finally, the seventeenth century produced a body of poetry not usually classified as Metaphysical but having some affinities with that tradition. Much of it is religious. Emblem poetry, best exemplified by Francis Quarles (1592-1644), was a mixed-media art including a print that depicted a scene of religious or moral significance, a biblical quotation, a related poem, another quotation, and, in most cases, a concluding epigram. The engravings in emblem books are frequently more interesting than the poems, but the form seems to have made its mark on Spenser, Shakespeare, and several of the Metaphysical poets, notably Herbert and Crashaw. Herbert's great book *The Temple* (1633) contains several poems that, arranged to form figures, become in effect emblems of their subject matter. Another poet, Henry More, in his fondness for allegory and the Spenserian stanza points to one large influence, but often reminds the reader of the Metaphysicals in his choice and handling of imagery, even though his work is more justly charged with obscurity than theirs. At the same time, More is one of the few seventeenth century poets who is known to have studied René Descartes and to have been directly influenced by the Cartesian dualism of mind and matter. If, as Basil Willey has argued in *The Seventeenth Century Background* (1934), Cartesian thought undermined confidence in the "truth" of poetry, it is in More that one should be able to read the signs of the decline, but More seems as sure of the truth of his poetical utterances as of his *Divine Dialogues* (1668) in prose. Other Metaphysically tinged poetry will be considered part of the mid-century transition below.

## BEN JONSON

From a twentieth century perspective Ben Jonson (1573-1637) was overshadowed by Shakespeare as a playwright and by Donne as a lyric and reflective poet, but his importance in his time is difficult to overestimate. Before his time, England had produced classical scholars who edited texts, produced grammars and other educational tools, and wrote significant prose. Not until Jonson, however, did an Englishman combine classical learning with great poetic ability. Jonson's interpretation of the classical heritage, which involved (besides the drama) imitations of such distinctly classical forms as the epigram, ode, and verse epistle; the translation into verse of Horace's *Ars poetica* (c. 17 B.C.E.; *The Art of Poetry*) and the employment of poetry as an ethical, civilizing influence not only enriched poetry but also defined classicism itself for generations of Englishmen. Even present-day classicists are likely to conceive of its essential spirit as comprising such virtues as simplicity, clarity, symmetry, detachment, and restraint, although such qualities are hardly the hallmarks of Euripides, Pindar, Ovid, and any number of other Greek and Roman poets. Jonsonian classicism proved to be a timely antidote to Elizabethan verbosity and extravagance, however, and generated some of the best poetry of the seventeenth century.

All Jonson's favorite classical forms had been practiced in the sixteenth century, though often in an eclectic and self-indulgent way. Jonson showed that the discipline of strict classicism could be liberating. Bush has pointed out that his imitations of Martial not only capture the temper of the greatest Roman epigrammatist better than did any of his predecessors, but also display more originality than earlier poems in this genre. Although not a great love poet, Jonson wrote a series of song lyrics that are models of their type, one of them, "Drink to me only with thine eyes" being familiar to millions of people who know nothing of classicism or of Jonson himself. His verse letter "To Penshurst," though initially unexciting to a reader accustomed to Donne's pyrotechnics, achieves an unobtrusive but unforgettable effect. When, at the end, he contrasts the Sidney family mansion with other houses—"their lords have built, but thy lord dwell"—he has accomplished a tribute worth all the fulsome compliments that Elizabethans heaped on their benefactors. It was through his study of Horace, a quiet bastion of civility in the noisy Roman Empire, that Jonson was able to produce such an effect.

Like Donne, Jonson not only wrote fine poems but inspired others of a high order as well. Robert Herrick (1591-1674), to whom Jonson was "Saint Ben," sometimes approached his master in the art of epigram and sometimes exceeded him in the writing of cool, elegant lyrics. Poets such as Edmund Waller (1606-1687) who reached the heights only infrequently probably could not have done so at all without Jonson's example (and occasionally Donne's also). The delicacy of Waller's "Go, lovely rose" is an inheritance of the Tribe of Ben. If the same poet's Penshurst poems fall short of Jonson's, Marvell's "Upon Appleton House" is both marvelously original and indebted to Jonson. William Alexander McClung, in *The Country House in English Renaissance Poetry* (1977), has shown how the poets after Jonson were able to set forth both an ideal of environment and an ideal of virtue through their reflection in a house.

Neither Jonson nor his followers necessarily came by their Horatian restraint and moderation naturally. As a young man, Jonson flashed the same hot temper that many another Elizabethans did not bother to control. In 1598, he plunged a rapier six inches into the side of a fellow actor named Gabriel Spencer, killing him instantly. He escaped with a branding on the thumb by pleading benefit of clergy—a dubious privilege possible for an educated man in or out of holy orders. Pen in hand, however, he modeled his work on that of Horace, who counseled, and perhaps practiced, moderation as a "golden mean." Horace did not prevent Jonson from lashing out verbally at his critics from time to time, but the Roman poet probably saved the impetuous Jonson from many a poetical gaucherie.

Many of Jonson's followers were political conservatives, advocates of royal supremacy and others who had most to fear from the intransigent Puritans, whose power grew steadily throughout the first half of the century until they forced Charles I from his throne and, in 1649, beheaded him for treason. Thus Jonsonian classicists overlapped, but did not subsume, the Cavalier lyric poets, who celebrated the not particularly Horatian virtues of war, chivalry, and loyalty to the monarchy. Just as paradoxically, the great classicist of the generation after Jonson turned out to be Latin secretary of Oliver Cromwell's Commonwealth, the militant Puritan Milton.

At their best, the Jonsonians wrote graceful and civilized lyrics reflecting a philosophy that was, in the best sense of the term, Epicurean. Like the Elizabethans, they were attracted to the theme of human mortality, but whereas the earlier poets had responded to the inevitability of decline and death with lugubrious melancholy, the Tribe of Ben had imbibed Horace's advice: carpe diem, or "seize the day." They wrote the most beautiful lyrics on this theme ever written in English: Herrick's "To Daffodils," "To the Virgins, to Make Much of Time," and "Corinna's going A-Maying," Waller's "Go, lovely rose," and Marvell's "To His Coy Mistress."

Another subject dear to the heart of Jonsonians was one relatively rare in previous (and many later) eras: children. Jonson wrote, with deep feeling yet immense restraint, of the deaths of two children. "On My First Daughter" does not repeat the personal pronoun of the title, although the reader learns that her name was Mary. The parents, however, are referred to in the third person, only the final phrase, "cover lightly, gentle earth!" betraying the speaker's involvement in the child's demise. An even finer poem, "On My First Son," has only six couplets and yet achieves enormous poignancy through the most economical means. Jonson could have expressed his love no more forcefully than by saying: "Here doth lie/ Ben Jonson his best piece of poetry." The lesson he draws is more Horatian than Christian: "For whose sake, henceforth, all his vows be such/ As what he loves may never like too much." Although Jonson wrote a few religious lyrics, it seems to be the classical legacy that he cherished most deeply.

Among those who gathered with Jonson at the Mermaid Tavern, Corbett also wrote of family members, including one poem "To His Son, Vincent" in which he characteristically sets forth moderate wishes for his offspring, "not too much wealth, nor wit," and on the positive side, the graces of his mother, friends, peace, and innocence at the last. Among the poets who wrote poems about other people's children was William Cartwright, who expressed wishes for a friend's newborn son, and Herrick, who penned two short epitaphs and two graces for children to recite at meals. Obviously the range of childhood poems in the seventeenth century is very narrow, even if Traherne's mystical poems "Shadows in the Water," "Innocence," and others are included. Even so, that children figure in poetry at all is an indication that Jonson's disciples do not consider commonplace subjects beneath their notice.

As might be expected of admirers of Horace and Martial, Jonsonians favored short lines and short stanzas, though without the intricacy and irregularity often seen in Metaphysical lyrics. They often wrote in couplets, though the form known as the heroic couplet does not appear much before mid-century and does not become important until the age of Dryden. The couplets mirror the unassuming quality of so much early English classicism but commonly betray careful craftsmanship. The diction is rather plain, the metaphors few, and not often unusual. The words and images are carefully chosen, however, with an eye to precision and euphony. The tone is tender and affectionate toward friends and loved ones, sarcastic toward those who, like fools, deserve it. There are few high flights, but neither are Jonsonian lapses likely to be very gross. Speech, Jonson wrote, in *Timber: Or, Discoveries Made upon Men and Matter* (1641) is "the instrument of society." Furthermore, "words are the people's." The poet is someone who uses the people's resources for the people's good.

BAROQUE POETRY

Probably because it arose as a reaction against a Renaissance classicism that had no parallel in England before Jonson, the Baroque movement, beginning around 1580 and continuing for the better part of a century, had few manifestations in English poetry. First applied to architecture and later to sculpture and painting, the term described in particular the style of certain sixteenth century Venetian painters, particularly Jacopo Robusti Tintoretto, and of those, such as El Greco, who were influenced by the Venetians. The Baroque disdained formal beauty and placidity in favor of asymmetrical composition, rich color, energy, and even contortion.

Applied to prose style, "baroque" signifies the revolt against full and rounded Ciceronian elegance, a tendency to place the main sentence element first, the avoidance of symmetry by varying the form and length of constructions, and a greater autonomy for subordinate constructions, which tend to follow the main sentence element. English had developed a Ciceronian prose style, but a recognizably anti-Ciceronian prose arose in the seventeenth century, notably in such works as Robert Burton's *The Anatomy of Melancholy* (1621) and Sir Thomas Browne's *Religio Medici* (1642).

In poetry, the Baroque has some affinities with the Metaphysical, but the differences are suggested by the adjectives used to describe the Baroque: "ornate," "sensuous," "pictorial," and "emotional." The Baroque is more likely to reject logic and reason, which are useful to Metaphysical poets of an argumentative bent. In his *European Metaphysical Poetry*, Frank J. Warnke distinguishes between a Baroque inclination to use contrast and antithesis for the purpose of separating opposites and a Metaphysical preference for paradox and synthesis to produce a fusion of opposites. The Baroque was cultivated chiefly—not exclusively—by Roman Catholics as an expression of the Counter-Reformation spirit; it stands in contrast to the austerity of much northern European Protestant art.

The only English poets commonly associated with the Baroque are Fletcher and Crashaw (c. 1612-1649). Although Crashaw left more than four hundred poems, he is best known for his Saint Teresa poems, especially his florid "Upon the book and picture of the seraphical Saint Teresa" called "The Flaming Heart." The poem blazes to a finish in a series of oaths that illustrate the Baroque manner:

By thy large draughts of intellectual day,
And by thy thirsts of love more large than they;
By all thy brim-filled bowls of fierce desire
By thy last morning's draught of liquid fire. . . .

By these and other oaths he asked to be emptied of self and enabled to imitate her example. It is no surprise to learn that Crashaw lived for some years on the Continent, that he renounced his Anglican priesthood to become a Roman Catholic, and that he died in Italy.

Fletcher (c. 1585-1623), on the other hand, stands as a caution against too facile generalizations. He is best known for his devotional poem, *Christ Victorie, and Triumph in Heaven, and Earth, Over, and After Death* (1610). He remained English and Anglican, and although his poetry reminds some readers of the baroque pioneer Guillaume du Bartas, he usually causes readers of Spenser to think of *The Faerie Queene*. The case of Fletcher underlines the fact that English writers of the earlier seventeenth century felt no compulsion to wage war with the Renaissance, since its greatest nondramatic poet, far from being a doctrinaire classicist, synthesized elements classical, medieval, and Renaissance.

The Baroque style in poetry, as in the visual arts, contained more than the usual number of the seeds of decadence. Baroque poets were liable to grotesqueness, obscurity, melodrama, and triviality. Its excesses no doubt helped pave the way for the later neoclassical resurgence. Again by analogy with architecture, some literary historians have seen the Baroque also leading to the rococo, understood as a fussy, overdecorative, playful style that nevertheless might serve a serious purpose for a neoclassicist engaged in playful satire. The most obvious example in English literature, Alexander Pope's *The Rape of the Lock* (1712), comes early in the eighteenth century.

### MID-CENTURY TRANSITION

To argue for too neat a mid-century transition between the earlier classical, Metaphysical, and Baroque styles, on the one hand, and the neoclassical age on the other, is perhaps to betray an obsession with the neoclassical virtue of symmetry, but in a number of ways the mid-century marks a turning point. England's only interregnum straddles the century's midpoint, while on the Continent the Thirty Years' War came to an end with the treaties of the Peace of Westphalia in 1648. Both of these political events involved poetry and poets, the English Civil War more strikingly. The continental wars, insofar as they involved Protestant-Catholic clashes, represented nothing new, but they exhibited several modern features. Because they involved most European states in one way or another and required a general congress of nations to achieve even temporary peace, these conflicts augured the modern situation, in which local conflicts can trigger unforeseen large-scale involvement. Armorers preparing soldiers for battle had to devise protection against traditional weapons such as the sword and also new ones such as the pistol; the latter were often used as a kind of last resort, as clubs, or thrown at enemies more often than they were fired. All over Europe men were getting a preview of the mass destruction they could expect in future wars. The necessity of compromise and toleration—never before recognized as virtues—was beginning to dawn. More and more it seemed essential that reason and judgment, not passion and force, reign.

England had embarked on its internal war in 1642. The Puritans, who had already succeeded in closing London's theaters, alarmed conservative Englishmen by closing down the monarchy itself. The execution of Charles I and the proclamation of the Commonwealth in 1649 culminated nearly a decade of violence that had driven Sir John Denham, Sir William Davenant, and Thomas Hobbes, among others, into exile, and the Cavalier poet Richard Lovelace into prison, where he penned several immortal poems. The political transition ended in 1660. Young Dryden wrote *Astraea Redux* (1660), an elaborate poetic tribute to a great event: the return of Charles II, son of the executed king, in glory. The adjustments made by all the former belligerents signal a new era. The next revolution, in 1688, despite ingredients seemingly as volatile as those which had precipitated the mid-century war, was not bloody.

Miner (*The Metaphysical Mode from Donne to Cowley*) has referred to the decade between 1645 and 1655 as a "microcosm" of the century as a whole. Certainly it was a productive time for poets. In only the first half of that decade appeared Waller's *Poems* (1645), Sir John Suckling's *Fragmenta Aurea* (1646), Crashaw's *Steps to the Temple* (1646, 1648), Herrick's *Hesperides: Or, The Works Both Humane and Divine of Robert Herrick, Esq.* (1648), Lovelace's *Lucasta: Epodes, Odes, Sonnets, Songs, &c. to Which Is Added Aramantha, a Pastorall* (1649), and Vaughan's *Silex Scintillans* (parts 1 and 2, 1650, 1655), all studded with still familiar anthology favorites. Although Marvell's posthumous poems are difficult to date, at least some of his best are presumed to have been written in the early 1650's, as were a number of the finest of Milton's sonnets, while *Paradise Lost* (1667, 1674) was evolving in Milton's imagination. Miner's point, however, is that the poets at work at this time are difficult to classify as Cavalier, Puritan, Metaphysical, or neoclassical. The distinctive earlier voices—those of Donne and Jonson and Herbert—had been stilled, and the most distinctive later one had not yet developed. The teenage Dryden's notorious foray into Metaphysical imagery in his 1649 poem "Upon the Death of the Lord Hastings," where Hastings's smallpox blisters are compared to "rosebuds stuck in the lily-skin about," and where "Each little pimple had a tear in it/ To wail the fault its rising did commit," presages the great neoclassicist only in its use of rhymed pentameter couplets—and those are not yet particularly "heroic."

That particular form, the end-stopped couplet with its potential for balance, antithesis, and memorable precision, was being hammered out in the 1640's by such poets as Waller, Denham, and John Cleveland (otherwise remembered chiefly as a decadent Metaphysical) in a series of spirited anti-Puritan satires. The latter's 1642 poem, "Cooper's Hill," now faded, looks forward to the Augustan Age with its blend of Horatian and Vergilian sentiments, its lofty abstractions, and its skillful handling of rhythm. The pentameter couplet was as old as Geoffrey Chaucer, but as a distinct unit, sometimes virtually a stanza in itself, it was capable of generating quite different effects. Detachable, quotable, suited for uttering the common wisdom, the great truths apparent to all, it embodied the neoclassical concept of wit, which was variously defined from this period on, but most memorably (because so well-expressed in a couplet, of course) by Pope in 1711: "True wit is nature to advantage dressed,/ What oft was thought, but ne'er so well expressed."

At the very middle of the century appeared a work by a man whose profession was neither poet nor critic but whose terse genealogy of a poem marks off the distance between the ages of Donne and Dryden. Hobbes was responding to remarks on epic made by Davenant in the preface to his fragmentary heroic poem *Gondibert* (1651) when he wrote:

> Time and education beget experience; experience begets memory; memory begets judgment and fancy; judgment begets the strength and structure, and fancy begets the ornaments of a poem.

It is impossible to imagine Donne countenancing the splitting asunder of "structure" and "ornaments," or for that matter acknowledging "ornaments" at all—for where were they in his poetry?

The following year, 1651, saw the publication of Hobbes's magnum opus, the *Leviathan*. There he made explicit what his answer to Davenant had implied: "In a good poem ... both judgment and fancy are required: but the fancy must be more eminent." In other words, "ornament" is more important than "structure." To be sure, Hobbes was only stating succinctly a view that had already surfaced in Francis Bacon's philosophy: Poetry is make-believe ("feigned history," as Bacon put it in *The Advancement of Learning* back in 1605) and has nothing to do with truth. This reproach becomes more damning when seen in the context of the linguistic theories set forth elsewhere by Hobbes and by the Royal Society of London in the following decade.

Another work of the mid-century marks a beginning rather than a transition. In 1650, *The Tenth Muse Lately Sprung Up in America* was published in London. Supposedly the manuscript had been spirited across the Atlantic without its author's consent. It was the first book of poems by an American woman, Anne Bradstreet. Discounting the doggerel of such works of piety as *The Bay Psalm Book* (1640), it was in fact the first book of poems by any American. More than two hundred years would pass before another woman poet would do as well as Bradstreet, who, twenty years earlier, as a teenage bride, had emigrated to Massachusetts.

POETRY AND THE SCIENTIFIC REVOLUTION

Of the nonliterary forces on seventeenth century poets, the New Science may well have been the most uniformly pervasive throughout the Western world. Whereas social, political, and even religious developments varied considerably in nature and scope, the scientists were busy discovering laws that applied everywhere and affected the prevailing worldview impartially. Some artists and thinkers discovered the New Science and pondered its implications before others, but no poet could fall very many decades behind the vanguard and continue to be taken seriously. The modern reader of, say, C. S. Lewis's *The Discarded Image* (1964) and E. M. W. Tillyard's *The Elizabethan World Picture* (1943) observes that the Elizabethan "picture" had not changed substantially from the medieval "image" described by Lewis. Between 1600 and 1700, however, the worldview of educated people changed more dramatically than in any previous century. Early in the century Donne signaled his awareness of science's challenge to the old certitudes about the world. By Dryden's maturity, the new learning had rendered the Elizabethan brand of erudition disreputable and its literary imagination largely incomprehensible.

In *The Breaking of the Circle* (1960), Marjorie Hope Nicolson uses a popular medieval symbol, the circle of perfection, to demonstrate the effect of the New Science on the poets' perception of their world. The universe was a circle; so was Earth and the human head. The circle was God's perfect form, unending like himself, and all its manifestations shared in the perfection. It was easy—one might almost say "natural"—for Donne to begin one of his sonnets: "I am a little world made cunningly." Significantly, Donne did not say that he was *like* a little world. Not only did he use a metaphor instead of a simile, but also he used the metaphor confident that he was expressing a truth. In another sonnet, Shakespeare refers to his soul as "the center of my sinful earth." Two thousand years earlier, Aristotle had said that "to make metaphors well is to perceive likeness," and this judgment still stood firm. Already, however, a succession of thinkers from Nicolaus Copernicus in 1543 to Sir Isaac Newton in 1687 were at work breaking up the circle of perfection.

A special irony attaches to the contribution of Copernicus, a pious Roman Catholic who took the concept of the circle of perfection for granted when he set forth his heliocentric theory of the solar system. His insight was to see the Sun, not Earth, as the center of God's operations in the visible world. To him, it was perfectly obvious that God would impart perfect circular motion to the planets. Unfortunately his new model provided even less accurate predictability of planetary motions than the old geocentric theory that it was intended to replace. Thus he had to invent an ingenious system of subordinate circles—"eccentrics" and "epicycles"—to account for the discrepancies between the simple version of his model and his observations of what actually went on in the heavens. Thus, although his heliocentric theory incurred condemnation by Protestant and Catholic alike, his cumbersome model did not attract many adherents, and for decades intelligent people remained ignorant of his theory and its implications.

Two contemporaries of Donne changed all that. In 1609, Galileo built a telescope; by the next year, he was systematically examining not just the solar system but other suns beyond it. Johann Kepler discovered, virtually at the same time, the elliptical orbit of Mars. He did this by breaking the old habit—his own as well as humankind's—of regarding physical events as symbols of divine mysteries, and thereby swept Copernicus's eccentrics and epicycles into a rubbish heap. When Donne wrote *An Anatomy of the World: The First Anniversary*, in 1611, he showed his familiarity with the new astronomy:

> And new philosophy calls all in doubt,
> The element of fire is quite put out;
> The sun is lost, and the earth, and no man's wit
> Can well direct him where to look for it.

Even before the confirmation of Copernicus's theory, the greatest literary geniuses of his century raised versions of the great question provoked by the new science. Michel Eyquem de Montaigne put it most simply in his *Essais* (books 1-2 1580; rev. 1582; books 1-3, 1588; rev. 1595; *The Essays*, 1603): "What do I know?" The word "essays" signifies "attempts," and the work can be described as a series of attempts to answer his question. Miguel de Cervantes, setting out with the rather routine literary motive of satirizing a particularly silly type of chivalric romance, stumbled on his theme: the difficulty of distinguishing appearance from reality—even for those who, unlike Don Quixote, are not mad. The second part of Cervantes's novel, *El ingenioso hidalgo don Quixote de la Mancha* (1605, 1615; *The History of the Valorous and Wittie Knight-Errant, Don Quixote of the Mancha*, 1612-1620; better known as *Don Quixote de la Mancha*), written like the first out of an understandable but pedestrian literary ambition (to reclaim his hero from the clutches of a plagiarist), raises the disturbing possibility that the madman interprets at least some aspects of reality more sensibly than the "sane" people among whom the idealistic Don Quixote was floundering. Shakespeare, having already endorsed the ancient concept of the poet as a divinely inspired madman in *A Midsummer Night's Dream* (pr. c. 1595-1596), created, at the very beginning of the new century, a "mad" hero who raises an even more profound question: Can knowledge of the truth, even if attainable (and Hamlet gains the knowledge of the truth that concerns him most—the circumstances of his father's death—through ghostly intervention), lead to madness and paralysis of the will?

Unlike Eliot's twentieth century figure of J. Alfred Prufrock, who asks, "Do I dare disturb the universe?," medieval man did not disturb, and was not disturbed by, the universe. Even the presumed decay of the world from its original golden age did not alarm him, for it was all part of the plan of a wise and loving Creator. In *An Anatomy of the World*, the decay of the world has become profoundly disturbing, for the very cosmic order itself seems to be coming apart: "'Tis all in pieces, all coherence gone." Shortly before writing this poem—and perhaps afterward—Donne was able to write poetry of the sort quoted earlier, in which he moves easily from macrocosm to microcosm; but he also recognized that the "new philosophy calls all in doubt."

Astronomical discoveries were not the only form of knowledge. In 1600, William Gilbert wrote a book on magnetism. He was, like Copernicus, a good sixteenth century man and could talk about lodestones as possessing souls; his important discovery, however, was that the earth is a lodestone. In 1628, when William Harvey published his findings on the circulation of the blood, he referred to the heart as the body's "sovereign" and "inmost home," but in the process, he taught the world to regard it as a mechanism—a pump. The old worldview was being destroyed quite unintentionally by men whose traditional assumptions often hampered their progress, but whose achievement made it impossible for their own grandchildren to make the same assumptions or to take the old learning seriously. As a result of Robert Boyle's work, chemistry was banishing alchemy, a subject taken seriously not only by poets but also by the scientists of an earlier day. At century's end, to talk of a person as a "little world" was mere quaintness, for Harvey had taught everyone to regard the body as one sort of mechanism, while the astronomers insisted that the solar system was another. It was merely idle to make connections between them.

As the scientists focused more clearly on their subjects, the poets' vision became more blurred. Astronomy is only one such subject area, but it is a particularly useful one for the purpose of demonstrating the change. Around 1582 Sidney's Astrophel could exclaim: "With how sad steps, O moon, thou climb'st the skies,/ How silently, and with how wan a face." Astrophel is a disappointed lover, of course, and need not be taken too seriously. What strikes the reader is the ease with which his creator sees parallels between the moon and the earthbound lover. In a more serious context, Herbert addresses a star: "Bright spark, shot from a brighter place/ Where beams surround my Savior's face." Herbert almost surely knew what Galileo had been doing, but his "brighter place" still lay, as it were, beyond the reach of the telescope. In 1650, Vaughan could begin a poem: "I saw Eternity the other night/ Like a great Ring of pure and endless light,/ All calm, as it was bright." The reader's first inclination is perhaps to marvel at the facility of the utterance, but is the tone as matter-of-fact as it seems? Might not Donne and Herbert have seen eternity every night? On second thought one wonders whether the moments of insight are getting rarer. Five years later, Vaughan published "They are all gone into the world of light," a poem reflecting an awareness of the transience of the heavenly vision:

> And yet, as Angels in some brighter dreams
> Call the soul, when man doth sleep:
> So some strange thoughts transcend our wonted themes,
> And into glory peep.

At the end of the poem the speaker begs God to "disperse these mists." Any reader can verify that in later Metaphysical poetry the view of heaven gets cloudier. Traherne, almost surely writing in the Restoration, sees heaven not through the earthly eye but mystically with a sight often blurred by dream, shadows, and mists. In "My Spirit," for example, his soul "saw infinity/ 'Twas not a sphere, but 'twas a power/ Invisible." In *Religio Laici*, Dryden can see none of this and counsels submission to the Church. By 1733, Pope has banished all thought of reading heavenly meanings in the heavens: "The proper study of Mankind is Man"—unless, of course, one happens to be an astronomer.

## NEOCLASSICISM FROM 1660 TO 1700

By the Restoration, the poets had turned their attention primarily to public and social themes. The comedy of this period has given readers the impression of a licentious age determined to bury the memory of Puritanistic domination and live as fast and loose an existence as possible. Such behavior could not have characterized more than a tiny percentage of the people of later Stuart England. It was an age struggling for order through compromise. Wit might entertain, but life required sober judgment.

The classical tradition survived the New Science better than did the Metaphysical. It did not aspire to compete with science in the realm beyond everyday human and social experience. The Jonsonian tradition of short lyric and reflective poems no longer flourished, but the neoclassicists of the Restoration rediscovered satire and the heroic poem—the latter primarily in the remarkable triad of Miltonic poems published between 1667 and 1671: *Paradise Lost* (1667, 1674), *Paradise Regained* (1671), and *Samson Agonistes* (1671). Horace was not neglected, but the study and translation of the Homeric and Vergilian epics gained in popularity. The time might have been ripe for a great patriotic epic (Milton considered a true Arthurian epic that would rectify the deficiencies of Spenser's episodic one before he finally settled on the yet nobler idea of justifying God's way to humans), but whether because Milton's accomplishment had preempted the field or because history as Restoration poets knew it could not be hammered into the Vergilian mold, it was not written.

Instead, Dryden produced something new: a political satire in a heroic style based on a contemporary controversy over the attempt to exclude Charles II's Roman Catholic brother James from the royal succession. It was a serious matter, laden with danger for the principal in the struggle, for Dryden, and for the nation. He did not use blank verse, as Shakespeare and Milton had in their greatest works, but the heroic couplet, a form that Dryden had been honing for twenty years. The result is a poem of peculiar urgency, yet by virtue of Dryden's skillful representation of Charles II as the biblical King David and of the earl of Shaftesbury as "false Achitophel," who attempts to turn Absalom (Charles's illegitimate son, the duke of Monmouth) against his father, the poem takes on universality. It is by far the most impressive poem of the period: *Absalom and Achitophel* (1681, 1682).

The drama aside, satire is the greatest literary achievement of the Restoration, and it is also the most diverse. From Samuel Butler's low burlesque of the Puritans in *Hudibras* (1663, 1664, 1678, parts 1-3) to Dryden's sustained high style in *Absalom and Achitophel*, from a butt as small as one undistinguished playwright (Thomas Shadwell in Dryden's 1682 mock-epic *Mac Flecknoe: Or, A Satyre upon the True-Blew-Protestant Poet, T. S.*) to one as large as humankind, vain aspirer to the status of rational being (the earl of Rochester's "A Satire Against Mankind," printed in 1675), verse satire flourished, providing models for even greater achievements in the first part of the following century. The Renaissance notion of decorum as the delicate adjustment of literary means to ends, of the suitability of the parts to the whole, governed these diverse attempts at diminishing the wickedness and folly that Restoration poets considered it their duty to expose and correct. Even *Hudibras*, with its slam-bang tetrameter couplets and quirky rhymes, seems the perfect vehicle for flaying the routed Puritans, and its levels of irony are far more complex than superficial readers suspect. When satire began to invade prose, as it increasingly did in the eighteenth century, its narrative possibilities increased, but it lost subtle effects of rhythm, timing, and rhyme.

Compared with the first sixty years of the century, the Restoration seems a prosaic age. A considerable number of its most accomplished writers—John Bunyan, the diarists Samuel Pepys and John Evelyn, Sir William Temple, John Locke—wrote no poetry worth preserving, and Dryden himself wrote a large proportion of prose. Does the preponderance of prose and satire confirm Eliot's early charge that a "dissociation of sensibility" had set in by the time of the Restoration? Is it true that writers no longer could fuse thought and feeling, with the consequence that prose was used for conveying truth and poetry for the setting forth of delightful lies?

Hobbes, who had little use for poetry in general, praised the epic as conducive to moral truth, and he admitted that satire can be defended on moral grounds also. The Restoration poets in England were the successors of a classical tradition that emphasized the ethical value of poetry, so they might as plausibly be considered carrying out, on a somewhat larger scale, the dictates of Jonson as those of Hobbes. The Royal Society of London, of which Dryden was a member, was founded in 1662 for "the improving of natural knowledge," and among its ambitions it numbered the improving of the language by waging war against "tropes" and "figures" and "metaphors." One cannot imagine Donne having anything to do with such an organization, all the more because the Society on principle did not discuss "such subjects as God and the soul." It is difficult to see how Dryden's association with it substantiates the charge of dissociated sensibility, however, for there is certainly both thought and feeling together in *Absalom and Achitophel*, even if it is, like the Royal Society itself, earthbound and relatively unmetaphorical, and, while it is no doubt instructive, generations of readers have taken delight in it also.

One is tempted to offer a different explanation for Restoration writers' greater attachment to prose and to satire. The reading audience expanded greatly in the seventeenth century, and increasingly it became the business of the writer to satisfy its interests, which for a variety of reasons were political and social. The early Metaphysical writers possessed a very small audience (one another and a few more who shared the same interests); very much the same situation obtained for Jonson and his followers. When the readership increased, poets modified their work accordingly. When Dryden did write of religion, he wrote of it as he and his contemporaries understood it. That Dryden took little delight in Donne's poetry is clear from his remarks in "A Discourse Concerning the Original and Progress of Satire" (1693):

> Donne affects the metaphysics, not only in his amorous verses, where nature only should reign; and perplexes the minds of the fair sex with nice speculations of philosophy, when he should engage their hearts and entertain them with the softnesses of love.

Dryden did not understand Donne's intentions very well, but he understood his own political intentions very well indeed.

In his own and the century's final years, Dryden worked primarily at translation, promising in his "Preface to *Fables Ancient and Modern*" (1700), "if it should please God to give me longer life and moderate health." He added another provision: "that I meet with those encouragements from the public, which may enable me to proceed in my undertaking with some cheerfulness." This is the remark of a public figure—a former poet laureate, author of a stream of plays and published books since the 1600's, a veteran attraction at Will's Coffee House in London.

Poets had not always expected such encouragements. When Donne died in 1631, only four of his poems had been published. Herbert, Marvell, and Traherne saw few or none of their poems in print. Jonson, on the other hand, had offered his work to the public, even inviting ridicule in 1616 by boldly calling his volume *Works*. Like Dryden after him, he had developed a healthy sense of audience in his career as a playwright. He had even more reason to fear an unhappy audience than Dryden, for along with John Marston and George Chapman, he had been imprisoned and very nearly mutilated by a gang of Scots retainers of James I whom the trio had outraged by some of their jests in their play *Eastward Ho!* (pr., pb. 1605). Nevertheless, Jonson promised a translation of Horace's *Ars poetica* (c. 17 B.C.E.; *The Art of Poetry*), with no provisions whatsoever, that same year. The fact that he did not deliver the translation until long afterward does not seem to have had anything to do with readers' wishes. Jonson usually conveyed the impression that whatever he had to say amounted to nothing less than a golden opportunity for any sensible reader or listener.

Even if one assumes that Dryden's hope for encouragement may have been only an expression of politeness, that politeness itself signifies a change of relationship with the "public." Most of the poetry written in the time of Donne and Jonson has the quality of being overheard. It is as if the poet is praying, making love, or rebuking a fool, and the reader has just happened to pass by. If the poem is a verse epistle, the reader experiences the uncomfortable feeling that he is reading someone else's mail—and quite often that is so. By 1700, the poet seems conscious of producing a document for public inspection and proceeds accordingly, with all the implications—fortunate and unfortunate—of such a procedure. He will not tax the public with too many difficulties, for some of them—too many, perhaps—will not understand. He had better polish his work, and he had better not be dull. He might produce one of those "overheard" lyrics once in a while, but the chances are that they will yield few excellences not imitative of earlier poets whose circumstances favored that type of poem.

The neoclassical sense of audience would continue, as the neoclassical period would continue, for nearly another century—at least in those poets with access to a public. The poet's public stance would give rise to more fine satire and reflective poems of great majesty and sustained moral power. The knack of lyric would be largely lost, and, when recovered, the lyrics would be romantic. No one would ever write poems like "A Valediction: Forbidding Mourning" or "To His Coy Mistress" again.

BIBLIOGRAPHY

Baker, David J. *Between Nations: Shakespeare, Spenser, Marvell, and the Question of Britain*. Stanford, Calif.: Stanford University Press, 1997. Fusing historiography and literary criticism, this book places Renaissance England and its literature at a meeting of English, Irish, Scottish, and Welsh histories.

Barbour, Reid. *English Epicures and Stoics: Ancient Legacies in Early Stuart Culture.* Amherst: University of Massachusetts Press, 1998. Part of the Massachusetts Studies in Early Modern Culture series. Portrays the intricate dialectical influence of the ancient Greek philosophies of Epicureanism and Stoicism on seventeenth century England and analyzes how these disparate legacies served as touchstones for discourse in the theater, poetry, and political, religious, and scientific literature of the period.

Campbell, Gordon, and Thomas N. Corns. *John Milton: Life, Work, and Thought*. New York: Oxford University Press, 2008. A biography by two eminent Milton scholars, emphasizing the relationship between Milton's imaginative works and the rapidly changing times in which he lived. Includes illustrations and maps. Extensive notes and bibliography. Index.

Cummings, Robert, ed. *Seventeenth-Century Poetry: An Annotated Anthology*. Malden, Mass.: Wiley-Blackwell, 2000. A selection from the works of more than fifty poets, including all the major figures of the period, as well as a number of writers recently added to the literary canon, many of them women. Modernized spelling and in-depth annotations. Index of authors, index of titles and first lines, and bibliography.

Cunnar, Eugene R., and Jeffrey Johnson. *Discovering and (Re)Covering the Seventeenth Century Religion Lyric*. Pittsburgh, Pa.: Duquesne University Press, 2001. A collection of fifteen essays whose primary purpose is to consider devotional lyricists of the seventeenth century who have previously been neglected. Among those discussed are Robert Southwell, Aemilia Lanyer, William Alabaster, William Austin, and Mary Carey. Bibliography and index.

Fowler, Alistair, ed. *The New Oxford Book of Seventeenth Century Verse*. 1992. Reprint. New York: Oxford University Press, 2008. This indispensable anthology contains 861 selections from works of major and minor poets and from a wide range of genres, including popular verse. Notes, index of first lines, and index of authors.

Lewis, Jayne, and Maximillian E. Novak, eds. *Enchanted Ground: Reimagining John Dryden*. Toronto: University of Toronto Press, 2004. A volume in the University of California, Los Angeles, Clark Memorial Library series. Subjects of these essays by various scholars include Dryden's political poetry, religious beliefs, connections to the literary heritage, plays, and songs. An audio compact disc of Dryden's songs is included with the book. Illustrated. Bibliographical references and index.

Mapstone, Sally, ed. *Older Scots Literature*. Edinburgh: John Donald, 2005. The third part of this volume contains essays on seventeenth century Scottish poets, including those associated with Scotland's James VI after he ascended the English throne. Bibliographical references and index.

Morotti, Arthur F. *Manuscript, Print, and the English Renaissance Lyric*. Ithaca, N.Y.: Cornell University Press, 1995. Examines the tradition of manuscript transmission of poetic works and explains how the change to print publication was effected. Morotti notes the ways in which the new process altered not only the creative process but also the cultural milieu. Bibliography and index.

Post, Jonathan F. S., ed. *Green Thoughts, Green Shades: Essays by Contemporary Poets on the Early Modern Lyric*. Berkeley: University of California Press, 2002. Twelve noted contemporary poets contemplate the poetry of their sixteenth and seventeenth century predecessors in the first publication of its kind. The keen insights and the lively style of these essays has elicited enthusiastic comments from scholars and critics. Highly recommended. Index.

Rawson, Claude, and Aaron Santesso, eds. *John Dryden (1631-1700): His Politics, His Plays, and His Poets*. Newark: University of Delaware Press, 2004. Essays produced for Yale University's celebration of the tercentenary of Dryden's death. Part 1 of the volume focuses on Dryden's plays, part 2, on connections between Dryden and other poets. Bibliography and index.

Reid, David Stuart. *The Metaphysical Poets*. Harlow, England: Longman, 2000. The author devotes a chapter to each of the six major Metaphysical poets, emphasizing their unique qualities as well as their similarities. The theme of diversity is then carried into a concluding chapter, which deals with other types of "seventeenth century wit" and with the differences between Metaphysical poets and the Augustans. A brief biography precedes each of the six main chapters. Illustrations, bibliographical references, and index.

Young, R. V. *Doctrine and Devotion in Seventeenth-Century Poetry: Studies on Donne, Herbert, Crashaw, and Vaughan.* Studies in Renaissance Literature 2. Rochester, N.Y.: D. S. Brewer, 2000. Argues that the devotional poetry of John Donne, George Herbert, Henry Vaughan, and Richard Crashaw owed more to the tradition of continental Catholicism than to Protestantism. The author also challenges postmodern interpretations by pointing out that such matters as subjective identity have long been basic to Christian thought. A landmark scholarly study. Bibliography and index.

Zwicker, Steven N., ed. *The Cambridge Companion to John Dryden.* New York: Cambridge University Press, 2004. Among the topics of the essays in this diverse collection are Dryden's plays, his satire, his politics, and his poetics. Chronology, bibliography, and index.

*Robert P. Ellis*

# THOMAS CAMPION

**Born:** London, England; February 12, 1567
**Died:** London, England; March 1, 1620

### OTHER LITERARY FORMS

Thomas Campion (KAM-pee-uhn) wrote a critical essay of poetics, *Observations in the Art of English Poesie* (1602), and a book of music theory, *A New Way of Making Fowre Parts in Counter-point* (c. 1617), the one work of his that remained in print throughout the seventeenth century.

### ACHIEVEMENTS

England has always had a strong claim to one of the finest literatures in the West. Most critics agree, moreover, that the literature of the late English Renaissance—stretching from Edmund Spenser through William Shakespeare to John Milton—was the true golden age. With music, however, it is a different story; usually England imported rather than exported musical ideas. The Germans, George Frideric Handel (later naturalized as a British subject) in the eighteenth century and Felix Mendelssohn in the nineteenth, dominated English music. For two brief periods, however, England was Europe's musical innovator—the mid-fifteenth century, when John Dunstable's music taught Continental composers the new style, and the decades spanning the sixteenth and seventeenth centuries, when William Byrd, Thomas Morley, Thomas Wheelkes, and especially John Dowland ushered in England's musical golden age. Baldassare Castiglione's *Il Cortegiano* (1528; *The Courtier*, 1561) advises the Renaissance gentleman to be adept at both poetry and music, and most educated persons had some level of expertise in both, but only one man in that twin golden age deserves to be called both a first-rate poet and a first-rate composer: Thomas Campion. Most composers would either set words by others, as John Dowland did—often producing truly moving music to inferior words, as in his famous "Come heavy sleep"—or they would write their own words with even worse literary results, as Campion's friend Philip Rosseter did in his half of *A Booke of Ayres*, which he jointly produced with Campion. Most poets would entitle a work, hopefully, "Song" and wait for a composer to do his share—as John Donne did, for example, in "Song: Goe and Catch a Falling Star." Campion, however, wrote both words and music and thus is the distillation of the English Renaissance.

## BIOGRAPHY

Thomas Campion was born into a circle of lawyers. His father, John Campion, was a legal clerk in the Chancery Court, with social ambitions left unrealized at his death in 1576, when his son was nine years old. Campion's mother, Lucy, was a middle-class woman with some property inherited from her family. She had earlier married another lawyer, Roger Trigg, and had a daughter, Mary. Trigg died in 1563, and a year later, she married John Campion, bearing Thomas and his sister Rose. After John's death, she again waited a year and married yet another lawyer, Augustine Steward. When she died and Steward married a woman named Anne Sisley, Campion was left orphaned at the age of fourteen, living with foster parents, who immediately (1581) sent him with Thomas Sisley, Anne's child from a previous marriage, to Peterhouse, Cambridge.

While at Cambridge, Campion was a friend of Thomas Nashe and may have met other literary figures there also—fellow students Christopher Marlowe, Thomas Kyd, and Robert Greene, as well as Edmund Spenser's friend, the don Gabriel Harvey, who theorized about quantitative meter. Cambridge, the nurturing ground of early Puritanism, left Campion uninterested in religion—a fact that may have contributed to his decision to leave in 1584 without the usual clerical degree—but it was there that he first developed an interest in literature and music.

After a hiatus of nearly two years, Campion resumed his education by entering Gray's Inn, London, to study law—a move that his family connections made nearly inevitable. At Gray's Inn, however, Campion preferred literature and music to his legal studies, earning no degree in his eight years there and seemingly being interested mostly in the periodic revels, especially student dramatic productions. He contributed some songs to masques—good preparation for his later career as masque writer to the Jacobean nobility. It is possible that Campion met William Shakespeare at this time, for *The Comedy of Errors* was performed at Gray's Inn between 1592 and 1594, shortly before Campion left. Like his younger contemporary and fellow law student, John Donne, Campion was circulating his poetry privately and gaining a solid reputation as a poet before he appeared in print; it is also probable that Campion was singing his songs to his own lute accompaniment at this time. Five of these songs appeared pseudonymously at the end of the 1591 edition of Sir Philip Sidney's *Astrophel and Stella*.

During his years at Gray's Inn, Campion accompanied the military expedition led by the earl of Essex to Brittany to help the French fend off a Spanish invasion (1591). His poetic achievements there were more notable than his military ones: No record of his activities survives aside from two Latin poems he composed about his experiences, the epigrams "De Se" and "In Obitum Gual. Devoreux fratris clariss. Comitis Essexiae." Latin, indeed, was Campion's favored language at this time; his first published volume of poetry, *Poemata*, is a lengthy volume of Latin poems, mostly epigrams.

Soon after he abandoned law and Gray's Inn, he met the lutenist Philip Rosseter, who remained Campion's closest friend for the rest of his life. It was Rosseter who changed the direction of Campion's career. Latin was a fashionable language in the English Renaissance for those with literary ambitions; even as late as Milton, poets were expected to produce in Latin as well as English. Its accessibility to the general public, however, was limited. At this time, Campion began serious production of poetry whose main intent was to entertain—first his lute songs and then his masques. In 1601, he published jointly with Rosseter *A Booke of Ayres*, containing forty-two songs, the first twenty-one by Campion and the last twenty-one by Rosseter.

The following year, Campion published a work in prose that gained him some fame—*Observations in the Art of English Poesie*. Possibly a reflection of the literary interests of his Cambridge days, the treatise is the last—and best—defense of quantitative meter in English verse. In the 1580's, a group of men led by Gabriel Harvey, Edmund Spenser, and Sir Philip Sidney began an attempt to rescue English poetry from the dreary fourteeners and poulter's measures that everyone seemed to be writing. Influenced by French theorists, they tried to write poetry based on duration (quantity) of syllables rather than stress (accent). Such an attempt was, perhaps, inevitable in the English Renaissance, for, like so much else, it was based on Greek and Latin models. The failure of the attempt, however, was inevitable because English inherited the strong Germanic accent from the Anglo-Saxon language and thus could not be forced to do what Greek and Latin, without the strong Germanic accent, could do naturally. Some of Spenser's and Sidney's more unreadable pieces are quantitative; then they abandoned the attempt and became great poets. Campion's *Observations in the Art of English Poesie* is actually a resurrection of this dead theory, and as a resurrected body should be, his theory was considerably stronger than the dead one. Instead of calling for an exacting measurement of long and short vowels and count of neighboring consonants, Campion appealed to variety: Use of the eight basic feet of quantitative meter would rescue English poetry from the monotony of the unending alternation of stresses and non-stresses. Campion made two mistakes in his treatise, however: First, he overlooked the fact that varying stressed instead of quantitative feet would do the job better, and second, he called the drab accentual verse that he was arguing against "rhyme." Samuel Daniel thus responded with his eloquent *The Defence of Ryme* (1603) and finally put to rest the English quantitative theory without a reply from Campion.

Campion, however, had left the field. Late in 1602 or thereabouts, he went to France and enrolled in the University of Caen to study medicine. One might expect that Campion's stay at Caen would be similar to those at Cambridge and Gray's Inn, especially considering Caen's reputation for revels and entertainments of all sorts. This time, however, Campion persevered and received his degree, returning to London in 1605 to establish a medical practice. His reputation as a poet and musician was still strong, and this perhaps attracted sufficient patients among the nobility to keep his practice going on a secure if not lucrative level. His later verse reveals an occasional medical metaphor.

Campion wrote little during the next few years while he was establishing himself in his profession, publishing nothing between his *Observations in the Art of English Poesie* in 1602 and his five major works in his most productive year of 1613, except for *Lord Hay's Masque* in 1607. With the accession of James I to the English throne in 1603, the masque moved from the universities and inns of court to the homes of the fashionable nobility. Prospero's masque celebrating the engagement of Miranda and Ferdinand in act 4 of Shakespeare's *The Tempest* (pr. 1611) gives a good indication of the nature and function of the masque to the Jacobeans: A noble family would celebrate an important occasion, especially a wedding, with an entertainment combining music, drama, and visual spectacle, based on classical myth and employing allegory. Campion, Ben Jonson, and a number of other poets became popular as masque writers in the early seventeenth century, Campion producing five masques or masquelike entertainments, three of them in 1613.

One of the three, *The Somerset Masque* (pr. 1613), involved Campion in one of Jacobean England's worst scandals. In 1611, Robert Carr, King James's favorite and later earl of Somerset, began a liaison with Frances Howard, the countess of Essex. The relationship was partly a political one, since it was part of an attempt by the powerful Howard family to gain more power. The countess's marriage to Essex was annulled, and Somerset, against the advice of his close friend Sir Thomas Overbury, married her in late 1613. Campion's *The Somerset Masque* provided part of the nuptial entertainment. Out of spite, Somerset and his wife maneuvered Overbury into insulting the king and thus landed him in the Tower of London, where their agents slowly poisoned him to death. Part of the money paid by Somerset to the agents was conveyed by two unwitting accomplices, Sir Thomas Munson and Thomas Campion. At the subsequent trial, Campion was questioned, but no charges were brought against him, while Munson was wrongly sentenced to imprisonment in the Tower. He was imprisoned until 1617, when he was exonerated, but by that time his health had broken. Campion was the physician who attended him.

In addition to his courtly entertainments, Campion published four books of *ayres* to add to his earlier one: *Two Bookes of Ayres* published jointly in 1613 and *The Third and Fourth Booke of Ayres*, also published jointly, in 1617. The third book was dedicated to the recently released Munson and the fourth book to Munson's son, indications of Campion's loyalty to his friends. In 1618, he published *The Ayres That Were Sung and Played at Brougham Castle*—in honor of the king's visit there—a hybrid work sharing characteristics with his other books of airs and also his masques. His last work, generating a symmetry of closure, was similar to his first: *Thomae Campiani Epigrammatum Libri II*, a long collection of Latin poems, mostly epigrams, some of which appeared in his earlier volumes.

One other publishing event in Campion's life, however, needs to be mentioned. The date of *A New Way of Making Fowre Parts in Counter-point* has not yet been determined by scholars, some preferring 1617-1619 and others 1613-1614. The work is a short treatise on music theory and thus is a complement to his *Observations in the Art of English Poesie*. Before Campion, music was largely polyphonic, with each voice contributing its own melody to a rather complex whole. Campion's system minimized the melodic independence of the three lower voices. It seemed to work well enough, for it produced pleasant music, and his treatise was included in John Playford's popular *Introduction to the Skill of Music* (1660) and appeared in subsequent editions of that book until 1694, when a treatise by Henry Purcell replaced it.

Campion died on March 1, 1620. He was fifty-three years old, a lifelong bachelor. He left his very modest estate, valued at twenty-two pounds, to his friend and collaborator, Philip Rosseter.

### ANALYSIS

In one sense, Thomas Campion was typically Elizabethan: Classical mythology, amorous encounters with either distant courtly ladies or willing country maids, and superficial religious emotions provided his subjects and themes. Although much of his verse lacks the substance of that of William Shakespeare, Ben Jonson, and John Donne, it is highly musical poetry, in which the careful modulation of sounds produces the illusion of music even when divorced from a musical setting. Campion's poetry depends, in short, on the ear more than most; if one is not fortunate enough to have a recording of "Never Weather-Beaten Sail" or "I Care Not for These Ladies," one should at least read these poems aloud to gain some idea of their music. This is the quality that draws Campion out of the ranks of mediocre Renaissance poets who wrote on similar conventional themes.

Campion was most successful in the writing of short poems. His airs, on which his reputation rests, include some of the best art songs written in English. Even his longer masques are appealing because they are essentially a succession of short pieces linked together; their mythological/allegorical plots contribute little to their success, for the frequent beautiful songs and the occasional interesting speech generate the ceremonious pageantry necessary to the masque. Critics have called Campion a miniaturist, and that description is apt.

Campion learned quantitative meter at first hand by studying and writing Latin poetry. His two volumes of Latin verse, which stand at opposite ends of his creative life, largely consist of epigrams and occasional poems. Epigrams poking fun at his friend, the inept poet Barnabe Barnes, praising famous people such as Francis Drake, Prince Henry, Sir Philip Sidney, William Camden, and Francis Bacon, consoling his friend Thomas Munson, extolling imaginary ladies with Roman names, and celebrating ordinary objects such as portable clocks, remind one of Ben Jonson's similar works in English. One rather long epigram, "In Obitum Gual. Devoreux fratris clariss. Comitis Essexiae," is an elegy for Walter Devereux, brother of the second earl of Essex, who died at the siege of Rouen (1591); Campion was there and wrote the poem while the battle was still in progress. One particularly short epigram, interesting for its subject, provides a good example:

> About the Epigram
> Similar to biting pepper, the acid epigram
> Is not gracious to each taste: no one denies its use.

Among these short, useful, and sometimes acrid poems, Campion included several longer, more ambitious works, including a somewhat epic poem of 283 lines, "Ad Thamesin," celebrating the English victory over the Spanish Armada, and the 404-line Ovidian *Umbra* (1619), recounting the story of Iole, who conceived a child by the god Phoebus while she was asleep—an erotic situation that recurs in Campion's airs. These longer pieces lack the pungency of the short epigrams and are by no means first-rate poems. They do, however, contain some of the music of Campion's English airs and represent his longest productions of purely quantitative meter. The relative lack of success of these longer poems, together with the appeal of many of the shorter ones, is an indication that Campion was a miniaturist in both languages.

The famous argument between Jonson and his stage designer Inigo Jones about which element of the masque was the more important—the plot or the mechanical contrivances generating the masque's spectacle—could easily have had Campion as a third participant. Campion's masques are distinguished neither for their elaborate stage design, even though the ingenious Jones was his frequent collaborator, nor for their drama, but for their music. In contrast to Jonson's masques, Campion's appear dramatically thin: There is never a plot, only a situation, and characters are little more than mouths to deliver speeches and sing songs. It is arguable, however, that the success of a masque depends only on those qualities generating pageantry, and dramatic energy is not necessarily one of them.

## LORD HAY'S MASQUE

Campion's *Lord Hay's Masque* was presented in 1607 to celebrate the marriage of King James's favorite, the Scotsman James Hay, and the English lady Honora Denney. The political situation of a recently crowned Scottish king on the English throne attempting to consolidate his two realms provides the background for this, Campion's most successful masque. There are thus three levels of meaning in the masque: the marriage of Hay and Denney, the union of Scotland and England, and the mythological reconciliation between Diana (allegorically Queen Elizabeth), who wished to keep her maids of honor virgins, and Apollo (allegorically King James), who wished to marry them to his knights. In anger, Diana has changed Apollo's knights into trees, and in the course of the masque, they regain their rightful shapes. Campion's song "Now hath Flora rob'd her bowers" is a moving poem in praise of marriage; its music is best described as majestic.

## THE LORD'S MASQUE

*The Lord's Masque*, presented as part of the ceremonies attending Princess Elizabeth's wedding to Frederick, elector of Palantine (February 14, 1613), and *The Caversham Entertainment*, presented the following April to entertain Queen Anne on her way to Bath to recover from her depression brought on by the wedding, are related pieces, this circumstantial link being strengthened by their joint publication. *The Lord's Masque* is a stately allegory in which Orpheus, representing music, frees Entheus, representing "poetic fury," from the control of Mania, or madness. The result of that liberation is a Latin poem recited by a Sybil praising the marriage of the young couple. *The Caversham Entertainment*, in contrast, is lighthearted and totally lacking in plot. A Cynic, a Traveller, and a Gardener appear severally and together before the queen, sing some rural songs, and debate issues such as the necessity of human companionship and the value of music.

## THE SOMERSET MASQUE

*The Somerset Masque* is unintentionally ironic, given the outcome of the sorry marriage it celebrates. Delegates from the four corners of the globe are attacked by the allegorical figures Error, Rumour, Curiosity, and Credulity as they sail toward England to attend the marriage. The allegorical characters cause confusion and chaos until the Fates, Eternity and Harmony, appear to restore order. The irony is that the rumors circulating about Robert Carr and his bride Frances Howard and the murder of Sir Thomas Overbury were true. A further irony is that with this masque, Campion's career as entertainer to the Jacobean nobility came to an end; it is unprovable but likely that his connection with Lord Somerset was the reason.

## A BOOKE OF AYRES, TWO BOOKES OF AYRES, AND THE THIRD AND FOURTH BOOKE OF AYRES

Campion's five books of airs—*A Booke of Ayres*, *Two Bookes of Ayres*, and *The Third and Fourth Booke of Ayres*—are somewhat misleadingly titled because the first, published jointly in 1601 with Rosseter, stands apart from the numbering, which starts with his second. All five are fairly homogeneous, containing a mixture of amorous and religious verse, between twenty-one and twenty-nine airs per book. The Rosseter collection contains, perhaps, the highest proportion of truly first-rate airs. The later books contain slightly more religious airs than the earlier (except for the first book, which is solely religious, and the second book, which is solely amorous), but this is counterbalanced by the increased earthiness of the later amorous airs, as for example in "Beauty, since you so much desire," from the fourth book, which is an almost word-for-word rendition of "Mistress, since you so much desire" from the Rosseter collection except for the important fact that the seat of "Cupid's fire" is no longer in the lady's eyes but in her genitals. Campion is even called on to apologize for some of these lyrics, telling the reader that he may turn the page if he wishes and that Chaucer was guilty of greater breaches of taste than he is.

Campion's airs are his most important contribution to literature. They are short poems, usually two or three stanzas, on conventional Renaissance subjects characterized by sensitive modulations of sound, especially vowels. They are, moreover, set to music exceptional for both melodic skill and aptness to the words. The technique of mirroring in music what is stated in words is called word painting, and Campion was a master of it. For example, in "Fire, fire, fire" from the third book, the refrain contains the repeated words "O drown both me, O drown both me," and the music descends from a higher to a lower pitch. Similarly, in "Mistress, since you so much desire" from the Rosseter collection and its revision "Beauty, since you so much desire" from the fourth book, the refrain repeats the words "But a little higher" four times, each time ascending the scale. Again, in "When to her Lute Corinna Sings" from the Rosseter collection, the line "the strings do break" is set with a quick sixteenth note musical phrase; in order to maintain the tempo, a lutenist would play this measure percussively.

This type of word painting, clever as it is, is not without dangers, as Campion himself admits in his prologue to the Rosseter collection, likening the excessive word painting of some of his contemporaries to an unskilled actor who, whenever he mentions his eyes, points to them with his finger. Much of Campion's word painting is subtle, as in "Though you are young," from the Rosseter collection, where the air's main theme, the strength of age as compared to the ephemerality of youth, is mirrored in the lute accompaniment that repeats a chord in an inverted position, that is, a lower string sounding a note higher than its next highest neighbor. Subtle in a different way is Campion's famous and much anthologized "There is a Garden in Her Face" from the fourth book. Part of the refrain, "Till cherry ripe," is repeated several times to a London street-seller's cry, with the indication that the lady celebrated in this air may be had for a price—an irony lost to the reader innocent of the music. "Never weather-beaten sail" from the first book is, perhaps, Campion's most subtle and most successful attempt at word painting. The subject of the air is the world-weariness of the singer and his desire to die and thus, like a storm-tossed ship, reach a safe harbor. A lesser composer would have set the words to music mirroring the distress and weariness of the words, but Campion writes a melody that can be described only as confident and joyous—a tension creating two perspectives, the earthly and the heavenly, and forcing the listener to see earthly troubles from a divine point of view.

OTHER MAJOR WORKS

PLAYS: *Lord Hay's Masque*, pr., pb. 1607; *The Caversham Entertainment*, pr. 1613 (masque); *The Lord's Masque*, pr., pb. 1613; *The Somerset Masque*, pr. 1613.

NONFICTION: *Observations in the Art of English Poesie*, 1602; *A New Way of Making Fowre Parts in Counter-point*, c. 1617.

BIBLIOGRAPHY

Booth, Mark W. *The Experience of Songs*. New Haven, Conn.: Yale University Press, 1981. Booth's chapter "Art Song" is an exhaustive reading of the musical and lyrical aspects of Campion's "I Care Not for These Ladies," an "anticourtly" pastoral song. Although he devotes some attention to the music of the poem, Booth focuses on the lyrics, finding them more complex than earlier critics had believed.

Coren, Pamela. "In the Person of Womankind: Female Persona Poems by Campion, Donne, Jonson." *Studies in Philology* 98, no. 2 (Spring, 2001): 225-250. Analysis of the use of the female persona in Campion's "A Secret Love or Two, I Must Confesse."

Davis, Walter R. *Thomas Campion*. Boston: Twayne, 1987. Devotes separate chapters to Campion's biography, poetry, music, theory, masques (the Renaissance "multimedia show"), and reputation. Contains a two-page chronology, extensive notes, a selected bibliography with brief annotations, and an index. Essential for Campion scholars.

Lindley, David. *Thomas Campion*. Leiden, the Netherlands: E. J. Brill, 1986. Discusses Campion's poetry, his music, the relationship between his music and poetry, and his masques. Provides literary, musical, and political contexts but focuses on the works. Contains extensive analyses of individual masques and poems and a select bibliography.

Lowbury, Edward, Timothy Salter, and Alison Young. *Thomas Campion: Poet, Composer, Physician*. New York: Barnes & Noble, 1970. Despite its title, the book stresses music. Reviews Campion's critical reputation, provides a biographical chapter, discusses the relationship between music and poetry, and examines his masques, his poem/songs, and his literary and music criticism. Six pages are devoted to "interactions." Select bibliography.

Ryding, Erik S. *In Harmony Framed: Musical Humanism, Thomas Campion, and the Two Daniels*. Kirksville, Mo.: Sixteenth Century Journal Publishers, 1993. Contrasts the poetic and musical work of the Daniel brothers, John and Samuel, with Thomas Campion. The author categorizes Campion with the Renaissance humanists. Includes a bibliography.

Wilson, Christopher. *Words and Notes Coupled Lovingly Together: Thomas Campion—A Critical Study*. New York: Garland, 1989. Contains a biographical outline, a review of Campion's scholarship, an examination of the Campion canon, brief discussions of the poetry and the music, and thorough treatments of *Observations in the Art of English Poesie* and his musical theories. Includes an extensive commentary on the masques and a comprehensive bibliography.

*Robert E. Boenig*

# THOMAS CAREW

**Born:** West Wickham, Kent, England; 1594
**Died:** London, England; March 22, 1640

PRINCIPAL POETRY

*Poems*, 1640, 1642
*Poems, with a Maske, by Thomas Carew Esquire*, 1651
*Poems, Songs and Sonnets, Together with a Masque*, 1671
*The Poems of Thomas Carew with His Masque*, 1949 (Rhodes Dunlap, editor)

### OTHER LITERARY FORMS

Thomas Carew (KEHR-ee, also kuh-REW) wrote a number of songs for plays that were presented at the court of Charles I. The only other major work he produced, however, was his masque *Coelum Britannicum* (pr. 1634).

### ACHIEVEMENTS

To discuss the achievements of Thomas Carew is a difficult, if not an impossible, task because the first printed edition of his work did not appear until after his death. As a result, his poems were not widely known—which is no reflection on their merit. Whatever impact he had on the literary climate of the Caroline period was limited to a small audience at court who knew his poems from the manuscript copies that were circulated. With this qualification in mind, Carew's accomplishments can be counted as significant. Although Carew was a minor poet, he was one of the best writing at a time when minor poetry had reached a high level. Certainly Carew achieved this high level in "An Elegie upon the Death of the Deane of Pauls, Dr. John Donne," his unquestioned masterpiece. He more often produced verse that was trite or contrived. Somewhere between these two levels of achievement, however, lies a body of genuinely agreeable poetry that is valuable to the student of literature not so much because of its own innate merit but because it so effectively captures the spirit of Cavalier poetry. Indeed, one can gain a satisfactory knowledge of the themes and techniques of the Cavaliers through reading Carew alone, for he is in a sense the perfect example of the court poet during the reign of Charles I.

### BIOGRAPHY

Despite the recurring popularity of his verse and his reputation as a significant Cavalier poet, little is known about the life of Thomas Carew other than that which one might infer from his poems or speculate about the life of a courtier at the court of Charles I. Carew was born in Kent in 1594. His father, Matthew, was a master in Chancery, and his mother, Alice Rymers, was descended from a noble family. Although nothing is known of Carew's boyhood, there is a record of his having begun study at Merton College, Oxford, in 1608. In 1610, he entered Cambridge, and apparently he took his degree in 1612. Again, one can only speculate about Carew's academic career, but he no doubt studied the basic curriculum in rhetoric, mathematics, and philosophy.

After graduating from Cambridge, Carew studied law, although his father's letters about his son's preparation for the bench suggest that Carew's inclinations were not toward a legal career. Rhodes Dunlap, in *The Poems of Thomas Carew* (1949), speculates that Carew may have been distracted by the notoriously frivolous life of an Inns of Court student. Matthew Carew shared this and other concerns with his friend Sir Dudley Carleton, English ambassador to Italy, who, at the request of his friend, employed the youthful Carew in 1613. Although records do exist about Carleton's Italian activities, no mention is made of Carew. No doubt the intelligent and lively Carew availed himself of the opportunities for learning and licentiousness that Italy offered until he was released from Carleton's employ in 1616, apparently the result of Carew's making a rather foolish suggestion in writing about Lady Carleton's lack of fidelity to her husband.

Carew returned to England, where he apparently fell ill with syphilis. Perhaps it was this bout with the illness that led to one of the better anecdotes concerning Carew. Apparently thinking himself to be dying, he sent for John Hale, a former school fellow from Merton College who had gone into the ministry. On his deathbed, or so he thought, Carew asked for absolution and repented his wayward life. Carew recovered and continued his ways. When he again lay ill and sent for Hale, he was refused by his former friend. Matthew Carew tried to heal the wounds between his son and Carleton, but to no avail. No doubt the elder Carew was still completely frustrated with his son when he died in 1618.

A year later, Carew attended Sir Edward Herbert on his embassy to Paris. In 1624, Carew was recalled to England, and soon after his poetry began to circulate in manuscript form (only a few of his poems were published during his lifetime). In 1630, Carew was appointed to a court position, where he remained until his death.

Little is known about Carew's life at court. In 1634, his masque *Coelum Britannicum* was presented there; the designer was the famous architect Inigo Jones, who had worked closely with Ben Jonson. Carew was highly regarded by contemporary literary figures, counting among his friends John Donne, Ben Jonson, Sir William Davenant, James Shirley, and Richard Lovelace, with whom he apparently had a close relationship. Like so many of the Tribe of Ben, Carew was a staunch Royalist.

Another interesting anecdote told about Carew is that he saved the queen from being caught in a compromising position with Jermyn, Lord Saint Albans. He had obviously learned something from the affair with Lady Carleton. For saving her secret, the queen apparently rewarded Carew with her highest devotion.

Carew died in 1640, probably after joining the king in his Scottish campaign. He was buried next to his father at St. Anne's Chapel. No trace of either grave is discernible today.

ANALYSIS

A man with many masters—Donne, Jonson, Giambattista Marino—Thomas Carew was slave to none, although as a Cavalier poet he has been generally regarded as one of Jonson's followers. Like Jonson, Carew commanded many lyric forms, and his lines often read as beautifully as do those of Jonson. In fact, many of Carew's verses have been effectively set to music. Proficiency with meter, however, was only part of Carew's art. He used the conceit effectively, although at times his images strain to such an extent as to warrant Samuel Johnson's attacks on the Metaphysical poets. Carew more effectively associated himself with the Metaphysical school with his use of paradox and argument, adding an intellectual quality to his poems that he so highly valued in Donne.

Jonson and Donne account for the main influences on Carew. He was equally capable of borrowing from Petrarch, Edmund Spenser, or Marino, however, for both theme and technique. In fact, because most of Carew's poems deal with the theme of love, the forsaken lover in particular, writers such as Petrarch and Spenser were often models better suited to his purpose.

### "UPON SOME ALTERATIONS IN MY MISTRESS, AFTER MY DEPARTURE INTO FRANCE"

There has been a fair amount of speculation about whether Carew's love poems, particularly those addressed to Celia (probably a pseudonym) or to the unidentified mistress, have an autobiographical basis. Such speculation aside, the poems are interesting for both their lyric excellence and their range of themes. The peak of Carew's lyric accomplishment occurs in "Upon some Alterations in my Mistress, after my Departure into France," where the central image of the lover lost on the troubled ocean of his lady's altered affections is enhanced by the equally varying meters, thus well fusing theme and structure. Thematically, one sees in Carew a movement from Petrarchan despair to bitter vindication against his inconstant mistress. The very range of Carew's work thus demands admiration.

What this brief analysis suggests is that Carew's work reveals many of the themes and techniques that had dominated Elizabethan and Jacobean poetry and that were equally important to the Caroline poets. Carew also polished his use of the rhyming couplet in anticipation of the Augustan Age. Despite his limitations, Carew paints an accurate picture of poetic achievement and direction in the late Renaissance.

"Upon some Alterations in my Mistress, after my Departure into France" warrants comment, first, because it demonstrates an attitude in love poetry that Carew would reject for the bitter vindictiveness of later poems, such as "Disdaine returned," and second, because Carew's technique in the poem, even when not effective, is interesting. The poem is more likely autobiographical than are many of his other love poems. The poem appears to be Carew's response to his mistress's change of feeling after he had gone to France with Sir Edward Herbert. Unlike later works showing Carew bitter about his lady's rejection, this short lyric poem presents the poet as a forlorn Petrarchan lover. Appropriately, its theme is developed in the extended image of a poet lost on the troubled ocean of inconstant love and his lady's waning affections.

Carew's use of the extended image is interesting not only because it is so typical of Petrarchan poetry, but also because this technique varies from his general approach, which, like Donne's, usually fuses diverse elements. In this poem, the first stanza quickly presents the image that will be elaborated:

> Oh gentle Love, doe not forsake the guide
> Of my fraile Barke, on which the swelling tide
> Of ruthless pride
> Doth beat, and threaten wrack from every side.

It was a well-worn figure by the time Carew came to employ it, and Carew in no way used it with originality. The varied line lengths and metrical feet, however, suggesting the tempestuous seas, show Carew effectively combining idea and form.

Carew's reference to the "mystie cloud of anger" in the second stanza identifies the alterations to which the title refers. Still, Carew follows this line by calling his lady his "faire starre," seeming to say that despite her alterations, she remains for him a guiding passion. The last line of the poem, however—"In the deep flood she drown'd her beamie face"—suggests the more defiant train of thought of his later poems as he turns his back on his lady and tells her that her own treatment of him will be her destruction.

## "SONG, TO MY INCONSTANT MISTRESS"

In Carew's "Song, To my inconstant Mistress," as in "Disdaine returned," he pictures himself as the scorned Petrarchan lover, though, rather than suffering in frustration, he methodically points out why his mistress will at some point regret her attitude. This intellectual response to an emotional situation is characteristic of the school of Donne, while the lyric excellence of the poem, in five-line tetrameter stanzas rhyming *ababb*, follows the influence that governed the Tribe of Ben. Carew thus illustrates his ability to absorb diverse influences.

Underlying the entire thematic structure of "Song, To my inconstant Mistress" is the poet's paralleling of love and religion. The opening stanza portrays him as a man with a "strong faith," while his mistress is a "poor excommunicate." These early parallels suggest a point that the poet will later develop: that true faithfulness in love will, as in religion, be rewarded by salvation. The focus of this poem, however, is on the damning of the unfaithful mistress.

The second stanza develops one of Carew's typical themes, that love demands an equal commitment by both parties. The poet says that his inconstant mistress will be replaced by a "faire hand" and that this new love and the poet will be "both with equall glory crown'd." At this point, Lynn Sadler suggests, the tone of the poet has something of the "swagger of bravado." The point is well taken; moreover, the swagger is to become more bitter in the final stanza.

In the third stanza, the implications of the first are at last fulfilled. The poet has already established the bliss he will enjoy because of his constancy to the ideal of love. His main point, however, is to show the despair that awaits the one who has violated the spirit of love. Her reward, moreover, will be equal to her sin, for she will suffer to the degree that she caused suffering. Finally, again in religious terms, she will be "Damn'd for (her) false Apostasie."

"Song, To my inconstant Mistress" is one of Carew's best lyric love poems. His fusion of religious and erotic imagery enhances the latter without mocking or trivializing the former, an achievement that distinguishes the poem from the common run of Cavalier lyrics.

### "DISDAINE RETURNED"

One of Carew's best-known poems, "Disdaine returned," demonstrates two significant aspects of his art: the lyric beauty that he inherited from Jonson and his smooth integration of several typical Elizabethan and Jacobean themes. The basic structure of the poem is simple. It has three six-line stanzas in tetrameter, rhyming *ababcc*. In the last stanza, however, the closing couplet varies slightly in its meter and thus draws the poem to a decisive close, suggesting that the poet has cured himself of his lovesickness. Unlike many of the other Celia poems in which Carew expounds the poet's frustrations in love with a typical Petrarchan lament, "Disdaine returned" shows the spirit and style that were characteristic of Donne in such poems as "The Broken Heart." The poem opens with a carpe diem statement, "As old Time makes these decay/ So his flames must waste away." Rather than using these lines to make the basic live-for-the-moment argument, however, Carew suggests a feeling of depressed reconciliation; his lady has lost the opportunity for a genuine love that would not fade with the passing of time or the loss of beauty. The second stanza justifies the claim as Carew defines in basically Platonic terms his ideas about love that his mistress has not been able to accept: "Hearts with equal love combined kindle never-dying fires."

In the third stanza, the frustrated poet, whose love is genuine, is forced to return his lady's rejection. As the second stanza suggests, there must be equal commitment for the relationship to prosper. The poet says, however, that he has not found his love returned: "I have searched thy soul within/ And find naught but pride and scorn." He decides to return these feelings of disdain, ending his pointless suffering.

### "An Elegie upon the Death of the Deane of Pauls, Dr. John Donne"

Generally accepted as Carew's best poem, "An Elegie upon the Death of the Deane of Pauls, Dr. John Donne" is one of the few poems by Carew to be published during his own lifetime. It was published in 1633, although it was probably written much nearer the time of Donne's death in 1631.

The poem opens with an indictment of an age that finds only "unkneaded dowebak't prose" to praise the loss of its greatest poet. Carew's frustration with this situation is intensified throughout the poem as he reviews the many changes in the use of language that Donne had wrought. He freed the poet from "senile imitation" of the ancients and then "fresh invention planted." Carew devotes a large part of the poem, in fact, to making this point, using a concept that Donne would have appreciated: Donne paid the "debts of our penurious bankrupt age," which had so long struggled in borrowed images and forms. So great was Donne's power, Carew says, that "our stubborne language bends, made only fit/ With her tough-thick-rib'd hoopes to gird about/ Thy Giant phansie."

Because Donne is gone, Carew declares, the advances that he initiated are vanishing as well, since they are "Too hard for Libertines in Poetrie." To further build on this theme, the poet uses the image of the wheel that will cease to turn after losing its "moving head." Still, Carew's final image is that of the phoenix, a popular image in Donne's poetry, to suggest that perhaps from the ashes the spirit of Donne will rise in another era.

Finally, Carew apologizes for his poor effort by saying that Donne is "Theme enough to tyre all Art." He then presents the closing epitaph:

> Here lies a King, that rul'd as hee thought fit
> The universall Monarchy of wit;
> Here lie two Flamens, and both those, the best,
> Apollo's first, at last, the true God's Priest.

This best of Carew's poems is a rather accurate projection of what would be the course of poetic achievement after the death of Donne. Not until Alexander Pope, about one hundred years later (excluding John Milton), did England see a genius to compare with Donne, yet between these two giants, such poems as this one by Carew kept alive the spirit of poetic achievement that distinguished the Renaissance.

### Other major work

PLAY: *Coelum Britannicum*, pr. 1634 (masque).

### Bibliography

Benet, Diana. "Carew's Monarchy of Wit." In *"The Muses' Common-Weale": Poetry and Politics in the Seventeenth Century*, edited by Claude J. Summers and Ted-Larry Pebworth. Columbia: University of Missouri Press, 1988. Argues that Carew, using the absolutist rhetoric of James and Charles, consciously constructs a realm of wit in which the writer reigns supreme. Shows the problems faced by writers in the Stuarts' attempts to limit free speech.

Corns, Thomas N., ed. *The Cambridge Companion to English Poetry: Donne to Marvell.* New York: Cambridge University Press, 1993. Presents a brief but balanced biography of Carew and an analysis of his work.

Parker, Michael P. "'To my friend G. N. from Wrest': Carew's Secular Masque." In *Classic and Cavalier: Essays on Jonson and the Sons of Ben,* edited by Claude J. Summers and Ted-Larry Pebworth. Pittsburgh, Pa.: University of Pittsburgh Press, 1982. Surveys the seventeenth century genre of the country-house poem and places Carew's piece as the turning point between Jonson's "To Penshurst" and Marvell's "Upon Appleton House." Supplies information about Wrest and its owners, which was for many years obscured through historical error. Shows how the structure of the poem owes much to the masque tradition.

Ray, Robert H. "The Admiration of Sir Philip Sidney by Lovelace and Carew: New Seventeenth Century Allusions." *ANQ* 18, no. 1 (Winter, 2005): 18-22. Notes how Richard Lovelace and Carew were influenced by Sidney and examines Carew's poem "To My Worthy Friend Master George Sandys, on His Translation of the Psalmes."

Sadler, Lynn. *Thomas Carew.* Boston: Twayne, 1979. This critical biography presents a straightforward introduction to Carew's life, times, and works. Covers his entire output, emphasizing the better-known lyrics at the expense of the country-house poems and Carew's masque. Perhaps the most accessible single work on Carew for the general reader. Includes a well-selected bibliography with annotations.

Selig, Edward I. *The Flourishing Wreath.* New Haven, Conn.: Yale University Press, 1958. Reprint. Hamden, Conn.: Archon Books, 1970. The first full-length serious study of Carew's verse, this remains the most thorough attempt to justify Carew's fame in his own time. Selig's chapter on the poet's song lyrics is still valuable; he points out that a third of Carew's poems were written for singing, and sixty settings survive. The book's examination of patterns of imagery in Carew is also useful.

Semler, L. E. *The English Mannerist Poets and the Visual Arts.* Madison, N.J.: Fairleigh Dickinson University Press, 1998. Includes an introduction to mannerism as it applies to visual as well as poetic work. Each of the five poets covered, including Carew, is shown to have one or more of the characteristics of the mannerist style.

Sharpe, Kevin. "Cavalier Critic? The Ethics and Politics of Thomas Carew's Poetry." In *Politics of Discourse: The Literature and History of Seventeenth-Century England,* edited by Kevin Sharpe and Steven Zwicker. Berkeley: University of California Press, 1987. Distances Carew from the usual image of the Cavalier and argues that he was a serious writer with an orderly and hierarchical vision of a kingdom of nature and love. Emphasizes Carew's often misunderstood, positive view of marriage and connects this idea to his political vision.

Walton, Geoffrey. "The Cavalier Poets." In *From Donne to Marvell.* Vol. 3 in *New Pelican Guide to English Literature*, edited by Boris Ford. New York: Penguin Books, 1982. Stresses Carew's complexity and range, and singles out for praise the sense of social responsibility shown in Carew's two country-house poems, "To Saxham" and "To my friend G. N., from Wrest."

*Gerald W. Morton*

# GEORGE CHAPMAN

**Born:** Near Hitchin, Hertfordshire, England; c. 1559
**Died:** London, England; May 12, 1634

<small>PRINCIPAL POETRY</small>
*The Shadow of Night*, 1594
*Ovid's Banquet of Sense*, 1595
*Hero and Leander*, 1598 (completion of Christopher Marlowe's poem)
*Euthymiae Raptus: Or, The Tears of Peace*, 1609
*An Epicede or Funerall Song on the Death of Henry Prince of Wales*, 1612
*Eugenia*, 1614
*Andromeda Liberata: Or, The Nuptials of Perseus and Andromeda*, 1614
*Pro Vere Autumni Lachrymae*, 1622

<small>OTHER LITERARY FORMS</small>
In his own time, George Chapman was equally well known for his poetry and plays. As a leading playwright for the children's companies that performed at the Blackfriars Theatre, he achieved distinction in both tragedy and comedy. His greatest success in tragedy was *Bussy d'Ambois* (pr. 1604, 1641), followed by a sequel, *The Revenge of Bussy d'Ambois* (pr. c. 1610). His other tragedies include the two-part *The Conspiracy and Tragedy of Charles, Duke of Byron* (pr., pb. 1608), as well as *The Tragedy of Chabot, Admiral of France* (pr. c. 1635; with James Shirley) and *The Wars of Caesar and Pompey* (pr. c. 1613). Chapman also composed the first comedy of humors, *An Humourous Day's Mirth* (pr. 1597), and romantic and satiric comedies, including *The Blind Beggar of Alexandria* (pr. 1596), *The Gentleman Usher* (pr. c. 1602), *All Fools* (pr. c. 1604), *Monsieur d'Olive* (pr. 1604), *The Widow's Tears* (pr. c. 1605), and *May Day* (pr. c. 1609).

<small>ACHIEVEMENTS</small>
George Chapman regarded his English translations of Homer's *Odyssey* (c. 725 B.C.E.; English translation, 1614) and *Iliad* (c. 750 B.C.E.; English translation, 1611) as "the work that I was born to do." An arduous, demanding task that occupied him for thirty years, his translation was commissioned by the youthful son of James I, Prince Henry, whose untimely death at the age of eighteen left the poet without a patron. Although he continued to work in spite of the lack of patronage, he turned to the stage and to original verse to make his living. That John Keats found looking into Chapman's Homer a thrilling discovery, which he subsequently immortalized in a sonnet, is a tribute to the quality of this work, which has not been generally admired. Chapman's transla-

tion has receded into obscurity as an archaic and quaint achievement.

Chapman's original poetry, which is characterized by a remarkable range of theme and style, is often considered difficult or even obscure for the modern reader. A largely philosophical poet, Chapman incorporates challenging intellectual concepts and images in his verse. Some of his more explicitly philosophical poems, such as *The Shadow of Night*, are rich in Neoplatonic thought, an abstruse subject. Others, such as his continuation of Christopher Marlowe's unfinished *Hero and Leander*, convey ideas through emblematic and iconographic techniques. In the poem *Ovid's Banquet of Sense*, he writes partly in the manner of the erotic epyllion and partly in the more Metaphysical vein of sharply intellectual conceits, while in *Euthymiae Raptus*, he writes more in the style of satiric allegory, with pointed, polished heroic couplets. Some of his poems are occasional, such as the *Andromeda Liberata*, which celebrates the notorious marriage of the king's favorite, Robert Carr, to Lady Frances Howard, later implicated in the murder of Thomas Overbury. Chapman's choice of the Andromeda myth to represent Frances's unconsummated marriage with the young earl of Essex was extremely tactless, and the poet had to publish a justification and explication of what was interpreted as an insulting poem. Some of his poems are mystical, as is the first section of *Euthymiae Raptus*, where he relates his encounter with the flaming vision of Homer's spirit, which inspired him to his translation, and as is the "Hymn to Our Savior," included in the collection called *Petrarch's Seven Penitential Psalms* (1612), and concerned with the theme of transcending fleshly experience. Finally, Chapman also wrote two fine elegies, *Eugenia*, written on the death of Lord Russell, and *An Epicede or Funerall Song on the Death of Henry Prince of Wales*, on the death of the much loved and genuinely lamented Prince Henry.

## BIOGRAPHY

Although George Chapman was born into a fairly wealthy and well-connected family, it was his fate to suffer poverty because he was the younger son. Not much is known about his early years. He spent some time at Oxford but did not take a degree there. After a brief period of service in the household of a nobleman, he saw military action on the Continent, participating in the Low Country campaigns of 1591-1592. His first literary accomplishment was the publication of *The Shadow of Night*, an esoteric poem reflecting his association with a group of erudite young scholars, including Sir Walter Ralegh, all of whom reputedly dabbled in the occult. His publication of a continuation of Marlowe's *Hero and Leander* clearly established his relationship with the ill-fated younger playwright.

His own early career as a playwright barely supported him, and he was imprisoned for debt in 1600. After his release, he attempted to supplement his income from the stage by seeking patronage for his nondramatic poetry. The youthful Prince Henry, a genuine patron of the arts, offered to support Chapman's proposed translation of the complete works of Homer. Unfortunately, the death of the young prince put an end to such hopes, and Chapman was never to be completely free from the specter of poverty. When he collaborated with Ben Jonson and John Marston on the city comedy *Eastward Ho!* (pr., pb. 1605), Chapman found himself in prison again, this time for the play's supposed slander against Scots. Largely through his own epistolary efforts directed toward both the king and other dignitaries, Chapman and fellow prisoner Jonson were released without having their noses slit, the usual punishment for the given offense.

After his release from prison, Chapman continued to write both plays and poetry and to continue the laborious work of translation even without the aid of patronage. He eventually became an acknowledged literary success in all these endeavors, honored in Joshua Poole's *The English Parnassus* (1657), lauded by the critic Francis Meres as one of the best in both comedy and tragedy, and believed by some modern critics to have been the "rival poet" of William Shakespeare. Although little is known about his later years, historian Anthony à Wood's description of the elderly poet as "reverend, religious, and sober" suggests his continuing dedication to the serious art of poetry and to the subtle art of life.

When Chapman died at the age of seventy-four, his monument was fashioned by Inigo Jones, the noted theatrical designer with whom Chapman had collaborated on court masques. His Latin inscription was "Georgis Chapmanus, poeta Homericus, Philosophers verus (etsi Christianus poeta)."

## ANALYSIS

George Chapman's poetry is unusually diversified. It does not reveal a consistent individual style, technique, or attitude, so that an initial reading does not immediately divulge a single creative mind at work. A skilled experimenter, Chapman tried the Metaphysical style of John Donne and the satirical heroic couplet in a manner anticipating John Dryden, and in his translations reverted to the archaic medieval fourteener. His poetry is also unusually difficult. His allusions are often esoteric, his syntax strained or convoluted, and his underlying ideas verging on the occult. His is not primarily a lyrical voice, and his verses are almost never musical. For Chapman, the content of poetry is supreme, and the poet's moral calling is profound. His work, in consequence, is essentially didactic.

Chapman's poetics, as expressed in scattered epistles and dedications attached to his verses, help clarify his intentions and to reveal the purpose behind what may strike the reader as willful obscurity. Philosophically, Chapman was a Platonist, and he was well read in Neoplatonic writings. His poetic theories are a metaphorical counterpart to Platonic dualism. The fact that precious minerals are buried in the ground rather than easily available on the surface suggests to Chapman that the spirit of poetry must lie beneath the obvious surface meaning of the words. The body of poetry may delight the ear with its smooth, melodious lines, but the soul speaks only to the inward workings of the mind. Thus, Chapman rejects the Muse that will sing of love's sensual fulfillment in favor of his mistress Philosophy, who inspires the majesty and riches of the mind. The reader must not be misled by the outer bark or rind of the poems, to use another of his analogies, but should rather seek the fruit of meaning deep within. Scorning the profane multitude, Chapman consecrates his verses to those readers with minds willing to search.

## ALLEGORY AND EMBLEM

Two of the techniques that Chapman employs most often to achieve his somewhat arcane didactic purposes are allegory and emblem. His poems are frequently allegorical, both in the sense that he introduces personified abstractions as spokespeople for his ideas and in the sense that a given event or personage stands for another. He reveals his allegorical cast of mind in dealing with such objects as love, war, or learning by envisioning them as personified abstractions, clothing them in appropriate iconographical garments, and situating them in emblematic tableaux. His use of emblems thus grows out of his allegorical mode of thought. Drawing on the popular emblem books of the Renaissance, he depicts scenes or images from nature or mythology as iconographic equivalents of ideas. A torn scarf, for example, becomes a confused mind, and an uprooted tree a fallen hero. The technique is symbolic and highly visual, but static rather than dramatic.

Since Chapman regarded his Homeric translations as his major poetic mission in life, he did not consider his own poetry as a great achievement. He regarded the calling of the poet with great seriousness, however, and his poems as a result have much of importance to say. In spite of their difficulty and partly because of it, his unusual poems speak to the sensitive reader willing to dig below the often formidable surface.

## THE SHADOW OF NIGHT

Chapman's first published poem, *The Shadow of Night*, consists of two complementary poems, "Hymnus in Noctem" and "Hymnus in Cynthiam." The first is a lament, the second a hymn of praise. The first is concerned with contemplation, the second with action. Both celebrate the intellect and assert the superiority of darkness over daylight. Sophisticated in structure, esoteric in allusion, and steeped in the philosophy of Neoplatonism, the work is a challenge to the general reader.

The object of lament in "Hymnus in Noctem" is the fallen state of the world. Chapman contrasts the debased world of the present day, rife with injustice, to the primal chaos that existed when night was ruler. In that time before creation, there was harmony, for chaos had soul without body; but now bodies thrive without soul. Humans are now blind, experiencing a "shadow" night of intellect that is a reversal of genuine night. The poet then calls upon the spirit of night to send Furies into the world to punish humans for their rampant wickedness. He will aid the Furies by castigating sinful humankind in his verses and by writing tragedies aimed at moral reformation.

As night is praised for its creative darkness, the source of inner wisdom, daylight is regarded negatively, associated with whoredom, rape, and unbridled lust. Chapman warns the great virgin queen, here equated with the moon goddess, that an unwise marriage would eclipse her virtue, removing her from the wise mysteries of the night and exposing her to brash daylight. The poem ends with an emblematic scene, as Cynthia appears in an ivory chariot, accompanied by comets, meteors, and lightning.

"Hymnus in Cynthiam" proclaims praise for Cynthia as pattern of all virtue, wisdom, and beauty, at once moon goddess, divine soul of the world, and Queen Elizabeth I. Cynthia is portrayed here in her daytime role, and the active life of daylight is contrasted to night as the time for contemplation. During the day, Cynthia descends from the moon to earth, where she fashions a nymph named Euthymia, or Joy, out of meteoric stuff. Out of the same vapors, she creates a hunter and his hounds. Chapman's narrative of a shadowy hunting scene is probably based on the myth of Acteon and his hounds. The poet's allegorical version of the myth depicts the hunt as appropriate to the daylight, a time of sensual and otherwise sinful behavior. The object of the hunt is debased joy, which attracts the base affections (the hunting hounds), and the rational souls, submitting to passion (the hunters on their horses), follow after. This pageant of desire is essentially unreal, however, as daytime itself is unreal, and Cynthia promptly disposes of the hounds when night arrives. The mystical darkness offers an opportunity for true joy found only in the spiritual and intellectual fulfillment made possible by contemplative, nocturnal solitude.

The major themes of this two-part poem are thus the Platonic vision of inward contentment, the true joy afforded by contemplation, and the superiority of darkness over daylight. Writing partly in the ancient tradition of the Orphic hymns, Chapman veils his meaning in a mysterious religious atmosphere. The allegorical hunt and the emblematic scenes are, however, vividly described and poetically clear. The poem ends with a tribute to the immutability of Cynthia. Although the original harmony of primal darkness is gone, Cynthia will try to restore virtue to the degenerate world.

### OVID'S BANQUET OF SENSE

Prefacing the volume of poems featuring Chapman's next major poem, *Ovid's Banquet of Sense*, is a brief statement of the poet's convictions about his craft. Here he admits that he hates the profane multitude, asserts that he addresses his intentionally difficult poetry to a select audience, and appeals to those few readers who have a "light-bearing intellect" to appreciate his arcane verses. At first reading, the 117 stanzas of this poem do not seem very esoteric at all. Ostensibly, *Ovid's Banquet of Sense* follows the currently popular mode of the erotic epyllion, as exemplified in William Shakespeare's *Venus and Adonis* (1593). If one follows Chapman's warning, however, one feels committed to search beneath the surface for deeper meaning.

The narrative structure of the poem follows the experience of Ovid in the garden of his mistress Corinna. In the garden, he is able to feast his senses on her while he remains hidden from her view. The first of his senses to be gratified is hearing, or *auditus*, as Corinna plays on her lute, fingering the strings and sweetly singing delightful lyrics. Then, as Ovid draws somewhat nearer to where she is seated at her bath, he is greeted by the overpowering fragrance of the spices she uses in bathing her body. His sense of smell, or *olfactus*, is now enchanted. Moving closer to the arbor to see her more clearly, Ovid is next able to feast his eyes on her inviting nakedness. The longest section of the poem is devoted to this languorous satisfaction of sight, or *visus*. The poet indulges in lavish sensual imagery to describe the experience. Ovid's intense pleasure in the sight of his unclothed mistress ends abruptly, however, when she looks into her glass and suddenly sees him staring at her. Quickly wrapping herself in a cloud, she reproaches him for his immodest spying on her private bath. Ovid defends himself very convincingly, arguing that since his senses of hearing, smell, and sight have already been satisfied, he has a right to ask for a kiss to satisfy his sense of taste, or *gustus*. She grants him the kiss, which is also described in richly provocative language, but the ingenious would-be lover then argues for gratification of the ultimate sense, touch, or *tactus*.

Corinna is responsive to Ovid's seductive plea, and when he lightly touches her side, she starts as if electrified. Like Ovid, the reader is aroused by the prolonged erotic buildup, but both are doomed to a letdown. At this climactic moment, the scene is interrupted by the sudden appearance of several other women, Corinna's friends, who have come to paint in the garden. Having led both his hero and his reader to expect more, the poet now drops the narrative with a somewhat smug remark that much more is intended but must be omitted.

In the final stanza, Chapman refers to the "curious frame" of his poem, suggesting that it resembles a painting, wherein not everything can be seen and some things having to be inferred. The meaning beneath the surface, about which Chapman warned the reader, emerges from this awareness. The reader, like Ovid, has been put in the position of voyeur. Chapman has tricked the reader into false expectations and into assuming a morally ambiguous role. Indeed, the frustration seems worse for the suspenseful reader than for the abandoned lover, for Ovid is not disappointed by the anticlimax but instead is inspired to write his *Ars amatoria* (c. 2 B.C.E.; *Art of Love*, 1612). It is the reader who is trapped forever inside the curious frame. In spite of this trickery, *Ovid's Banquet of Sense* is likely to be one of Chapman's most appealing poems for the general reader. The primarily pictorial imagery, the undercurrent of irony, the escalating narrative movement through the five sensory experiences, and the vivid sensuality of Ovid's responsiveness to his mistress combine to make it at once a dramatic and lyrical reading, unlike Chapman's usual heavy didacticism.

## "A CORONET FOR HIS MISTRESS PHILOSOPHY"

The didactic point of view is supplied by "A Coronet for His Mistress Philosophy," the series of interlinked sonnets that follow *Ovid's Banquet of Sense*. Offering a moral perspective on the ambiguity of *Ovid's Banquet of Sense*, this series is circular, as its title implies, with the last line of each sonnet becoming the first line of the next, coming full circle at the end by repeating the opening line. Here Chapman renounces the Muses that sing of love's "sensual emperie" and rejects the violent torments of sexual desire in favor of devotion to the benevolent mistress, Philosophy. The poet's active and industrious pen will henceforth devote itself to the unchanging beauty of this intellectual mistress, whose virtues will in turn inspire him to ever greater art.

## HERO AND LEANDER

Chapman's continuation of Christopher Marlowe's *Hero and Leander* is also a narrative love poem. Marlowe's premature death in 1594 left unfinished his poetic version of this tragic love story from the classical world. What survives of Marlowe's work is two sestiads, which leave the narrative incomplete. Chapman undertook to finish the poem, publishing his own four sestiads in 1598. Chapman claims that he drank with Marlowe from the fountain of the Muses, but acknowledged that his own draft inspired verse more "grave" and "high." Whereas Marlowe had been concerned with the physical beauty of the lovers and exalted their passion, Chapman takes a moral approach to their relationship, condemning their failure to sacramentalize physical love through marriage.

In the third sestiad, the goddess Ceremony descends from heaven to reproach Leander. Her body is as transparent as glass, and she wears a rich pentacle filled with mysterious signs and symbols. In one hand, she carries a mathematical crystal, a burning-glass capable of destroying Confusion, and in the other, a laurel rod with which to bend back barbarism. Her awesome reproof of Leander likens love without marriage to meat without seasoning, desire without delight, unsigned bills, and unripened corn. Leander immediately vows to celebrate the requisite nuptial rites. Meanwhile, Hero lies on her bed, torn between guilt and passion. Her conflict gradually gives way to resolution as thoughts of her lover's beauty prevail over her sense of shame. In the end, love triumphs over fear.

In the fourth sestiad, Hero offers a sacrifice to the goddess Venus, who accuses her devotee of dissembling loyalty to her. Venus darts fire from her eyes to burn the sacrificial offering, and Hero tries to shield herself from the rage of the deity with a picture of Leander. The divinely repudiated offering is clearly a bad omen.

The fifth sestiad is introduced with Hero's expression of impatience for night to bring her lover. The marriage theme is also reinforced in the form of an allegorical digression about a wedding staged and observed by Hero to make the time seem to pass more quickly and pleasantly. The wedding scene also introduces a wild nymph, Teras, a name given to comets portending evil. Teras sings a tale to the wedding party, following it with a delicately lyrical epithalamium. As she finishes the song, however, she suddenly assumes her comet nature, and with her hair standing on end, she glides out of the company. Her back appears black, striking terror into the hearts of all, especially Hero, who anxiously awaits her lover.

Night finally arrives in the sixth sestiad, bringing with it the tragic climax of the poem. Determined to swim the Hellespont to see Hero, Leander takes his fatal plunge into the stormy sea. Vainly he calls upon first Venus, then Neptune, for help against the violent waves tormenting his body, but the swimmer is doomed. Angry Neptune hurls his marble mace against the fates to forestall the fatal moment, but to no avail. The god then brings the drowned body of Leander on shore, where Hero sees him and, grief-stricken, dies calling his name. Moved by pity, the kindly god of the sea transforms the lovers into birds called Acanthides, or Thistle-Warps, which always fly together in couples.

Although Chapman's continuation lacks the classical grace and sensuous imagery of Marlowe's first two sestiads, it is poetically successful. His poem has a variety of styles, ranging from classical simplicity to Renaissance ornateness. The inevitable tragic plot is deepened by Chapman through the theme of moral responsibility and the role of form and ritual in civilization. He uses personified abstractions effectively, as in the case of the imposing goddess Ceremony, and he demonstrates his mythmaking skills in the person of the comet-nymph Teras. His emblematic verse intensifies the visual effects of the poem, often making it painterly in the manner of *Ovid's Banquet of Sense*. In his poem, his didacticism is happily integrated with story and character rather than being imposed from without. Of all of Chapman's poems, *Hero and Leander* is the most accessible to the contemporary reader.

### EUTHYMIAE RAPTUS

*Euthymiae Raptus* is a substantial (1,232-line) allegorical poem. The immediate occasion that called it forth was the truce in the war with the Netherlands, which had been brought about through the mediation of King James, and the poem is dedicated to the young Prince Henry. It is, however, much more than an occasional poem. Partly autobiographical and partly philosophical, as well as partly topical, it is a major achievement.

The opening *inductio* has primary autobiographical value. Here Chapman relates his personal, mystical encounter with the spirit of Homer. The poet had been meditating when he suddenly perceived a figure clothed in light with a bosom full of fire and breathing flames. It is at once obvious that the apparition is blind, though gifted with inward sight. The spirit then identifies itself as Homer, come to praise Chapman for his translations and to reveal the reason why the world has not achieved a state of peace. Invisible until this moment, Homer has been inspiring Chapman's poetry for a long time. At the end of this section, Homer shows Chapman a vision of the lady Peace mourning over a coffin, despairing the death of Love. A brief *invocatio* follows, spoken by the poet, while Peace, pouring out tears of grief, prepares to speak.

The third and major section of the poem is structured as a dialogue between Peace and the poet as Interlocutor. This section is essentially a thoughtful and impassioned antiwar poem. Typical of Chapman's philosophical cast of mind, the poem probes the cause of war throughout human history. Peace's lament for Love clearly relates the fact of war to the death of Love, but why has Love died? Peace attributes the demise of Love to lack of learning among people in general. Genuine learning, according to Peace, implies a capability for original thought, without which humans can never arrive at a true knowledge of God. It is this deprived state of mind and soul that has made war possible. The failure of learning keeps humans from knowing God, thereby bringing about the end of Love, and Love is necessary to sustain Peace.

The concept of learning elucidated in this poem is not so much intellectual as ethical. Learning is viewed as the art of good life. Chapman cites three classes of men in particular who are dangerous enemies of this ideal: first, the active men, who aim only at worldly success and reject learning in favor of ruthlessly pursuing ambition; second, the passive men, who simply neglect learning while they waste time in mere pleasures; and, finally, the intellective men, who debase learning because they pursue their studies only for the sake of social and financial reward. Genuine learning, to be attained for its own sake, empowers the soul with control over the body's distracting passions and perturbations. Those who are called scholars in this world are all too often mere "walking dictionaries" or mere "articulate clocks" who cannot "turn blood to soul" and who will therefore never come to know God. These three categories of nonlearners and perverters of learning willingly enter the destructive toils of war.

## LEGACY

These four long poems, along with the elegies *Eugenia* and *An Epicede or Funerall Song on the Death of Henry Prince of Wales* and the occasional pieces, *Andromeda Liberata* and *Pro Vere Autumni Lachrymae*, represent most of Chapman's original verse. There are also a few short pieces called *Petrarch's Seven Penitential Psalms*, consisting largely of translations. The body of Chapman's original poetry is thus limited in scope but impressive in quality. Although *The Shadow of Night* is occasionally obscure in poetic diction, and although *Euthymiae Raptus* at times proves slow going in its didacticism, both of these poems are nevertheless rich in thought and are distinguished by several passages of high poetic caliber. *Ovid's Banquet of Sense* and *Hero and Leander* are actually two of the finest narrative poems of the English Renaissance.

The modern reader has much to gain from Chapman. His subtlety and irony appeal to the intellect, and his emblematic and metaphorical language pleases the aesthetic imagination. His is a distinctive Renaissance voice not circumscribed by the formulaic patterns of that highly conventional age. He is above all a serious writer, committed to the lofty calling of poetry as a vehicle of ideas through the medium of figurative language.

OTHER MAJOR WORKS

PLAYS: *The Blind Beggar of Alexandria*, pr. 1596 (fragment); *An Humourous Day's Mirth*, pr. 1597; *Sir Giles Goosecap*, pr. c. 1601 or 1603; *The Gentleman Usher*, pr. c. 1602; *All Fools*, pr. 1604 (wr. 1599; also known as *The World Runs on Wheels*); *Bussy d'Ambois*, pr. 1604, 1641; *Monsieur d'Olive*, pr. 1604; *Eastward Ho!*, pr., pb. 1605 (with John Marston and Ben Jonson); *The Widow's Tears*, pr. c. 1605; *The Conspiracy and Tragedy of Charles, Duke of Byron*, pr., pb. 1608; *May Day*, pr. c. 1609; *The Revenge of Bussy d'Ambois*, pr. c. 1610; *The Masque of the Middle Temple and Lincoln's Inn*, pr. 1613 (masque); *The Wars of Caesar and Pompey*, pr. c. 1613; *The Ball*, pr. 1632 (with James Shirley); *The Tragedy of Chabot, Admiral of France*, pr. 1635 (with Shirley).

TRANSLATIONS: *Iliad*, 1598, 1609, 1611 (of Homer); *Petrarch's Seven Penitential Psalms*, 1612; *Odyssey*, 1614 (of Homer); *Georgics*, 1618 (of Hesiod); *The Crown of All Homer's Works*, 1624 (of Homer's lesser-known works).

BIBLIOGRAPHY

Beach, Vincent W. *George Chapman: An Annotated Bibliography of Commentary and Criticism*. New York: G. K. Hall, 1995. A reference work providing extensive bibliographical information on Chapman. Index.

Bradbrook, Muriel C. *George Chapman*. London: Longman, 1977. This brief general overview of Chapman's life and work contains sections on the lyric poetry, including *Hero and Leander* and the translations of Homer and Hesiod. The individual chapters on the comedies and tragedies conclude that Chapman's modern reputation will have to be based on only the best of the lyrics plus two tragedies, *Bussy d'Ambois* and the two parts of the Byron play.

Donno, Elizabeth Story. "The Epyllion." In *English Poetry and Prose, 1540-1674*, edited by Christopher Ricks. New York: Peter Bedrick Books, 1986. Donno's essay provides an excellent introduction to Elizabethan narrative poetry, especially the mythological variety. Her account of Chapman's narrative verse is sound; another chapter covers his dramatic poetry. The index offers good cross-referencing. Includes a select bibliography.

Hulse, Clark. *Metamorphic Verse: The Elizabethan Minor Epic*. Princeton, N.J.: Princeton University Press, 1981. Hulse has accomplished the most complete redefinition of Elizabethan narrative poetry of modern times. His account of Chapman and his contribution is thorough and complete. The bibliographical apparatus is professional.

Huntington, John. *Ambition, Rank, and Poetry in 1590's England*. Urbana: University of

Illinois Press, 2001. Huntington uncovers a form of subtle social protest encoded in the writings of aspiring Elizabethan poets, and argues that these writers invested their poetry with a new social vision that challenged a nobility of blood and proposed a nobility of learning instead. Huntington focuses on the early work of Chapman and on the writings of others who shared his social agenda and his nonprivileged status.

Kermode, Frank. "The Banquet of Sense." In *Shakespeare, Spenser, Donne*. London: Routledge & Kegan Paul, 1971. Presents a revelatory commentary on Chapman's narratives; the insights are simply unparalleled. Includes substantial notes, a bibliography, and an index.

MacLure, Millar. *George Chapman: A Critical Study*. Toronto, Ont.: University of Toronto Press, 1966. This full-scale critical analysis of all of Chapman's writings includes extensive coverage of his narrative poetry and integrates it well with the rest of his life's work. MacLure pays particular attention to his diction and his use of poetic devices. Contains an index, notes, and a bibliography.

Snare, Gerald. *The Mystification of George Chapman*. Durham, N.C.: Duke University Press, 1989. The title is slightly misleading. This first-rate critical analysis actually attempts to demystify Chapman and his work, which had suffered from a prevailing view that it was unnecessarily obscure and contorted. Snare's discussions are lucid. Includes good notes, an index, and a bibliography.

Spivack, Charlotte. *George Chapman*. New York: Twayne, 1967. An admiring study accessible to the nonspecialist, the book begins with a biographical section and then reviews Chapman's literary work. Spivack considers him an important poet, a great playwright, and a consistent philosopher—a more favorable assessment than that of other critics.

Striar, Brian. "Chapman's *Hero and Leander* V. 62." *Explicator* 66, no. 4 (Summer, 2008): 202-204. A focused analysis of the phrase, "Teras with the ebon thigh," in *Hero and Leander*, in which the author suggests that Chapman might have meant "ebur," short for "eburin" (ivory and ox-blood), instead.

Waddington, Raymond B. *The Mind's Empire: Myth and Form in George Chapman's Narrative Poems*. Baltimore: The Johns Hopkins University Press, 1974. Focuses exclusively on Chapman's poems; analyzes them exhaustively and relates them to their cultural and historical backgrounds. Emphasis is on structural analysis. Contains an extensive bibliography, index, and complete notes.

*Charlotte Spivack*

# ABRAHAM COWLEY

**Born:** London, England; 1618
**Died:** Chertsey, England; July 28, 1667

PRINCIPAL POETRY
*Poeticall Blossomes*, 1633
*The Mistress: Or, Several Copies of Love Verses*, 1647
*Poems*, 1656 (also known as *Miscellanies*)
*Verses Lately Written upon Several Occasions*, 1663
*Poemata Latina*, 1668

## OTHER LITERARY FORMS

From time to time, Abraham Cowley (KOW-lee) interrupted his poetic activity with bits of drama and prose. The former were light, immature attempts: a pastoral drama, *Loves Riddle* (pb. 1638); a Latin comedy entitled *Naufragium Joculare* (pr., pb. 1638); another comedy, *The Guardian* (pr. 1641), hastily put together when Prince Charles passed through Cambridge, but rewritten as *Cutter of Coleman-Street* (pb. 1663). His serious prose is direct and concise, although the pieces tend to repeat the traditional Renaissance theme of solitude. His most notable prose work was a pamphlet, *A Proposition for the Advancement of Experimental Philosophy* (1661), which may have hastened the founding of the Royal Society.

## ACHIEVEMENTS

In the 1930's, the respected critic and literary historian Douglas Bush suggested that Abraham Cowley needed to be seen and understood as a man of his own age, rather than as an artist whose appeal is timeless. That statement may well be the key to assessing Cowley's achievement. During his own day, he secured a considerable reputation as a poet that endured well into the eighteenth century. Then, in 1779, Samuel Johnson issued, as the initial piece to what became *Lives of the Poets* (1779-1781), his *Life of Cowley*. With his usual rhetorical balance, Johnson described Cowley as a poet who had been "at one time too much praised and too much neglected at another." The London sage, through laborious comparison, classified his subject among the Metaphysical poets of the first half of the seventeenth century—a group that he could not always discuss in positive terms. Johnson, however, did single out Cowley as the best among the Metaphysicals and also the last of them. In general, Johnson praised the "Ode of Wit" (1668), turned a neutral ear toward the *Pindarique Odes* (1656), and evaluated the prose as possessing smooth and placid "equability." Cowley was all but forgotten during the nineteenth century, and not until after World War I, when critics such as Sir Herbert J. C.

Grierson and T. S. Eliot began to rediscover Metaphysical verse, did his achievement begin to be understood.

Perhaps Cowley's greatest achievement as a poet was that, even in retirement, he stood willing to consider the intellectual challenges of a new world, a world at the edge of scientific and political revolution. He seemed extremely sensitive to the need for the poem as a means for expressing the intellectual essence of that new world, yet he never forsook the Renaissance tradition in which he had been taught. Cowley gave to English poetry a sensible mixture of seriousness, learning, imagination, intelligence, and perception. Although he often wrestled with himself, caught between authority and reason, between the rational and the imaginative, between the rejected past and the uncertain future, he managed to control his art, to triumph over the uncertainty and confusion of his time. Through poetry, Cowley searched for order; through poetry he achieved order—classical, scientific, and religious order—in a world that had itself become worn from passion. The achievement of Cowley is that he showed his successors—especially the Augustans of the early eighteenth century—that a poet should seek and find new material and new methods without having to sever the strong cord of the past.

## BIOGRAPHY

Abraham Cowley was born in the parish of St. Michael le Quern, Cheapside, in London, sometime after July, 1618, the seventh child and fifth son (born posthumously) of Thomas Cowley, a stationer and grocer, who left £1000 to be divided among his seven children. His mother was Thomasine Berrye, to whom Thomas Cowley had pledged his faith sometime in 1581. The widow did the best she could to educate her children through her own devices and then managed to send the boys off to more formal institutions. Thus, she obtained young Abraham's admission as a king's scholar at Westminster School, to which he proceeded armed with some acquaintance with Edmund Spenser. By the age of fifteen, he was already a published poet; his first collection of five pieces, entitled *Poeticall Blossomes*, was followed by a second edition three years later. One of the poems, "Pyramus and Thisbe," some 226 lines long, had been written when he was ten; another, "Constantia and Philetus," was written during the poet's twelfth year.

Cowley's scholarly skills unfortunately did not keep pace with the development of his poetic muse. Apparently the boy balked at the drudgeries of learning grammar and languages; furthermore, his masters contended that his natural quickness made such study unnecessary. In the end, he failed to gain election to Cambridge University in 1636 and had to wait until mid-June of the following year, at which time he became a scholar of Trinity College. Cambridge proved no deterrent to young Cowley's poetic bent; in 1638, he published a pastoral drama, *Loves Riddle*, written at least four years previously. Then, on February 2, 1638, members of Trinity College performed his Latin comedy, *Naufragium Joculare*, which he published shortly thereafter. After taking his

B.A. in 1639, Cowley remained at Cambridge through 1642, by which time he had earned the M.A. The year before, when Prince Charles had passed through Cambridge, the young poet had hastily prepared for the occasion a comedy entitled *The Guardian*; the piece was acted a number of times before its publication in 1650 and it continued to be performed, privately, of course, during the Commonwealth and the suppression of the theaters.

Leaving Cambridge in 1643, Cowley continued to write poetry, principally at St. John's College, Oxford, where he had "retired" and become intimate with Royalist leaders. Joining the family of Jermyn (later St. Albans), he followed the queen to France in 1646, where he found a fellow poet, Richard Crashaw. The exiled court employed Cowley for a number of diplomatic services, particularly on missions to Jersey and Holland; other activities included transmitting a correspondence in cipher between Charles I and his queen. During this period, several of Cowley's works appeared in London, including a collection of poems entitled *The Mistress*. His poetic output was restricted, however, because his diplomatic work occupied all his days and most of his evenings. In 1656, his employers sent him to England on what can only be termed an espionage mission under the guise of seeking retirement. He was arrested, but only because the authorities mistook him for someone else; released on bail, he remained under strict probation until Charles II reclaimed the throne of England in 1660.

For Cowley, however, the big event of 1656 was the publication of his most important collection, *Poems*—including the juvenile pieces, the elegies to William Hervey and Crashaw, *The Mistress*, the *Pindarique Odes*, and *Davideis*. The last item, an epic of four books (out of twelve that he had originally planned), actually belonged to the poet's Cambridge period, and Cowley finally admitted that he had abandoned plans to complete it. After the publication of the *Poems*, Cowley, still in the employ of the exiled Royalists in France, suddenly took up the study of medicine—as a means of obscuring his espionage activities. Seemingly without difficulty, he earned his medical doctor's degree at Oxford in December, 1657, and then retired to Kent, where he studied and produced a Latin poem, "Plantarum Libri duo" (published in 1662). After the Restoration, Cowley's best poetry and prose appeared: "Ode upon the Blessed Restoration" (1660), *A Vision, Concerning His Late Pretended Highnesse, Cromwell the Wicked* (1661), *A Proposition for the Advancement of Experimental Philosophy*, "Ode to the Royal Society" (1661), and *Verses Lately Written upon Several Occasions*.

Cowley's early employer, Jermyn, by then the earl of St. Albans, helped to obtain for him some royal land at Chertsey, where he could spend the remainder of his days in easy retirement. There he settled in April, 1665. His health began to decline, however, and the fact that his tenants balked at paying their rents did little to improve his physical and emotional condition. In late July, 1667, after being outdoors longer than necessary, he caught a severe cold; he died on the twenty-eighth of that month. Cowley was buried with considerable ceremony in Westminster Abbey, near Geoffrey Chaucer and

Edmund Spenser, and for the rest of the seventeenth century, poets and critics continued to view him as the model of cultivated poetry.

## ANALYSIS

Abraham Cowley is a transitional figure, a poet who tended to relinquish the emotional values of John Donne and George Herbert and grasp the edges of reason and wit. He was more versatile than the early Metaphysicals: He embraced the influence of Donne and Ben Jonson, relied on the Pindaric form that would take hold in the eighteenth century, conceived of an experimental biblical epic in English (*Davideis*) well in advance of John Milton's major project, and demonstrated an open-mindedness that allowed him to write in support of Francis Bacon, Thomas Hobbes, and the Royal Society. Cowley's elegies on the deaths of William Hervey and Richard Crashaw are extremely frank poems of natural pain and loss, while at the same time the poet recognized the need for the human intellect to be aware of "Things Divine"—the dullness of the earthly as opposed to the reality of the heavenly.

Indeed, Cowley's versatile imagination ranged far and wide, and he easily adapted diverse subjects to fit his own purposes. Unlike the poets of the Restoration and the early eighteenth century who followed him, he ignored various current fashions and concentrated on economy, unity, form, and imagination; he did not have to force the grotesque on his readers, nor did he have to inundate them with a pretense of art. Cowley was a master at what Bishop Thomas Sprat termed, in 1668, "harmonious artistry." He turned his back on wild and affected extravagance and embraced propriety and measure; he applied wit to matter, combined philosophy with charity and religion. Even when writing amorous verse, he took inspiration both from the courtier and from the scholar—the passion of the one and the wisdom of the other.

## POETICALL BLOSSOMES

Cowley launched his career as a serious poet at the age of fifteen, while still a student at Westminster School, with the publication of *Poeticall Blossomes*. In fact, there is evidence that the volume had been prepared in some form at least two years earlier. At any rate, what appeared was a rather high level of poetic juvenilia, five pieces in which both sound and sense reflected an ability far beyond the poet's youth. The first, "Pyramus and Thisbe," 226 lines, does not differ too markedly from Ovid's tale, although Cowley's Venus seems overly malevolent and the (then) ten-year-old poet carried to extremes the desired but untasted joys of love. Otherwise, the piece evidences a sense of discipline and knowledge often reserved for the mature imagination, as young Cowley attempted to control his phrasing and his verse form. The second poem in the collection, "Constantia and Philetus," may serve as a companion to "Pyramus and Thisbe," although it is certainly no mere imitation. Cowley, now about twelve, again chose as his subject a tragic love story, keeping hold on Venus, Cupid, and other deities. However, he shifted his setting from ancient Rome to the suburban surroundings of an Italian villa, there to unfold a rather conventional poetic narrative: two lovers, a rival favored by the parents, a sympathetic brother, and a dead heroine. He adorned the entire scene with amorous conceits and characters yearning for the beauties of the country and the consolations of nature.

In addition to the larger pieces, *Poeticall Blossomes* contained an interesting trio of shorter efforts. In "A Dream of Elysium," Cowley, seemingly engaged in an exercise in poetic self-education, parades before a sleeping poet a host of classical favorites: Hyacinth, Narcissus, Apollo, Ovid, Homer, Cato, Leander, Hero, Portia, Brutus, Pyramus, and Thisbe. The final two poems of the volume constitute the young writer's first attempts at what would become, for him, an important form—the occasional poem. Both pieces are elegies: One mourns the death of a public official, Dudley, Lord Carleton and Viscount Dorchester, who attended Westminster School, served as secretary of state, and died in February, 1632; the other was occasioned by the death of Cowley's cousin, Richard Clerke, a student at Lincoln's Inn. Naturally, the two poems contain extravagant praises and lofty figures, no doubt reflecting what the boy had read in his favorite, Spenser, and had been taught by his masters. There are those who speculate that had Cowley died in adolescence, as Thomas Chatterton did in the next century, the verses of *Poeticall Blossomes* would have sustained at least a very small poetic reputation in a very obscure niche of literary history. Cowley, however, despite a number of purely political distractions during his adult life, managed to extend his poetic talents beyond childhood exercises, and it is to the products of his maturity that one must turn for the comprehension and appreciation of his art.

## POEMS

Perhaps Cowley's most important contribution to poetry came in 1656 with the publication of his extensive collection, *Poems*, several additions to which he made during his lifetime. Of more than passing interest is the preface to this volume, wherein Cowley attempts, by reference to his own personal situation, to explain the relationship between the poet and his environment. In 1656, he had little desire to write poetry, mainly because of the political instability of the moment, his own health, and his mental state. He admitted that a warlike, unstable, and even tragic age may be the best for the poet to write about, but it may also be the worst time in which to write. Living as he did, a stranger under surveillance in his own homeland, he felt restricted in his artistic endeavors. "The soul," he complained in the preface, "must be filled with bright and delightful ideas when it undertakes to communicate delight to others, which is the main end of poesy." Thus, he had given serious thought to abandoning Puritan England for the obscurity of some plantation in the Americas, and the 1656 *Poems* was to be his legacy to a world for whose conflicts and confrontations he no longer had any concern.

The *Poems* contain four divisions: the *Miscellanies*, including the *Anacreontiques*;

*The Mistress*, a collection of love poems; *Pindarique Odes*; and the *Davideis*, a heroic epic focusing on the problems of the Old Testament king. In subsequent editions, Cowley and his editors added "Verses on Various Occasions" and "Several Discourses by Way of Essays in Prose and Verse." Cowley himself informed his readers that the *Miscellanies* constituted poems preserved from earlier folios (some even from his school days); unfortunately, he made no distinction between the poor efforts and those of quality. Thus, an immature ode, "Here's to thee, Dick," stands near the serious and moving elegy "On the Death of Mr. William Hervey," in which he conveys both universal meaning and personal tragedy and loss. Cowley, however, rarely allowed himself to travel the route of the strictly personal; for him, poetry required support from learning, from scholastic comparisons that did not always rise to poetical levels. The fine valedictory "To the Lord Falkland," which celebrates the friendship between two interesting but divergent personalities, is sprinkled with lofty scientific comparisons to display the order that reigns in the crowded mind of his hero. Indeed, there are moments in Cowley's elegies when the reader wonders if the poet was more interested in praising the virtues of science and learning than in mourning the loss of friends. Such high distractions, however, do not weaken the intensity of Cowley's sincerity.

## THE MISTRESS

*The Mistress*, originally published as a separate volume in 1647, comprises one hundred love poems, or, in Cowley's own terms, feigned addresses to some fair creature of the fancy. Almost apologetically, the poet explains in the prefatory remarks that all writers of verse must at one time or another pay some service to Love, to prove themselves true to Love. Unfortunately, Cowley evidences difficulty in warming to the occasion, perhaps held back by the prevalent mood of Puritan strictness that then dominated the art. Thus, many of his physical and psychological images of Love come from traditions rather than from the heart: Love is an interchange of hearts, a flame, a worship, a river frozen by disdain. On the other hand, Cowley's original, nontraditional images and similes are often wildly incongruous, even unintentionally comical, and lacking in true feeling.

Tears are made by smoke but not by flame; the lover's heart bursts on its object "Like a grenado shot into a magazine"; a love story cut into bark burns and withers the tree; a young lady's beauty changes from civil government to tyranny. Certainly, *The Mistress* reveals that Cowley could employ an obvious degree of playfulness in verse; he could counterfeit, with ease and ingenuity, a series of love adventures; he could sustain some semblance of unity in a seeming hodgepodge of romantic episodes; he could amuse his readers. For those of his age who took their love poetry seriously, however—for those who expected grace, warmth, tenderness, even truth—*The Mistress* must have been rather disappointing.

## PINDARIQUE ODES

There is some confusion concerning the form of the *Pindarique Odes*. Cowley may have wanted readers to believe that he was writing the true Pindaric ode: strophe, antistrophe (alike in form), and epode (different in form from the first two divisions), with varying meter and verse lengths within a strophe, but nevertheless regular metrical schemes established for corresponding divisions. Actually, he created a new form, an irregular ode: He discarded the usual stanza patterns, varied the length of lines and the number of lines within the strophes, and varied the meter with shifts in emotional intensity. He obviously knew what he was doing and probably chose the title for the section to disguise a questionable innovation. In fact, he doubted (in the preface) whether the form would be understood by most of his readers, even those acquainted with the principles of poetry. Nevertheless, he employed sudden and lengthy digressions, "unusual and bold" figures, and various and irregular numbers. Cowley's purpose throughout was to achieve a sense of harmony between what he viewed as the liberty of the ode and the moral liberty of life, the latter combining responsibility and freedom. Through moral liberty, he hoped to find simplicity, retirement, and charm; the liberty of the ode, he thought, might allow for a greater participation in intellectual exercise.

In practice, the ode allowed Cowley the opportunity to subject his readers to a host of what he had termed "bold figures," images that would have occurred to no one other than he. Thus, on one occasion he asks his Muse to "rein her Pindaric Pegasus closely in," since the beast is "an unruly and a hardmouthed horse." At another time, the Muse appears in her chariot, with Eloquence, Wit, Memory, and Invention running by her side. Suddenly, Cowley stops the action to compare the Muse with the Creator and with the two worlds that they have created. Such comparisons, with their accompanying "bold" images, allowed the poet to display his learning, to set down explanatory notes of definition, explication, and interpretation—whether his readers needed them or not. As long as he could serve as his own explicator, there seemed no limit to his invention. Generally, though, Cowley's odes fall short of their intentions as complete pieces of poetry. The digressions—the instruments of the poet's new-found intellectual freedom—may strike and impress the reader momentarily, but they also distract and divert the attention from the main idea of the poem.

Not all of Cowley's odes fall short of the mark. He succeeded when his subject interested him enough to say something substantive about it. In both "To Mr. Hobbes" and "Brutus" he followed the serious thinkers of his time. The first poem finds him looking beyond the transitory troubles of the moment to a new day. The second allows him to observe Oliver Cromwell, the Caesar of his time and, like the conscientious Royalist of the period, seek contemplation rather than action. He looks to history and philosophy to explain the evils of tyranny and to find parallels with other evils that eventually gave way to good. In the ode to Hobbes, Cowley finds solace in the fact that all ideas and concepts of permanent value must remain young and fresh forever. In the ode to Brutus, the poet discovers that odd events, evil men, and wretched actions are not themselves sufficient to destroy or even obscure virtue. Again, the particular circumstances of the moment and his deep personal disappointment gave Cowley the conviction to express what he actually felt.

### DAVIDEIS

It is tempting to dismiss *Davideis* as another example of Cowley's juvenilia. Of the twelve books planned, only four were finished, and those were written while Cowley was still at Cambridge. By 1656, and perhaps even before, Cowley had lost his taste for the epic and determined not to finish it. If anything can be salvaged from *Davideis* it may be found in the preface, where the poet makes an eloquent plea for sacred poetry. Cowley complains that for too long wit and eloquence have been wasted on the beggarly flattery of important persons, idolizing of foolish women, and senseless fables. The time has come, he announces, to recover poetry from the devil and restore it to the kingdom of God, to rescue it from the impure waters of Damascus and baptize it in the Jordan.

Unfortunately, the epic that follows never rises to the elegance or merit of the prefatory prose. The poem simply sinks from its own weight. Cowley's Hell, for example, is a labyrinth of cosmic elements: caverns that breed rare metals; nests of infant, weeping winds; a complex court of mother waters. The journey there is indeed long and laborious, and the relationship between all those cosmic details (gold, winds, voices, tides, and tidelessness) and Hell is never made clear. Cowley himself acknowledged the immaturity and weakness of the epic, but he also saw it as an adumbration of the poetic potential of biblical history. Eleven years after the publication of *Davideis* in the collected *Poems*, John Milton published *Paradise Lost* (1667, 1674).

### "HYMN TO LIGHT"

Cowley added to the collected editions of his poems as they were issued between 1656 and his death in 1667. As with the contents of the first edition, the pieces vary in quality. In "Hymn to Light," the poet manages to achieve a proper balance between his learning and his imagination. The reader senses that Cowley has actually observed the "winged arrows" shooting from the "golden quiver of the sky," the result of a long succession of fresh and bright dawns rising in the English countryside. Those very dawns seem to have frightened "sleep, the lazy owl of night," turning the face of "cloudy care" into a "gentle, beamy smile." During those blessed years of retirement, away from the unnatural complications and intrigues of the political world, Cowley turned more and more toward the beauty of nature as a source of pleasure. Although in "Hymn to Light" he labels light an offspring of chaos, its very beams embrace and enhance the charms and beauty of the world, while at the same time tempting the selfish and inconsiderate by shining on valuable elements. Toward the end of the poem, he conceives of light as a "clear river" that pours forth its radiance from the vast ocean of the sky; it collects in pools and lakes when its course is opposed by some firm body—the earth, for example. Such a conceit may appear overly abstract and abstruse, but it is perhaps the most extreme figure of the poem, demonstrating the degree to which the mature Cowley had advanced beyond his juvenile epic endeavors.

## "ODE TO THE ROYAL SOCIETY"

There are critics who assert that with the "Ode to the Royal Society" (1667), Cowley rose to his highest level. That is debatable, but it is certainly his last important poem. The poem was written at the request of Cowley's friend, the diarist John Evelyn, who asked for a tribute to the Royal Society to complement the official history being undertaken by Thomas Sprat, bishop of Rochester. The poem, published the same year as Sprat's *History of the Royal Society*, focused not so much on the institution in question or even on science in general but on the evolution of philosophy, which Cowley placed into two chronological periods: before and after Francis Bacon. The poet dwells briefly on the constrictions of the early philosophies, which merely wandered among the labyrinths of endless discourse, with little or no positive effect on humankind. Then follows an impassioned attack on pure authority, which arrived at erroneous scientific and intellectual conclusions and stubbornly clung to them.

Cowley compares Francis Bacon—who, with his *Advancement of Learning* (1605), *Novum Organum* (1620), and *De Augmentis Scientiarum* (1623), had initiated a new age of philosophy—to Moses; men of intellect were led out of the barren wasteland of the past to the very borders of exalted wit. Only Bacon, maintains Cowley, was willing to act and capable of routing the ghostlike body of authority that had for so long misled people with its dead thoughts. The philosophers of the past were but mechanics, copiers of others' work; Bacon summoned the mind away from words, the mere pictures of thoughts, and redirected it toward objects, the proper focus of the mind. Thus, the poet paid tribute to the philosopher as the proper predecessor of the Royal Society; his investigations paved the way for the significant accomplishments of that institution. The immediate success of the poem may have been due in part to Cowley's personal ties with the Royal Society—particularly as a friend of both Sprat and Evelyn and as the author of *A Proposition for the Advancement of Experimental Philosophy*. Those critics who have praised the piece for its pure poetic merit, however, have rightly identified it as the culmination of Cowley's contributions to the English ode.

## LEGACY

Beginning with Joseph Addison's negative criticism (*The Spectator* 62, May, 1711) and extending through the critique in Samuel Johnson's *Lives of the Poets*, Cowley's reputation has endured the accusations of mixed wit and strained metaphysical conceits. Obviously, Addison and Johnson, even though they represent opposite chronological poles of the eighteenth century, were still too close to their subject to assess him objectively and to recognize him as a transitional figure. Cowley lived during the end of one intellectual age and the beginning of another. He belonged alongside John Donne, Richard Crashaw, George Herbert, Henry Vaughan, Thomas Traherne, and Andrew Marvell; he owed equal allegiance to the writers of the early Restoration, to such classicists as John Denham and Edmund Waller. Thus, his poetry reflects the traditions of one period and the freshness of another, the extravagances of youth and the freedom to combine ingenuity with reason and learning. Cowley also had the distinct advantage of a point of view resulting from the mastery of several positive sciences and of practically all the literature of Europe. Knowledge, reflection, control, clear judgment: These he carried with him from the Puritan Revolution into the Restoration and then to his own retirement. He belonged to an age principally of learning and of prose; he wrote poetry with the sustained rhetorical and emotional force that often results in greatness. Unfortunately, his meteor merely approached greatness, flaring only for a brief moment on the literary horizon.

OTHER MAJOR WORKS

PLAYS: *Loves Riddle*, pb. 1638; *Naufragium Joculare*, pr., pb. 1638; *The Guardian*, pr. 1641 (revised as *Cutter of Coleman-Street*, pb. 1663).

NONFICTION: *A Proposition for the Advancement of Experimental Philosophy*, 1661; *A Vision, Concerning His Late Pretended Highnesse, Cromwell the Wicked*, 1661; *Several Discourses by Way of Essays in Prose and Verse*, 1668.

MISCELLANEOUS: *The Works of Mr. Abraham Cowley*, 1668, 1681, 1689.

BIBLIOGRAPHY

Dykstal, Timothy. "The Epic Reticence of Abraham Cowley." *Studies in English Literature* 31, no. 1 (Winter, 1991): 95. An analysis of Cowley's *Davideis* and John Milton's *Paradise Lost*.

Hinman, Robert B. *Abraham Cowley's World of Order*. Cambridge, Mass.: Harvard University Press, 1960. Summarizes Cowley's scholarship, outlines his notions about art, examines the influence of Francis Bacon and Thomas Hobbes, reads the poems in terms of "order," and evaluates Cowley's position as a poet. Contains an extensive bibliography.

Nethercot, Arthur H. *Abraham Cowley: The Muse's Hannibal*. 1931. Reprint. New York: Russell & Russell, 1967. The definitive biography, this book discusses Cowley's literary work, citing his composition of the first religious epic in English, his development of the Pindaric ode, and his literary criticism. Includes an extensive bibliography, several illustrations, and some documents, one of which is Cowley's will.

Pebworth, Ted-Larry. "Cowley's *Davideis* and the Exaltation of Friendship." In *The David Myth in Western Literature*, edited by Raymond-Jean Frontain and Jan

Wojcik. West Lafayette, Ind.: Purdue University Press, 1980. Essay concerns the friendship of David and Jonathan, which is compared to the classical friendships of Damon and Pythias, Cicero and Atticus, and Orestes and Pylades and the topical friendship of Cowley and William Hervey. Examines the friendship in *Davideis* in terms of the three-step Neoplatonic progression of love.

Revard, Stella P. "Cowley's *Pindarique Odes* and the Politics of the Inter-Regnum." *Criticism* 35, no. 3 (Summer, 1993): 391. An examination of Royalist celebration and resistance in Cowley's *Pindarique Odes*. It is assumed that these texts and the political agenda they encode were produced under censorship.

Taaffe, James G. *Abraham Cowley*. New York: Twayne, 1972. An excellent overview of Cowley's literary work. Contains readings of many of Cowley's works, with extensive commentary on *Davideis*. Of the shorter works, "The Muse," the poems on the deaths of Richard Crashaw and William Hervey, and the Cromwell poem are treated in some detail. Includes a chronology and an annotated select bibliography.

Trotter, David. *The Poetry of Abraham Cowley*. Totowa, N.J.: Rowman & Littlefield, 1979. Tends to downplay political and social contexts and to stress the role of form in Cowley's work. The lyric poems (especially *The Mistress*), the sacred poems, the Pindaric odes, and Cowley's relationship to Richard Crashaw are treated in separate chapters. Contains a helpful bibliography.

Walton, Geoffrey. "Abraham Cowley." In *From Donne to Marvell*. Vol. 3 in *A Guide to English Literature*, edited by Boris Ford. London: Cassell, 1956. Walton regards Cowley as the bridge between Metaphysical wit and neoclassical poetry and relates Cowley's poetry back to Jonson and Donne and ahead to Dryden and Pope. Walton's focus, though, is on Cowley's neoclassical verse, especially in the shaping of the Pindaric ode and the creation of the first neoclassical epic in English, *Davideis*.

Welch, Anthony. "Epic Romance, Royalist Retreat, and the English Civil War." *Modern Philology* 105, no. 3 (February, 2008): 570. Welch discusses the effect that the stalemate of Charles I's army at the First Battle of Newbury had on the Royalist epic poem that Cowley was writing about the Civil War.

Williamson, George. *Six Metaphysical Poets: A Reader's Guide*. New York: Farrar, Straus and Giroux, 1967. Williamson's chapter on Cowley provides a good overview of the metaphysical elements in Cowley's poetry. Contains several one-page discussions of individual poems and concludes with an informative comparison between Cowley and Donne. For Williamson, Cowley's love poetry is located between Donne's Metaphysical poetry and Waller's verse.

*Samuel J. Rogal*

# RICHARD CRASHAW

**Born:** London, England; c. 1612
**Died:** Loreto (now in Italy); August 21, 1649

PRINCIPAL POETRY
*Epigrammatum Sacrorum Liber*, 1634
*Steps to the Temple*, 1646, 1648
*Carmen Deo Nostro*, 1652
*Poems: English, Latin, and Greek*, 1927, 1957
*Complete Poetry of Richard Crashaw*, 1970

## OTHER LITERARY FORMS

Richard Crashaw (KRASH-aw) wrote primarily religious poetry reflecting the life of Christ and the symbols of Christianity.

## ACHIEVEMENTS

Richard Crashaw occupies his niche in literary history as a sort of maverick Metaphysical whose poetry, although displaying many of the techniques and characteristics of John Donne and George Herbert, is unique in its baroque flamboyance and its strong Roman Catholic sensibilities. A poet of fluctuating popularity, Crashaw has had his work treated as decadent Metaphysical poetry, as an outstanding example of ornate wit, as conventional Catholic devotion, and as intensely personal expression. His poems are longer and more elaborate than those of his model George Herbert, although his themes are narrower in focus. Crashaw is sometimes ranked with Donne and Herbert as a major Metaphysical poet; alternately, he is linked with such significant but minor writers as Abraham Cowley and Henry Vaughan.

In his intense rendering of Counter-Reformation Roman Catholic spirituality, as well as in his use of powerful visual experiences, Crashaw is distinctive. His poetry, widely popular in his own day, continued to attract readers and critical appreciation through the end of the seventeenth century and early in the eighteenth; it waned with the pre-Romantics and their successors and received relatively little notice until early in the twentieth century, when a host of major critics rediscovered religious poetry.

## BIOGRAPHY

The only child of William Crashaw, Richard Crashaw was born in London in either 1612 or 1613. His mother died when he was an infant; William Crashaw's second wife, Elizabeth, died when Richard was seven.

William Crashaw, Anglican divine, seems an unlikely parent for one of England's most famous converts to Roman Catholicism. Staunchly Low Church (some say Puritan) in his theology and in his lifestyle, the elder Crashaw devoted his life to preaching and writing, partly against the Laudian or High Church excesses in the Church of England but principally against what he perceived as the far greater dangers of the Church of Rome itself. In his efforts to know the full strength of the enemy, William Crashaw amassed an impressive collection of "Romish" writings; the critic can only speculate what effect these works, as well as his father's convictions, may have had on the spiritual development of Richard Crashaw.

After two years at London's famed Charterhouse School with its austere regime and classical curriculum, Crashaw was admitted, in 1631, to Pembroke College at Cambridge University. He would receive his A.B. in 1634 and his A.M. in 1638. He came to Pembroke with something of a reputation as a poet, a reputation that grew steadily as he produced Latin and Greek epigrams as well as English models, translations of the Psalms, and various occasional verses. These works form the basis of his 1634 publication, *Epigrammatum Sacrorum Liber*, the only work Crashaw himself would see through the printing process.

In 1635, Crashaw was appointed to a fellowship at Peterhouse College and sometime shortly thereafter was ordained to the Anglican priesthood. At Peterhouse, he was in direct contact with a circle of Laudian churchmen whose devotion, emphasis on liturgical ceremony and propriety, and reverence marked another step in Crashaw's eventual spiritual journey to Rome. Between 1635 and 1643, Crashaw also learned Spanish and Italian, moving with ease into the reading of the Spanish mystics, among them Teresa of Ávila and John of the Cross, as well as the rich tradition of Italian devotional literature. This material would strongly influence his later poetry, to the extent that his work is sometimes described as Continental rather than English.

Another significant event of the Peterhouse years was Crashaw's acquaintance with the community at Little Gidding, the religious retreat founded by George Herbert's friend Nicholas Ferrar. At Little Gidding, daily communal prayers and other religious observances were prescribed and orderly; the ancient church building was restored by the community to a Laudian elegance; the sanctuary fittings were rich and reverent. Although Ferrar and his followers steadfastly maintained their allegiance to Canterbury, the community was sometimes criticized as Papist.

These same criticisms were being levied at Peterhouse, where John Cosin, master of Peterhouse and a friend of Crashaw, was restoring and adorning the college chapel with equal devotion. Reports of the candles, incense, and crucifixes at Peterhouse continued to arouse Puritan suspicions; in the early 1640's, Cosin, along with Crashaw, was censured for "popish doctrine." In 1643, Parliament, goaded by the growing Puritan forces, forbade all altar ornaments as well as all pictures of saints. In these early years of the Civil Wars, Cosin, Crashaw, and four others were formally expelled from their fellowships and forced to depart.

The last six years of Crashaw's life, the key years of his conversion and the flowering of his poetry, are difficult to trace with any certainty. In 1644, he wrote from Leyden, speaking of his poverty and his loneliness. He may have revisited England, probably only for a short period. At some point, he made the acquaintance of Queen Henrietta Maria, who, as a devout Catholic, took up his cause in a letter to Pope Innocent. Somewhere in his physical and spiritual travels, Crashaw decided—or discerned a call—to commit himself to Roman Catholicism; this central experience cannot be dated. He continued to write, completing the poems his editor would entitle *Steps to the Temple* (a humble compliment to George Herbert's *The Temple*, 1633), revising many of his earlier poems, and working on the pieces that would form his last volume, *Carmen Deo Nostro*.

Crashaw spent time in Rome and in Paris, absorbing the rich art of these cities as well as their expressions of Catholicism. In Paris, he was befriended by the poet Abraham Cowley who, appalled at his friend's physical condition, obtained care and financial assistance for him. Back in Rome, Crashaw was appointed to the service of a cardinal and subsequently was sent to Loreto, the house where, according to Catholic tradition, the Virgin Mary received word of the Annunciation. Crashaw had barely reached this Marian shrine when he fell ill; he died August 21, 1649.

## ANALYSIS

Richard Crashaw's poetry may be divided into three groups of unequal significance for the scholar: the early epigrams, the secular poetry, and the religious poetry. The early epigrams and translations are studied, meticulous, and often occasional. The 178 Latin epigrams in *Epigrammatum Sacrorum Liber* show the influence of Martial and other classical writers. Crashaw also uses biblical motifs, particularly for his several English epigrams, displaying in his treatment of these themes an example of the close reading that will underlie his later work.

As a book of poetry, these early pieces are significant for the discipline they reveal and for their fascination with wordplay—puns, quips, repetitions, conceits—which Crashaw will later elevate to such exuberance. They are finger exercises, and if they lack the genius of John Milton's college ventures, they nevertheless suggest later greatness.

### DELIGHTS OF THE MUSES

Crashaw's second body of verse, the secular or nonsacred poetry, comprises much of the work found in *Delights of the Muses*, the volume appended to and published with *Steps to the Temple*. In that volume, Crashaw displays the Donnean Metaphysical, writing poems with titles such as "Wishes. To His (Supposed) Mistress," "A Picture Sent to a Friend," "Venus Putting on Mars His Armor," and "Loves Horoscope." Witty, polished, urbane, these poems show an accomplished and sophisticated writer delighting in the possibilities of English poetry. Intensely visual, these poems often select a single image and elaborate it in a manner reminiscent of the earlier emblem tradition. The classical tradition is still strong but the metrics are clearly English.

Although the poems in *Delights of the Muses* are often Donne-like in their wit, there is a certain reticence to them. The robust speaker of Donne's songs and sonnets is absent in Crashaw; there is relatively little use of the personal pronoun and none of the speechlike abruptness that makes so many of Donne's poems memorable. The meter is usually highly regular, most often iambic tetrameter or pentameter, and the cadences are smooth. There is an unsubstantiated tradition that Crashaw was a trained musician; these poems would support that claim.

From time to time, there is a baffling half-revelation, for example in the two-line "On Marriage," when the speaker declares that he would "be married, but I'd have no wife,/ I would be married to the single life." Whether this is witty posturing, cynical disclaimer, or an honest account of his own state (Crashaw never married), the reader cannot tell. Crashaw's work would appear in anthologies even if he had written only the secular poetry, but his name would definitely be in smaller type. The poet himself spent far less effort in revising these secular poems, suggesting that he too considered them of secondary importance.

## STEPS TO THE TEMPLE AND CARMEN DEO NOSTRO

Turning to Crashaw's major works, those rich poems that he wrote and revised for the collections that would become *Steps to the Temple* and *Carmen Deo Nostro*, one is confronted with a lavish, even bewildering, highly sensuous, celebration of the Christianity that so fired the poet. If Donne argues with God in his Holy Sonnets and Herbert prays through *The Temple*, then Crashaw contemplates and exclaims. Apparently gifted with mystical experiences even in the midst of his English tradition, Crashaw's mode of prayer is much more akin to that of Teresa of Ávila than to the Book of Common Prayer. Like Teresa, who said that she could meditate for hours on the opening two words of the Lord's Prayer, Crashaw, confronted by the mysteries of Christ's life, death, and resurrection, meditates, celebrates, sorrows, refines, ponders, sees. Faced with mystery, he expresses it in paradox and strains to reconcile the opposites. Christianity does, after all, continually join flesh and spirit, God and humanity, justice and mercy, life and death. Crashaw's poetry does the same: It reveals rather than persuades. Unlike Henry Vaughan and especially Thomas Traherne, whose religious poetry is almost unflaggingly optimistic, Crashaw focuses on both the joys and sufferings of Christianity and more on the sufferings of Christ and the Virgin Mary, although he involves himself in the joyous mysteries of Christianity as well.

## "IN THE HOLY NATIVITY OF OUR LORD"

"In the Holy Nativity of Our Lord," one of Crashaw's best-known, most tightly written poems, makes a most appropriate introduction to the poet. Starting with the paradox of the revelation of Christ's birth to humble shepherds, Crashaw structures his hymn in a series of dualities and paradoxes: "Loves noone" meets "Natures night," frost is replaced by flowers, a tiny manger provides a bed for "this huge birth" of God who becomes man. The dualities in the poem are underscored by the shepherds themselves, classically named Tityrus and Thursis, who alternate verses and sing the chorus together.

The contrasts lead to the central question of the hymn, where to find a "fit" bed for the infant Jesus. When the "whitest sheets of snow" prove pure but too cold and the "rosie fleece" of angels' wings is warm but cannot "passe for pure," the shepherds return to the nativity scene to discover that the Christ child has vividly and dramatically reached his own solution:

> See see, how soone his new-bloom'd cheeke
> Twixt's mother's brests is gone to bed.
> Sweet choice (said I!) no way but so
> Not to lye cold, yet sleep in snow.

The paradox is resolved in the person of the Virgin Mother, Mary; the "I" of the shepherds becomes the "we" of all the faithful; the celebration of "Eternitie shut in a span/ Summer in winter, day in night,/ Heaven in Earth and god in man" ends in a full chorus, followed by an anthem of liturgical joy.

Several traits elevate this poem well above the countless conventional, albeit sincere, Nativity poems of this period. The central image is vivid and personal; the Christ child is presented not as king but as nursing infant. Crashaw brilliantly takes the biblical motif of the Son of man, who has no place to lay his head, and transforms it into image. The poem moves gracefully from opening question to resolution, celebrating that resolution and concluding with the offering: "at last . . . our selves become our owne best sacrifice." It is a poem of liturgical color: The images of white and gold that weave through the stanzas are reminiscent of the vestments worn for the Christmas liturgy as well as the sunrise of Christmas Day.

One of Crashaw's simpler poems because of its traditional subject matter, "In the Holy Nativity of Our Lord" exemplifies the gifts of the poet. Crashaw is a worker with color: gold and silver, red and crimson and scarlet, and blinding white fill the poems along with modifiers such as "bright," "rosy," "radiant," and a score of others. The poet is highly conscious of textures and surfaces, forever describing his images as "soft," "rough," "slippery." Predominantly Anglo-Saxon in his diction (his most repeated nouns are monosyllables—"die," "birth," "sun," "flame," "heart," "eyes"), Crashaw betrays his early fondness for Latin in some of his favorite adjectives: "immortal," "triumphant," "illustrious," and "supernatural." He alliterates constantly, playing with vowel and consonant sounds to achieve unity of tone as well as musical qualities.

## "SAINTE MARY MAGDALEN"

Ironically, Crashaw's most characteristic gifts as a poet, particularly his enthusiasm for the refined and elaborate image, are responsible for some of his most-criticized efforts. Of these, the most famous is "Sainte Mary Magdalen: Or, The Weeper," a long poem commemorating the legend of Mary Magdalene, the sinner forgiven by Jesus, who, according to tradition, wept tears of repentance for many years. The motif is a beloved one in the seventeenth century; poems celebrating (and recommending) tears abound, often with Mary Magdalene, Saint Peter, or another grieving Christian as the focal point. Crashaw's poem is really not about Mary Magdalene at all; rather it is about the tears themselves, which, after falling from Mary Magdalene's eyes, follow a circuitous, thirty-seven stanza route, develop a speech of their own, and finally go up to Heaven to meet "a worthy object, Our Lords Feet." In between his opening salutation of Magdalene's eyes ("Ever bubling things! Thawing crystall! Snowy hills!") and the final image of Jesus, Crashaw scatters images and conceits with such abandon as to bewilder the unwary. Some of these conceits are richly apt: Magdalene is "pretious prodigall! Faire spendthrift of thy self!" Others (and there are many more of these) are extravagant, incredible, even ludicrous:

> And now where e're he strayes
>
> . . . . . . . . . .
>
> He's follow'd by two faithfull fountaines,
> Two walking Bathes; two weeping motions;
> Portable and compendious Oceans.

"Sainte Mary Magdalen" has been cited as the prime example of all that is bad, even bathetic, in Crashaw, and surely today's reader, accustomed to a leaner poetic style and certainly to a less visible religious expression, confronts major problems. These can be partially alleviated, however, with at least some consideration of the traditions out of which Crashaw is writing. He is, in a sense, doing in "Sainte Mary Magdalen" what Teresa of Ávila is doing with the Lord's Prayer: He is taking a single image and pondering it at length, refining and embroidering and elaborating the object of his meditation until it reaches a conclusion.

Crashaw is also influenced by the Christian tradition of litanies. A litany is a long series of short prayers, each one a single phrase or epithet, often recited by a priest with responses ("pray for us" or "have mercy on us") from the congregation. A litany does what the poem does: It presents aspect after aspect of the holy person or mystery so that the faithful may, in some sense, see. The petitions of a litany are not related to one another but to the person or mystery they are celebrating: The Virgin Mary, for example, is called Ark of the Covenant, Morning Star, Mystical Rose, Tower of Ivory, not because these phrases have any relationship to one another, but because they are figures or conceits of her. Depending on one's scriptural background or perhaps spiritual disposition, some phrases suggest more devotion than others.

Much has been said of Crashaw's affinities with the movement in art called Baroque—that richly decorative aesthetic that suggests tension, opposites pulling at each other, extravagant gestures and ornate detail, and that somehow connotes a sense of unworldliness or otherness. "The Weeper," in its maze of images and conceits, suggests that it contains a significant truth that readers cannot follow but at which they can only guess. The poem is perhaps less baroque than some of Crashaw's other works, but it has that same energy, tension, and movement.

Finally, one might consider the fact that the poem celebrates Mary Magdalene, who wept repeatedly, even for years. The poem, too, celebrates repeatedly, with a focus on image after image, indeed perhaps doing the very thing it celebrates. Like Mary Magdalene, the poem reverences the Lord again and again. Read in this sense, "Sainte Mary Magdalen" may well be a hieroglyph, the term used by Joseph Summers to describe George Herbert's poetry (*George Herbert: His Religion and Art*, 1954).

All the above is not intended as a defense of "Sainte Mary Magdalen" so much as an attempt to view Crashaw in his contexts. Like many of the mystics, he has little need for discursive structure, preferring instead the intuitive, associative mode for communicating his experiences. If some images are banal, they are still a part of his contemplation and they stay in the poem. It is an unfamiliar aesthetic but not one without some validity. It is worth noting that nearly all Crashaw's numerous revisions of his poetry are toward length; he rarely discarded and never shortened.

## SAINT TERESA POEMS

As a Roman Catholic, Crashaw was more free than his Church of England contemporaries to consider the lives of the saints. Although the biblical Mary Magdalene and the Virgin Mary were appropriate for the devotions of at least High Church Anglicans, saints such as Teresa of Ávila were less so, even though Teresa's works had appeared in English as early as 1611 and would surely have been familiar to devout readers. It is not known whether Crashaw possessed a copy of Teresa's classic *El castillo interior: O, Tratado de las moradas* (wr. 1577, pb. 1588; *The Interior Castle*, 1852); if he did, and if he preached against it, there is an intriguing poetic justice in his son's selection of Teresa for his richest poems. The two Saint Teresa poems rank among Crashaw's finest.

The poems contrast as well as match; "A Hymn to the Name and Honor of the Admirable Saint Teresa" is a legend or story made into a lesson, whereas "The Flaming Heart" is a meditation on an image, possibly the painting by the Antwerp artist Gerhard Seghers, or perhaps the more famous Gian Lorenzo Bernini statue in the Coronaro Chapel, Saint Maria della Vittoria, Rome. Crashaw could have seen either representation, and he may well have seen both.

"A Hymn to the Name and Honor of the Admirable Saint Teresa" begins with the story of the child Teresa, who, wanting martyrdom and heaven for her faith, persuades her little brother to go off with her in search of the Moors, who will, she hopes, put them to death. The poet, meditating on the greatness of heart in the six-year-old Teresa, is both witty and moving when he breaks in, "Sweet, not so fast!" A richer, more demanding martyrdom awaits the adult Teresa; she will be called to the contemplative life, reform the Carmelite order, write magnificent works, and give herself totally to the love of God. Dying to the self in the most ancient tradition, she will indeed be a spiritual martyr. The poem combines, in the richest Metaphysical tradition, intellect and emotion, tough demands and profoundly intuitive responses. Teresa is not free to choose her martyrdom any more than were the first Christians; she can only respond to the choice that God makes for her.

In the poem, Crashaw is working in the best tradition of Anglican preaching as well as with Roman Catholic sensitivity. He begins with a story, an exemplum, good clear narrative, aphorisms ("Tis Love, not years nor limbs, that can/ Make the Martyr, or the man"), vivid drama, and a totally believable picture of the child Teresa and her ardent love of God. The regular tetrameter lines with their *aabb* rhymes move the story gracefully, even inevitably, along. Then, with "not so fast," the poet moves into a new vein altogether, summoning back Teresa—and the reader—to contemplate what giving oneself to God really means. The poetry moves from narrative to lyrical, intuitive expression and is filled with images, exclamations, and apostrophes. Instead of martyrdom as a child, Teresa will face numerous mystical deaths, which will prepare her for the final death that brings total union with the Lord; these mystical deaths "Shall all at last dye into one,/ And melt thy soules sweet mansion." The diction becomes more and more simple as the concepts underneath the poetry become increasingly mystical. The poem concludes in a dazzling combination of Anglican neatness ("decorum") and Roman Catholic transcendence: The one who wishes to see Jesus "must learne in life to dye like Thee." The poem is simultaneously a meditation on a holy life and a lyrical celebration of one who was chosen by God to live totally for him. The women in Crashaw's poetry, whether the Virgin Mary, Magdalene, Teresa, or even that "not impossible she" of the poem "Wishes. To His (Supposed) Mistress," are all great souled, larger than life, intensely vivid, and visual. Later, Crashaw would write "An Apologie" for the hymn as "having been writt when the author was yet among the protestantes"; one wonders whether its discursive, even preachy, tone is a manifestation of this state of mind. Surely, the poem needs no "apologie."

In the second Teresa poem, "The Flaming Heart," Crashaw keeps his tetrameter rhymed couplets but adopts a totally different stance, moving from story-with-lesson to contemplation. The thirteenth century theologian Thomas Aquinas defines contemplation as simultaneously knowing and loving one of the divine mysteries, and the poem illustrates that definition. The speaker is gazing at a picture or statue of Teresa in which she is visited by a seraphim, a celestial being, who, holding a burning dart, prepares to transfix the saint. The scene is taken from Teresa's own journal account of her divine revelations and translates the momentary interior apprehension into external narration.

Teresa's language is explicitly sexual; the cherub with the dart, the piercing, the pain followed by ecstatic joy, all these are a part of that long tradition that uses the language of physical love for God's encounters with his people. It is the language of Donne's Holy Sonnets. Catholic artists, directed by the Council of Trent to make the mysteries of faith more vivid for believers, are drawn to this incident; it is not surprising that the newly converted Crashaw, already enamored of image and mystery, would be drawn to the story of Teresa, another "not impossible she."

"The Flaming Heart" welcomes "you that come as friends" almost as though the readers are pilgrims to the church where the image is displayed. The faithful viewers are, however, immediately corrected by the wit of the speaker; although "they say" that one figure is the seraphim and the other is Teresa, the speaker assumes the role of correcting guide, asking, "be ruled by me." The figures must be reversed; the saint is the seraphim.

With that flashing insight, "Read HIM for her and her for him," the poet moves into the entire burden of the long poem, constantly juxtaposing Teresa and the seraph, celebrating her angelic virtues and total love of God, casting the seraph in the role of a "rivalled lover" who needs to veil his face, singing praise of the "flaming heart" of Teresa that is so afire with love. The couplets race in their eagerness to show this instant, moving from abstract to concrete, from Teresa to the seraph. The colors are rich here, crimson, golden, and fiery; the sense of pain becoming joy is almost tangible; the transcendence of the moment breaks out of the visual representation as the speaker also moves out of time and space and into the world of mystical prayer. The closing lines, perhaps Crashaw's most intense and most often cited, are litany, prayer, celebration, vision.

BIBLIOGRAPHY

Bertonasco, Marc F. *Crashaw and the Baroque.* Tuscaloosa: University of Alabama Press, 1971. Traces Crashaw's key images to seventeenth century emblem books and finds Saint Francis de Sales's meditative method the major influence on Crashaw's spiritual development. Provides a detailed analysis of "Sainte Mary Magdalen" that demonstrates these influences. The appendix contains a review of Crashaw's scholarship, and a bibliography.

Cefalu, Paul. *English Renaissance Literature and Contemporary Theory: Sublime Objects of Theology.* New York: Palgrave Macmillan, 2007. Cefalu uses modern philosophy and cultural theory to analyze the religious poems of Crashaw, John Milton, and John Donne.

Cousins, Anthony D. *The Catholic Religious Poets from Southwell to Crashaw: A Critical History.* London: Sheed & Ward, 1991. History of the criticism and interpretation of these English poets from a Christian perspective. Bibliographical references, index.

Healy, Thomas F. *Richard Crashaw.* Leiden, the Netherlands: E. J. Brill, 1986. Explains that Crashaw's poetry owes much to his Cambridge years at Pembroke and Peterhouse, when the religious, intellectual, and poetic environment shaped his ideas and his work. Includes extended criticism of "Musick's Duell" and, particularly, "To the Name of Jesus."

LeVay, John. "Crashaw's 'Wishes to His (Supposed) Mistresse.'" *Explicator* 50, no. 4 (Summer, 1992): 205. A critique of Crashaw's "Delight of the Muses," which includes a wishful reverie of the poet's ideal woman.

Mintz, Susannah B. "The Crashavian Mother." *Studies in English Literature* 39, no. 1 (Winter, 1999): 111-129. A study of the history of critical thought regarding Crashaw's relationship to women.

Parrish, Paul A. *Richard Crashaw*. Boston: Twayne, 1980. Surveys Crashaw's life and work and contains several relatively long explications of individual Crashaw poems. Provides a biography, followed by chapters on Crashaw's early work, the secular poems, *Steps to the Temple*, the major hymns, and the Teresa poems. Includes a selected, annotated bibliography.

Sabine, Maureen. *Feminine Engendered Faith: The Poetry of John Donne and Richard Crashaw*. London: Macmillan, 1992. Examines these two poets' religious imagery and content with particular emphasis on the impact of the Virgin Mary. Contains bibliographical references, index.

Young, R. V. *Doctrine and Devotion in Seventeenth-Century Poetry*. Rochester, N.Y.: D. S. Brewer, 2000. History and criticism of Christian poetry in seventeenth century England. The works of Crashaw, George Herbert, Henry Vaughan, and John Donne are analyzed. Includes bibliographic references.

_____. *Richard Crashaw and the Spanish Golden Age*. New Haven, Conn.: Yale University Press, 1982. Places Crashaw within a metaphysical context and argues that Crashaw's poetry is impersonal and public, that he was familiar with contemporary Spanish literature, and that his poems about saints and feast days ("The Flaming Heart," "Hymn to the Name of Jesus," and "A Hymn to the Name and Honor of the Admirable Saint Teresa") deserve the extended criticism he devotes to them.

*Katherine Hanley*

# THOMAS DEKKER

**Born:** London, England; c. 1572
**Died:** London, England; August, 1632

*The Whole History of Fortunatus*, 1599 (commonly known as *Old Fortunatus*, play and poetry)
*The Shoemaker's Holiday: Or, The Gentle Craft*, 1600 (based on Thomas Deloney's narrative *The Gentle Craft*, play and poetry)
*The Wonderful Year*, 1603 (prose and poetry)
*The Honest Whore, Part I*, 1604 (with Thomas Middleton, play and poetry)
*The Honest Whore, Part II*, c. 1605 (play and poetry)
*The Double PP*, 1606 (prose and poetry)
*Lanthorn and Candlelight*, 1608, 1609 (prose and poetry; revised as *O per se O*, 1612; *Villanies Discovered*, 1616, 1620; *English Villanies*, 1632, 1638, 1648)
*Dekker, His Dream*, 1620 (prose and poetry)
*The Virgin Martyr*, c. 1620 (with Philip Massinger, play and poetry)
*The Witch of Edmonton*, 1621 (with William Rowley and John Ford, play and poetry)
*The Sun's Darling*, 1624 (with Ford, play and poetry)

## OTHER LITERARY FORMS

Thomas Dekker (DEHK-ur) was a prolific author. Although his canon is not easily fixed because of works presumed to be lost, disputed authorship, and revised editions, the sheer number of his publications is impressive. Dekker was primarily a dramatist. By himself, he composed more than twenty plays, and he collaborated on as many as forty; more than half of these are not extant today. His plays come in all the genres that theater-hungry Elizabethans loved to devour: city comedies, history plays, classical romances, and domestic tragedies. Additionally, Dekker published about twenty-five prose tracts and pamphlets that catered to a variety of popular tastes: descriptions of London's lowlife, collections of humorous and scandalous stories, and jeremiads on the nation's sins and its impending punishment at the hands of an angry God. Dekker found time between writing for the theater and the printing press to compose complimentary verses on other poets' works and to twice prepare interludes, sketches, and songs for the pageants honoring the Lord Mayor of London.

The best edition of the plays, *The Dramatic Works of Thomas Dekker* (1953-1961), is edited by Fredson Bowers in four volumes. Those tracts dealing with the calamities befalling Stuart London are represented in *The Plague Pamphlets of Thomas Dekker*

(1925; F. P. Wilson, editor). The bulk of Dekker's prose and verse is collected in the occasionally unreliable *The Non-Dramatic Works of Thomas Dekker* (1884-1886, 4 volumes; Alexander B. Grosart, editor). A more readable and more judicious sampling of the tales and sketches is found in *Selected Prose Writings* (1968; E. D. Pendry, editor).

### ACHIEVEMENTS

A writer such as Thomas Dekker, so prolific in output, necessarily produces a lot of chaff with his wheat. His plays often lack tightly knit plots and carefully proportioned form; his prose works, especially those satirizing the moral lapses of contemporaries, sometimes belabor the point. Two literary virtues, however, continue to endear Dekker to readers, virtues common to both plays and pamphlets, to both verse and prose.

First, Dekker is always a wordsmith of the highest rank. Although Ben Jonson complained of Dekker and his collaborators that "It's the bane and torment of our ears/ To hear the discords of those jangled rhymers," hardly any reader or critic since has shared the opinion. Since the seventeenth century, Dekker has been universally acknowledged as a gifted poet whose lyrical ability stands out in an age well-stocked with good lyric poets. Charles Lamb's famous pronouncement that Dekker had "poetry for everything" sums up the commonplace modern attitude. Not only Dekker's verse in the plays, however, but also his prose deserves to be called poetic. Dekker's language, whatever its form, is characterized by frequent sound effects, varied diction, and attention to rhythm. Thoroughly at home with Renaissance habits of decorative rhetoric, Dekker seemingly thought in poetry and thus wrote it naturally, effortlessly, and continually.

Second, Dekker's heart is always in the right place. His sympathetically drawn characters seem to come alive as he portrays the people, sights, and events of Elizabethan London. Dekker is often compared with Geoffrey Chaucer and William Shakespeare for his sense of the *comédie humaine*, for knowing the heights and depths of human experience and for still finding something to care about afterward. Dekker's keen observations of life underlie his sharp sense of society's incongruities.

### BIOGRAPHY

Few specifics of Thomas Dekker's life are known. He was probably born in 1572, although this date is conjectural. He may have served as a tradesman's apprentice or a sailor before beginning (in 1595?) to write plays for companies of actors. By playwriting and pamphleteering, he kept himself alive for the next thirty-seven years. The date of his marriage is uncertain, but it is known that his wife, Mary, died in 1616. Dekker lived his life almost completely in London, first in Cripplegate and later in Clerkenwell. He was imprisoned for debt on three occasions and once for recusancy. Presumably the Thomas Dekker who was buried in August, 1632, in Clerkenwell parish was the playwright and pamphleteer.

Although Dekker's personal life is mostly subject to conjecture, his professional career can be more closely followed. It revolves around three intertwining themes: the dramatic collaborations, the pamphlets, and a lifelong struggle against poverty. No one knows how Dekker's career started, but by 1598, he was writing plays alone or jointly for Philip Henslowe. Henslowe owned and managed the Rose Theatre, where he commissioned writers to compose plays for his prime tenants, an acting company called the Lord Admiral's Men. In 1598 alone, Dekker had a hand in fifteen plays (all now lost) that Henslowe commissioned. The sheer quantity indicates how audiences must have clamored for new productions, and some of the titles indicate the taste of the age for popularizations of history (*The First Civil Wars in France*), reworkings of classical tales (*Hannibal and Hermes*), and current stories of eccentric persons or scandalous events (*Black Batman of the North*). All the plays on which Dekker worked had catchy titles: *The Roaring Girl: Or, Moll Cutpurse* (pr. c. 1610), *The Honest Whore*, *The Witch of Edmonton*, and *Match Me in London* (pr. c. 1611-1612), to name a few.

As early as 1600, Dekker was writing for companies other than the Lord Admiral's Men. In the course of his career, he would write for the leading acting companies of the time: the Children of St. Paul's, the Prince's Men, the Palsgrave's Men, and the Players of the Revels. More varied than his employers were his collaborators: As a young man Dekker worked with Michael Drayton, Jonson, George Chapman, Henry Chettle, and even Shakespeare. When he returned to the theater as an older man, the new young scriptwriters—a veritable "Who's Who" of Jacobean dramatists, including John Ford, Samuel Rowley, John Marston, Philip Massinger, and John Webster—worked with him.

Since his employers and collaborators changed so often, it is not surprising that at least once the intense dramatic rivalry characteristic of the age embroiled Dekker in controversy. In 1600, he was drafted into the brief but vitriolic "War of the Theatres," which had begun in the previous year when Marston satirized Jonson as a boorish and presumptuous poet. Jonson returned the compliment by poking fun at Marston in two plays and tried to anticipate a Marston-Dekker rejoinder with a third play, *Poetaster: Or, His Arraignment* (pr. 1601), which compares them to "screaming grasshoppers held by the wings." Marston and Dekker retaliated with *Satiromastix: Or, The Untrussing of the Humourous Poet* (pr. 1601), an amalgam of tragic, comic, and tragicomic plots, portraying Jonson as a slow-witted and slow-working poet for hire.

In 1603, Dekker was forced to find another line of work when an outbreak of the plague closed the theaters. He produced a pamphlet, *The Wonderful Year*, which recounted the death of the queen, Elizabeth I, the accession of James I, and the coming of the disease that scourged humankind's folly. In the next six years, Dekker published more than a dozen pamphlets designed to capitalize on readers' interest in current events and the city's criminal subculture. In his pamphlets, as in his plays, Dekker provides a panorama of cutpurses, pimps, courtesans, apprentices, and similar types; he paints scenes of busy streets and records the sounds of loud voices, creaking carriages, and thumped pots. Dekker's purpose is not that of the local colorist who preserves such scenes simply because they typify a time and place. Rather, his interest is that of the moralist who sees the side of city life that the upper classes would like to ignore and that the academics shrug off as part of the necessary order of things.

Dekker himself knew this low world intimately—at least he never seems to have gotten into the higher. Unlike his fellow writers Jonson and Shakespeare or the actor Edward Alleyn, Dekker could not or did not take advantage of the aristocracy's interest in the theater to secure for himself consistent patronage and financial stability. Playwriting seems to have brought Dekker only a few pounds per play: Despite his prodigious outburst of fifteen collaborations in 1598, he was arrested for debt that year and the next. Fourteen years later, while both publishing pamphlets and writing plays, Dekker was again imprisoned for debt at the King's Bench, a prison notorious for its mismanagement. He remained in debtors' prison for six or seven years (1613-1619).

No wonder, then, that money is one of Dekker's favorite themes and gold one image to which he devotes loving attention. He neither worships the almighty guinea nor scorns sinful lucre. On one hand, Dekker likes money: His best characters make shrewd but kindly use of the stuff; they work, and their labor supports them. He sometimes sees even confidence games as offshoots of a healthy capitalistic impulse. Old Fortunatus's claim, "Gold is the strength, the sinnewes of the world,/ The Health, the soule, the beautie most divine," may be misguided, but Dekker understands the impulse. He forgives prodigals easily. On the other hand, Dekker expects generosity from moneymakers. Even virtuous persons who do not use their wealth well come to bad ends; those who refuse to help the needy he assigns to the coldest regions of hell. According to Pendry in *Selected Prose Writings*, the use of money is for Dekker an index of morality: Virtue flows from its proper use and vice from its improper.

The last decade of Dekker's life was a repetition of the previous three. He wrote for the theater, published pamphlets, and teetered on the edge of debt. Though his life was hard and his social rank was low, Dekker generally wrote as if his literary trade was, like the shoemaker's, a truly gentle craft.

### ANALYSIS

Most of Thomas Dekker's best poetry is found in his plays; unfortunately, since most of his plays were collaborations, it is often difficult to assign particular poetic passages to Dekker, and perhaps even harder to assign the larger poetic designs to him. He is, however, generally credited with most of the poetry in *Old Fortunatus* and *The Honest Whore, Parts I* and *II*. He wrote the delightfully poetic *The Shoemaker's Holiday* almost unaided. Mother Sawyer's eloquent poetry in *The Witch of Edmonton* so closely resembles portions of his long pamphlet-poem, *Dekker, His Dream*, as to make it all but certainly his. Songs and verses occupy varying proportions of his journalistic works, from a few lines in *The Wonderful Year*, to several songs in *Lanthorn and Candlelight*, to most of *The Double PP*. In all his plays, verse comprises a significant part of the dialogue.

While the quality of thought and care in organization vary from work to work and almost from line to line in a given work, the quality of the sound rarely falters. According to George Price in *Thomas Dekker* (1969), one poem long attributed to Dekker, *Canaan's Calamitie* (1598), has been excluded from the canon largely because of the inferior music of its verse. Critics often attach words such as "sweet," "lovely," "gentle," and "compassionate" to Dekker's most popular passages, and the adjectives seem to cover both sound and theme in works such as *Old Fortunatus* and *The Shoemaker's Holiday*.

## OLD FORTUNATUS

An old-fashioned production in its own day, *Old Fortunatus* weaves a morality pageant in which the goddess Fortune and her attendants witness a power struggle between Virtue and Vice with a loose chronicle play about a man to whom Fortune grants a choice. Instead of health, strength, knowledge, and wisdom, old Fortunatus chooses riches. His wealth and native cunning enable him to steal knowledge (in the form of a magic hat). After Fortune claims the old man's life, his sons Ampedo and Andelocia, inheriting his magic purse and hat, make no better use of them than their father had done. Greedy Andelocia abducts a princess, plays assorted pranks at various courts, and ends up strangled by equally greedy courtiers; virtuous Ampedo wrings his hands, eventually burns the magic hat, and dies in the stocks, unmourned even by Virtue. Structurally, *Old Fortunatus* has the odd elegance of medieval drama. Fortune, Virtue, and Vice enter the human world five times, usually with song and emblematic show designed to judge men or to point out the choices open to them.

The play's allegorical pageantry demanded elaborate costuming and equally elaborate verse, ranging from songs in varied meters and tones to dialogues that are often more incantation than blank verse speech:

> *Kings:* Accursed Queen of chaunces, damned sorceresse.
> *The Rest:* Most pow'rfull Queen of chaunce, dread soveraignesse.
> *Fortune:* . . . [*To the Kings*] curse on: your cries to me are Musicke
> And fill the sacred rondure of mine eares
> With tunes more sweet than moving of the Spheres:
> Curse on.

Most of the chronicle play that is interwoven with the morality pageant employs blank verse liberally sprinkled with prose passages and rhymed couplets. Renaissance notions of decorum set forth rather clear-cut rules governing the use of prose and poetry. An iambic pentameter line was considered the best medium for tragedy and for kings' and nobles' speeches in comedy. Madmen, clowns, and letter-readers in tragedy and lower-class characters in comedy can speak prose. Dekker refines these guidelines. He uses prose for musing aloud, for French and Irish dialects, for talking to servants, and for expressing disappointment or depression: The sons mourn their dead father and have their most violent quarrel in prose. Dekker keys form to mood much as a modern songwriter does when he inserts a spoken passage into the lyrics. Even Dekker's prose, however, is textured like poetry; except for the lack of iambic pentameter rhythm, prose passages are virtually indistinguishable from verse. Typical are the lilting rhythms of the following passage (one of the cruelest in the play): "I was about to cast my little little self into a great love trance for him, fearing his hart was flint, but since I see 'tis pure virgin wax, he shall melt his belly full."

Sound itself is the subject of much comment in the play. Dekker's natural gift for pleasing rhythms, his knack for combining the gentler consonant sounds with higher frequency vowels, and his ear for slightly varied repetitions all combine to make *Old Fortunatus* strikingly beautiful poetry.

The fame of *Old Fortunatus*, however, rests on more than its sound. Dekker's imagery deserves the praise it consistently gets. The Princess's heartless line is one of many that connect melting with the play's values—love, fire, gold, and the sun—in ways that suggest both the purification of dross through the melting process and the fate of rich Crassus. Other images connect the silver moon and stars with music, and both precious metals with an earth producing fruit-laden trees that men use wisely or unwisely. The allegorical figures with their emblematic actions and costumes would heighten the effectiveness of such imagery for a viewing audience, just as hearing the poetry greatly magnifies its impact over silent reading.

## THE SHOEMAKER'S HOLIDAY

In *The Shoemaker's Holiday*, Dekker shows a more sophisticated use of poetry. As in *Old Fortunatus*, he shifts between poetry and prose, depending somewhat on the characters' social class but more on mood, so that in a given scene a character can slip from prose to poetry and back while those around him remain in their normal métier. In the earlier play, however, he made little attempt to connect certain characters with certain sounds or images. In *The Shoemaker's Holiday*, characters have their own peculiar music.

The play combines three plots. In the first, Rowland Lacy disguises himself as Hans, a Dutch shoemaker, to avoid being shipped off to war in France, far from his beloved Rose Otley. His uncle, the earl of Lincoln, and her father, Sir Roger Otley, oppose the love match. In the second, the shoemaker Rafe leaves his young wife, Jane, to do his country's bidding; later, lamed and supposed dead, he returns to find Jane missing. He rediscovers her just in time to stop her marriage to the rich but shallow Hammon. In the third, master shoemaker Simon Eyre, the employer of Lacy, Rafe, and a crew of journeymen and apprentices, rises by common sense and enthusiastic shop management to become London's merriest Lord Mayor.

Two relatively minor characters illustrate Dekker's poetic sense. The earl of Lincoln, despite his blank verse, speaks less poetically than most of the other characters, and Eyre's journeyman, Firke, despite his freer prose rhythms, speaks much of the best poetry. Lincoln's decasyllables in the opening scene, for example, summarize Lacy's situation with few rhetorical figures:

> 'Twas now almost a year since he requested
> To travel countries for experiences.
> I furnished him with coin, bills of exchange,
> Letters of credit, men to wait on him.

Lincoln's speech is not absolutely unpoetic. Its rhythm is varied, quickened by added syllables and made natural by inverted feet—but that is all. Lincoln has a prosaic mind; to him Lacy's love is mere nuisance, a mild threat to the family name. Dishonest about his own motives, he presumes that others are likewise motivated by self-interest. Thus, when he speaks, his words slip easily off the tongue, but rarely figure forth the imaginative connections between things that Dekker's other characters display.

By contrast, Firke's lines have more of poetry's verbal texture than does most modern free verse. Asked the whereabouts of the eloped Rose and Lacy, he answers in a pastiche of poetic allusions and a pun on the gold coin that Elizabethans called angels: "No point: shall I betray my brother? no, shall I prove *Judas* to Hans? no, shall I crie treason to my corporation? no, I shall be firkt and yerkt then, but give me your angell, your angell shall tel you." The passage shouts an emphatic dance rhythm, forcefully repeats the focal "no, shall I," employs assonance ("*Judas* to *Hans*"), alliteration ("betray my brother"), and rhyme ("treason to my corporation" and "firkt and yerkt"). It speeds along, then slows to a perfectly cadenced close. The speaker, a boisterous, rowdy, practical joker, is always ready to burst into song, or something so close as to be indistinguishable from song.

Dekker gives these minor characters distinctive poetic voices. To the major characters, he gives individualizing linguistic habits. Bluff Simon Eyre's trick of repeating himself would be maddening in a less kindly fellow. He is the only character capable of speaking prose to the king. Hammon, suitor both to Rose and Jane, speaks courtly compliment in light, rhymed couplets in which vows about "life" and "wife" play too heavy a part. Though he enjoys the banter of stichomythic verse, his images are stuffily conventional. As wellborn characters, Lacy and Rose naturally speak blank verse. Lacy's voice, however, turns to a quick prose dialect when he is disguised as Hans; Rose occasionally startles by slipping out of her romantic preoccupations into a few lines of practical yet polished prose.

Perhaps the play's best poetry is that which Dekker gives to shoemaker Rafe and seamstress Jane. Surrounded by shopkeepers and unaccustomed to courtly compliment, these two must invent their own poetic images and rhythms. "I will not greeve you,/

With hopes to taste fruite, which will never fall," says Jane to Hammon. Hearing of Rafe's death, she dismisses her persistent suitor with lines remarkable for homespun grace. Rafe, in turn, gives the entire play its thematic unity in two passages that raise shoemaking from a craft to a communal act of love. As he leaves for France, Rafe gives Jane a parting gift: not the jewels and rings that rich men present their wives, but a pair of shoes "cut out by *Hodge*, Sticht by my fellow *Firke*, seam'd by my selfe,/ Made up and pinckt, with letters for thy name." The shoes are the epitome of the shoemaker's art, and they are individually Jane's. Dekker returns to the image at a pivotal point after Rafe comes home from the war. The shoes, now old and needing replacement, lead Rafe to reunion with the missing Jane. His homely poetry, the most original in a play full of original language, is more touching than preposterous:

> . . . this shoe I durst be sworne
> Once covered the instep of my *Jane:*
> This is her size, her breadth, thus trod my love,
> These true love knots I prickt, I hold my life,
> By this old shoe I shall find out my wife.

The simple language fits Rafe as well as the shoe fits Jane. In *The Shoemaker's Holiday*, craftsmen know their work as confidently as the master wordsmith Dekker knows his characters' individual voices.

Critics generally agree that the play is Dekker's poetic masterpiece. His other plays contain excellent poetry, nicely tuned to suit persona in sound, mood, and imagery, but none has the range and grace of *The Shoemaker's Holiday*. Of special interest to the student of Dekker's verse are two of the speeches in *The Honest Whore* plays. In *Part I*, Hippolito's furious diatribe against whoredom is a virtual monologue, rising in a hundred lines to a fine crescendo, which deserves careful metrical and figural analysis. Its counterpart in *Part II*, Bellafront's long argument against her former profession, deserves similar attention.

## PAMPHLETS

Dekker's pamphlets continue the habit of mixing prose and verse; most of them contain some poetry, if only in the rhymed couplets signifying closure. As early as 1603, in *The Wonderful Year*, he was writing essentially dramatic poetry. In that pamphlet, he includes two poems supposed to be the prologue and a summary of the action of a play—the "play" of England's reaction to Elizabeth I's death. The poetic section ends with three short epigrams of a deliberately homespun sort. *Lanthorn and Candlelight* further reflects the dramatic in Dekker's poetry. In the opening chapter, poems are couched in cant, a special thieves' jargon. "To cant" means "to sing," but since "canters" are strange, they sing strangely: "Enough! With boozy cove maund nase,/ Tower the patring cove in the darkman case." Dekker includes both a "Canter's Dictionary" (largely plagiarized) and "Englished" translations. His habit of using dramatic voices in poetry finds a logical conclusion in such songs.

Poetry is sporadic in most of Dekker's pamphlets; in *The Double PP* and *Dekker, His Dream*, however, it dominates. The former alternates sections of prose and poetry in an exhibition of English nationalism as complete as Simon Eyre's. In an elaborate rhetorical figure, Dekker presents ten kinds of papists as ten chivalric shields attacked by ten well-armed classes of English Protestants. The generally shallow but occasionally penetrating stereotypes show the influence of the current fad for Overburian Characters.

## DEKKER, HIS DREAM

*Dekker, His Dream* is a much better poem. Published shortly after his release from seven years in debtor's prison, the work is ostensibly autobiographical. Dekker claims to relate a dream he had after almost seven years of imprisonment in an enchanted cave. Using lines of rhymed iambic pentameter that vary with his subject in tone and tempo, Dekker describes the last day of the world, the final judgment, heaven, and hell. Periodically he interrupts the narrative to justify his vision by quoting in prose from scripture or church authorities.

Structurally, *Dekker, His Dream* is among his best works, building slowly to a climactic conclusion in which Dekker turns out to be, as William Blake said of John Milton, "of the devil's party." The poem begins with covert reminders of what Dekker himself has recently suffered, then moves vividly through the tale of Earth's destruction. Calmly, it relates the majestic coming of Christ and the harmonious rewards given the good, then turns rather quickly to hell. (In fact, Christ and Heaven occupy eight of Dekker's fifty-two pages.) Like Dante, Dekker secures permission to walk among the damned; he finds a two-part hell. In the first, the cold region, he sees the "rich dogs" who refused to help the poor and sick. Tormented by whips, diseases, snakes, and salamanders, they react with "Yels, teeth-gnashing, chattering, shivering." Then he moves into the traditional fires to find the drunkards, gamblers, adulterers, and gluttons—"millions" of them, whipped and stung with their own longings and with the "worme of conscience." Among them is a young man cursing God and proclaiming loudly as the whips descend that he does not deserve eternal punishment. Dekker gives him a perfectly logical defense: He had only thirty years of life, fifteen of which were spent asleep, five more in childishness, and some at least in good deeds. Nature had given him little— drops of gall from her left breast instead of milk—and his sins were small. His lengthy defense contains some of Dekker's best images and rhythms; it is interrupted by a booming angelic voice that shouts about justice until the rest of the damned, angered, outshout it, waking the poet. Dekker, hands shaking from the experience, concludes that, reading the world, "I found Here worse Devils than are in Hell."

The dream vision has been largely misinterpreted, but close study of the quality of the imagery and the proportions of the whole indicate that Dekker was indeed leading his readers to question the justice shouted by the avenging angel. It is a subtly and effectively composed poem, deserving more attention than it has had.

OTHER MAJOR WORKS

PLAYS: *Patient Grissell*, pr. 1600 (with Henry Chettle and William Haughton); *Satiromastix: Or, The Untrussing of the Humourous Poet*, pr. 1601; *Sir Thomas Wyatt*, pr. 1602 (as *Lady Jane*, pb. 1607); *Westward Ho!*, pr. 1604 (with John Webster); *Northward Ho!*, pr. 1605 (with Webster); *The Whore of Babylon*, pr. c. 1606-1607; *The Roaring Girl: Or, Moll Cutpurse*, pr. c. 1610 (with Thomas Middleton); *If This Be Not a Good Play, the Devil Is in It*, pr. c. 1610-1612 (as *If It Be Not Good, the Devil Is in It*); *Match Me in London*, pr. c. 1611-1612; *The Noble Soldier: Or, A Contract Broken, Justly Revenged*, pr. c. 1622-1631 (with John Day; thought to be the same as *The Spanish Fig*, 1602); *The Wonder of a Kingdom*, pr. c. 1623; *The Welsh Embassador: Or, A Comedy in Disguises*, pr. c. 1624 (revision of *The Noble Soldier*); *The Dramatic Works of Thomas Dekker*, 1953-1961 (4 volumes; Fredson Bowers, editor).

NONFICTION: *News from Hell*, 1606; *The Seven Deadly Sins*, 1606; *The Bellman of London*, 1608; *A Work for Armourers*, 1609; *Four Birds of Noah's Ark*, 1609; *The Gull's Hornbook*, 1609; *Penny-Wise, Pound-Foolish*, 1631; *The Plague Pamphlets of Thomas Dekker*, 1925 (F. P. Wilson, editor).

MISCELLANEOUS: *The Magnificent Entertainment Given to King James*, 1603 (with Ben Jonson and Middleton); *The Non-Dramatic Works of Thomas Dekker*, 1884-1886 (4 volumes; Alexander B. Grosart, editor); *Selected Prose Writings*, 1967 (E. D. Pendry, editor).

BIBLIOGRAPHY

Adler, Doris Ray. *Thomas Dekker: A Reference Guide*. Boston: G. K. Hall, 1983. An annotated bibliography of works on Dekker. Index.

Champion, Larry S. *Thomas Dekker and the Tradition of English Drama*. 2d ed. New York: Peter Lang, 1987. This straightforward commentary deals primarily with the dramatic structure and tone of the plays, but also shows how Dekker often experiments with new approaches. Also discusses Dekker's links with his contemporaries.

Conover, James H. *Thomas Dekker: An Analysis of Dramatic Structure*. The Hague, the Netherlands: Mouton, 1966. Traces the development of the plots of Dekker's major plays (including *The Shoemaker's Holiday*, *The Honest Whore*, *Old Fortunatus*, and *Satiromastix*) and concludes with a chapter on the structural traits he believes are peculiar to Dekker's works.

Dekker, Thomas. *The Shoemaker's Holiday*. Edited by Stanley Wells and Robert Smallwood. 3d ed. London: Metheun Drama, 2008. More than a reprint of the play, this edition provides a study of the text and the editors' historical introduction, including an examination of the play's relationship with contemporary life and drama and its place in Dekker's work, a stage history, analysis, and a reprint of source materials.

Gasper, Julia. *The Dragon and the Dove: The Plays of Thomas Dekker.* New York: Oxford University Press, 1990. A critical analysis of Dekker's plays that focuses on his treatment of kings and rulers as well as of Protestantism. Bibliography and index.

Hoy, Cyrus Henry. *Introductions, Notes, and Commentaries to Texts in "The Dramatic Works of Thomas Dekker."* 4 vols. Edited by Fredson Bowers. 1980. Reprint. New York: Cambridge University Press, 2009. The work edited by Bowers focused on the text of the plays, but this work places the plays in their critical context and provides details of the their writing, including collaborations and sources.

Hunt, Mary Leland. *Thomas Dekker: A Study.* 1911. Reprint. Philadelphia: R. West, 1977. The first book-length study of Dekker's life and work—prose as well as plays. It remains useful not only for the critical summaries of the works but also for its chronological treatment of the poet's life. Of special interest are the comments about Dekker's friendships in the theater and his collaborators.

Price, George R. *Thomas Dekker.* New York: Twayne, 1969. Price provides all the standard virtues of the Twayne volumes: a succinct chronology, a chapter on the life, and three chapters of analysis followed by a summarizing conclusion. The detailed notes and annotated bibliography make this study an excellent starting place for students of Dekker.

Waage, Frederick O. *Thomas Dekker's Pamphlets, 1603-1609, and Jacobean Popular Literature.* 2 vols. Salzburg: University for English Language and Literature, 1977. These two scholarly volumes are full of commentary on Dekker's ideas and his life. The first chapter on Dekker's career, 1603-1609, is informative, and the seventeen-page bibliography offers researchers a good beginning point.

Wells, Stanley. *Shakespeare and Co.: Christopher Marlowe, Thomas Dekker, Ben Jonson, Thomas Middleton, John Fletcher, and the Other Players in His Story.* London: Penguin, 2007. While the main focus is William Shakespeare, this work also treats Dekker, especially in his association with Shakespeare.

*Robert M. Otten and Elizabeth Spalding Otten*

# JOHN DONNE

**Born:** London, England; between January 24 and June 19, 1572
**Died:** London, England; March 31, 1631

### OTHER LITERARY FORMS

Although John Donne (duhn) is known chiefly as a lyric poet, the posthumous volume *Poems, by J.D.*, which includes the lyrics, represents only a small part of his literary output. Donne was famous in his own age mainly as a preacher; in fact, he was probably the most popular preacher of an age when preaching held the same fascination for the general public that the cinema has today. Various sermons of Donne's were published during his lifetime, and several collections were published in the following decades. Without a commitment to Donne's religious values, however, few today would want to read through many of his sermons. Donne must, however, be credited with the careful articulation of the parts of his sermons, which create a resounding unity of theme; and his control of prose rhythm and his ingenious imagery retain their power, even if modern readers are no longer disposed to see the majesty of God mirrored in such writing.

Excerpts from Donne's sermons thus have a continuing vitality for general readers in a way that excerpts from the sermons of, for example, Lancelot Andrewes cannot. In the early seventeenth century, Andrewes had been the most popular preacher before Donne, and, as bishop of Winchester, he held a more important position. He also had a greater reputation as a stylist, but for modern readers, Andrewes carries to an extreme the baroque fashion of "crumbling a text" (analyzing in minute detail). The sermons of Andrewes are now unreadable without special training in theology and classical languages. On the other hand, though also writing for an educated audience with a serious interest in divinity, Donne wears his scholarship more easily and can still be read by the general student without special preparation. His sermon to the Virginia Company is the first sermon in English to make a missionary appeal.

The single most famous of Donne's sermons was his last. *Death's Duell* (1632), preached before King Charles on February 25, 1631, is a profound meditation on mortality. Human mortality is always a major theme with Donne, but here he reaches a new eloquence. Full of startling imagery, the sermon takes as its theme the paradox that life is death and death is life—although Christ's death delivers humankind from death.

*John Donne*
(Library of Congress)

When this last sermon of Donne's was published, Henry King, bishop of Chichester, re-marked that "as he exceeded others at first so at last he exceeded himself."

A work of similar theme but published by Donne in his own lifetime is the *Devotions upon Emergent Occasions* (1624). Composed, as R. C. Bald has shown, with extreme rapidity during a serious illness and convalescence in 1623, this work is based on the structured meditational technique of Saint Francis de Sales, involving the sensuous evo-cation of scenes, although, as Thomas F. Van Laan has suggested, the work is perhaps also influenced by the *Ejercicios espirituales* (1548; *The Spiritual Exercises*, 1736) of Saint Ignatius of Loyola. It is divided into twenty-three sections, each consisting of a meditation, an expostulation, and a prayer. The work is an artfully constructed whole of sustained emotional power, but the meditations have achieved a special fame with their vivid evocations of the theme that sickness brings people closer to God by putting them in touch with their frailty and mortality. Various meditations from the *Devotions upon Emergent Occasions* present famous pictures of the tolling of the death knell, of the body as a microcosm, and of the curious medical practices of the day, for example, the application of live pigeons to Donne's feet to try to draw the vapors of fever from his head. By this last practice, Donne discovers that he is his own executioner because the vapors are believed to be the consequence of his melancholy, and this is no more than the studiousness required of him by his calling as a preacher. Although in past centuries most readers found the work's self-consciousness and introspection alienating, the contemporary sensibility finds these characteristics especially congenial. The three meditations on the tolling of the bells have, in particular, provided titles and catchphrases for popular writers.

A posthumously published early study of mortality by Donne is *Essayes in Divinity* (1651). Written in a knotty, baroque style, the work is a collection of curiously impersonal considerations of the Creation and of the deliverance of the Israelites from bondage in Egypt. The essays show none of the fire of the sermons and of the *Devotions upon Emergent Occasions*. A very different sort of contemplation of mortality is provided in *Biathanatos* (1646). The casuistical reasoning perhaps shows evidence of Donne's Jesuit background. The same approach to logic and a similar iconoclasm are apparent in *Juvenilia: Or, Certaine Paradoxes and Problemes* (1633; the first complete version was, however, not published until 1923).

The earliest of Donne's publications were two works of religious controversy of a more serious nature. These works also show Donne's Jesuit background, but in them, he is reacting against his upbringing and presenting a case for Anglican moderation in the face of Roman Catholic—and especially Jesuit—pretensions. *Pseudo-Martyr* (1610) was written at the explicit request of King James, according to Donne's first biographer, Izaak Walton. Here and throughout his subsequent career, Donne is a strongly committed Erastian, seeing the Church as properly subordinate in this world to secular authority.

The other of these early works of controversy, *Ignatius His Conclave* (1611), which appeared in Latin as well as English, is still amusing to modern readers who are unlikely to come to it with quite the strong partisan feeling of its original audience.

## ACHIEVEMENTS

John Donne was a remarkably influential poet in his day. Despite the fact that it was only after his death that a substantial body of his poetry was published, the elegies and satires (and to a lesser extent the divine poems and the songs and sonnets) had already created a new poetic mode during Donne's lifetime as a result of circulating in manuscript. Thomas Carew, in a memorial elegy published in the first edition of Donne's poems, described him as ruling the "universal monarchy of wit." The poetry of the School of Donne was usually characterized in its own day by its "strong lines." This characterization seems to have meant that Donne and his followers were to be distinguished from the Sons of Ben, the poets influenced by Ben Jonson, chiefly by their experiments with rough meter and conversational syntax; Jonson, however, was also—somewhat confusingly—praised for strong lines. Donne's own characteristic metrics involve lines densely packed with syllables. He makes great use not only of syncope (dropping of an unstressed vowel within a word) and elision (dropping of an unstressed vowel at the juncture between words) but also of a device almost unique to Donne among English poets—synaloepha (speeding up of adjacent vowels at the juncture between words with no actual dropping). By hindsight, Donne, Edward Lord Herbert of Cherbury, Henry King, George Herbert, John Cleveland, Richard Crashaw, Abraham Cowley, Henry Vaughan, Andrew Marvell, and others of the School of Donne share not only strong lines but also a common fund of imagery. Eschewing for the most part classical allusions, these poets turned to the imagery of everyday life and of the new learning in science and philosophy.

In the middle of the seventeenth century, there occurred what T. S. Eliot has memorably described as a "dissociation of sensibility," after which it became increasingly difficult to see Donne's secular and religious values as part of a consistent whole. The beginnings of this attitude were already apparent in Donne's own day; in a letter, for example, he describes *Biathanatos* as the work not of Dr. Donne but of the youthful Jack Donne. Toward the end of the century, the change of perspective is complete when John Dryden describes Donne unsympathetically as one who "perplexes the Minds of the Fair Sex with nice Speculations of philosophy." The Restoration and the eighteenth century had lost Donne's sense of religious commitment and thus scrutinized a style in isolation from the content it intended to express. Donne's poetry was condemned as artificial, and his reputation disappeared almost overnight.

This was the situation when Samuel Johnson wrote the famous strictures on Donne in his *Life of Cowley*. That these remarks occur in the *Life of Cowley* is perhaps a commentary on the fallen stature of the earlier poets: Donne did not himself merit individual treatment in *Lives of the Poets* (1779-1781). Conceding that to write like Donne "it was at least necessary to read and think," Johnson describes the wit of the School of Donne—accurately enough—as the "discovery of occult resemblances in things apparently unlike." Although many readers of the earlier seventeenth century and of the twentieth century would consider the description high praise, for Johnson it was a condemnation. For him, the "most heterogeneous ideas are yoked by violence together." He popularized the term "Metaphysical poetry" for this yoking; the term had, however, been used earlier, even in Donne's own day.

Donne's stature and influence in the twentieth century and beyond are equal to his great stature and wide influence in the seventeenth century, but the attitude represented by Johnson remained the norm for the centuries between. Donne's modern-day prestige is based on values different from those that accounted for his prestige in his own day. The seventeenth century took its religion seriously but understood religion as part of the whole fabric of life. Donne's stature as a preacher was for this reason part of his prestige as a poet. In addition, the fact that he wrote love poetry and sometimes used graphic erotic imagery did not in his own day seem incongruous with his calling as a preacher.

The twentieth century did not, of course, recover the intense religiosity of the early seventeenth century, but what T. S. Eliot, Ezra Pound, and other poets of their circle had discovered in the 1920's was an aestheticism as intense as this religiosity. Their values naturally led them to praise lyric poetry in preference to epic and to prize intensity of emotion in literary work of all kinds. They disparaged the poetry of John Milton because it was an expression of ideas rather than of feeling and offered Donne as a model and a more appropriate great author for the period. The restoration of Donne's prestige was remarkably complete; but, paradoxically, precisely because the triumph of Donne was so complete, the denigration of Milton never quite occurred. The values that Eliot and others praised in Donne were looked for—and discovered—in Milton as well.

Although Donne was perhaps a more exciting figure during his mid-twentieth century "rediscovery" than he is in the twenty-first century, because to appreciate him meant to throw over the eighteenth and nineteenth century allegiance to Milton as the great poet of the language, Donne's stature as a major figure has become assured. Modern-day scholarly opinion has, however, been moving inevitably toward seeing the divine poems as the capstone of his career. Scholarly opinion has, in fact, moved beyond Eliot's position and come to value literary works simply because they have religious content, since intensity of feeling will surely be found in a poetry of religious commitment. This is not a way of appreciating Donne and the Metaphysicals that would have been understood in the seventeenth century.

### BIOGRAPHY

Born in St. Nicholas Olave Parish, London, sometime between January 24 and June 19, 1572, John Donne came from a Welsh paternal line (originally Dwn) with some claim to gentility. His father, however, was an ironmonger, although important enough to serve as warden of his professional guild. On his mother's side, Donne's connections were distinguished for both their intellectual attainments and their recusancy—that is, allegiance to the Church of Rome in the face of the Elizabethan Church Settlement. Donne's maternal grandfather was the epigrammatist and playwright John Heywood. A great-grandfather, John Rastell, was a minor playwright. Two of Donne's uncles were Jesuits who died in exile for their faith, as did his great-uncle Judge William Rastell; and another great-uncle, the monk Thomas Heywood, was executed, having been caught saying Mass. Finally, a great-grandmother was the sister of Thomas More, whose skull Donne inherited and very characteristically kept as a memento mori. Donne's brother, Henry, died in prison, where he had been sent for harboring a seminary priest; and Donne justifiably said in *Pseudo-Martyr* that no family had suffered more for the Roman Church.

His father died while Donne was still in infancy. His mother married twice more. The stepfather of Donne's youth was a prominent physician. At first educated at home by Roman Catholic tutors, in 1584, Donne and his younger brother, Henry, were admitted to Hart Hall, Oxford. Although they were a precocious twelve and eleven at the time, they were entered in the register as even younger to circumvent the requirement that students of sixteen and over subscribe to the Oath of Supremacy. Donne spent probably three years at Oxford altogether.

Although records are lacking for the next period of Donne's life, one theory is that he spent some of this time in travel abroad. With his brother, Donne eventually took up residence at the Inns of Court to prepare for a legal career. Unsettled in these career plans by the arrest and death of Henry, Donne began serious study of the relative claims of the Anglican and Roman Churches and finally abandoned the study of law entirely.

In 1596, he participated in the earl of Essex's military expedition to Cadiz. Donne's affability and his growing reputation as a poet—sustained by the private circulation of some of his elegies and lyrics—recommended him to a son of Sir Thomas Egerton who had also participated in the sack of Cadiz, and Egerton, who was Lord Keeper, was persuaded to appoint Donne as his secretary. In this position and also in Parliament, where he served briefly in 1601, he had many opportunities to meet people of note, and he improved his reputation as a poet by composing satires and occasional poems as well as additional lyrics.

In 1601, Donne was already in his late twenties, and, during Christmastide, he contracted a secret marriage with Anne More, the sixteen-year-old niece of Lady Egerton. Because the marriage was contrary to her father's wishes, Donne was imprisoned for his offense; he also permanently lost his position as Egerton's secretary, and the couple were forced to live for several years on the charity of friends and relations. A comment made at the time, sometimes attributed to Donne himself, was, "John Donne, Anne Donne, Undone."

Although his career hopes had been dashed by the impetuous marriage, his winning personality and poetic skill won for him new friends in high places. He traveled abroad with Sir Walter Chute in 1605; he became a member of the salon of Lucy, countess of Bedford; and he even attracted the attention of King James, who saw what a useful ornament Donne would be to the Church and urged him to take orders. Not completely resolved in his conscience to do so, Donne, for a considerable time, temporized. However, his activity during this period led him inevitably toward this step. A substantial body of Donne's religious verse was written during this period and sent to Magdalen Herbert, mother of George Herbert and Lord Herbert of Cherbury. Finally, he committed himself to seeking advancement within the Anglican Church with the publication of *Pseudo-Martyr*, a work of religious controversy on a problem strongly vexing the King—the refusal of Roman Catholics to subscribe to the Oath of Allegiance. Thereafter, the king refused to consider Donne for any post outside the Church. In 1610, Oxford University awarded an honorary master's degree to Donne, who had been prevented by his former religion from taking an undergraduate degree.

Having composed the *Anniversaries* under the patronage of Sir Robert Drury of Hawsted, he accompanied Sir Robert to Paris and then to Frankfort. After the return of the party to England in 1612, Donne and his family resided with Sir Robert. Although he continued to write occasional verse, Donne had definitely decided to take orders. Having prepared himself through further study, he was ordained early in 1615, and numerous avenues for advancement immediately became available to him. The king made him a royal chaplain. Cambridge awarded him the degree of doctor of divinity by royal command. Lincoln's Inn appointed him reader in divinity to the Society. In addition, he was able to turn down offers of fourteen country livings in his first year as a priest, while accepting two. The one blight on his early years as a priest was the death of his wife in 1617. In 1619, Donne took time out from his regular duties to serve as chaplain accompanying Lord Doncaster on an embassy to Germany.

Donne's fame as a preacher had been immediate, and it continued to grow each year. As Walton reports, even his friends were surprised by the continuous growth of his pulpit eloquence after such a striking beginning. Such genius received its proper setting in 1621, when Donne was appointed dean of St. Paul's Cathedral. The position was also a lucrative one, and the dean's residence was as large as an episcopal palace.

The winter of 1623-1624 was a particularly eventful time in Donne's life. Having contracted relapsing fever, he was on the verge of death, but with characteristic dedication—and also characteristic self-consciousness—he kept a meticulous record of his illness as an aid to devotion. The resulting work, *Devotions upon Emergent Occasions*, was published almost immediately. During the same period, Donne's daughter, Constance, married the aging Elizabethan actor Edward Alleyn, founder of Dulwich College. From circumstances surrounding the wedding, the publishing history of *Devotions upon Emergent Occasions* has been reconstructed. It now seems clear that Donne composed this highly structured work in just a few weeks while still physically incapacitated.

In 1624, he took on additional duties as vicar of St. Dunstan's-in-the-West. After the death of King James in the following year, Donne was chosen to preach the first sermon before the new king. This and other sermons were printed at the request of King Charles. Also printed was his memorial sermon for Lady Danvers, as Magdalen Herbert had become.

Even when Donne again became gravely ill in 1629, he would not stop preaching. Ever conscious of his mortality during these last months, he sat for a portrait wearing his shroud. When he delivered his last sermon on Ash Wednesday in 1631, it was the famous *Death's Duell*. Walton gives a vivid account of the writing and preaching of this sermon during Donne's last illness, and some of the sermon's special urgency is perhaps explained by the fact that the king's household called it Donne's own funeral sermon. Indeed, a few weeks later, on March 31, 1631, he died, having been preceded only a few months before by his aged mother.

## ANALYSIS

The traditional dichotomy between Jack Donne and Dr. Donne, despite John Donne's own authority for it, is essentially false. In the seventeenth century context, the work of Donne constitutes a fundamental unity. Conventional wisdom may expect devotional poetry from a divine and feel a certain uneasiness when faced with love poetry, but such a view misses the point in two different ways. On one hand, Donne's love poetry is philosophical in its nature and characterized by a texture of religious imagery; and on the other hand, his devotional poetry makes unexpected, bold use of erotic imagery. What Donne presents is two sides of a consistent vision of the world and of the mortality of man.

In the nineteenth century, when Donne's poetry did occasionally attract some attention from the discerning, it was not for the lyrics but for the satires. The satirical mode seemed the most congenial use that Donne had found for his paradoxical style. This had also been the attitude of the eighteenth century, which, however, valued metrical euphony too highly to accept even the satires. In fact, Alexander Pope tried to rescue Donne for the eighteenth century by the curious expedient of "translating" his satires into verse, that is, by regularizing them. In addition to replacing Donne's strong lines and surprising caesurae with regular meter, Pope, as Addison C. Bross has shown, puts ideas into climactic sequence, makes particulars follow generalizations, groups similar images together, and untangles syntax. In other words, he homogenizes the works.

Although Donne's lyrics have become preferred to his satires, the satires are regarded as artistically effective in their original form, although this artistry is of a different order from that of the lyrics. Sherry Zivley has shown that the imagery of the satires works in a somewhat different way from that of the imagery of the lyrics, where diverse images simply succeed one another. With images accumulated from a similarly wide range of sources, the satires build a thematic center. N. J. C. Andreasen has gone even further, discerning in the body of the satires a thematic unity. Andreasen sees Donne as having created a single persona for the satires, one who consistently deplores the encroaching materialism of the seventeenth century.

### "KIND PITY CHOKES MY SPLEEN"

Satire 3 on religion ("Kind pity chokes my spleen") is undoubtedly the most famous of the satires. Using related images to picture men as engaging in a kind of courtship of the truth, the poem provides a defense of moderation and of a common ground between the competing churches of the post-Reformation world. Although written in the period of Donne's transition from the Roman Catholic Church to the Anglican, the poem rejects both of these, along with the Lutheran and the Calvinist Churches, and calls on men to put their trust in God and not in those who unjustly claim authority from God for churches of their own devising.

In addition to the fully developed satires, Donne wrote a small number of very brief epigrams. These mere witticisms are often on classical subjects and therefore without the occasional focus that turns Ben Jonson's epigrams into genuine poetry. This is the only place where Donne makes any substantial use of classical allusion.

In his own day, Donne's most popular poems were probably his elegies. Although the term "elegy" is applied only to a memorial poem in modern usage, Donne's elegies derive their form from a classical tradition that uses the term, as well, for poetry of love complaint written in couplets. Generally longer than the more famous songs and sonnets, the elegies are written on the model of Ovid's *Amores* (c. 20 B.C.E.; English translation, c. 1597). Twenty or more such poems have been attributed to Donne, but several of these are demonstrably not his. On the basis of manuscript evidence, Dame Helen Gardner has suggested that Donne intended fourteen poems to stand as a thematically unified Book of Elegies and that "The Autumnal" (elegy 9), which has a different manuscript history, and "The Dream" (elegy 10), which is not in couplets, although authentic poems by Donne, do not form a part of it.

### "The Autumnal"

Elegy 9, "The Autumnal," praises older women as more seasonable to the appetite because the uncontrollable fires of their youth have passed. There is a long tradition that this poem was specially written for Magdalen Herbert. If so, it is particularly daring since, although not a seduction poem, it is frankly erotic in its praise; inasmuch as Magdalen Herbert did take as her second husband a much younger man, however, it may be supposed that she would have appreciated the general recognition that sexual attractiveness and interest can endure and even ripen. On the other hand, the poem's praises are not without qualification. The persona admires autumnal beauty, but he can see nothing attractive in the truly aged, whom he rejects as death's heads from which the teeth have been scattered to various places—to the vexation of their souls since the teeth will have to be gathered together again for the resurrection of the body at the Last Judgment. Thus the poem shows Donne's typical combination of eroticism and contemplation of mortality in a mode of grotesque humor.

### "To His Mistress Going to Bed"

In elegy 19, "To His Mistress Going to Bed," the persona enthusiastically directs his mistress in her undressing. Aroused, he uses his hands to full advantage to explore her body. In a famous passage, he compares his amazement to that of someone discovering a new land. He next directs her to bare her body to him as fully as she would to the midwife. This graphic request is followed by the poem's closing couplet, in which the persona points out that he is naked already to show his mistress the way and thus poignantly reveals that he is only hoping for such lasciviousness from her and not already having his wanton way. Even this poem uses religious imagery—most clearly and most daringly when it advocates a woman's baring of her body to her lover by analogy with the baring of the soul before God. In an influential explication, Clay Hunt suggests that Donne is, in fact, ridiculing the Neoplatonic school of love that could seriously advance such an analogy. If so, Donne is clearly having it both ways and making the analogy available for its own sake as well.

## "THE CANONIZATION"

The songs and sonnets, as the other love poems are usually called, although no sonnets in the conventional sense are included, show an imaginative variety of verse forms. They are particularly famous for their dramatic, conversational opening lines. In addition, these poems are a great storehouse of the kind of verbal ambiguity that William Empson has shown the modern world how to admire.

In "The Canonization," the persona justifies his love affair in explicitly sacred terms by explaining that his relationship with his beloved makes the two of them saints of love. John A. Clair has shown how the structure of "The Canonization" follows the five stages of the process of canonization in the Roman Catholic Church during the Renaissance: proof of sanctity, recognition of heroic virtue, demonstration of miracles, examination of relics and writings, and declaration of worthiness of veneration. The poem is thus addressed to a devil's advocate who refuses to see the holiness of erotic love. It is this devil's advocate in love who is asked to hold his tongue, in the famous first line. "The Canonization" illustrates Donne's typical use of ambiguity as well as paradox, not as merely decorative wit, but to reveal deepest meanings. William H. Machett suggests that, for example, when the lovers in this poem become a "piece of chronicle," the word "piece" is a triple pun meaning masterpiece, fragment, and fortress. There is also a much more obvious meaning—piece of artillery—a meaning that interacts with the title to give a richer texture to the whole poem: The poem is about not only the making of saints of love, but also the warfare between this idea and conventional notions of sex and religion. Consequently, yet another meaning of "piece" comes into play, the sexual.

## "THE FLEA"

"The Flea" is a seduction poem. Like many of the songs and sonnets, it takes the form of a logical argument making full use of the casuistries and indeed sophistries of the dialectic of Peter Ramus. In the first of the poem's three stanzas, the persona asks the lady to contemplate a flea he has discerned on her person. Because his blood and hers are mingled in the flea that has in succession bitten each of them, the mingling of the bloods that takes place during intercourse (as was then believed) has already occurred.

In the second stanza, the persona cautions the lady not to kill the flea. By joining their bloods, the flea has become the place of their joining in marriage, so for her to kill the flea would be to murder him and also to commit both suicide and sacrilege.

In the last stanza, the persona discovers that the lady has ignored his argument and killed the flea, but he is ready with another argument. When the lady triumphantly points out that they have survived this death of the flea, surely she is also showing how false her fears of sex are, because sex involves no greater loss of blood and no greater death. Implicit in these last lines is the traditional pun on "death," which was the popular term for sexual climax.

The pun and the poem as a whole illustrate Donne's characteristic mingling of the sacred and the profane. It should be noted that a love poem on the subject of the lady's fleas was not an original idea with Donne, but the usual treatment of the subject was as an erotic fantasy. Donne's originality is precisely in his use of the subject for dialectic and in the restraint he shows in ending the poem before the lady capitulates, in fact without indicating whether she does.

## "THE ECSTASY"

"The Ecstasy," the longest of the songs and sonnets, has, for a lyric, attracted a remarkable range of divergent interpretations. The poem is about spiritual love and intermingling as the culmination of physical love, but some critics have seen the Neoplatonism, or spiritualizing of love, as quite serious, while others have insisted that it is merely a patently sophistical ploy of the persona to convince his mistress that, since they are one soul, the physical consummation of their love is harmless, appropriate, inevitable. If the critics who see "The Ecstasy" as a seduction poem are right, the conclusion is even more salacious than they have supposed, since it calls on the addressee to examine the lovers closely for the evidence of true love when they have given themselves over to their bodies—in other words, to watch them make love. In fact, the poem, like so many of Donne's, is quite content to be theological and erotic by turns—beginning with its very title, a term used of both religious experience and sexual experience. That the perfect soul brought into being by the union of the lovers should combine the flesh and spirit eternally is an understandable religious hope and also a good sexual fantasy. In this way, the poem illustrates Donne's philosophy of love. Although not all his poems use this theme, Donne has, in fact, a unique ability for his day to perceive love as experienced by equals.

## "A VALEDICTION: FORBIDDING MOURNING"

Another famous poem of love between equals is "A Valediction: Forbidding Mourning." The poem rushes through a dazzling spectrum of imagery in just the way deplored by Samuel Johnson. In addition, in the *Life of Cowley*, Johnson singles out the poem for his ultimate condemnation, saying that in the extended metaphor of the last three stanzas "it may be doubted whether absurdity or ingenuity has the better claim." During the present century, ingenuity has once again become respectable in poetry, and modern readers come with more sympathy than Johnson did to this famous extended metaphor, or conceit, comparing lovers who have to suffer a temporary separation to a pair of pencil compasses. Even the improbability of the image—which Johnson castigated as absurdity—has been given a context by modern scholarship. W. A. Murray, for example, has shown that the circle with a dot in the center, which is inscribed by the compasses reflecting the lovers who are separated yet joined, is, in fact, the alchemical symbol for gold, mentioned elsewhere in the poem and a traditional symbol of perfection. More ingeniously, John Freccero has seen Donne's compasses as inscribing not simply a circle but, as they close, a spiral. The spiral has some history of use in describing the motion of the planets. Because the spiral is also a conventional symbol of humanity, this spiral reading helps readers see in "A Valediction: Forbidding Mourning" Donne's characteristic balance of the celestial and the personal.

In fact, Donne's inclusiveness is even wider than it is usually assumed to be. He collapses not only physical and spiritual but also male and female. Donne has the unusual perspicacity to make the persona of "Break of Day" explicitly female, and although no critic has made the point before, there is nothing to prevent seeing a similar female persona in "A Valediction: Forbidding Mourning." Such a reading has the advantage of introducing some erotic puns in the compass conceit as the man (the fixed center in this reading) harkens after his beloved as she roams and then grows erect when she returns to him. More important, such a reading makes further sense out of the image of a circle inscribed by compasses. The circle is a traditional symbol of woman, and woman's life is traditionally completed—or, as the poem puts it, made just—with a man at the center. Because the circle is a natural sexual image for woman, in this reading, the poem illustrates the practical sex as well as the theoretical sociology behind its imagery as the lover's firmness makes the woman's circle taut. An objection that might be made to this reading is that the poem's various references to parting show that it is the speaker who is going away. Although a woman of the seventeenth century would be unlikely to do extensive traveling apart from her lover (or even in his company), a woman may have to part as well as a man, and lovers might well think of themselves as roaming the world when kept apart only by the daily round of pedestrian business. There is no more reason in the poem for believing that the absent one will literally roam than for believing that this absent one will literally run.

Although Walton assigns this poem to the occasion of Donne's trip to France with Sir Robert Drury in 1611, the apocryphal nature of Walton's story is sufficiently indicated by the fact that it does not appear until the 1675 version of his *Life of Donne*. This dating would, at the least, make "A Valediction: Forbidding Mourning" extremely late for the songs and sonnets. Nevertheless, were the poem occasioned by Donne's preparation to travel to France in 1611, reading it as spoken by a woman would still be appropriate, since Donne prepared for this trip by sending his wife and children to stay with relatives on the Isle of Wight several months before he was himself able to embark. In addition, a general knowledge of how poets work suggests that a lyric inspired by a specific occasion is seldom in every particular a document congruent with the poet's actual experience. Perhaps the poem finally says that a woman can make a virtue of necessary separation as well as a man can.

## "TWICKHAM GARDEN"

Among the songs and sonnets are a few poems that seem to have been written for patrons. Since Twickenham is the seat of the earls of Bedford, "Twickham Garden" is assumed to have been written for Lucy, countess of Bedford. According to the poem, the garden is a refuge like Eden, but the persona admits that with him the serpent has been let in. He wishes he were instead an aphrodisiac plant or fountain more properly at home in the place. In the last stanza, he seems to become such a fountain, but he is disappointed to discover that all the lovers who visit the garden are false. The poem ends—perhaps rather curiously for a patronage poem—with the obscure paradox that the only true woman is the one whose truth is killing.

## "A NOCTURNAL UPON ST. LUCY'S DAY, BEING THE SHORTEST DAY"

A similar depersonalization characterizes the riddling poem "A Nocturnal upon St. Lucy's Day, Being the Shortest Day." While the ironies of darkness and light and of the changing movement of time (*Lucy* means light, but her day provides less of it than any other) would have recommended the subject to Donne anyway, it must have been an additional stimulus that this astronomically significant day was the saint's day of one of his patrons. Clarence H. Miller, seeing the poem as unique among the songs and sonnets in describing the union with the lady as exclusively sacred without any admixture of the profane, relates the poem to the liturgy for Saint Lucy's Day. In the body of the poem, however, the persona sees himself as the epitaph for light, as every dead thing. Finally, he becomes Saint Lucy's Day itself—for the purpose of providing lovers with a longer nighttime for lust. Despite a certain bitterness or at least coarseness of tone, the poem is usually seen as a lament for the countess's death (1627); the death of Donne's wife, however, has also been suggested, although Anne More has no special association with Saint Lucy and his love for her could not have been exclusively spiritual. Richard E. Hughes has considered the occasion of the poem from a different point of view and usefully suggested that, though commemorating the countess of Bedford, the poem is not an improbably late lyric for the songs and sonnets but a lament from an earlier period for the loss of the countess's friendship. If the tone is considered in the least charitable light, the poem might even be read as an accusation of patronage withdrawn.

## VERSE LETTERS

The familiar letter came into its own as a genre during the seventeenth century, and collections even began to be published. About two hundred of Donne's letters survive. This is a larger number than for any other figure of the English Renaissance except Francis Bacon, and Bacon's correspondence includes many letters written in his official capacity. Because the familiar letter had only begun to surface as a genre, much of the impersonality and formality of earlier letter writing persist in Donne's correspondence. Donne's son was a rather casual editor, and in light of the sometimes general nature of

Donne's letters, the date and intended recipient of many remain unknown. One curiosity of this period of epistolary transition is the verse letter. Almost forty of Donne's letters are written in verse. Some of these are true occasional poems datable from internal evidence, but many are of a more general, philosophical nature.

The most famous of the verse letters are "The Storm" and "The Calm," the first certainly and the second probably addressed to Christopher Brooke. Traditionally, shipwrecks and other dangers of the sea are used to illustrate the unpredictability of fortune in men's lives, but, as B. F. Nellist has shown, Donne does not follow this convention; instead, he teaches that frustration and despair are to be accepted as part of man's lot.

## EPITHALAMIA

While many of the verse letters seem to have been exchanged with friends as *jeux d'esprit*, some are attempts to influence patrons. A group of poems clearly written with an eye to patronage are the epithalamia. Among the weddings that Donne celebrated was that of Princess Elizabeth to Frederick V, elector of the palatinate and later briefly king of Bohemia. Donne also celebrated the wedding of the royal favorite Robert Carr, earl of Somerset, to Frances Howard, countess of Essex. Since the countess was shortly afterward convicted of murdering the essayist Sir Thomas Overbury for having stood in the way of her marriage, this epithalamion must later have been something of an embarrassment to Donne. An occasional poem for which no occasion is ascribed is the "Epithalamion Made at Lincoln's Inn." This is the most interesting of the epithalamia to contemporary taste. Its satiric tone, verbal crudities, and scoffing are a pleasant surprise in a genre usually characterized by reverence, even obsequiousness. The problem of what wedding could have been appropriately celebrated with such a poem has been resolved by David Novarr's suggestion that the "Epithalamion Made at Lincoln's Inn" was written for a mock wedding held as part of the law students' midsummer revels.

## MEMORIAL VERSE

Other poems written for patrons are those usually called the epicedes and obsequies. These are eulogies for the dead—elegies in a more modern sense of the term than the one Donne seems to have in mind. Donne was one among the many poets who expressed regret at the death of Prince Henry, the hope of the dynasty.

Also in the general category of memorial verse are the two poems known as *Anniversaries* (*An Anatomy of the World: The First Anniversary* and *Of the Progress of the Soule: The Second Anniversary*), but these two poems are so unlike traditional eulogies as to defy inclusion in the genre. In their search for moments of intense feeling, the Metaphysical poets, with their love of paradox, did not often try to write long poems. Most of the attempts they did make are unsatisfactory or at least puzzling in some fundamental way. The *Anniversaries* are, indeed, primary texts in the study of the difficulties of the long poem in the Metaphysical mode.

Ostensibly written as memorial poems to commemorate Elizabeth Drury, who died as a child of fourteen and whom Donne had never seen, these poems range over a broad canvas of history. "Shee," as the subject of the two poems is called, is eulogized in an extravagant fashion beyond anything in the obsequies. While O. B. Hardison has shown that these poems were not regarded as bizarre or fulsome when originally published, they were the first of Donne's works to lose favor with the passing of time. Indeed, of *An Anatomy of the World*, Ben Jonson objected to Donne himself that "if it had been writ of the Virgin Marie it had been something." Donne's answer is reported to have been that he was describing not Elizabeth Drury specifically but the idea of woman; but this explanation has not been found wholly satisfactory. Many candidates have been suggested for Shee of the *Anniversaries*—from Saint Lucy and Astraea (Goddess of Justice) to the Catholic Church and Christ as Divine *Logos*. Two critics have suggested Queen Elizabeth, but one finds her eulogized and the other sees her as satirized, indicting in a particularly striking way the problematic nature of these difficult, knotty poems.

Hardison and, later, Barbara Kiefer Lewalski, made the case for the poems as part of a tradition of epideictic poetry—poetry of praise. In this tradition, extravagant compliments are the norm rather than the exception, and all of Donne's individual extravagances have precedents. What such a reading leaves out of account is, on one hand, the extraordinary density of the extravagant praise in Donne's *Anniversaries* and, on the other, the presence of satire, not only the possible satire of the heroine but also explicit satire in the exploration of the decay of nature that forms the subject of the poems. Marjorie Hope Nicholson sees the *Anniversaries* as companion poems, the first a lament for the body, the second a meditation on mortality. Louis L. Martz suggests, further, that the *Anniversaries* are structured meditations. Martz sees *An Anatomy of the World* as a mechanical application of Ignatian meditation and *Of the Progress of the Soule* as a more successful organic application. Meditation theory, however, fails to resolve all the interpretive difficulties. Northrop Frye's theory that the poems are Menippean satire and Frank Manley's that they are wisdom literature also leave unresolved difficulties.

Perhaps these interpretive difficulties are fundamentally beyond resolution. Rosalie L. Colie has usefully pointed out that, in the *Anniversaries*, Donne seems not to be trying to bring his disparate materials to a conventional resolution. The poems accept contradictions as part of the flux of life and should be seen within the Renaissance tradition of paradox. Donne is demonstrably a student of paradox in many of his other works. More specifically, Daniel B. Rowland has placed *An Anatomy of the World* in the Mannerist tradition because in it Donne succeeded in creating an unresolved tension. His purpose may be just to raise questions about the relative weight of praise and satire and about the identity of the heroine Shee. Mario Praz goes further—perhaps too far—when he sees all the work of Donne as Mannerist, as illustrative not of wit but of the dialectics of passion; Mannerism does, however, provide a useful description for what modern taste finds a strange combination of materials in the *Anniversaries*.

## "INFINITATI SACRUM"

An even more difficult long poem is an unfinished one called "Infinitati Sacrum." This strange parable of Original Sin adapts Paracelsus's theory of the transmigration of souls to follow through the course of subsequent history the spirit of the apple plucked by Eve. W. A. Murray has seen in this poem the beginnings of a *Paradise Lost* (1667, 1674). While few other readers will want to go so far, most will agree with Murray and with George Williamson that "Infinitati Sacrum" is a preliminary use of the materials and themes treated in the *Anniversaries*.

Donne has been called a poet of religious doubt in contrast to Herbert, a poet of religious assurance; but Herbert has real doubts in the context of his assurance, and the bold demand for salvation in audacious, even shocking language characteristic of the Holy Sonnets suggests, on the contrary, that Donne writes from a deep-seated conviction of election.

## HOLY SONNETS

Louis Martz, Helen Gardner, and others have shown the influence of Ignatian meditation in the Holy Sonnets. Dame Helen, in fact, by restoring the manuscript order, has been able to see in these poems a sequential meditative exercise. The sensuous language, however, suggests not so much the meditative technique of Saint Ignatius of Loyola as the technique of Saint Francis de Sales. In addition, Don M. Ricks has argued cogently that the order of the poems in the Westmorland Manuscript may suggest an Elizabethan sonnet sequence and not a meditative exercise at all.

Holy Sonnet 14 (10 in Dame Helen's numbering), "Batter my heart, three-personed God," has been seen by Arthur L. Clements and others as hieroglyphically illustrating the Trinity in its three-part structure. This poem opens with the striking dramatic immediacy typical of Donne's best lyrics. Using both military and sexual imagery, Donne describes the frightening, ambivalent feelings called up by the thought of giving oneself over to God's power and overwhelming grace. The soul is a town ruled by a usurper whom God's viceroy, Reason, is inadequate to overthrow. The soul is also the beloved of God though betrothed to his enemy and longing for divorce. The resolution of this sonnet turns on a paradoxical sexual image as the persona says that his soul will never be chaste unless God ravishes him. A similar complex of imagery is used, though in a less startling fashion, in Holy Sonnet 2 (1), "As due by many titles I resign."

Holy Sonnet 9 (5), "If poisonous minerals," begins audaciously by accusing God of unfairness in the consequences He has decreed for Original Sin. In the sestet, the persona abruptly realizes that he is unworthy to dispute with God in this way and begs that his tears of guilt might form a river of forgetfulness inducing God to overlook his sins rather than actually forgiving them. Although this poem does not turn on a sexual image, it does contrast the lot of fallen man unfavorably with that of lecherous goats, who have no decree of damnation hanging over them.

Holy Sonnet 18 (2 in Dame Helen's separately numbered group from the Westmorland Manuscript), "Show me, dear Christ, Thy spouse so bright and clear," has some of the most shocking sexual imagery in all of religious literature. Although the tradition of using erotic imagery to describe the soul's relationship with God has a long history, particularly in exegesis of the Song of Songs, that is helpful in understanding the other Holy Sonnets, the imagery here is of a different order. Like Satire 3, the poem is a discussion of the competing claims of the various Christian churches, but it goes well beyond the courtship imagery of the satire when it praises the Anglican Church because, like a promiscuous woman, it makes itself available to all men.

A distinctly separate series of Holy Sonnets is "La Corona." Using paradoxes such as the fact that the Virgin is her Maker's maker, and including extensive allusions to the divine office, this sequence of seven poems on the life of Christ has been called by Martz a rosary of sonnets, not so much because of the devotional content as because of the interlaced structure: The last line of each poem is repeated as the first line of the next. Although the ingenious patterning renders the sequence less personal than Donne's best religious poetry, within its exquisite compass it does make a beautiful statement of the mysteries of faith.

In "A Hymn to Christ, at the Author's Last Going into Germany," Donne exaggerates the dangers of a Channel crossing to confront his mortality. Then even in the face of death, the persona pictures Christ as a jealous lover to be castigated if he withdraws his love just because it is not reciprocated; yet the persona does call for a bill of divorcement from all his lesser loves. The poem ends with the thought that, just as dark churches (being free of distractions) are best for praying, death is the best refuge from stormy seas.

"Good Friday, 1613: Riding Westward" is a witty paradox built on Ramist dialectic. Forced to make a trip to the West on Good Friday, the persona feels his soul drawn to the East. Although the heavens are ordered for westward motion, he feels a contradiction even as he duplicates their motion because all Christian iconology urges him to return to the East where life began—both human life in Eden and spiritual life with the Crucifixion. He reasons that through sin he has turned his back on the Cross—but only to receive the correction that his sins merit. He hopes such flagellation will so change his appearance that he will again become recognizable to God as made in his own image. Then he will at last be able to turn and face God.

Another divine poem of witty paradox is "A Hymn to God the Father." Punning on "Son/sun" and on his own name, Donne demands that God swear to save him. Having done so, God will at last have Donne. Because of its frankness and its very personal use of puns, this poem is not really a hymn despite its title—although it has been included in hymnals.

The chapter headings of *Devotions upon Emergent Occasions* as laid out in the table of contents should also be included among the divine poems. Joan Webber has made the illuminating discovery that this table of contents is a Latin poem in dactylic hexameters.

This is a particularly surprising element of artistry in a work composed in such a short time and under such difficult conditions. Thus even more self-conscious than had been supposed, *Devotions upon Emergent Occasions* can finally be seen as an explication of the Latin poem.

OTHER MAJOR WORKS

NONFICTION: *Pseudo-Martyr*, 1610; *Ignatius His Conclave*, 1611; *Devotions upon Emergent Occasions*, 1624; *Death's Duell*, 1632; *Juvenilia: Or, Certaine Paradoxes and Problemes*, 1633, 1923; *Six Sermons on Several Occasions*, 1634; *LXXX Sermons*, 1640; *Biathanatos*, 1646; *Fifty Sermons*, 1649; *Essayes in Divinity*, 1651; *Letters to Severall Persons of Honour*, 1651; *A Collection of Letters*, 1660; *XXVI Sermons*, 1660.

BIBLIOGRAPHY

Bloom, Harold, ed. *John Donne and the Metaphysical Poets*. New York: Bloom's Literary Criticism, 2008. A collection of critical analysis of Donne's poetry and that of the other Metaphysical poets.

Carey, John. *John Donne: Life, Mind, and Art*. Rev. ed. Boston: Faber & Faber, 1990. Carey's exposition of the whole range of Donne's poetry is exact and detailed. Its arrangement is thematic rather than biographical, which produces some forceful new appraisals. Includes an index.

Edwards, David L. *John Donne: Man of Flesh and Spirit*. Grand Rapids, Mich.: William B. Eerdmans, 2002. Biography of Donne that looks at how his life influenced his works.

Guibbory, Achsah, ed. *Cambridge Companion to John Donne*. New York: Cambridge, 2006. Covers both criticism and biography. Topics include Donne's political and religious world, his satires, his erotic poems, an explication of his poems, and gender and death in his poetry.

Johnson, Jeffrey. *The Theology of John Donne*. New York: D. S. Brewer, 1999. A portrayal of the religious writings of Donne as the result of a well-founded knowledge of Christian theology and Donne as a full-fledged religious thinker. Includes bibliographic references and an index.

Saunders, Ben. *Desiring Donne: Poetry, Sexuality, Interpretation*. Cambridge, Mass.: Harvard University Press, 2006. An examination of desire and love in the poetry of Donne that examines the seventeenth century perspective on love and desire.

Sherwood, Terry. *Fulfilling the Circle: A Study of John Donne's Thought*. Toronto, Ont.: University of Toronto Press, 1984. Attempts to trace Donne's understanding of the complex interrelationship of body and soul back from his later, more mature work. Theological and psychological perspectives are central. Includes an index.

Stubbs, John. *John Donne: The Reformed Soul*. New York: W. W. Norton, 2007. A readable and scholarly biography of the poet.

Sugg, Richard. *John Donne*. New York: Palgrave Macmillan, 2007. Provides a coherent overview of Donne's life and work and explains the Renaissance world in which he lived.

Targoff, Ramie. *John Donne, Body and Soul*. Chicago: University of Chicago Press, 2008. Targoff explains the seemingly disparate nature of Donne's writings by arguing that Donne's theme was always the union of body and soul.

*Edmund Miller*

# GEORGE HERBERT

**Born:** Montgomery, Wales; April 3, 1593
**Died:** Bemerton, near Salisbury, Wiltshire, England; March 1, 1633

*Musae Responsoriae*, 1620, 1662 (printed)
*Lucus*, 1623
*Passio Discerpta*, 1623
*Memoriae Matris Sacrum*, 1627
*The Temple*, 1633
*Poems*, 1958, 1961
*Sundrie Pieces: A New Selection of George Herbert's Poetry, with Samples of His Prose*, 2003 (illustrated by Sarah van Niekerk)

### OTHER LITERARY FORMS

George Herbert's most important work besides *The Temple* is his prose treatise *A Priest to the Temple: Or, The Country Parson His Character and Rule of Holy Life*, written when he was in fact a country parson at Bemerton during the last years of his life, though not published until 1652. However idealized it may be, *A Priest to the Temple* gives a good picture of the life of humble service that Herbert offered to his God and his parishioners. The volume of *Outlandish Proverbs Selected by Mr. G. H.*, published in 1640, testifies to Herbert's lifelong interest in the proverb, a form of literary and moral expression that is prominent throughout the poems in *The Temple*. Other minor works include a translation of *A Treatise of Temperance and Sobrietie of Luigi Cornaro* (1634), and a series of "Briefe Notes" appended to, but indicating various disagreements with, *The Hundred and Ten Considerations of Signior Iohn Valdesso* (1638).

### ACHIEVEMENTS

George Herbert has always been and perhaps will continue to be read somewhat in the shadow of John Donne, arguably the greatest and most influential of the seventeenth century Metaphysical poets. At the same time, however, Herbert has rarely lacked an audience well aware of his remarkable poetic abilities and unique voice. During his lifetime, Herbert's English poems were most likely circulated in manuscript, no doubt within a rather restricted circle of friends, and were evidently highly regarded. Upon publication in 1633, the year of his death, *The Temple* began to reach an ever-widening group of readers, the number and variety of whom say something about Herbert's appeal. It is not enough to note that Herbert was extremely popular, though he certainly was that: At least eleven editions of *The Temple* came out in the seventeenth century.

Perhaps more interesting is the fact that unlikely bedfellows shared an interest in Herbert and claimed him as their own. Members of the so-called High Church party found Herbert's deep attachment to Anglican ceremonial beauty particularly congenial, and they read *The Temple* as a record of how spiritual conflicts might evaporate in the face of simple faith, humility, and conformity. Several important poets, including Henry Vaughan and Richard Crashaw, along with a host of minor poets, including Christopher Harvey, Ralph Knevet, and Henry Colman, looked to Herbert as a guide in their devotions and a model for their poems. Other aspects of Herbert, however, appealed to many readers who could be called, for lack of a better term, Puritans. Though the Puritans are often criticized for a disinterest in, if not hostility to, art as an enemy of truth, Herbert's characteristic plainness, simplicity, and sincerity, coupled with his constant stress on the Bible as the center of the holy life, made him attractive to readers who were otherwise not greatly devoted to poetry. Richard Baxter and, later, John Wesley were extremely fond of Herbert, and it is no surprise that many poems from *The Temple* were subsequently adapted as hymns.

That Herbert could be appropriated so easily by such divergent readers indicates the richness of *The Temple*. Modern writers as varied as Gerard Manley Hopkins, T. S. Eliot, Dylan Thomas, Elizabeth Bishop, and Simone Weil have each in his or her own way learned from Herbert: as a poet who has a distinctive voice that nevertheless does not exclude other voices, particularly from the Bible and the Book of Common Prayer; as a man of purity and simplicity who is yet rarely naïve and often painfully sensitive to the intricacies of sin and self-deception; as a Christian, indeed a priest, wedded to humility but well aware that the resources of art can serve as resources of devotion.

### BIOGRAPHY

George Herbert was born on April 3, 1593, into one of the most distinguished families of Montgomeryshire, active both in local politics and court service. The fifth son in a family of seven sons and three daughters, he was reared principally by his mother (his father died in 1596), by all reports a remarkable woman who left a deep impression on her children. Magdalene Herbert not only shrewdly managed an extremely large household—unlike the modern-day nuclear family, the upper-class household of the seventeenth century might contain upward of a score of children, relatives, servants, and visitors—but also supervised the education of her children. Perhaps more important, as Donne relates in his commemorative sermon on her, she was a model of piety and took a great interest in the spiritual development of her family. Herbert's early childhood thus well prepared him for a life of distinction and devotion, two clusters of values that he later spent much time trying to reconcile.

Herbert's formal education began at Westminster School, and upon entering Trinity College, Cambridge, he soon established himself as a young man of great promise. Moving quickly through A.B. and A.M. degrees and positions as a minor, then a major fellow, Herbert became the university orator in 1620. Such an appointment not only indicates the great verbal and oral skills that Herbert must have demonstrated, skills that he would later use to great advantage as both a poet and a preacher, but also testifies to the high regard in which he was held. The orator was in some respects the public spokesperson for the university, constantly communicating with government officials and dignitaries, and it was only a small step to graduate from this office to a more prestigious position at court or in state service.

This was not, however, to be Herbert's path. Perhaps his attendance at two particularly troubling terms of Parliament (in 1624 and 1625) discouraged him from a life of secular employment. Perhaps the death of King James and the accession of Charles I left him without a strong group of supporters to back any possible ambitions. Perhaps as he grew older, passed through several serious illnesses, and deepened his devotions, he came to see that a secular career did not, in the long run, have nearly as much to offer as a life of holy service. For whatever reason, Herbert chose to be ordained as a deacon by 1626, and four years later, he became a priest. With his wife, whom he married in 1629, Herbert lived the remaining years of his life at Bemerton, a small parish near Salisbury. He died on March 1, 1633.

Herbert's poetry is often deeply personal, so that many readers insist on looking at *The Temple* as a kind of veiled autobiography. Surely the major themes of his life are indeed the major themes in his poetry: On one level, *The Temple* dramatizes Herbert's conflicting drives toward secular achievement and religious retreat, his search for a satisfying vocation, and his apparently constant self-doubts and worries about his unworthiness to be a lowly servant of God, let alone a priest. *The Temple* is ultimately, however, far more than autobiographical, and the reader should not assume that every statement made by Herbert the poet is literally true of Herbert the man. The persona who narrates and undergoes a variety of experiences in *The Temple* is very much like Herbert but also very much like the readers of *The Temple*. Herbert's purpose in writing his poems was not so much to express his personal concerns as it was to clarify and perhaps resolve certain important problems that all Christians—some would broaden this to include all thoughtful readers—share. The details of Herbert's life thus figure largely in his poems, but as part of a design that is much more inclusive.

## ANALYSIS

*The Temple* is unquestionably one of the most inventive and varied collections of poems published in the seventeenth century, and a reader can go a long way toward appreciating George Herbert by studying this inventiveness and variety. At the same time, though, the full range of Herbert's intentions and impact may be missed if his technical virtuosity is seen as an end in itself. Everything known about Herbert suggests that he would not want to be described as a master craftsman or skilled technician of poetry unless it was also stressed that every effort of his artistry served a central purpose: helping him to know, love, and praise God, and to understand better his place in a world filled with sin but governed and redeemed by Christ. Such poems as "Jordan" (I) and (II) and "The Posie" are in fact critical of certain styles of poetry and show that Herbert is more than occasionally impatient with the subterfuge, indirection, and even pride that seem inevitable in producing a well-written work. Ultimately, however, poetic creativity and devotion are welded together in *The Temple*. As the title suggests, Herbert imagines himself to be a builder, and nearly all the details, both large and small, of the structure he raises show it to be a place of intricate beauty as well as sacred worship.

## THE TEMPLE

Understanding the design of *The Temple* as a whole is no easy matter, in part because Herbert's natural inclination seems to be to "play" with structure, rather than to adopt a fixed schema as the pattern for the entire work. *The Temple* is divided into three parts, as though the reader is going to be led step-by-step through a physical temple. "The Church-porch," by far Herbert's longest single poem, offers a great deal of advice on moral matters to prepare a youth who is otherwise not yet ready for more serious devotions. After such an initiation, the reader is ready to enter the section called "The Church," a collection of lyrics that continues to describe various places or objects in the church (the altar, stained glass windows, and so on) but that in doing so dramatizes the spiritual conflicts of a believer trying to secure his faith. The final section, "The Church Militant," turns from the life of the individual believer to the corporate body of the church, which, like each individual, must endure a series of successes and failures throughout its history. While the tripartite structure of *The Temple* thus has a certain obvious coherence, there are limits to the usefulness of such a scheme. Though Herbert never completely drops his theme of tracing out the contours of the physical temple, he quickly shows that his main interest is in exploring the temple within the heart and mind of the worshiper.

Herbert's flexible and open-ended play with structure, his ability to make patterns that are stable enough to support a great weight of meaning but loose enough to avoid dull predictability, is seen to a great advantage in the way he arranges the poems of "The Church." Far from being a random miscellany, "The Church" is a carefully ordered collection in which the individual poems are placed in sequences and other kinds of groups, sometimes with poems that stand nearby in the volume, at other times with ones located many pages away. Although even a superficial reading of the poems soon advises the reader that he must watch closely how they relate to one another, Herbert provides a good description of his method and a clue to where he learned it in his poem "The H. Scriptures" (II). Despite its many parts, the Bible, he suggests, has a basic unity, and in order to understand any particular story the reader needs to trace how "This verse marks that, and both do make a motion/ Unto a third, that ten leaves off doth lie." Like the Bible, "The Church" has a basic unity, and the reader understands the poems fully only when he or she takes into account how they comment on and echo one another.

Sometimes the patterns and sequences of the poems are rather straightforward. "The Church" opens with a series that moves through the events celebrated during Easter Week, and the cumulative effect of such poems as "The Sacrifice," "The Agonie," "Good Friday," "Easter," and "Easter-wings" is to reinforce a sense of the importance of this part of the Christian calendar. In another group, the typical progress of a Christian life is reflected in the succession of titles: "Affliction," "Repentance," "Faith," "Prayer," and "The H. Communion." Even when Herbert does not fully develop a sequence, there are many examples of paired poems, where one answers, corrects, or otherwise responds to another. "Church-monuments," one of Herbert's most impressive poems even though its theme is the body's inevitable decay, is immediately followed by "Church-musick," which focuses on the high-flying freedom of the soul once it is released from the body. The desperate pleas that fill "Longing" are short-lived; by the first line of the next poem, "The Bag"—"Away despair! My gracious Lord doth heare"—the pleas have been answered.

Toward the end of "The Church," the speaker in the poem "The Invitation" calls out to God, inviting him to a feast; the following poem, "The Banquet," shows not only that the invitation has been accepted but also that the feast is far more glorious than the speaker had imagined. The more the reader follows the many links drawing the poems closer and closer together, the more apparent it becomes that one aspect of Herbert's design in "The Church" is to use the entire collection to trace a believer's gradual attainment not only of wisdom but also, more important, of peace. Read as one long, continuous sequence, the poems of "The Church" do seem to have a general plot, as the tribulations so much in evidence early in the work gradually give way to a more subdued questioning and heightened moments of bliss. Many commentators have noted that Herbert marks out this general plot very clearly for his reader: At the beginning of "The Church" the reader is invited to "approach, and taste/ The churches mysticall repast," and the final poem in the section, "Love" (III), concludes quite simply—"So I did sit and eat"—showing that this task has been completed.

Without disregarding the broad movement in "The Church" from immaturity to maturity, pain to comfort, it is equally important to note that Herbert by no means presents a simple tale of easily achieved spiritual progress. The plot traced out by the lyrics in "The Church," while ultimately a hopeful one, is at the same time densely textured, complicated, filled with moments of weakness, backsliding, and lessons improperly learned. Numerous short sequences suggest that humanity's needs are answered by Christ, who is always nearby; for example, the momentary sense that Christ has vanished, and that even when he is near he is unapproachable, expressed in "The Search," "Grief," and "The Crosse," gives way to the blooming of joy in "The Flower"—joy that is both surprising and expected: "How fresh, O Lord, how sweet and clean/ Are thy returns! ev'n as the flowers in spring."

If comfort is predictable, though, so is despair, and many short sequences show how quickly people move back again from wonder to worry; the exhilaration of "The Temper" (I), for example, is extremely precarious, over and done with, even by the time the next poem, "The Temper" (II), begins: "It cannot be. Where is that mightie joy,/ Which just now took up all my heart?" As confusing and frustrating as these constant oscillations may be, Herbert's purpose is not to undermine the reader's security. By linking his poems in a variety of ways, often teasing and challenging his reader, Herbert expands the limits of the lyric form, setting the entire collection up to do what no one lyric possibly could: to dramatize and analyze the various moods and rhythms of a faithful believer.

## POETIC STRUCTURE

Herbert's structural skill is evident not only in the overall plan and order of *The Temple* but also in the individual poems. His playful sense of poetic structure, though, has often been misunderstood and held against him. Such obviously patterned poems as "The Altar" and "Easter-wings," both of which are typographically shaped to resemble the objects named in the title, often strike some readers as quaint at best. Eighteenth century critics, for example, viewed these poems rather condescendingly as typical of Herbert and did not hesitate to consider him as a "false wit," incapable of more noble and creative effects.

Looked at more sympathetically, though, "The Altar" and "Easter-wings" are typical of Herbert only in suggesting how important poetic form is for him. Besides being a statement and a dramatization, a poem by Herbert is also an artifact, whose structure, sometimes simply, at other times subtly, reinforces a particular theme. At one end of the scale, there are directly imitative poems such as "Paradise," a poem about pruning in which the rhyme words are, in fact, pruned; "Heaven," in which the last word of the speaker's questions echoes in a following line as an answer; and "Trinitie Sunday," composed of a trinity of three-line stanzas. Other poems show more subdued but nevertheless effective pictorial designs: The shape of the stanzas in "The Agonie" suggests the image of the winepress mentioned in the poem, which calls to mind the association between Christ's sacrificial blood and sacramental wine; and each stanza in "The Bag" seems to contain an open space, literally like the bag mentioned in the poem used to take messages from humans straight to God.

Such directly imitative devices help to prepare the reader for Herbert's far more challenging uses of poetic form in other places in *The Temple*. The structure of "Church-monuments," for example, is meant not so much to imitate a gravestone, as the title seems to suggest, as to help the reader imagine the decay described in the poem that will sooner or later overcome gravestones, bodies, and the entire physical world. Because the lines are only occasionally end-stopped, the rhythm becomes somewhat unsettling, even ominous, and since the word "dust" is repeated again and again, the entire poem momentarily becomes like the hourglass mentioned in the last few lines, "which holds the dust/ That measures all our time; which also shall/ Be crumbled into dust."

Similarly, the theme and mood of the speaker in "The Collar" are powerfully and immediately conveyed by its structure: The poem is apparently unshaped, with irregularly alternating lines of different length to suggest the disordered mind of a man who has lost all control. By the concluding lines, though, the structure of the poem communicates the achievement of order. As the speaker exhausts himself to a moment of calmness, "normal" poetic form also surfaces in the relatively stable *abab* rhyme scheme of the last four lines: "But as I rav'd and grew more fierce and wilde/ At every word,/ Me thoughts I heard one calling, *Child!!* And I reply'd, *My Lord.*" Because he so often shapes his poems to have a visual impact, Herbert is compared with the emblem writers of his time, whose verses were either appended to illustrative plates or were at least meant to call to mind and interpret such illustrations. Such poems as "Church-monuments" and "The Collar," however, show that one of Herbert's particular skills is an ability to use the structure of his poems to imitate not only objects and static scenes but also dramatic processes.

## LANGUAGE

Herbert's attention to structure is matched by his loving care for the language of his poems. Especially when compared with other works of his period, *The Temple* seems remarkably simple and direct, with little of the straining against meaning that characterizes so many of William Shakespeare's sonnets, and with hardly any of Donne's self-conscious roughness and almost inconsiderate obscurity.

As many critics have noted, though, Herbert's simplicity marks the triumph, not the abandonment, of art. The language of *The Temple* is that of the Bible (especially in the King James or Authorized Version, published in 1611) and the Book of Common Prayer: austere but resonant and multileveled. Herbert's delight in language reflects not only the deep influence of God's words, the Holy Scriptures, but also his awareness that human words, returned to God in prayer, praise, song, and poetry, are at least an acceptable celebration of God's Word made flesh in Christ.

Throughout "The Church," Herbert struggles with the dilemma that humans in poetry, as in all things, can give to God only what God has already given them; but though this undermines any pretense of human self-sufficiency, it is an arrangement in which Herbert ultimately finds a great deal of comfort. The heartfelt simplicity of the three poems titled "Praise" and the two titled "Antiphon," among many others in "The Church," signifies not only a poetic choice but also an acceptance of humanity's subservient place in God's world.

At the same time, however, Herbert's humility allows him to exploit the richness of the English language. Modern readers who consider puns to be at best a low form of wit need to be reminded that Herbert, like most other seventeenth century poets, used puns and wordplay not only for comic effects but also for much more serious purposes: to indicate deep correspondences between various things in the world, between language and reality and between different levels of experience.

In "The Sonne," Herbert confesses "I like our language well," in part because it lends itself so easily to one especially significant pun: The reader is led quickly through the multiple meanings of the title word, from "son" to "sun," and finally to Christ, who combines these meanings as Son of Man, Son of God, and the guiding and warming light of Christians: their sun. There may well be even another concealed pun here: "The Sonne" is written in the form of a sonnet. The title "The Holdfast" is also a pun that takes the reader into the central conflict of the poem: A "holdfast" is something one can cling securely to, in this case God; in addition, "holdfast" is a term for a stingy, self-reliant man, such as the speaker of the poem, who must first relax his hold on himself before he can truly understand "That all things were more ours by being his," that is, Christ's.

Though it is sometimes difficult to determine where Herbert's wordplay leaves off and the reader's invention begins, the title "The Collar" sets off a series of associations that are relevant to the lines that follow: The collar is perhaps first and foremost the Christian's yoke of discipline and obedience from which the speaker flees; this word also suggests "choler," the anger and distress of the speaker as he raves on and on; finally, by a slight adjustment it also sounds like the "caller," alluding not only to the situation of the speaker calling out in anguish but also to the infinitely patient God who calls even his unruly servant "Child."

Herbert occasionally uses puns and wordplay to construct a puzzle, the explanation of which points the reader toward a comforting observation. In "Jesu," for example, the title word is "deeply carved" in the speaker's heart. When his heart is broken by "A great affliction," the letters become scattered, but even so they spell out an important message: the fragments *J* (often printed as *I* in the seventeenth century), *ES*, and *U* form the statement "I ease you," a welcome affirmation of the power of Christ. Not all Herbert's poems are puzzles, but his constant reliance on puns keeps his otherwise short and compact lyrics from one-dimensional simplicity. Even the smallest details in a poem are liable to expand into several important meanings. In "Christmas," for example, when he describes the "glorious, yet contracted light" of the Christ child, he not only marvels at how the greatness of God has taken the diminutive form of a baby, but also celebrates the fact that humanity is bound, by legal contract or covenant, to God.

When Herbert questions, in the ominously titled poem "Discipline," "Who can scape his bow?" the various interpretations of the last word provide comforting associations. Besides being a weapon of war and traditional instrument of justice and wrath, the "bow" also calls to mind Cupid's bow and arrow, which are instruments of love; the rainbow, the sign after the Flood that God will change his ways of wrath; the bowlike cross, a common comparison found in many biblical commentators; and Christ's "bowing," taking human form to save humankind. Throughout *The Temple*, Herbert carefully avoids the two most common dangers of the pun—he is rarely ostentatious or ridiculous—and as a result his wordplay almost always adds a great deal of allusiveness and depth to his poems.

## "THE CHURCH"

What makes Herbert an enduring poet is not simply his structural and stylistic expertise but also the application of these technical skills to themes of great importance. The general subject of *The Temple* is, in Herbert's own words as reported by Izaak Walton, his seventeenth century biographer, "the many spiritual Conflicts that have passed betwixt God and my Soul." Knowing this, it should be no surprise to see that the poems in "The Church" are constantly dramatic, most often revolving around a dual focus: humanity's inevitable sins and misunderstandings, and the processes through which humanity is comforted, instructed, and corrected.

Before telling humanity's tale, however, Herbert places human life within the frame of one larger event, the Crucifixion. Christ's drama must be told first, and, accordingly, the poem on "The Sacrifice" is placed near the beginning of "The Church." Although this poem is in many respects unusual for Herbert—it is very long, and uses Christ not only as the subject but also as the speaker—its pattern recurs in many other places: Unlike such poets as Donne and Crashaw, who often try to sustain a high dramatic pitch for an entire poem, Herbert, here and elsewhere, normally works with quick, unexpected, striking dramatic moments. "The Sacrifice" has a startling immediacy as Christ narrates the humiliating events of his crucifixion, and yet the reader also senses a curiously triumphant detachment. Even though Christ's repeated refrain is "Was ever grief like mine?" his voice is calm and ironic as he lists in obsessive detail the incongruities of his situation, the Son of God tortured by the people he offers to serve and save. After more than two hundred lines showing Christ's rather impassive power, Herbert breaks his carefully established format: Christ suddenly cries out in anguish *"My God, my God—,"* a broken, unfinished line that the reader presumably completes by adding, "why has thou forsaken me?" The refrain then changes in this stanza to the simple statement, "Never was grief like mine." Because of this sudden breakdown, the reader is drawn more surely into a fuller understanding of the sacrifice: Christ is not only serene and all-powerful but also, at least for one moment, vulnerable, human. Once "The Sacrifice" establishes to what extent Christ, despite his torment, is humanity's benefactor, the reader can realize more fully that the "spiritual Conflicts" in Herbert's poems are not truly between humanity and God but between humans and themselves.

Throughout "The Church," the focus is on the many ways that people find to resist God. Like Donne, Herbert is convinced of humans' basic and inescapable sinfulness, and some of his poems, like Donne's Holy Sonnets, explore arrogant intellectual pride ("Vanitie" [I] and [II]), disobedience ("Affliction" [I], "The Collar"), and the general blackness of the human soul ("Sinne" [I] and [II]). Beyond these themes, however, and in a manner that distinguishes him from Donne, Herbert is primarily interested in dramatizing far more intricate modes of self-deception and far less obvious subtleties of pride. The speaker in "The Thanksgiving," for example, seems genuinely moved by his meditation on Christ, and his exuberant plant to dedicate his life to charitable works probably strikes every reader as praiseworthy. In a turn that is characteristic of Herbert, however, the last two lines suddenly undermine all that has come before. At the height of his confident offering to Christ, the speaker stumbles: "Then for thy passion—I will do for that—/ Alas, my God, I know not what." Herbert is by no means ridiculing the speaker or banishing exuberance and charity from the devotional life, but he dramatizes very effectively how evasive one can be even when trying to dedicate oneself to following Christ's example.

A similar reversal occurs in "Miserie." Here the speaker clearly abhors sin and spends most of his time criticizing humanity's foolishness in choosing a filthy life of "strange pollutions" over the moral purity that might have been within reach. The accusations are extreme but compelling, and it takes little arguing to convince the reader that humanity is "A lump of flesh, without a foot or wing/ To raise him to a glimpse of blisse:/ A sick toss'd vessel, dashing on each thing." The last line, however, changes the focus of the poem entirely: After seventy-seven lines describing the "strange wayes" around him, the speaker suddenly realizes that "My God, I mean my self." In this way, Herbert shows that abhorrence of sin, while perhaps admirable, may be a mode of pride unless one includes oneself in the indictment.

"The Thanksgiving" and "Miserie" are also good examples of how Herbert typically includes the reader in his dramatic revelations and reversals. Although it might be overstating the case to say that Herbert traps his readers, many assent to and often identify with his speakers from the start of a poem. Because they accept their premises—the statements in both "The Thanksgiving" and "Miserie" seem plausible, if not praiseworthy, until the very end—they also share in their fall. The self-deception and pride of the speakers in many of Herbert's lyrics are thus, in a certain sense, duplicated in the reader, and as the speakers are dramatized, explored, and corrected, so is the reader.

## LYRICS OF COMFORT

Throughout *The Temple*, Herbert's subject is not merely the correction of humanity's numerous flaws: Equally dramatic are the lyrics of recovery and comfort where the speaker overcomes not pride but feelings of unworthiness, uselessness, and weakness. For all his moments of self-scrutiny and criticism, Herbert is a remarkably gentle poet, and he knows when to remind his readers how securely he feels that they are ground in God's mercy. Without God, he explains, human beings are nothing—a premise that many modern readers find extremely discouraging—but he goes on to add that human beings need not be without God. For Herbert, humans are constantly cheered and renewed by God's presence: In "Aaron," feelings of worry about being a priest give way to calm confidence as soon as one sees that Christ "is not dead,/ But lives in me while I do rest"; in "The Flower," sadness about the fragility of life and poetry turns into a heightened sense of joy and beauty, truly "thy wonders"; and in "The Elixir," all human effort, as long as it is done "for thy sake," becomes "drudgerie divine," pleasant and ennobling.

## "LOVE"

God's voice and presence appear throughout the volume, but nowhere so movingly as in the last poem of "The Church," "Love" (III). Here God and man meet face to face, and though a lesser poet might not have been able to withstand the temptation to over-embellish the scene, Herbert's dramatic lyric is as understated as it is powerful. God is love, "quick-ey'd Love," whose every word and movement is meant to comfort an extremely shy human guest who is humbly aware that he is "Guiltie of dust and sinne." Humanity's unworthiness, however, is finally beside the point: Stated in its simplest possible terms, God knows, forgives, accepts, and redeems humanity.

Simple words of paraphrase, however, can never tell the whole story. "Love" (III) is not a statement but an enactment, not a bit of theological argument or explanation but a dramatization of a devotional gesture. From the beginning of "The Church," as he notes at the conclusion of "The Reprisall," one of Herbert's main tasks is to show how "In thee [Christ] I will overcome/ The man, who once against thee fought." The particular action and quiet tone of the last lines of "Love" (III)—"You must sit down, sayes Love, and taste my meat:/ So I did sit and eat"—confirm that the battle, against God and against himself, is over, celebrated by a meal that is simultaneously a lover's banquet, a communion service, and his first true taste of heavenly joy.

### OTHER MAJOR WORKS

NONFICTION: *A Treatise of Temperance and Sobrietie of Luigi Cornaro*, 1634 (translation); *Outlandish Proverbs Selected by Mr. G. H.*, 1640 (also known as *Jacula Prudentum*, 1651); *A Priest to the Temple: Or, The Country Parson His Character and Rule of Holy Life*, 1652 (wr. 1632; also known as *The Country Parson*).

MISCELLANEOUS: *The Works of George Herbert*, 1941, 1945 (F. E. Hutchinson, editor).

### BIBLIOGRAPHY

Blythe, Ronald. *George Herbert in Bemerton*. Salisbury, England: Hobnob Press, 2005. This biography of Herbert examines his later years, which were spent in Bemerton.

Clarke, Elizabeth. *Theory and Theology in George Herbert's Poetry: Divinitie, and Poesie, Met*. Oxford, England: Clarendon Press, 1997. Explores the relationship between Herbert's poetry and the notion of divine inspiration rooted in devotional texts of his time. Includes bibliographical references and indexes.

Cruickshank, Frances. *Verse and Poetics in George Herbert and John Donne.* Burlington, Vt.: Ashgate, 2010. This study of Herbert's poetry compares it with that of Donne and pays extra attention to the techniques used.

Hodgkins, Christopher. *Authority, Church, and Society in George Herbert: Return to the Middle Way.* Columbia: University of Missouri Press, 1993. A critical analysis in which Hodgkins demonstrates that Herbert's poetry is predominantly nostalgia for old English social, political, and religious customs. Identifies the changes in his poetry as reflections of the changing times.

_____, ed. *George Herbert's Pastoral: New Essays on the Poet and Priest of Bemerton.* Newark: University of Delaware Press, 2010. This collection of essays present critical analysis of Herbert's work, particularly his pastoral poems.

Malcolmson, Cristina. *George Herbert: A Literary Life.* New York: Palgrave Macmillan, 2003. A reconsideration of Herbert, his poetry and his politics. This insightful biography sheds new light on the poet's intentions and his contemporary audience.

Miller, Greg. *George Herbert's "Holy Patterns": Reforming Individuals in Community.* New York: Continuum, 2007. Examines Herbert's religious beliefs as they influenced his poetry and how Herbert's verse can be seen as moving people toward faith.

Stewart, Stanley. *George Herbert.* Boston: Twayne, 1986. In this brief study, Stewart surveys Herbert's life and writings in both poetry and prose and counters emphasis on Herbert's Protestantism by emphasizing his close connection with medieval Catholicism and High Anglican devotion. He concludes with a fine chapter on Herbert's influence on other seventeenth century poets and a helpful annotated list of key critical works on Herbert.

Strier, Richard. *Love Known: Theology and Experience in George Herbert's Poetry.* Chicago: University of Chicago Press, 1983. Offers penetrating critical readings of many of the key poems of *The Temple,* examining in particular how they confirm Herbert's deep debt to Protestant theology, especially that of Martin Luther. For Strier, Herbert's poems focus repeatedly on the unreliability of reason and the drama of human unworthiness rendered inconsequential by divine love.

Vendler, Helen. *Invisible Listeners: Lyric Intimacy in Herbert, Whitman, and Ashbery.* Princeton, N.J.: Princeton University Press, 2007. Vendler, who focuses on close readings that stress poetic and emotional complexity, compares and contrasts the writings of Herbert, Walt Whitman, and John Ashbery.

*Sidney Gottlieb*

# BEN JONSON

**Born:** London, England; June 11, 1573
**Died:** London, England; August 6, 1637

### OTHER LITERARY FORMS

Ben Jonson's fame has rested mainly on his comic drama, especially on the master-pieces of his maturity, *Volpone: Or, The Fox* (pr. 1605), *Epicœne: Or, The Silent Woman* (pr. 1609), *The Alchemist* (pr. 1610), and *Bartholomew Fair* (pr. 1614). Surviving earlier comedies are *The Case Is Altered* (pr. 1597), *Every Man in His Humour* (pr. 1598), *Every Man Out of His Humour* (pr. 1599), *Cynthia's Revels: Or, The Fountain of Self-Love* (pr. c. 1600-1601), *Poetaster: Or, His Arraignment* (pr. 1601), and *Eastward Ho!* (pr., pb. 1605, with George Chapman and John Marston). Later comedies are *The Devil Is an Ass* (pr. 1616), *The Staple of News* (pr. 1626), *The New Inn: Or, The Light Heart* (pr. 1629), *The Magnetic Lady: Or, Humours Reconciled* (pr. 1632), and *A Tale of a Tub* (pr. 1633). Jonson wrote two tragedies, *Sejanus His Fall* (pr. 1603) and *Catiline His Conspiracy* (pr., pb. 1611). Two uncompleted works date apparently from the end of his life: the pastoral *The Sad Shepherd: Or, A Tale of Robin Hood* (pb. 1640) and the tragedy *Mortimer His Fall* (only a few pages).

Jonson's court masques and entertainments may conservatively be said to number about thirty, differing tallies being possible depending on whether minor entertainments of various kinds are counted. Besides plays, masques, and original nondramatic verse, Jonson wrote and translated a few other works that help to place him in the Renaissance humanistic tradition; all were first published in *The Works of Benjamin Jonson* (1640-1641). As a vernacular humanist, Jonson wrote *The English Grammar* (1640); he translated Horace's *Ars poetica* (as *Horace His Art of Poetry*) in 1640; finally, he compiled and translated extracts from classical and modern authors, mostly having to do with ethics, education, and rhetoric; the collection is titled *Timber: Or, Discoveries Made upon Men and Matter* (1641).

## ACHIEVEMENTS

Ben Jonson's achievements as a writer of verse can best be summarized by saying that he founded English neoclassicism. Although Jonson wrote several decades before what is usually thought of as the neoclassic age, his work clearly foreshadows that of John Dryden and Alexander Pope. His, like theirs, was a mode of poetry generally imitative of ancient Roman forms, concerned, as major Roman writers had been, with behavior on a specifically human stage of action, and sometimes heroic, often satirical, in tone and stance.

## BIOGRAPHY

Benjamin Jonson's father, a minister, died a month before his son's birth. Ben's mother remarried, apparently fairly soon thereafter, the stepfather being a master bricklayer of Westminster. A friend enrolled Jonson at Westminster School, but (as he told William Drummond) he was taken from school at about the age of sixteen and put to a "Craft," presumably bricklaying. Unable to endure this occupation, Jonson escaped briefly into the wars with the Netherlands. The next few years (roughly, his early twenties) are the most obscure of Jonson's life. At some point during this time, he married and began having children, although practically nothing is known about his wife or family.

Jonson reappears in the late 1590's in theatrical records as an actor and part-time playwright. In these years, Jonson was repeatedly at odds with the law, usually because of his involvement with satirical or political drama. He also attracted the authorities' hostility through his conversion to Roman Catholicism. (Eventually he returned to the Church of England and later in life expressed, above all, distaste for those who claimed complete theological certainty.) In the series of comedies of humours beginning with *Every Man in His Humour*, Jonson coined an original form of satirical comedy based on the caricature of psychological types. In 1600 to 1601, he temporarily abandoned the open-air public playhouses to present his comical satires at the more fashionable indoor private theater at Blackfriars. The move was part of the provocation of the stage quarrel, or war of the theaters, in which Jonson, Thomas Dekker, and John Marston traded plays lampooning one another. Jonson's earliest datable nondramatic poetry also belongs to these years. From the first, Jonson wrote occasional and panegyric verse addressed to the aristocracy, invoking their patronage.

The first decade and a half of the seventeenth century were the years of Jonson's superb creativity and greatest popularity as a playwright. During those years, he was in social contact with fellow playwrights such as William Shakespeare, and also with scholars such as William Camden and John Selden. Jonson's associations, however, were not limited to the theatrical and the learned; he was steadily employed as the writer of court masques throughout the reign of James I. Both the king and the aristocrats at the court responded to Jonson's work for many years with notable offers of support. The years from 1616 through 1624 probably marked the height of his prestige. In 1616, he published *The Workes of Benjamin Jonson* in folio. A royal pension came in the same year

*Ben Jonson*
(Library of Congress)

and, in 1619, an honorary degree from Oxford. Also gratifying was the gathering around Jonson of the Tribe of Ben, a circle of poetic sons, including Thomas Carew and Robert Herrick, who adopted him as their mentor.

The accession of Charles I to the throne in 1625 ended Johnson's tenure as regular writer of masques for the court, and in other respects also, the last dozen years of Jonson's life contrast with the preceding successful decades. At some points during these last years, he was clearly in financial need, and he suffered a stroke in 1628. He was writing comedies again for the popular stage, but none of them won much acclaim. Against such bleak circumstances, however, stands a persistence of poetic energy, embodied in much outstanding verse attributable to these years. Jonson held the regard of his circle of poetic sons until his death in 1637, and beyond: One of them, Sir Kenelm Digby, finally assembled and published Jonson's later along with his earlier *Works* in 1640-1641.

### ANALYSIS

Until the last few decades, attention to Ben Jonson's poetry focused largely on the famous songs and the moving epitaphs on children. Such choices were not ill-advised, but they are unrepresentative. The works in these modes certainly rank among Jonson's most successful, but they differ in tone from Jonson's norm.

Songs such as "Kiss me, sweet: the wary lover" and "Drink to me only with thine eyes" evoke emotions beyond the world of reason or fact, partly through reference to extravagant gestures and implausible experiences: hundreds and thousands of kisses, a wreath that will not die after the beloved has breathed on it. Through rhythms that are stronger and less interrupted than Jonson usually created, the songs activate the capacity to respond sensually and irrationally to language. Some of them create magical secret worlds where sense and emotion are to be experienced in disregard of troubling or quali-fying context (the "silent summer nights/ When youths ply their stol'n delights" in "Kiss me, sweet: the wary lover"). Exactly such worlds are created, but also subjected to critique, in *Volpone* and *The Alchemist*.

The epitaphs, particularly those on Jonson's own children ("On My First Son," "On My First Daughter") are so effective because in them subjective emotions strain against rational conviction. Jonson's statement in each of these poems is doctrinal and exem-plary, involving resignation to the will of God, but part of the power of the affirmation of belief arises from Jonson's undertone of grief over which faith has won out. Regret and despair have not been reasoned away but are being rationally controlled; consolation is not easy.

Such richly concentrated poems obviously deserve attention; that they should have received exposure to the virtual exclusion of Jonson's less lyrical or emotive verse, however, perhaps represents a holdover from Romantic or Victorian taste for rhapsodic expressions of feeling and imaginative vision in poetry. In fact, the renewal of contact with the Metaphysical sensibility achieved by T. S. Eliot and other critics in the 1920's and 1930's, which brought about the displacement of Victorian approaches to a number of seventeenth century writers, did not do so, immediately or directly, in the case of Jonson as a nondramatic poet. Some of Jonson's works are recognizably close to the secular reaches of John Donne's writing, but the speaker's psychological self-discovery through metaphor, so often the business of a Donne poem, is only occasionally Jonson's way. The contrast is especially clear between Jonson's poetic range and the realm of the meditative, intense, often all-but-private Metaphysical religious lyric. Jonson wrote very few strictly devotional poems; the ode "To Heaven" is probably the only strikingly successful work that could bear that label. In poems such as the ode to Sir Lucius Cary and Sir Henry Morison and the funeral elegies, where the afterlife is mentioned, the rela-tion of humanity as such to divinity is not the real focus of attention. The poems involve tensions mainly between diverse human levels, between more ordinary experience on one hand and, on the other, an excellence or superiority of nature that Cary, Morison, Lady Jane Pawlet, and the other exemplary figures achieve.

At most, only on the peripheries of Jonson's nondramatic verse can it be seen to ap-proximate pure emotive lyricism, or can it be cast in Metaphysical terms. Only in the late twentieth century did criticism achieve a modern reunderstanding of Jonson's achievement, involving a strongly positive evaluation of his central, typical poetic work. Jonson emerges in this criticism as decisively a neoclassic artist, the intellectual background of whose poetry is Renaissance humanism.

## TIMBER

Jonson appears as a humanistic thinker in *Timber*, and his career reflected humanistic motivations and aspirations. Fundamentally, Jonson conceived of learning, thought, and language as phases of people's active life. Humanists conceived of education as the initiation of patterns of wise and effective behavior in the student's life. Humanistic education was largely linguistic because of the traditional importance of the persuasive linguistic act, the centrality of oratory (or, for the Renaissance, the counseling of the prince and nobles) in the repertory of practical, political skills. Patterns both of moral behavior in general and of speech specifically were normally learned through imitation of the deeds and words of figures from the past; for most humanists, and very definitely for Jonson, this did not mean that modern men were supposed to become mere apes of their predecessors, but rather that, through first following models, men should exercise and organize their own capacities to a point where they could emulate and rival the ancients, becoming effective on their own terms as the ancients were on theirs.

As a nonaristocratic humanist in a stratified society, Jonson essentially followed a pattern marked out since the time of Thomas More and Thomas Elyot early in the preceding century when he attached himself to noble households and the court. Debarred by birth from directly wielding the largest measure of power in his society, he engaged in action obliquely by speaking to the powerful, counseling and offering praise to encourage the elite in the wise conduct of life and authority. This was the light in which Jonson saw his masques, not only as celebrations, but also as reminders of ideals, such as justice, which should inform the court's activity. A great many of Jonson's moralizing poems addressed to noblemen and others also clearly exhibited actual hortatory intent.

Jonson's thought includes, as one might expect, special factors that set it off somewhat from humanism as it appears in other contexts. For one thing, while Jonson was not an unbeliever, it is certainly true that his humanism does not merge clearly and continuously into moralistic, pastoral Christianity, as had that of Desiderius Erasmus a hundred years before. The ethical universe of *Timber* is one of Roman, not obtrusively Christian, virtues; if anything, Jonson looks forward to later secular rationalism. Another characteristic of Jonson's humanism is the trace of influence from Seneca and Roman Stoicism, apparent in his writing, as elsewhere in early seventeenth century English expression. A main effect of Senecan influence on Jonson seems to have been to encourage a concern with and regard for what can best be called integrity; that is, the correlation of an individual's behavior with his inner nature rather than with outward circumstance. Such concern naturally belonged with the Senecan concept of specifically linguistic behavior that *Timber* expresses—a heightened awareness of style as emerging from and conveying an image of the "inmost" self.

Jonson's neoclassic verse is the poetic cognate of his quite secular, somewhat Senecan version of humanism. Splitting the relation into separate aspects only for the sake of analysis, one can say that in form Jonson's poems are above all linguistic acts, the talk of a persona to an implied (often, a designated) human audience. In content, the poems are orderings of levels or modes of human behavior.

## EPISTLES

Jonson's "An Epistle answering to One that asked to be Sealed of the Tribe of Ben" is identified by its title in terms of the act of communication that it imitates, the letter. Relatively few of Jonson's titles actually include the word "epistle," but many of them involve, or even simply consist of, the designation of an addressee—"To Katherine Lady Aubigny," "To Sir Robert Wroth," and so on. Thus the reader is asked to be aware of many of Jonson's poems not primarily in terms of any myths they may relate or images they may invoke, but as linguistic action, the linguistic behavior of a human speaker toward a human audience.

The fiction of speaker and audience is not an inert element but has an impact on the poem's other aspects. Many qualities of style are conditioned by the character of the addressee and his relation to the speaker. In the "Epistle to Master John Selden," the speaker states that he feels free to use a curt, "obscure," at times almost telegraphic style because "I know to whom I write": He knows that Selden is not only intelligent but also at home with the speaker's ways of thinking. Generally, the grandiloquence, expansiveness, and elaborate structure of public oratory will rarely be appropriate for an epistle or other poem addressed by one person to another.

Jonson's style in "An Epistle answering to One that asked to be Sealed of the Tribe of Ben" is fairly typical of that in a number of his poems. His diction is generally colloquial; Edmund Bolton's characterization of Jonson's "vital, judicious and practicable language" (in Edmund Bolton's *Hypercritica*, c. 1618) is an excellent general description of the style. Syntactic units in Jonson's poems are by and large brief and stopped abruptly so that one jumps (or stumbles) from clause to clause rather than making easy transitions. Units are typically not paired or otherwise arranged symmetrically in relation to one another. The effect in "An Epistle answering to One that asked to be Sealed of the Tribe of Ben" is one of rather blurting, unpremeditated speech, propelled by some emotional pressure. Structurally, too, the poem seems unpremeditated, beginning with appropriate introductory comments to the would-be disciple to whom Ben is writing, then falling away into contemptuous griping about phony elements in Jonson's society, circling down into what reads like underlying anxiety about Jonson's personal situation—and coming through this human situation to a now almost heroic assertion of what it means to be Ben or one sealed of his tribe.

In other poems, the style varies, within a generally informal range. Jonson's meaning can in fact be obscure when the syntax is very broken or a great deal of meaning is concentrated in one phrase; the effect is often that of a rather impatient intelligence, not using more words than it needs to communicate meaning to its immediate addressee. In extreme cases, the reader may feel like an outsider reading a communication not meant for him (see, for example, the "Epistle to Sir Edward Sackville"). Such privacy, immured by style, sets Jonson off somewhat from Augustan neoclassic writers such as Alexander Pope, who usually engage in smoother and more public address.

Titling the poem an epistle, besides drawing attention to its character as a linguistic act, also of course associates it with a generic tradition. Seneca was the most influential classical practitioner of the moral epistle as a prose form, Horace of the form in verse. Jonson's epistles and many of his other poems evoke these authors' works in content and style, sometimes through specific allusion. Clearly related to classical tradition, yet utterly topical and personal (with its references to the politics of "Spain or France" and to Jonson's employment as a writer of masques), "An Epistle answering to One that asked to be Sealed of the Tribe of Ben" is a successful act of humanistic imitation. Overt reference to tradition reveals the moral statement of Jonson's poetry in relation to the whole body of classical moral wisdom—and implies that Jonson is not afraid of the juxtaposition.

The particular wisdom of this poem is conveyed most clearly in the description of the course of conduct Jonson has "decreed" for himself, which comes after the middle of the poem's descriptions of a social environment of indulgence of appetite, empty talk, and illusory "Motions." Jonson's resolve is to "Live to that point . . . for which I am man/ And dwell as in my Center as I can." The image is one of withdrawal from concern for meaningless external situations; it is also a picture of a life standing in relation to some firm, definite principle, as opposed to the poem's earlier images of unfounded judgments and groundless chatter.

The ideas of withdrawal and of a "Center" within the personality are clearly reminiscent of Seneca and Horace. The most characteristic aspect of the poem's meaning is that it consists of definitions not so much of the ideal principle itself as of the behavior that is or is not oriented to it. Jonson is not much concerned with describing the Center except as such, as a point from which surrounding space takes orientation. He is concerned with describing centeredness, and distinguishing it from shapeless and unfocused conditions; or, to return from geometry to humanity, with describing what it is like to operate on a firm moral basis, and distinguishing this from the "wild Anarchy" in which those outside the Tribe of Ben live.

The focus on behavior that is or is not guided, rather than on the available guiding transcendent principle, corresponds to the specifically secular emphasis of Jonson's humanism. There is an almost (though certainly not quite) agnostic quality in Jonson's almost interchangeable references to the "point," the "Center," "heaven," and "reason" as the source of his wisdom and strength. Clearly it is the exemplification of those qualities in life that interests him. Such an interest makes Jonson stand out as strikingly modern against the backdrop, for example, of the highly articulated ideal world of Edmund Spenser; it links Jonson forward to the essence of English neoclassicism, such as in Pope's ethically oriented satires and moral essays.

It should be noted that the movement toward the Center involves choice and effort: Jonson must decree it to himself, and even those who have been once sealed to the tribe of Ben have still to fear the shame of possibly stumbling in reason's sight. For good or evil, no destiny holds Jonson's human beings in place. The ideal principle is only vaguely defined; it is merely an available, not a controlling, factor.

## EPIGRAMS

Like the epistles and other more or less epistolary longer poems, Jonson's epigrams are, in form, primarily linguistic acts. They are comments "on" or "to" someone. They are self-consciously brief remarks, aiming to capture the essence of a character—sometimes, implicitly, to reduce an object to its true dimensions (many of Jonson's epigrams are satirical).

The epigrammatic mode is closely related to the epistolary in Jonson's practice and in the tradition out of which he writes. Martial, the Roman epigrammatist whom Jonson regularly imitated, conceived of his works as epistles in brief. Jonson's style has the same constituents. The broken syntax sometimes seems part of epigrammatic compression; sometimes it promotes a casualness that is part of Jonson's reduction and dismissal of a satirized personality, as in epigram 21 ("On Reformed Gamester").

The pentameter couplets in which Jonson writes not only the epigrams but also the great bulk of his neoclassic verse are derived partly from normal English practice for nonlyric poetry going back through Geoffrey Chaucer. They are also, however, influenced by a classical form, the elegiac distich—a prosodic vehicle used by, among others, Martial. Readily recognizable and essentially symmetrical, the form tends to stand as a strong balancing, controlling, ordering presence in the poetry in which it appears. Part of its potential is as a structure for concentrated, gnomic, almost proverbial utterance, easy for the reader to carry away in his mind; this potential is best realized when the couplet is a tightly closed unit, as is normally the case in Pope.

Jonson uses the form in the several ways just mentioned. Couplet order underscores orderly, almost (for Jonson) patterned, praise of a firmly centered man in epigram 128 ("To William Roe"). Some epigrams consist of single gnomic couplets (epigram 34, "Of Death"), and others are memorable for neat, closed-couplet wit (epigram 31, "On Banck the Usurer"). Both Jonson's prestige and his virtuoso skill in testing the couplet's range of uses were important in establishing it as the standard neoclassic prosodic structure. Jonson's most characteristic way of exploiting the couplet, however, was not simply to employ, but simultaneously to violate, its order, to write across the prosodic structure as if in disregard of it. Actually, more often than not, in Jonson's verse, syntactic and phrasal breaks do not come at such points within a line as to facilitate the prosodic caesura, nor are they matched with line endings or even the ends of the couplets themselves (see, for example, epigram 46, "To Sir Luckless Woo-all"). The couplet may be opposed by meaning, along with grammar: Antitheses and other logical and rhetorical structures work at cross purposes with the prosody (epigram 11, "On Some-Thing, that Walks Some-Where").

In such circumstances, the couplet does not cease to be an obtrusive form. Jonson maintains the reader's awareness of it, precisely as a structure that is not managing to control or limit the autonomy of his grammar, rhetoric, and logic. The latter, of course, are the elements of the oratorical presence in the poetry—of Jonson's voice or speech. The net effect is to enhance the sense of the independent liveliness of the speaking persona, his freedom to move about, to understand and to explain in his own way, on his own terms. Jonson's handling of the couplet implies through form a quite radical version of secular humanism, a sense of the detachment of linguistic action (and of man the linguistic actor) from any containing structure.

Many of the same kinds of content are present in the epigrams as in the epistolary writings. The epigrammatic image of William Roe's stable personality, mentioned earlier, is obviously cognate with Jonson's self-image in "An Epistle answering to One that asked to be Sealed of the Tribe of Ben," as are such portrayals as those of Sir Henry Nevil (epigram 109), William, earl of Pembroke (102), and Sir Thomas Roe (98). (The latter contains one of Jonson's more gnomic statements of the concept of the inner-directed and self-sufficient man: "Be always to thy gathered self the same/ And study conscience, more than thou would'st fame.") Satire, often a phase in the epistles, can fill entire epigrams. Something, that Walks Somewhere, Sir Voluptuous Beast (epigrams 35 and 36) and Don Surly (epigram 38) are incisively but fully realized satiric characters, clearly inhabitants of the same world as the "humour" characters Corbaccio and Epicure Mammon in Jonson's plays. Something, that Walks Somewhere, the lord who walks in "clothes brave enough," "buried in flesh, and blood," unwilling to do and afraid to dare, is one of Jonson's most powerful pictures of pointless, disorganized life—almost of disorganized protoplasm. Jonson suggested in many indirect ways that he regarded Horace as his mentor, and his work certainly has many Horatian traits, but his satire sometimes seems to belong less in the Horatian than in the harsher Juvenalian category.

## "TO PENSHURST"

"To Penshurst," one of Jonson's most famous poems, celebrates a different kind of relatedness from the internal centering discussed so far. Here human life is benign because it stands within what people have recently learned to call an ecosystem: a web of connections between elements that feed and feed off one another and through interaction perpetuate one another's well-being. At Penshurst, the Sidney family's country estate, nature freely delivers its supply into the Sidneys' hands; fish and birds "officiously" serve themselves up; but here and even more in the very similar poem "To Sir Robert Wroth," one feels that the humans could have a harvesting function, culling what sometimes seems almost like a glut of natural abundance. In any case, the human lords of Penshurst themselves stand as the basis of further relations, providing a social center to which neighbors from a whole community and guests from farther away "come in." The neighbors bring even more food, and the "provisions" of Penshurst's "liberal board" flow back to them. The system yields more than it can use, and the superflux passes to the unenvied guest and is there, ready to be offered to the king, the regulator of a larger system and community, when he happens into this particular sphere. The system, though nature flows through it, is not mindless. From Penshurst's lady's "huswifery" up through "The mysteries of manners, arms and arts" that the house's children are learning, specifically human roles and human activities have their place in this strong and ample natural and human network; in fact, the sophisticated culture of an ancestral figure of the house, Sir Philip Sidney, can be alluded to without seeming out of place here.

A close modern analog to "To Penshurst" is W. H. Auden's "In Praise of Limestone," where people also mesh with landscape in a perfect way; Auden's description of the limestone system, however, is interrupted by accounts of less pleasing, more technological adjustments of the relation. In "To Penshurst," on the other hand, contrasting satiric pictures or references have less share than in almost any of Jonson's works. Only a few lines, mainly at the poem's beginning and end, succinctly insert Jonson's usual distinctions. Penshurst is Edenic. One is left with the uneasy feeling that the poem's being so much anthologized may be bound up with its being, for Jonson, atypically untroubled.

## ODES

Jonson's ode "To the Immortal Memory and Friendship of that Noble Pair, Sir Lucius Cary and Sir H. Morison" stands near the beginning of the history of English efforts to imitate Pindar's odes. It has a complex and stately stanzaic structure. Nevertheless, many traits are carried over from Jonson's epigrammatic and epistolary style, in particular the tendency toward syntax that is at odds with prosodic divisions, of which the poem contains egregious examples: For instance, a stanza break comes in the middle of the name "Ben/ Jonson." An epic, "Heroologia," which Jonson planned, would probably have represented another extension to a new genre of his characteristic manner and ethical matter. The epic was to be in couplets and was to deal with "the Worthies of his country, roused by fame" (reports William Drummond). Like Pope, Jonson actually wrote a mock-epic rather than the serious one; Jonson's work is the "merdurinous" "On the Famous Voyage" (epigram 133).

The ode to Cary and Morison is extreme in imagery as well as in syntactic prosodic tension. It opens with a notorious image, that of the "infant of Saguntum" who retreated back to the womb before it was "half got out," appalled by the horror and devastation of wartime scenes into which it was being born. Jonson goes on to surprise conventional taste even further by suggesting that this vaginal peripety represents a "summ'd" "circle . . . of deepest lore, could we the Center find." References to circle and center of course bring along a whole train of important imagery and structure in Jonson, as well as alluding to the structure of the whole poem, with its repeated peripeteia of "Turn," "Counter-Turn," and "Stand."

The will to shock, or at least to write in uncompromisingly extraordinary ways, may indirectly express the speaker's grief and sense of loss (the poem's occasion is Morison's death). It is certainly connected with a larger demand to see life in an unconventional way, which is the poem's essential consoling strategy. (Jonson speaks of the "holy rage" with which Morison "leap'd the present age"; readers are asked to do the same thing, in the same mood.) The distinction that Jonson insists on is between visions of life as "space" and as "act." In terms of the former—sheer duration—Morison's life was indeed lamentably cut off: He lived barely into his twenties. In terms of "act," Morison's life was perfect:

> A Soldier to the last right end
> A perfect Patriot, and a noble friend,
> But most a virtuous Son.
> All Offices were done
> By him, so ample, full and round,
> In weight, in measure, number, sound
> As, though his age imperfect might appear,
> His life was of Humanity the Sphere.

This is, notably, purely secular consolation. There are later references to a "bright eternal day," but it has less to do with Christian Paradise than with a pagan heaven of commemoration, in which Morison (and Cary) may persist as an "Asterism," a constellation. The poem's contrast with "Lycidas" marks the distance between John Milton's more old-fashioned Christian humanism and Jonson's secular mind.

Jubilation, rather than lamentation, over Morison's perfection of "act" is, like most of Jonson's higher choices, not easy to maintain. The speaker's own "tongue" "falls" into mourning at one point. Cary, Morison's great friend who survives him and to whom the poem is at least in part addressed, is exhorted to "call . . . for wine/ And let thy looks with gladness shine"—and to maintain connection. Like the centered men of the epigrams and epistles, and like the Sidneys of Penshurst, Cary is to act in relation, to "shine" on earth in conjunction with Morison's now heavenly light. The function of the poem vis-à-vis Cary is to establish this relation for him, and the broken but single name of Ben Jonson bridges over the two stanzas in which the relation of the two friends is most fully discussed.

The poem includes a satirical picture. Contrasting with the vital life of act, the vacuous life of space is personified as a futile careerist, "buoy'd . . . up" in the end only by the "Cork of Title." More than by alternation of satiric and positive images, however, the poem works by a tension constant throughout: the tension between the naturalistic sense of death as an end, which is never really lost, and the other vision on which Jonson is insisting. The poem is a celebration of secular heroism. It depicts that quality in its subjects ("Nothing perfect done/ But as a Cary, or a Morison"), enacts it in its language, and demands it of its readers. The tension and energy that the poem displays are the reasons for reading Jonson's verse.

OTHER MAJOR WORKS

PLAYS: *The Case Is Altered*, pr. 1597; *The Isle of Dogs*, pr. 1597 (with Thomas Nashe; no longer extant); *Every Man in His Humour*, pr. 1598, 1605; *Hot Anger Soon Cold*, pr. 1598 (with Henry Chettle and Henry Porter; no longer extant); *Every Man Out of His Humour*, pr. 1599; *The Page of Plymouth*, pr. 1599 (with Thomas Dekker; no longer extant); *Robert the Second, King of Scots*, pr. 1599 (with Chettle and Dekker; no longer extant); *Cynthia's Revels: Or, The Fountain of Self-Love*, pr. c. 1600-1601; *Poetaster: Or, His Arraignment*, pr. 1601; *Sejanus His Fall*, pr. 1603 (commonly known as *Sejanus*); *Eastward Ho!*, pr., pb. 1605 (with George Chapman and John Marston); *Volpone: Or, The Fox*, pr. 1605; *Epicœne: Or, The Silent Woman*, pr. 1609; *The Alchemist*, pr. 1610; *Catiline His Conspiracy*, pr., pb. 1611 (commonly known as *Catiline*); *Bartholomew Fair*, pr. 1614; *The Devil Is an Ass*, pr. 1616; *The Staple of News*, pr. 1626; *The New Inn: Or, The Light Heart*, pr. 1629; *The Magnetic Lady: Or, Humours Reconciled*, pr. 1632; *A Tale of a Tub*, pr. 1633; *The Sad Shepherd: Or, A Tale of Robin Hood*, pb. 1640 (fragment).

NONFICTION: *The English Grammar*, 1640; *Timber: Or, Discoveries Made upon Men and Matter*, 1641.

TRANSLATION: *Horace His Art of Poetry*, 1640 (of Horace's *Ars poetica*).

MISCELLANEOUS: *The Magnificent Entertainment Given to King James*, 1603 (with Dekker and Thomas Middleton); *The Workes of Benjamin Jonson*, 1616; *The Works of Benjamin Jonson*, 1640-1641 (2 volumes).

BIBLIOGRAPHY

Bloom, Harold, ed. *Ben Jonson*. Broomall, Pa.: Chelsea House, 2001. A collection of essays providing literary criticism of Jonson's major works.

Booth, Stephen. *Precious Nonsense: The Gettysburg Address, Ben Jonson's "Epitaphs on His Children," and "Twelfth Night."* Berkeley: University of California Press, 1998. Using three disparate texts, Booth shows how poetics can triumph over logic and enrich the reading experience. His presentation is playful yet analytical and his unique reading of "Epitaphs on His Children" is a valuable addition to critical thought on Jonson's work.

Cousins, A. D., and Alison V. Scott, eds. *Ben Jonson and the Politics of Genre.* New York: Cambridge University Press, 2009. Contains essays on Jonson and his writings, including one on his country house poems and another on epistles.

Dutton, Richard, ed. *Ben Jonson.* Longman Critical Readers. Harlow, England: Pearson Education, 2000. This study presents critical analysis and interpretation of Jonson's literary works. Bibliography and index.

Harp, Richard, and Stanley Stewart, eds. *The Cambridge Companion to Ben Jonson.* New York: Cambridge University Press, 2000. A companion to the writer and his works.

Loxley, James. *The Complete Critical Guide to Ben Jonson.* New York: Routledge, 2002. A handbook designed to provide readers with critical analysis of Jonson's works. Bibliography and index.

Miles, Rosalind. *Ben Jonson: His Life and Work.* London: Routledge & Kegan Paul, 1986. Miles's volume is a fine standard biography-study, especially for the literary background and Jonson's position in Jacobean courtly society. The scholarly apparatus is thorough: a chronology, an index, a select but extensive bibliography, notes, and an appendix.

Riggs, David. *Ben Jonson: A Life.* Cambridge, Mass.: Harvard University Press, 1989. This is a full-scale biography rather than a literary biography; the works illuminate the life rather than vice versa. The illumination is brilliant. Riggs reviews all the facts and assembles them in memorable order. He includes all the standard scholarly attachments, but the book deserves to be read simply for the revelations it contains for Jonson and his age, most of which are illustrated.

Summers, Claude J., and Ted-Larry Pebworth. *Ben Jonson.* Rev. ed. New York: Twayne, 1999. An introductory overview of Jonson's life and work. Includes bibliographical references and index.

Watson, Robert N., ed. *Critical Essays on Ben Jonson.* New York: G. K. Hall, 1997. A collection of previously published and new essays edited by an established authority on the life and work of Jonson. Includes an introduction that provides an overview of criticism of Jonson's work over his career. In addition, some previously unpublished interviews, letters, and manuscript fragments are included.

*John F. McDiarmid*

# CHRISTOPHER MARLOWE

**Born:** Canterbury, England; February 6, 1564
**Died:** Deptford, England; May 30, 1593

PRINCIPAL POETRY
*Hero and Leander*, 1598 (completed by George Chapman)
"The Passionate Shepherd to His Love," 1599 (in *The Passionate Pilgrim*)

### OTHER LITERARY FORMS

Christopher Marlowe's literary reputation rests primarily on the following plays: *Tamburlaine the Great, Part I* (pr. c. 1587); *Tamburlaine the Great, Part II* (pr. 1587); *The Jew of Malta* (pr. c. 1589); *Edward II* (pr. c. 1592); *Doctor Faustus* (pr. c. 1588). Two unfinished plays, *Dido, Queen of Carthage* (pr. c. 1586-1587; with Thomas Nashe and the fragmentary *The Massacre at Paris* (pr. 1593), round out his dramatic canon. He produced two important translations: *Elegies* (1595-1600), which treats three books of Ovid's *Amores* (c. 20 B.C.E.; English translation, c. 1597), and *Pharsalia* (1600), which treats Lucan's first book *Bellum civile* (60-65 C.E.; *Pharsalia*, 1614), and was first entered in the Stationers' Register as *Lucan's First Book of the Famous Civil War Betwixt Pompey and Caesar* (1600).

### ACHIEVEMENTS

Christopher Marlowe's plays established him as the foremost of the University Wits, a loosely knit group of young men, by reputation generally wild and rakish, that included Thomas Lodge, Thomas Nashe, George Peele, and the older, perhaps less unruly, John Lyly. Their work largely established the nature of the English drama that would reach its apogee in the work of William Shakespeare. Marlowe shares with Thomas Kyd the honor of developing the English conception of tragedy. Marlowe also developed the rather clumsy blank verse of the day into the flexible vehicle of his "mighty line," using it to flesh out his tragic characters as they fell from greatness. He shares the honor of reshaping the dramatically crude chronicle play into the mature and subtle history play. His *Edward II* bears comparison with William Shakespeare's *Richard III* (pr. c. 1592-1593) and anticipates Shakespeare's "Henriad."

Although Marlowe attracted much casual comment among his contemporaries, serious criticism of his work was rare until the nineteenth century. After the Puritan diatribe of T. Beard in *The Theatre of Gods* [sic] *Judgements* (1597) and W. Vaughn's consideration in *The Golden Grove* (1600), no serious criticism appeared until J. Broughton's article, "Of the Dramatic Writers Who Preceded Shakespeare" (1830). Beginning in 1883, with C. H. Herford and A. Wagner's article "The Sources of Tamburlaine,"

Marlovian criticism grew at an increasing rate. Two critics initiated the very extensive body of modern scholarship that began in the first decade of the twentieth century: Frederick S. Boas with his edition and commentary of the works (1901), and Brooke with an article, "On the Date of the First Edition of Marlowe's *Edward II*," in *Modern Language Notes* (1909). Boas's contribution culminated in the monumental *Marlowe: A Biographical and Critical Study* (1940). Although both writers concentrated on Marlowe's drama, they also began a serious examination of his poetry. From 1910 onward, the volume of criticism has been almost overwhelming.

Marlowe's nondramatic poetry has attracted an impressive, even a disproportionate, amount of critical attention, considering that it consists simply of one lyric poem, known in several versions, and one narrative poem, generally considered to be an 817-line fragment of a longer projected work. Had Marlowe's dramatic work been only middling, it is unlikely that his poetry, excellent as it is, would have been so widely noticed and esteemed. C. F. Tucker Brooke observes in his *The Works of Christopher Marlowe* (1964) that *Hero and Leander*, Marlowe's narrative fragment, was enormously popular with the Elizabethans and that the literature of the period is rich in allusions to the poem. His lyric poem "The Passionate Shepherd to His Love" also enjoyed an early and continuing popularity from its first appearance in *The Passionate Pilgrim* (1599) and *England's Helicon* (1600), two widely circulated collections of English verse. A version of the poem is included in Isaac Walton's *The Compleat Angler: Or, The Contemplative Man's Recreation* (1653).

While most of the criticism bears on concerns other than the poetry, criticism dealing with *Hero and Leander* and, to a lesser degree, with "The Passionate Shepherd to His Love," is more than respectable in quantity. Interest covers many aspects of the poems: the rhetorical and prosodic forms, with their implications for aesthetics and comedic intent; bibliographic matters dealing with publication history, textual variations, and their implications for questions about authorship; mythological bases and sources; possible autobiographical elements; and moral and ethical values, often centering on sexuality and implied homosexuality. The foregoing list is not exhaustive, and any given study is likely to include several of the aspects while using one of them to illuminate one or more of the others. Marlovian criticism boasts the names of many outstanding modern scholars; a sampling would include J. A. Symonds, T. S. Eliot, U. M. Ellis-Fermor, F. S. Tannenbaum, Mario Praz, J. Q. Adams, M. C. Bradbrook, J. Bakeless, L. Kirschbaum, W. W. Greg, Helen Gardner, F. P. Wilson, C. S. Lewis, and Louis L. Martz.

### BIOGRAPHY

Biographical interest in Christopher Marlowe has been keen and perhaps too often controversial. Public records are relatively numerous, considering that he was a sixteenth century Englishman who died before he was thirty years old. His baptism, progress through school and university to the M.A. degree, and the details of his death are documented. Contemporary references to Marlowe and his works are likewise plenti-ful. The variety of interpretation placed upon this evidence, however, is truly astonish-ing. What is quite clear is that Marlowe was born into a relatively affluent family of tradesmen in Canterbury. His father was in the shoe trade, possibly as a shoemaker, pos-sibly as an employer of shoemakers. In any case, in January, 1579, Marlowe entered King's School, an institution operating just beyond Canterbury Cathedral. In Decem-ber, 1580, he enrolled in Corpus Christi College, Cambridge, on a scholarship. In 1584, Marlowe graduated with a B.A. degree but continued his studies, still on scholarship. Marlowe's attendance was, at least occasionally, irregular, and he was engaged from time to time upon some sort of secret work for the government, the nature of which re-mains unclear despite much speculation. It involved travel on the Continent; it may have involved spying at home or abroad. When, in 1587, the university determined to with-hold the M.A. degree from Marlowe, the Privy Council intervened in the name of the queen and insisted that Marlowe's services to the Crown were sufficient grounds for granting the degree.

Upon leaving Cambridge, Marlowe immediately immersed himself in the political and intellectual life of London, on one hand, in the aristocratic circles of Sir Walter Ra-leigh and Sir Thomas Walsingham, and on the other, in the bohemianism of the London actors and playwrights. Both groups apparently contributed to the underworld contacts that tavern life and secret government service would suggest. As early as 1588, Robert Greene attacked Marlowe indirectly as an atheist, a charge that reappeared from time to time. In 1589, Marlowe was involved in a brawl with a certain William Bradley that ended with Bradley's death at the hands of one Thomas Watson. Both Marlowe and Watson were jailed temporarily because of the affair, which was finally adjudged to have been a case of self-defense.

By 1592, both *Tamburlaine the Great, Parts I* and *II*, and *Doctor Faustus* had been produced and published. Meanwhile, Marlowe's reputation as a dangerous fellow had grown. In that year, he had been bound over to keep the peace by a brace of frightened constables, and he appears to have been one of the atheist playwrights attacked in Rob-ert Greene's *Groatsworth of Wit Bought with a Million of Repentance* (1592). On May 12, 1593, Marlowe's fellow University Wit, friend, and former roommate, Thomas Kyd, during or shortly after torture, wrote a letter to the Lord Keeper, Sir John Pucker-ing, accusing Marlowe of ownership of papers, found in Kyd's room, which denied the divinity of Christ.

Whether or not Kyd's confession influenced them, the Privy Council issued a war-rant for Marlowe's arrest and ordered him to report to them daily. On May 30, Marlowe spent the day at the Bull Inn in Deptford in the disreputable company of the double-agent Robert Poley and two other possible spies, Nicholas Skeres and Ingram Frizer. The coroner's report indicates that they had walked in the garden during the day and then had eaten supper together. Following a quarrel about the bill, Marlowe is said to have taken Frizer's dagger from his belt and beaten him about the head with it. Frizer managed to grasp Marlowe's arm, reverse the blade, and force it into Marlowe's head. The jury found that the stab wound was the cause of death and declared the death to be instant and accidental.

On the whole, the jury was composed of competent men, the sequence of events plausible, and the jury's conclusion sound. Short, then, of the discovery of more telling evidence, all theories of a plot of premeditated murder against Marlowe must be taken as only more or less interesting conjectures. Perhaps it was inevitable that the facts about a famous man whose life was both colorful and secretive would excite equally colorful speculation about the facts that lie beyond the official records and public accusations.

ANALYSIS

Christopher Marlowe's lyric poem "The Passionate Shepherd to His Love" is known in several versions of varying length. C. F. Tucker Brooke's 1962 reprint of his 1910 edition of Marlowe's works cites the six-stanza version of *England's Helicon*, with variant readings provided in the notes. Frederick S. Boas, in *Christopher Marlowe: A Biographical and Critical Study*, puts the case for holding that only the first four stanzas are certainly Marlowe's. Fredson Bowers, in the second volume of his monumental *The Complete Works of Christopher Marlowe* (1973), offers a "reconstructed" four-stanza version of the original poem printed alongside the six-stanza version of *England's Helicon*. All versions provide a delightful and innocuous exercise in the pastoral tradition of happy innocent shepherds sporting in a bucolic setting. Simply put, a lover outlines for his sweetheart the beauties and pleasures she can expect if she will live with him and be his love. Nature and the rejoicing shepherds will provide the pair with entertainment, clothing, shelter, and all things fitting to an amorous paradise.

## "THE PASSIONATE SHEPHERD TO HIS LOVE"

The stanza is a simple quatrain rhyming in couplets. While it is a fine example of Elizabethan taste for decoration and is very pleasing to the ear, it presents nothing especially clever in its prosody. A few of the couplets are fresh enough in their rhymes, such as "falls/ madrigalls," "kirtle/ Mirtle," and "buds/ studs," but the rest are common enough. The alliteration falls short of being heavy-handed, and it achieves neither clearness nor subtlety. The poem's appeal, then, seems to lie mostly in its evocation of young love playing against an idealized background, its simple language and prosody forming part of its overt innocence.

Sir Walter Ralegh's famous response, "The Nymph's Reply to the Shepherd," also published in *England's Helicon*, sets all the cynicism associated with the carpe diem poetry of a John Donne or an Andrew Marvell against Marlowe's pose of innocence. Ralegh's shepherdess argues that the world and love are too old to allow her to be seduced by "pretty pleasures." She speaks of aging, of the cold of winter, of the sweet appearance that hides bitterness and approaching death. She scorns his offers of beauty, shelter, and love as things that decay and rot. Were youth, love, and joy eternal, and old age well provided for, then she might love. Both poems are set-pieces and imply nothing except that both poets were makers working within established traditions. The innocence of Marlowe's poem argues nothing about his own personality and much about his ability to project himself imaginatively into a character and a situation. In doing this, he produced a gem, and that is enough.

## HERO AND LEANDER

In contrast to the simple, single-leveled "The Passionate Shepherd to His Love," *Hero and Leander* is a more complex, more sophisticated poem. Whatever ultimate plans Marlowe may have had for the completed poem, the two completed sestiads are in the comic mode as they portray the fumbling yearnings and actions of two adolescents faced with passions with which they are totally unprepared to deal. The story of young love, then, is constantly undercut with one sort of comedy or another.

Perhaps the easiest clues to Marlowe's comic intention lie in his choice of epic style and heroic couplets, both of which lend themselves to witty parody because they are traditionally used seriously. The epic tradition allows Marlowe to pay his lovers elaborate, and obviously exaggerated, compliments through the use of epic similes and through comparison with the classical tales of gods and heroes. The heroic couplet allows him to emphasize the fun with variations of the meter and with comic rhymes, generally feminine ones.

The retelling of the famous tale of two ill-fated lovers—whose trysts require Leander to swim across the Hellespont to visit Hero in her tower—begins soberly enough, as a mock-epic should. By the ninth line, however, Marlowe begins a description of Hero's garments that is wildly ornate and exaggerated in style. Her dress, for example, is lined with purple and studded with golden stars; the sleeves are green and are embroidered with a scene of Venus, naked, viewing the slain and bloody Adonis; her veil reaches to the ground and is so realistically decorated with artificial vegetation that men mistake her breath for the odor of flowers and bees search it for honey. The picture, thus far, could pass as an example of Elizabethan taste for the gaudy, and becomes clearly comic only in retrospect.

The twenty-fifth line, however, presents a figure that sets the anticlimactic tone informing the whole piece. Hero's necklace is described as a chain of ordinary pebbles that the beauty of her neck makes shine as diamonds. Later on, her naked beauty causes an artificial dawn in her bedchamber, to Leander's delight. The improbabilities are piled on thickly: Her hands are not subject to burning because sun and wind alike delight in them as playthings; sparrows perch in her shell buskins; Cupid could not help mistaking her for his mother, Venus; and Nature itself resented having been plundered of its rightful beauty by this slip of a girl. Marlowe points up the comedy of the Cupid passage with a feminine rhyme: "But this is true, so like was one the other,/ As he imagined Hero was his mother." He signs the comic intent of the Nature passage with an outrageous conceit and compliment: "Therefore in sign of her treasure suffered wrack,/ Since Hero's time, hath half the world been black." Throughout the two sestiads, similar tactics are employed, including much additional use of comic feminine rhyme (Morpheus/ visit us, cunning/ running, furious/ Prometheus, kist him/ mist him, and yv'ry skin/ lively in) and mocking versions of the epic simile.

The compelling argument for Marlowe's comedic intent, however, lies in this treatment of situation, theme, and character. Boas reflects a view commonly held by critics at the turn of the twentieth century when he argues that Marlowe's purpose was to tell the stories of the lovers, working in as much mythology as possible. He does not see the comedy as anything but incidental, and congratulates Marlowe on rescuing the grossness of Ovidian comedy with "delicate humor." Brooke, also an early twentieth century Marlovian, regards *Hero and Leander* as an essentially original work to be judged independently of George Chapman's continuation of the poem. Brooke treats the poem as an extended example of masterful heroic verse with no hint that such verse could be used here as an adjunct of comedy.

The French critic Michel Poirier comes nearer to Marlowe's comedic intent in his biography *Christopher Marlowe* (1951, 1968), in which he describes the poem as belonging to the genre of Renaissance hedonism. He sees the poem as a "hymn to sensuality, tastefully done." He too sees the poem as erotic, but argues that it avoids equally ancient crudeness and the rough humor of the medieval fabliaux. Philip Henderson's essay "Christopher Marlowe" (1966) points up the by-then-dominant view by observing that *Hero and Leander* is not only a parody but also a very mischievous one, written by a poet who is so disengaged from his poem that he is able to treat it wittily and with a certain cynicism. John Ingram in *Christopher Marlowe and His Associates* (1970) harks back to an earlier view in claiming that no other Elizabethan poem equals it for purity and beauty. He notes nothing of the ironist at work.

A. L. Rowse, an ingenious if not always convincing literary historian and critic, sees *Hero and Leander*, in *Christopher Marlowe: His Life and Work* (1964), as a sort of rival piece to Shakespeare's *Venus and Adonis*. He goes so far as to suggest that Marlowe and Shakespeare read their poems to each other in a sort of combat of wit. However that may be, Rowse is probably right in seeing the poem as being carefully controlled, in contrast to the view, well-represented by Boas, that the poem is structurally a mere jumble. Rowse sees the poem as organically unified by the careful playing off of this mode and that technique against a variety of others.

In his essay "Marlowe's Humor," included in his most useful book *Marlowe: A Collection of Critical Essays* (1964), Clifford Leech rejects earlier criticism holding that the comic passages were the work of other writers and pits C. S. Lewis's denial, in his *Eng-*

*lish Literature in the Sixteenth Century* (1954), that *Hero and Leander* contains any humor at all against T. S. Eliot's assertion in *Selected Essays* (1950-1972) that Marlowe was at his best when writing "savage comic humor." Leech's position is that the poem is dominated by a humor at once gentle and delighting, not to say sly. He supports his position with a shrewd analysis of the subtle effects of tone and verse form. Louis L. Martz, in *Hero and Leander: A Fascimile of the First Edition, London, 1598* (1972), also sees Marlowe's tone as comic and as conveyed through the couplet, and he characterizes the poem as being carefully structured as a triptych, with the Mercury fable, usually viewed as a digression, as the central picture, flanked by tales depicting mortal love. He sees Marlowe's digression as intentional and Ovidian. Martz, as a whole, comes down firmly on the side of those who see the poem as a thoroughgoing comedy.

Philip Henderson keeps to the comedic interpretation but also brings boldly to the fore a factor in the story long recognized but generally treated as minor, incidental, and otherwise unaccountable—that of homosexuality as a theme. In *Christopher Marlowe* (second edition, 1974), he argues that the passage describing Leander's body is "rapturous," but that the element is reduced to farce by Leander's encounter with Neptune as he swims the Hellespont. At the same time, Henderson firmly denies that Rowse's description of Marlowe as clearly homosexual has any basis in fact. On balance, Henderson concludes that the critics' urge to find irony and sensational undertones obscures recognition of the beauty properly belonging to *Hero and Leander*, and he notes further that the insistence upon seeing comedy throughout Marlowe's work is a modern one. William Keach, tracing Marlowe's intentions in "Marlowe's Hero as 'Venus' Nun" (*English Literary Renaissance*, Winter, 1972), argues that Marlowe is largely indebted for the "subtleties and complexities" of his poem to hints from his fifth century Greek source, Musaeus. Keach sees both poets as ironists and argues that Hero's activities as a priestess of love who is puritanically virginal are essentially silly.

John Mills, in his study "The Courtship Ritual of Hero and Leander" (*English Literary Renaissance*, Winter, 1972), sees Hero at the opening as a compound of innocence and sexuality, with all the confusions that such a compound can make, both in her own mind and in those of men who observe her. Mills's interest lies, however, not so much in this condition itself as in the web of classical elements and allusions in which it is contained. He argues, in effect, that the poem depends upon an overblown, stereotypical, and mannered attitude toward romantic sex that he compares to Vladimir Nabokov's theory of "poshlust." Mills concludes that Marlowe's "poshlustian comedy" arises out of the actions being played out in a physical and material world of sexuality in such terms that Hero and Leander, and innocent readers, are persuaded that their activities are really spiritual. In another essay, "Sexual Discovery and Renaissance Morality in Marlowe's 'Hero and Leander'" (*Studies in English Literature, 1500-1900*, XII, 1972), published immediately after that of Mills, William P. Walsh argues that Marlowe is ironic in basing the story on love at first sight and making his characters slaves of their irrational passion. His notion is that the lovers themselves, not sexuality, are the objects of humorous comment with which they are not entirely out of sympathy. His development of the theme is detailed and astute, and he points out, in discussing the invented myth of the Destinies' love affair with Mercury, the generally overlooked argument that Marlowe makes for reproduction as the true object of sex, as against pleasure for its own sake. Walsh suggests that the inability of Hero and Leander to see beyond their dream of a sexual paradise at once positions them for the eventual tragic ending traditional to their story, yet keeps them reduced to comic stature in Marlowe's portion of the poem.

In writing *Hero and Leander*, then, Marlowe displayed ingenuity and erudition by telling an ironically comic tale of the mutual wooing and seduction of a pair of inexperienced but lusty young lovers. The telling is intricately and objectively organized and describes a rite of passage that is neither sentimentalized nor especially brutalized. The result is a highly skilled tour de force in the tradition of the Elizabethan maker, cynical enough, perhaps, but confessional or autobiographical only tangentially, if at all. Coupled with "The Passionate Shepherd to His Love," *Hero and Leander* establishes Marlowe's claim to a high place in the select company of those British poets who have produced a slender but superior body of lyric poetry.

OTHER MAJOR WORKS

PLAYS: *Dido, Queen of Carthage*, pr. c. 1586-1587 (with Thomas Nashe); *Tamburlaine the Great, Part I*, pr. c. 1587 (commonly known as *Tamburlaine*); *Tamburlaine the Great, Part II*, pr. 1587; *Doctor Faustus*, pr. c. 1588; *The Jew of Malta*, pr. c. 1589; *Edward II*, pr. c. 1592; *The Massacre at Paris*, pr. 1593; *Complete Plays*, pb. 1963.

TRANSLATIONS: *Elegies*, 1595-1600 (of Ovid's *Amores*); *Pharsalia*, 1600 (of Lucan's *Bellum civile*).

MISCELLANEOUS: *The Works of Christopher Marlowe*, 1910, 1962 (C. F. Tucker Brooke, editor); *The Works and Life of Christopher Marlowe*, 1930-1933, 1966 (R. H. Case, editor); *The Complete Works of Christopher Marlowe*, 1973 (Fredson Bowers, editor).

BIBLIOGRAPHY

Bloom, Harold, ed. *Christopher Marlowe: Modern Critical Views*. New York: Chelsea House, 1986. This volume consists of thirteen selections, mainly excerpts of previously published books that are landmarks in Marlowe criticism. The bibliography at the end of the volume includes most of the major critical studies of Marlowe.

Blumenfeld, Samuel L. *The Marlowe-Shakespeare Connection: A New Study of the Authorship Question*. Jefferson, N.C.: McFarland, 2008. Blumenfeld argues that Marlowe faked his death and continued writing plays and poetry as William Shakespeare.

Downie, J. A., and J. T. Parnell. *Constructing Christopher Marlowe*. New York: Cambridge University Press, 2000. This scholarly study contains essays on Marlowe's life and works. Includes bibliography and index.

Grantley, Darryll, and Peter Roberts, eds. *Christopher Marlowe and English Renaissance Culture.* Aldershot, Hants, England: Ashgate, 1999. This collection of essays covers topics such as Marlowe and atheism and the staging of his plays and provides in-depth analysis of most of his plays. Bibliography and index.

Hopkins, Lisa. *Christopher Marlowe: A Literary Life.* New York: Palgrave, 2000. A study of Marlowe's career and what is known of his life. Hopkins focuses on Marlowe's skepticism toward colonialism, family, and religion.

Nicholl, Charles. *The Reckoning: The Murder of Christopher Marlowe.* New York: Harcourt Brace, 1992. Nicholl examines the Marlowe's life, as well as the circumstances of his death.

Riggs, David. *The World of Christopher Marlowe.* New York: Henry Holt, 2005. This rich study of the poet/playwright, including both biography and analysis of Marlowe's works, is an excellent source of information about Marlowe's historical and social context.

Simkin, Stevie. *A Preface to Marlowe.* New York: Longman, 2000. Provides comprehensive and full analysis of all Marlowe's dramatic and non-dramatic works, brings the texts to life, and emphasizes the performance aspects of the texts. A controversial and challenging reading that reopens debates about Marlowe's status as a radical figure and as a subversive playwright. Bibliographical references and index.

Trow, M. J., and Taliesin Trow. *Who Killed Kit Marlowe? A Contract to Murder in Elizabethan England.* Stroud, England: Sutton, 2001. This discussion focuses on Marlowe's mystery-shrouded death, providing both the evidence that is available and the many theories that exist. Bibliography and index.

*B. G. Knepper*

# ANDREW MARVELL

**Born:** Winestead-in-Holderness, Yorkshire, England; March 31, 1621
**Died:** London, England; August 16, 1678

PRINCIPAL POETRY

*The First Anniversary of the Government Under His Highness the Lord Protector*,
   1655
*Miscellaneous Poems*, 1681
*Complete Poetry*, 1968

OTHER LITERARY FORMS

In 1672, with the publication of *The Rehearsal Transpros'd*, Andrew Marvell
(MAWR-vuhl) became a pamphleteer. In this animadversion on the works of Samuel
Parker, Marvell vigorously supported King Charles II's stand in favor of religious toleration. No other work by Marvell was so widely received in his lifetime as this urbane,
witty, slashing satire. According to Marvell's contemporary Gilbert Burnet, "From the
King down to the tradesman, his books were read with great pleasure." Parker's coun-
terattack quickly engendered Marvell's second pamphlet, *The Rehearsal Transpros'd:
The Second Part* (1673). *Mr. Smirke: Or, The Divine in Mode* (1676), was Marvell's defense of Herbert Croft, the bishop of Hereford, against Francis Turner's pamphlet attack. His next pamphlet, *An Account of the Growth of Popery and Arbitrary Government in England* (1677), resulted in the government's offering a reward for the identity
of the author. *Remarks upon a Late Disingenuous Discourse* was published posthumously in 1678. Some three hundred letters are also extant and available in Margoliouth's edition, as well as in those of Captain Edward Thompson and Alexander B.
Grosart.

ACHIEVEMENTS

In his own century and for some time afterward, Andrew Marvell's reputation rested
much more on his prose pamphlets, a few political poems, and his political activities,
than on his achievement as a lyric poet. Most of his poems, including all the lyrics, remained unpublished until the posthumous edition of 1681. By then the Metaphysical
mode was no longer in fashion, and the book of Marvell's poems seems to have been desired more for its excellent engraved portrait of the politician and pamphleteer than for
anything else. Appreciation of Marvell's poetry was increased by Charles Lamb's essay
of 1818, but it remained sporadic until after the publication of T. S. Eliot's essay on the
occasion of the tercentenary of Marvell's birth in 1921. Except for a quantity of imitations of his verse satires, some of which were attributed to him, his influence on other

*Andrew Marvell*
(Library of Congress)

poets was slight. By far his widest poetic audience is in the present day. He has had a modest influence on some twentieth century writers, such as Marianne Moore.

Today Marvell is recognized as a lyric poet of the first rank, although how uniformly excellent his poems are, individually or collectively, remains a subject of debate. Certainly the quality is somewhat irregular. Nevertheless, with a rather small corpus he has been awarded at least three apt distinctions. That three-quarters of his work is in eight-syllable form and much of it is brilliant has earned him the title master of the octosyllabic. A few fine poems on a difficult subject have caused him to be called Cromwell's poet. Finally, while his work includes civic, pastoral, and georgic material, he is, more than any other poet in English, the garden poet.

### BIOGRAPHY

Andrew Marvell was born on March 31, 1621, at Winestead-in-Holderness, Yorkshire. He was the fourth child and only surviving son of Andrew Marvell, Sr., a clergyman. In late 1624, the Reverend Marvell became lecturer at Holy Trinity Church in Hull, to which the family moved. The poet grew up there and was for the rest of his life associated with Hull, representing the city in Parliament for the last eighteen years of his life. On December 14, 1633, the young Marvell entered Trinity College, Cambridge. In 1637, Marvell was converted by Jesuits and ran away to London, whence his father retrieved him and returned him to Cambridge. Sometime in 1641, Marvell left Cambridge, having received the B.A. degree but without completing the requirements for the M.A.

Marvell may then have spent some time working in the commercial house of his brother-in-law, Edmund Popple, in Hull. His activities during the turbulent 1640's are not well recorded, but it is known that during that period he spent four years abroad, learning Dutch, French, Italian, and Spanish. He studied the gentlemanly art of fencing in Spain, and in Rome, he paid a visit to the impoverished English Catholic priest, Flecknoe, whom John Dryden would make the butt of a satiric poem. Engaged in this Grand Tour, Marvell seems to have avoided any direct part in the English Civil War. Marvell returned to England in the late 1640's, publishing a congratulatory poem (probably written in 1647) for a volume of Richard Lovelace's verse in 1649, and contributing one poem to a volume lamenting the death of the young Lord Hastings in June, 1649. From 1650 to 1652, Marvell was tutor to Mary Fairfax, daughter of the parliamentary general, Lord Fairfax, whose resignation in June, 1650, left Cromwell dominant. That same month, Marvell must have composed "An Horatian Ode upon Cromwell's Return from Ireland," in which he applauds Cromwell's activities up to that point and anticipates his success in the coming campaign against the Scots. Because the poem also shows great sympathy and regard for the late King Charles in the brief passage dealing with his execution, a good deal of critical attention has been paid to the question of whether Marvell's praise of Cromwell is genuine, ironic, or intended to create an image toward which it might be hoped that the real Cromwell would gravitate. Marvell is elsewhere so prone to see more than one side of a question that it does not really seem remarkable that he may have recognized good qualities in both King Charles and Cromwell. "Upon Appleton House" and "Upon the Hill and Grove at Bill-borow," which describe two Fairfax estates, must be presumed to date from Marvell's days with the Fairfaxes; it is likely that a number of the lyrics, including "The Garden" and the Mower poems, also date from that period.

In 1653, Marvell left the Fairfax employ and sought, through John Milton, a position with the Commonwealth government. When his association with Milton began is uncertain, but it is known that they became and remained very close friends. In September, 1657, Marvell received a government post, becoming Latin Secretary, sharing (with Milton) responsibility for correspondence with foreign governments. He retained this post until the dissolution of the Commonwealth government. During the Cromwell years, Marvell wrote a number of poems in praise of Cromwell. These include "An Horatian Ode upon Cromwell's Return from Ireland," *The First Anniversary of the Government Under His Highness the Lord Protector*, 1655, and "A Poem upon the Death of His Late Highness the Lord Protector." Although Cromwell and his son, and perhaps close associates, presumably saw these poems, they seem not to have been widely circulated. Only *The First Anniversary of the Government Under His Highness the Lord Protector* was printed, and that anonymously.

In 1659, the Corporation of Hull chose Marvell to represent them in Parliament. He remained a member for the rest of his life, being twice reelected. He seems to have made the transition to the Restoration of Charles II with relative ease, and from his position in Parliament joined other friends of Milton in protecting that poet from serious harm under the new regime. During this period Marvell's satiric talents blossomed. His satiric verse included three "advice to a painter" poems parodying a poem by Edmund Waller and lampooning various influential persons and their policies. More important by far were his prose pamphlets, especially the first, *The Rehearsal Transpros'd*. This was an attack on the pamphlets of Samuel Parker, a rising Church of England divine, who strongly supported conformity and had tangled in print with the nonconformists, especially John Owen. The question of toleration versus conformity was a very important one in the politics of 1672, with Charles II, for his own reasons, trying to put through a policy of toleration. Marvell's powerful and witty book quickly went through multiple editions. Parker strongly counterattacked with a new pamphlet, causing Marvell (despite an anonymous threat to cut his throat) to reply with *The Rehearsal Transpros'd: The Second Part*. Parker did not reply further. Marvell's last three pamphlets are of considerably less importance. *Mr. Smirke: Or, The Divine in Mode* used with less success and for a less crucial cause the techniques of the two parts of *The Rehearsal Transpros'd*. Next, *An Account of the Growth of Popery and Arbitrary Government in England* evoked the government offer of a reward for the name of the author, who died before action was taken on an informer's report. The title of this work precisely indicates the concerns that Marvell voiced in it, suggesting that leading government figures were involved in a plot to make England Catholic again. By 1674, Marvell himself was involved in clandestine activities as a member of a pro-Dutch "fifth column," apparently operating under the name of "Mr. Thomas" and making secret trips to Holland. Marvell's death, on August 16, 1678, was the result of his physician's treatment of a fever and not, as was suspected by some, a political murder. His last pamphlet, *Remarks upon a Late Disingenuous Discourse* is his least readable work and is of little importance.

### ANALYSIS

Andrew Marvell is firmly established today in the ranks of the Metaphysical poets, and there is no question that much of his work clearly displays the qualities appropriate to such a position. He reveals a kinship with the Metaphysical poets through his ingenious use of extended logic, even when dealing with emotions; his yoking of very dissimilar things, of the mundane (even profane) with the sublime, of large with small and far with near; and his analytic quality. His use of puns, often woven into intricate groups, may be added to the list. Like John Donne and the other Metaphysical poets, Marvell shapes his rhythm with careful attention to his meaning. Marvell's admiration for Donne shows not only in having written some strongly Donne-like poetry ("On a Drop of Dew," "Young Love," and parts of "Upon Appleton House," for example), but also in his gratuitously full use of one of Donne's poems in a pamphlet written late in Marvell's life. It might be added that Marvell's prose works, especially his most successful, show the same Metaphysical qualities.

Although Donne's best-known poetry (as well as Marvell's most Donne-like work) resembles puzzles from which attentive reading gradually extracts greater clarity, a similar approach to Marvell's best and most "Marvellian" passages (for example, "a green thought in a green Shade") causes them not to become more clear so much as more dazzling. Marvell has been called "many-sided," "ambiguous," "amphibian," "elusive," and "inconclusive." He is. He has been said to have a vision that is "complex," "double," or "ironic." He does.

Marvell's work often shows a remarkable ability to make opposites interdependent, to create a *concordia discors*. Such is the relationship of Cromwell and King Charles in "An Horatian Ode upon Cromwell's Return from Ireland," and of retirement and action in "Upon Appleton House" and "The Garden." Sometimes, no less remarkably, he achieves moments of what can only be called "fusion," as in the "annihilation of all that's made" in "The Garden," or in the last few lines of "To His Coy Mistress." He will at times surprisingly mix levity and gravity, as in "To His Coy Mistress" and parts of "Upon Appleton House." His use of qualifiers is unusual ("none, *I think*," or "*If* these the times").

Marvell employed decasyllabics for his last two Cromwell poems, inventing a stanza combining lines of eight and six syllables for the first. Three fourths of his work was in octosyllabics, however, and he has been rightly called the "master of the octosyllabic."

### "TO HIS COY MISTRESS"

Certainly the most widely anthologized and best known of Marvell's poems is "To His Coy Mistress." It is not only a seduction poem, but also a deduction poem, in which the theme of carpe diem is presented as a syllogism: (1) If there were world enough and time, the lady's coyness would not be a crime; (2) There is not world enough and time; (3) therefore, this coyness may or may not be a crime. Marvell must have been aware that his poem depended on flawed logic; he may have meant it to be ironically typical of the desperate reasoning employed by would-be seducers.

In the first section of the poem, the speaker describes the vast amounts of time ("An age at least to every part") and space (from the Ganges to the Humber) he would devote to his love if he could. This apparently gracious statement of patience is then juxtaposed with the striking image of "Time's wingéd chariot hurrying near" and the resultant

"Deserts of vast eternity." "Deserts," meaning "unpeopled places," is emphasized by the shift of the stress to the first syllable of the line. There follows the arresting depiction of the drawbacks of postmortem chastity, with worms "trying" the lady's "long-preserved virginity," as her "quaint honor" turns to dust.

Imagery of corruption was not unusual in carpe diem poems, and it also occurs (the memento mori theme) in visual arts of the period; Marvell's lines are, however, remarkably explicit and must have been devised to shock and disgust. The passage represents, as Rosalie Colie notes in *"My Ecchoing Song"* (1970), "sound psychology" in frightening the lady into the comfort of her lover's arms, an event that the next two lines suggest may indeed have occurred at this point, as the speaker rescues himself from the danger of excessive morbidity with the urbanely ironic comment, "The grave's a fine and private place,/ But none, I think, do there embrace." This makes the transition to the last section of the poem, wherein the speaker, having shown that however limitless time and space may intrinsically be, they are to mortals very limited, offers his solution. The answer is to take energetic action. The formerly coy mistress, now described (either in hope or in fact) as having a "willing soul" with "instant fires," is invited to join the speaker in "one ball" of strength and sweetness, which will tear "thorough the iron gates of life." This third section of the poem is an addition not typical of carpe diem poems, which usually suggest rather than delineate the consummation. The amorous couple, the speaker indicates, should enthusiastically embrace the inevitable and each other. Like the elder Fairfaxes in "Upon Appleton House," they should "make Destiny their choice" and devour time rather than waiting for time to consume them. In its three sections, "To His Coy Mistress" presents first a cheerful and generous offering of limitless time and space, then a chilling reminder that human life is very limited, and finally a frenzied but extraordinarily powerful invitation to break through and transcend all limits.

### "The Garden"

If "To His Coy Mistress" makes the case for action versus hesitation, "The Garden," the best-known hortensial work of the "garden poet," considers the question of action versus contemplation. Like much of Marvell's work, it employs a rich texture of wordplay and classical and Christian allusions. It is a retirement poem, in which the speaker begins by celebrating his withdrawal from the busy world of human endeavor. This theme is one rich in tradition, and would have been attractive during the uncertain and dangerous times in which Marvell lived. In this poem, however, the speaker retires not merely from the world of men, but, in a moment of ultimate retirement, from the world of material things. As the poet contemplates the garden, his mind and his soul momentarily transcend the material plane.

In the first stanza, the speaker comments on the folly of seeking human glory. Men "vainly" ("from vanity," and also "in vain") "amaze" themselves (surprise themselves/

trap themselves in a maze) in their efforts to achieve honors (represented by the palm, oak, and bay leaves used in classical victors' wreaths). Even the best such victory represents success in only one area of endeavor, for which the victor receives the decoration of a wreath woven from a single species, a wreath that in its singleness "upbraids" (braids up/rebukes) his "toyles" (coils of hair/efforts). In contrast, repose is rewarded by "all flowers and all trees." Addressing Quiet and Innocence personified, the speaker uses a typically Marvellian qualifier when he says that their sacred plants "if here below,/ Only among the plants will grow," suggesting that quiet and innocence may be really unobtainable on Earth. The solitude experienced by the lone visitor among the plants of the garden is nevertheless worth seeking, for, in comparison, "Society is all but rude"—society is nearly "coarse," or (an inversion and a pun) society is almost "rustic." The next three stanzas describe the physical, sensual values that the garden offers in contrast to those of the world. As the "society" of the garden is superior to that of men, so the sensuality of the garden is more intense than that of men: "No white or red was ever seen/ So amorous as this lovely green" (the colors of fleshly passion are less "amorous" than the green of the garden), and the beauties of the trees exceed those of any woman. The gods Apollo and Pan knew this, the speaker says, since they pursued the nymphs Daphne and Syrinx, not for their womanly charms, but in order to obtain their more desirable dendritic forms.

In the fifth stanza, the speaker reaches a height of sensual ecstasy as the various garden fruits literally thrust themselves on him, in what Rosalie Colie rightly calls a "climactic experience." It is powerfully sexual, yet the speaker is alone and in the garden, as Adam once was in Eden. And then the speaker, "stumbling" and "Insnared," falls, reminding the reader of the Fall in Eden. Marvell's speaker, however, is still alone and still—indeed, more than ever—in the garden. The next two stanzas describe what is occurring "Meanwhile" on the mental and spiritual planes. The mind withdraws from the lesser pleasures of the body to seek its own kind of happiness. Within the mind, an interior paradise, are the images of all things in the physical world, just as the sea was thought to contain creatures corresponding to all terrestrial species. Yet the mind, unlike the sea, can create, imaginatively, "Far other worlds and other seas," transcending the mundane, and "Annihilating all that's made/ To a green thought in a green shade," an image that R. I. V. Hodge in *Foreshortened Time* (1978) calls "arguably the most intriguing image in Marvell's poetry or in the whole of the seventeenth century." Many explications have been offered for this couplet; the central notion seems to be that through the action of the mind in creating the far other worlds and seas, the physical world ("all that's made") is compacted, or by contrast appears to be compacted, into a single thought. It is, however, a "green" thought—a living, fertile thought that is the source, through the action of the mind, of the transcendent worlds and seas. Indeed, perhaps the thinker himself has almost been annihilated; "in a green shade" could indicate not only that the thinker is shaded by the trees, but also that he is (for the moment) a shade, an insubstantial shadow of his physical self. The green thought is, perhaps, the Platonic pure idea of garden from which all gardens derive. It could be suggested that this is the true garden of the poem.

In stanza 7, the soul leaves the body in a flight indicative of its later, final flight to heaven. In the next stanza, the garden is compared explicitly to Eden—not merely Eden before the Fall, but Eden before Eve. Three times, in successive couplets, the speaker states that Paradise enjoyed alone is preferable to Paradise shared. Such praise of solitude can hardly be exceeded, even in the considerable Christian literature on the subject, and perhaps Marvell, relying on his readers' knowledge that Adam had after all requested Eve's company, expected his readers to identify this stanza as a momentary effusion, not shared by the poet himself, on the part of the poem's persona. The reader is reminded, at least, that mortals in the fallen world can only approximate paradisical ecstasy, not achieve it, until they leave this world for a better one. The speaker, now quite recalled from his ecstasy, observes "this dial new." The term may indicate a literal floral sundial, in which small plots of different plants marked the hours around a circle; it clearly and more importantly indicates the entire renewed postlapsarian world, under the mercy of God the "skillful gardener," who provides the "milder sun" (the Son, Christ, God's mercy). The bee, who is industrious rather than contemplative, "computes its time [thyme] as well as we!" This is a typically Marvellian paradox. The bee's industry is reminiscent of the negatively viewed "incessant labors" of the men in the first stanza; the bee, however, is performing wholesome activity in the garden, reckoned with flowers. The situation is analogous to that of the speaker in stanza 5 who fell, but did not Fall, remaining in the garden.

The poem's persona at first rejected the world of action for the garden's solitude and the contemplative exercise thereby made possible. Contemplation has led to physical, then to mental, then to spiritual ecstasy, but the ecstatic moment is limited because the speaker, dwelling in a world that remains thoroughly fallen, is not yet "prepared for longer flight." Refreshed by his experience and noting that the "dial" is *new*, the speaker can accept the action of the bee and recognize action, as well as contemplation, as an appropriate part of human existence.

## "UPON APPLETON HOUSE"

Another poem dealing with the question of withdrawal versus action is "Upon Appleton House," which clearly raises the issue of involvement in the English Civil War and subsequent disturbances. The poem falls into two halves, each depicting both action and retirement, and builds toward a resolution in the form of Lord Fairfax's daughter Mary, who was under Marvell's tutelage. A genre of the time was the "country house" poem, in which a country estate was described, and its inhabitants and their way of life thereby praised. "Upon Appleton House" begins in this manner, with the first nine stanzas devoted to the house itself. Employing a variety of conceits, Marvell finds the modest size and decoration of the structure preferable to the overblown grandeur of other houses. It is on a human scale, with "short but admirable Lines" that "In ev'ry Figure equal Man." Nevertheless, it is less modest than its owner, Lord Fairfax. When he arrives, the house sweats, and from its square hall sprouts a "Spherical" cupola, outdoing the proverbially impossible task of squaring the circle.

A source of building material for the house was the ancient nunnery whose ruins were still evident, wherein had dwelt the nuns whose order had in former times owned the estate. By recounting a historical episode connected with the nunnery, Marvell shows how it is also a source of the estate's present occupants. An ancestral Fairfax had wooed the "blooming Virgin" Isabel Thwaites, "Fair beyond measure" and an heiress. She was induced to enter the nunnery at Appleton, from which she could ultimately be extracted only by a Fairfacian raid. This tale, told in stanzas 11 to 35, falls into two distinct parts. The first (stanzas 11 to 28) is essentially a nun's eloquent invitation to Isabel to withdraw to the secluded life of the cloister. The joys of this "holy leisure," behind walls that "restrain the World without," are attractively and enthusiastically described, though Marvell would not wish to portray otherwise so Catholic an institution. The passage wherein Isabel is compared to the Virgin Mary, and the later picture of the nuns "in bed,/ As pearls together billeted,/ All night embracing arm in arm," may be meant to raise doubts in the reader's mind that would be confirmed when he is told that "The nuns smooth tongue has suckt her in." After debating what to do, the betrothed Fairfax decides to remove her from the nunnery by force. In a rather burlesque episode, the nuns, whose "loud'st cannon were their lungs," are dispossessed of their prize and, in the next stanza, which flashes forward to the Dissolution, of their nunnery.

Action in this case has been far superior to withdrawal. It leads ultimately, however, to another withdrawal, that of Sir Thomas Fairfax, son of the celebrated couple. After a heroic military career, he retired to Appleton House, but the flower beds there, which he shaped like the bastions of a fort, show that he was incapable of retiring fully. Stanzas 36 to 40 describe the flower-fort, wherein flower-cannons discharge salutes of scent and the bee stands sentinel. There follows (stanzas 41 to 45) a lamentation by the poet over the present unhappy state of England, "The garden of the world ere while," and praise of Fairfax, "Who, had it pleasèd him and God," could have prevented it. In this first half of the poem, then, Marvell has first described the house as an illustration of the greatness of its owner, then shown the virtue of action over withdrawal, then indicated that a man of great action can never fully retire. Finally, he has shown regretful acceptance of Fairfax's retirement, with the clear statement that England suffers without ameliorative action on someone's part. In the second half of the poem, the same ideas will be reiterated and enhanced, except in the last part, the focus will be not on Fairfax but on his daughter Mary ("Maria"), whose embodiment of the values of retirement and action will effect a resolution.

From the flower fort, the speaker can look down over the meadow (stanzas 46 to 60) onto the public world of action. It is a world capable of topsy-turvy, this "Abyss" of a meadow, from which it is a wonder that men rise alive. Men (seen from the hill) look like grasshoppers, but grasshoppers (perched on the tall grass) "are Gyants there." Cows look like beauty spots or fleas, and when the land is flooded, "Boats can over bridges sail" and "Fishes do the stables scale." It is a dangerous world, where the Mowers "massacre the grass," which is very tall, and the rail (humbly close to the ground) is accidentally killed: "Lowness is unsafe as hight,/ And chance o'retakes what scapeth spight." The earlier lamentation over England's condition in stanzas 41 to 43 invites the reader, if invitation were needed, to read this section as an allegory of England, although it may be carrying the allegory too far to see the hapless rail as Charles I, as has been suggested. The mowers who cause the carnage, leaving the field like a battlefield "quilted ore" with piles of hay that look like bodies, are not evil. As they dance in triumph, their smell is fragrant, and their kisses are as sweet as the hay. Marvell compares the meadow at the outset with stage scenery, constantly changing. Describing a series of scenes as the hay is harvested and piled and the cattle set loose in the field to crop the last few inches of grass, he ends with a flood. The flood is caused by the opening of sluices up-river, but the reader is meant to think of the biblical Flood.

Taking refuge from the drowned world, the speaker "imbarks" (embarks/encloses in bark) himself in the "green, yet growing ark" of an adjacent wood. The trees are as tightly woven together as are the families of Fairfax and Vere (Fairfax's wife's family). From without, the wood seems absolutely solid, but inside it is "passable" and "loose." The nightingale, a bird of solitude, sings here, and "highest oakes stoop down to hear,/ And listning elders prick the ear." The nightingale may represent Mary Fairfax, twelve years old when Marvell became her tutor, in which case the "Elders" would be her parents. At any rate, while the song of solitude is attractive, the "Sadder" sound of the stockdoves, whose necks bear "Nuptial Rings," is more pleasing. This indication, even within the wood, that private withdrawal may not be desirable, prepares for the later part of the poem, when Mary herself appears. In a lengthy section very reminiscent of "The Garden," the speaker revels in the delights and the security of the wood, a place "where the world no certain shot/ Can make, or me it toucheth not." He wishes never to leave the wood, and requests, in a passage that reminds many readers of Christ's crucifixion, that the vines and brambles fetter him and the "courteous Briars nail [him] through."

Noticing that the flood has subsided, he finds the meadow equally attractive. It is "newly washt," with "no serpent new." The "wanton harmless folds" of the river attract the speaker, who abandons himself to the pleasures of angling, achieving in stanza 81 such harmony with the landscape that it is difficult to distinguish between him and it. The sedge surrounds his temples, his side is a riverbank, and his "sliding foot" may remind the reader of the "Fountains sliding foot" in "The Garden." The sudden arrival of Maria, however, extracts him from this reverie by means of an odd inversion wherein she, the pupil, reminds the presumably adult speaker of his responsibility. Calling himself a "trifling Youth," he hastily hides his fishing gear.

Essentially the rest of the poem is devoted to praise of Maria, a creature neither of withdrawal nor of action, but a fusion of both. Among the imagery giving her awesome power are echoes of the Last Judgment: She has "judicious" eyes, she "already is the Law," and by her the world is "wholly vitrifi'd." Nature collects itself in silence, and the sun blushingly conceals himself. As the halcyon, flying "betwixt the day and night," paralyzes nature and turns it blue, so Maria gives her surroundings the stillness of glass and imbues them with her (their) qualities: "Tis She that to these Gardens gave/ That wondrous beauty which they have," and so also with the woods, meadow, and river. Intelligent (learning languages to gain wisdom, which is "Heavens Dialect"), without vanity, and raised in the "Domestick Heaven" of Appleton House, she is not the new branch that a male heir would be on the "Farfacian oak." Instead, she is a sprig of mistletoe that will one day be severed "for some universal good." Presumably this will be her marriage, which will be of considerable political importance. The product of the seclusion of Appleton House, she is thus the ideal person to take action to affect the world at large; in her the apparent opposites of withdrawal and action are harmoniously fused.

The final stanza of the poem features a pattern of conceits reminiscent of the first stanza, and compares the fishermen carrying their boats to tortoises, echoing the tortoise in stanza 2. The fishermen are "rational amphibii," amphibians who can think; but they are also thinkers who can operate in two mediums: Human beings need both contemplation and action. This concord of opposites, which is more powerful than compromise and is presented with reason and wit, represents those characteristics central to Marvell's work.

OTHER MAJOR WORKS

NONFICTION: *The Rehearsal Transpros'd*, 1672; *The Rehearsal Transpros'd: The Second Part*, 1673 (for modern editions of the two preceding entries, see *The Rehearsal Transpros'd and The Rehearsal Transpros'd: The Second Part*, 1971; D. I. B. Smith, editor); *Mr. Smirke: Or, The Divine in Mode*, 1676; *An Account of the Growth of Popery and Arbitrary Government in England*, 1677; *Remarks upon a Late Disingenuous Discourse*, 1678; *The Prose Works of Andrew Marvell*, 2003 (Martin Dzelzainis and Annabel Patterson, editors).

MISCELLANEOUS: *The Poems and Letters of Andrew Marvell*, 1927, 1952, 1971 (H. Margoliouth, editor).

BIBLIOGRAPHY

Chernaik, Warren L. *The Poet's Time: Politics and Religion in the Work of Andrew Marvell*. New York: Cambridge University Press, 1983. For Chernaik, Marvell is a poet-prophet whose political ideas are consistent, militant, and rooted in his religion. Also discusses Marvell's later (post-1666) satiric poetry and his political polemics.

Hunt, John Dixon. *Andrew Marvell: His Life and Writings*. Ithaca, N.Y.: Cornell University Press, 1978. Hunt's intent is to provide a context against which some of Marvell's major poems ("Upon Appleton House," "An Horatian Ode upon Cromwell's Return from Ireland," and "Last Instructions to a Painter") can be read. Profusely illustrated.

Klause, John. *The Unfortunate Fall: Theodicy and the Moral Imagination of Andrew Marvell*. Hamden, Conn.: Archon Books, 1983. In his extensive analyses of the Cromwell poems, "The Garden," and "Upon Appleton House," Klause finds Marvell "adapting" to political realities. Complemented by an extensive bibliography of primary and secondary sources.

Murray, Nicholas. *World Enough and Time: The Life of Andrew Marvell*. New York: St. Martin's Press, 2000. Even with the information uncovered in the three decades since the last biography of Marvell was written, little is known about long stretches of Marvell's career. Murray's narrative takes full advantage of what is available and provides a clear portrait of Marvell and his life in the Cromwell era and the Restoration.

Patterson, Annabel. *Marvell: The Writer in Public Life*. New York: Longman, 2000. Focuses on the intersection of Marvell's political and literary views.

Ray, Robert H. *An Andrew Marvell Companion*. New York: Garland, 1998. A useful, comprehensive reference guide to the life and works of the poet and political satirist. Includes a chronology of the poet's life and works, a bibliography, and suggestions for further research.

Rees, Christine. *The Judgment of Marvell*. London: Pinter, 1989. Rees argues that Marvell's poetry concerns choice or the impossibility of choosing, and his choices involve the life of pleasure, as well as those of action and contemplation. Using this threefold division, she offers extensive commentary on approximately twenty-five well-known poems.

Stocker, Margarita. *Apocalyptic Marvell: The Second Coming in Seventeenth Century Poetry*. Athens: Ohio University Press, 1986. Stocker's book offers a corrective view of Marvell, a poet committed to an apocalyptic ideology that informs all his poems. Supplemented by an extensive bibliography.

*C. Herbert Gilliland*

# THOMAS NASHE

**Born:** Lowestoft, Suffolk, England; November, 1567
**Died:** Yarmouth(?), England; c. 1601
**Also known as:** Thomes Nash

PRINCIPAL POETRY

*The Choise of Valentines*, 1899

### OTHER LITERARY FORMS

Almost all that Thomas Nashe wrote was published in pamphlet form. With the exception of a long poem (*The Choise of Valentines*), several sonnets and songs, and at least two dramas (*Summer's Last Will and Testament*, pr. 1592, and *The Isle of Dogs*, pr. 1597), all his work was prose. His prose works include *The Anatomie of Absurditie* (1589); *An Almond for a Parrat* (1590); a preface to Sir Philip Sidney's *Astrophel and Stella* (1591); *Pierce Penilesse, His Supplication to the Divell* (1592); *Strange News of the Intercepting of Certain Letters* (1592); *Christ's Tears over Jerusalem* (1593); *The Terrors of the Night* (1594); *The Unfortunate Traveller: Or, The Life of Jack Wilton* (1594); *Have with You to Saffron-Walden* (1596); and *Nashe's Lenten Stuffe* (1599).

### ACHIEVEMENTS

Thomas Nashe was more a journalist than an artist, if the definition of artist is one who follows the Aristotelian principles of using life as a source from which one creates a story with a beginning, middle, and end. Nashe informed and entertained his sixteenth century audience in the same way that a journalist pleases the public today. He was known in his time not as a poet or a dramatist, although he wrote both poetry and plays. He was known as the worthy opponent of the scholar Gabriel Harvey, as one who with lively rhetoric, biting invective, and soaring wit destroyed every argument the pompous Harvey could muster. He was also known to Elizabethans as the chief defender of the Anglican Church against the attack of the Puritans in the Martin Marprelate controversy. The magnificent invective found in the speeches of William Shakespeare's Falstaff, Prince Hal, and (more especially) Kent was almost certainly derived from the vituperation Nashe hurled at his adversaries.

Among modern students of literature, Nashe is remembered for his most unusual work, the picaresque novel of adventure, *The Unfortunate Traveller*. It is the story of a young page, Jack Wilton, who, after serving in the army of Henry VIII, travels to Europe to find means of earning a living. The underworld realism that Nashe presents in his descriptions of Jack's escapades has earned him a reputation for being something other than a hurler of invective. The book is not a unified work of art; its characters, other than Jack himself, are not particularly memorable. Its descriptions of the harshest elements of human life, such as disease, hunger, torture, rape, and murder, place it in stark contrast to the sweet absurdities of romance; it thus shows the way to the modern novel.

BIOGRAPHY

Thomas Nashe was born in November, 1567, the son of William Nashe, a minister in Lowestoft, Suffolk. Because no record exists of William's being a university graduate, it can be assumed that he was probably a stipendiary curate in Lowestoft, not a vicar. Although the title pages of *Pierce Penilesse, His Supplication to the Divell* and of *Strange News of the Intercepting of Certain Letters* refer to "Thomas Nashe, Gentleman," Nashe himself denied that he was of gentle birth. From his earliest years, indeed, he disliked the propensity he found in middle-class Englishmen to pretend to be something other than what they were.

In 1573, Nashe's father was granted the living in West Harling, Norfolk, where young Thomas probably spent his early years. Nothing is known of Nashe's basic education except that it was sufficient to allow him to enter St. John's College, Cambridge, in October, 1582. In March, 1586, he received his bachelor of arts degree and enrolled immediately to work toward the master of arts degree. In 1588, however, he left Cambridge without the degree. Perhaps financial difficulties forced him to leave the university, for his father had died the year before, in 1587. Without financial support from home, Nashe most likely would not have been able to continue his education; probably his college, dominated as it was by Puritans, would not look with favor in the form of financial assistance on the satirical young Nashe, who supported the pursuit of humanistic studies over the more narrow Puritan theology then in vogue at Cambridge.

Whatever his reasons for leaving Cambridge, Nashe certainly did not have the economic means to remain idle long. He followed the lead of two other Cambridge graduates who, armed with no wealth but their wits, turned to literature as a means of earning a livelihood. Both Robert Greene and Christopher Marlowe had gone to London to write, and both had found moderate success. Nashe may have been acquainted with both men at Cambridge, but he certainly knew them both in London. Like Nashe, both loved poetry and detested Puritans. In the same year that he left Cambridge, Nashe published *The Anatomie of Absurditie*, a work of inexperience and brashness.

A young writer of pamphlets in London had few opportunities to earn a living by his work. He was generally paid a flat amount for his manuscript, usually two pounds. If a pamphlet were well-received by the public, the patron to whom it was dedicated might be so flattered that he or she might feel disposed to grant the author a stipend to continue his work. Nashe's *The Anatomie of Absurditie*, dedicated to Sir Charles Blount, was, however, of so little literary merit that Nashe probably received no more than his original author's fee.

Nashe dedicated no more works to Sir Charles; but because he did need patrons, he dedicated later works to a variety of people in a position to offer him assistance. Finally, after the dedication of *The Unfortunate Traveller* to Henry Wriothesley, the earl of Southampton, Nashe decided that patrons were more trouble than they were worth. Hating hypocrisy in others and finding himself forced into hypocrisy in order to be paid for his work, Nashe turned to writing only for his readers and depended on them to reward his efforts.

Perhaps what gave Nashe his biggest literary boost was the famous Martin Marprelate controversy. Nashe's part in the verbal battle was limited to the pamphlet *An Almond for a Parrat*, but the style and the vigorous prose of Martin could not help influencing Nashe. Although he was hostile to Martin's Puritanical ideas, Nashe must nevertheless have learned much from the formidable prose of his Puritan adversary, for he attacks Martin with the same devices and force of language that the Puritan propagandist used.

Nashe's entry into the Martin Marprelate controversy brought with it rewards beyond what he might have hoped. Gabriel Harvey wrote disparagingly of Nashe's part in the controversy, thus starting a new fight: the Nashe-Harvey controversy. It was in this battle of wits that Nashe found his place as a writer. Here the verbal street-fighter had the great good fortune to be attacked by a man of reputation who was inferior in wit and writing ability to Nashe. Harvey's reputation never recovered from Nashe's fierce invective. Beginning with a slap at Harvey in his preface to Greene's *A Quip for an Upstart Courtier* (1592) and ending with *Have with You to Saffron-Walden*, Nashe earned a good reputation and a fair living from his anti-Harvey prose.

All his previous writings were practice for *The Unfortunate Traveller*, published in 1594. A kind of pamphlet itself, but longer and more complex, the work was not particularly popular during his lifetime, but today it is his best-known work.

Nashe was hounded from London in 1597 when the authorities decided that *The Isle of Dogs*, a play he had begun, and which Ben Jonson had finished, was "seditious." Jonson was jailed and Nashe sought, but the famous pamphleteer had fled to Yarmouth, in Norfolk. By 1598, he was back in London, where *Nashe's Lenten Stuffe* was entered in the Stationers' Register.

After *Nashe's Lenten Stuffe*, Nashe wrote no more, and in 1601, history records a reference to his death.

ANALYSIS

Thomas Nashe the satirical pamphleteer, who was wont to use language as a cudgel in a broad prose style, seldom disciplined himself to the more delicate work of writing poetry. Both his temperament and his pocketbook directed him to the freer and more profitable form of pamphlet prose. It is this prose that made his reputation, but Nashe did write poems, mostly lyrical in the manner of his time. No originator in poetic style,

Nashe followed the lead of such worthy predecessors as Geoffrey Chaucer, Henry Howard, earl of Surrey, Edmund Spenser, and Christopher Marlowe.

Nashe's interest in poetry was not slight. In typical Renaissance fashion, he believed poetry to be the highest form of moral philosophy. Following Sidney, he insisted that the best poetry is based on scholarship and devotion to detail. Not only does poetry, in his perception, encourage virtue and discourage vice, but also it "cleanses" the language of barbarisms and makes the "vulgar sort" in London adopt a more pleasing manner of speech. Because he loved good poetry and saw the moral and aesthetic value of it, Nashe condemned the "ballad mongers," who abused the ears and sensitivities of the gentle-folk of England. To him, the ballad writers were "common pamfletters" whose lack of learning and lust for money were responsible for littering the streets with the garbage of their ballads—a strange reaction for a man who was himself a notable writer of pamphlets. For the learned poetry of Western culture, Nashe had the highest appreciation.

Nashe's own poetic efforts are often placed in the context of his prose works, as if he were setting jewels among the coarser material, as did George Gascoigne, Thomas Lodge, Robert Greene, Thomas Deloney, and others. *Pierce Penilesse, His Supplication to the Divell*, "The Four Letters Confuted," and *The Unfortunate Traveller* all have poems sprinkled here and there. The play *Summer's Last Will and Testament*, itself written in quite acceptable blank verse, has several lyrics of some interest scattered throughout. Nashe's shorter poetic efforts are almost equally divided between sonnets and lyrical poems. The longer *The Choise of Valentines* is a narrative in the erotic style of Ovid.

## SONNETS

Among Nashe's poems are six sonnets, two of which may be said to be parodies of the form. Each is placed within a longer work, where its individual purpose is relevant to the themes of that work. Most of the sonnets are in the English form, containing three quatrains and a concluding couplet. Following the lead of the earl of Surrey (who is, indeed, the putative author of the two sonnets to Geraldine in *The Unfortunate Traveller*), Nashe uses a concluding couplet in each of his sonnets, including "To the Right Honorable the lord S.," which in other respects (as in the division into octave and sestet rhyming *abbaabba, cdcdee*) is closer to the Italian form.

In his first sonnet, "Perusing yesternight, with idle eyes," Nashe pauses at the end of *Pierce Penilesse, His Supplication to the Divell* to praise the lord Amyntas, whom Edmund Spenser had neglected in *The Faerie Queene* (1590, 1596). In "Perusing yesternight, with idle eyes," the famous poem by Spenser, Nashe had turned to the end of the poem to find sonnets addressed to "sundry Nobles." Nashe uses the three quatrains to rehearse the problem: He read the poem, found the sonnets addressed to the nobles, and wondered why Spenser had left out "thy memory." In an excellent use of the concluding couplet in this form, he decides that Spenser must have omitted praise of

Amyntas because "few words could not comprise thy fame."

If "Perusing yesternight, with idle eyes" is in the tradition of using the sonnet to praise, Nashe's second sonnet, "Were there no warres," is not. Concluding his prose attack on Gabriel Harvey in "The Four Letters Confuted," this sonnet looks forward to John Milton rather than backward to Petrarch. Here Nashe promises Harvey constant warfare. Harvey had suggested that he would like to call off the battle, but in so doing he had delivered a few verbal blows to Nashe. To the request for a truce, Nashe responds with a poetic "no!" Again using the three quatrains to deliver his message, the poet calls for "Vncessant warres with waspes and droanes," announces that revenge is an endless muse, and says that he will gain his reputation by attacking "this duns." His couplet effectively concludes by promising that his next work will be of an extraordinary type.

The next two sonnets may be thought of as parodies of the Petrarchan style and of the medieval romance generally. Nashe, like his creation Jack Wilton, had little use for the unrealistic in love, war, or any aspect of life. The exaggerated praise of women in the Petrarchan tradition sounded as false to him as it did to Shakespeare and to the later writers of anti-Petrarchan verse. Both "If I must die" and "Faire roome, the presence of sweet beauty's pride," found in *The Unfortunate Traveller*, are supposedly written by the lovesick Surrey to his absent love, Geraldine. Both poems are close enough to the real Surrey's own sonnets to ring true, but just ridiculous enough to be seen clearly as parodies.

The first is addressed to the woman Diamante, whom Surrey mistakes for Geraldine. The dying Surrey requests that his mistress suck out his breath, stab him with her tongue, crush him with her embrace, burn him with her eyes, and strangle him with her hair. In "Faire roome, the presence of sweet beauty's pride," Surrey, having visited Geraldine's room in Florence, addresses the room. He will worship the room, with which neither the chambers of heaven nor lightning can compare. No one, he concludes, can see heaven unless he meditates on the room.

Such romantic nonsense held no attraction for Jack or for Nashe. Jack makes fun of "suchlike rhymes" which lovers use to "assault" women: "A holy requiem to their souls that think to woo women with riddles." Jack, a much more realistic man, wins the favor of Diamante with a plain table.

The final two sonnets are also anti-Petrarchan in content. Addressed to a would-be patron to whom he dedicated *The Choise of Valentines*, both "To the Right Honorable the lord S." and "Thus hath my penne presum'd to please" ask pardon for presuming to address an overtly pornographic poem to a "sweete flower of matchless poetrie." In the octave of the former, Nashe excuses himself by declaring that he merely writes about what men really do. In the sestet, he proudly asserts that everyone can write Petrarchan love poems, full of "complaints and praises." No one, however, has written successfully of "loves pleasures" in his time—except, the implication is, him.

## LYRICS

Nashe's earliest two lyrics, although they are very different in content, are each in four stanzas of six lines of iambic pentameter. The rhyme in each case is *ababcc*. The later songs, those in *Summer's Last Will and Testament*, are in couplets and (in one case) tercets. Except for "Song: Spring, the sweete spring," all the lyrics are laments.

The most personal of the lyrics is "Why ist damnation," printed on the first page of Nashe's famous pamphlet *Pierce Penilesse, His Supplication to the Divell*. Trying to gain prosperity and failing, Nashe "resolved in verse to paint forth my passion." In a logical progression, the poet first considers suicide ("Why ist damnation to dispaire and die") but decides against it for his soul's safety. He then determines that in England wit and scholarship are useless. He asks God's forgiveness for his low mood, but despairs because he has no friends. Finally, he bids adieu to England as "unkinde, where skill is nothing woorth."

"All Soul, no earthly flesh," Nashe's second lyric, is more like the anti-Petrarchan sonnets that Nashe has the earl of Surrey write in *The Unfortunate Traveller* than it is like the other lyrics. Full of exaggerated comparisons (Geraldine is "pure soul," "pure gold"), comic images (his spirit will perch upon "hir silver breasts"), and conventional conceits (stars, sun, and dew take their worth from her), the poem is as far from Nashe as is John Lyly's *Euphues, the Anatomy of Wit* (1579).

In *Summer's Last Will and Testament*, Nashe includes four major lyrics and several minor ones. Some of the lyrics are cheery "Song: Spring, the sweete spring," "Song: Trip and goe," and "Song: Merry, merry, merry," for example. The general mood of the poems is sad, however, as the subject of the whole work would dictate: the death of summer. In watching summer die, readers, like Gerard Manley Hopkins's Margaret, see themselves. "Song: Fayre Summer droops" is a conventional lament on the passing of summer. Written in heroic couplets, the poem uses alliteration successfully in the last stanza to bring the song to a solid conclusion. "Song: Autumn Hath all the Summer's Fruitfull Treasure," also in heroic couplets, continues the theme of lament with lines using effective repetition ("Short dayes, sharpe dayes, long nights come on a pace"). Here, Nashe turns more directly to what was perhaps his central theme in the longer work: man's weakness in face of natural elements. The refrain, repeated at the end of each of the two stanzas, is "From winter, plague, & pestilence, good Lord, deliver us."

It was surely fear of the plague and of humanity's frailty in general that led Nashe to write the best of his lyrics, "Song: Adieu, farewell earths blisse," sung to the dying Summer by Will Summer. Nashe recognizes in the refrain that follows each of the six stanzas that he is sick, he must die, and he prays: "Lord, have mercy on us."

In a logical development, Nashe first introduces the theme of Everyman: "Fond are lifes lustful ioyes." In succeeding stanzas, he develops each of the "lustfull ioyes" in turn. "Rich men" are warned not to trust in their wealth, "Beauty" is revealed as transitory, "Strength" is pictured surrendering to the grave, and "Wit" is useless to dissuade

Hell's executioner. In a very specific, orderly manner and in spare iambic trimeter lines, Nashe presents humankind's death-lament and prayer for mercy. One stanza will show the strength of the whole poem:

> Beauty is but a flowre,
> Which wrinckles will deuoure,
> Brightnesse falls from the ayre,
> Queenes have died yong and faire,
> Dust hath closed Helens eye.
> I am sick, I must dye:
>  Lord, have mercy on vs.

## THE CHOISE OF VALENTINES

Nashe's last poem is by far his longest. *The Choise of Valentines* is an erotic narrative poem in heroic couplets running to more than three hundred lines. With the kind of specificity that one would expect from the author of *The Unfortunate Traveller*, Nashe tells of the visit of the young man Tomalin to a brothel in search of his valentine, "gentle mistris Francis." Tomalin's detailed exploration of the woman's anatomical charms, his unexpected loss of sexual potency, and her announced preference for a dildo all combine to present an Ovidian erotic-mythological poem of the type popular in Elizabethan England. Nashe's poem must, however, be set off from Shakespeare's *Venus and Adonis* (1593) and Marlowe's *Hero and Leander* (1598), which emphasize the mythological more than the erotic. Nashe clearly emphasizes the erotic, almost to the exclusion of the mythological. Why not? he seems to say in the dedicatory sonnet accompanying the poem: Ovid was his guide, and "Ouids wanton Muse did not offend."

Nowhere, with the exception of the excellent "Song: Adieu, farewell earths blisse," does Nashe rise to the heights of his greatest contemporaries, Spenser, Sidney, Marlowe, and Shakespeare. In that poem, in the sonnet "Were there no warres," and in perhaps one or two other poems his Muse is sufficiently shaken into consciousness by the poet's interest in the subject. The remainder of Nashe's poetry is the work of an excellent craftsperson who is playing with form and language.

## OTHER MAJOR WORKS

PLAYS: *Dido, Queen of Carthage,* pr. c. 1586-1587 (with Christopher Marlowe); *Summer's Last Will and Testament,* pr. 1592; *The Isle of Dogs,* pr. 1597 (with Ben Jonson; no longer extant).

NONFICTION: *The Anatomie of Absurditie,* 1589; Preface to Robert Greene's *Menaphon,* 1589; *An Almond for a Parrat,* 1590; Preface to Sir Philip Sidney's *Astrophel and Stella,* 1591; Preface to Robert Greene's *A Quip for an Upstart Courtier,* 1592; *Christ's Tears over Jerusalem,* 1593; *The Terrors of the Night,* 1594; *Have with You to Saffron-Walden,* 1596; *Nashe's Lenten Stuffe,* 1599.

MISCELLANEOUS: *Pierce Penilesse, His Supplication to the Divell,* 1592 (prose and poetry); *Strange News of the Intercepting of Certain Letters,* 1592 (prose and poetry; also known as *The Four Letters Confuted*); *The Unfortunate Traveller: Or, The Life of Jack Wilton,* 1594 (prose and poetry).

BIBLIOGRAPHY

Crewe, Jonathan V. *Unredeemed Rhetoric: Thomas Nashe and the Scandal of Author-ship.* Baltimore: The Johns Hopkins University Press, 1982. A study of the conflict between orthodox values and a cynical perception of society's injustice and exploitation that cuts across Nashe's career, complicating and adding tension to his work.

Helgerson, Richard. *The Elizabethan Prodigals.* Berkeley: University of California Press, 1977. Nashe and his colleagues Christopher Marlowe, Thomas Kyd, George Peele, Robert Greene, and Thomas Lodge, all with university training, formed a group of literary bohemians in London. Helgerson catalogs their escapades and relates them to their lives.

Hilliard, Stephen S. *The Singularity of Thomas Nashe.* Lincoln: University of Nebraska Press, 1986. Hilliard takes a fresh look at Nashe's life and writing, discovering the distinctive qualities of his wit and style and showing how they transformed both poetry and prose.

Holbrook, Peter. *Literature and Degree in Renaissance England: Nashe, Bourgeois Tragedy, Shakespeare.* Cranbury, N.J.: Associated University Presses, 1994. A historical study of political and social views in sixteenth century England.

Hutson, Lorna. *Thomas Nashe in Context.* New York: Oxford University Press, 1997. Considers Thomas Nashe within his social and historical milieu.

McGinn, Donald J. *Thomas Nashe.* Boston: Twayne, 1981. Contains insightful commentary on Nashe's life and works. Focuses on Nashe's works as portrayals of the various types of middle-class Londoners—their appearance, their manners, and their customs.

Nicholl, Charles. *A Cup of News: The Life of Thomas Nashe.* London: Routledge & Kegan Paul, 1984. This scholarly biography sets a high standard. In addition to substantial discussions of Nashe's life and writings, Nicholl includes illustrations of portraits and scenes, as well as reproductions of relevant documents.

Nielson, James. *Unread Herrings: Thomas Nashe and the Prosaics of the Real.* New York: Peter Lang, 1993. This study examines Nashe's use of realism in his works. Bibliography.

*Eugene P. Wright*

# SIR WALTER RALEGH

**Born:** Hayes Barton, Devon, England; c. 1552
**Died:** London, England; October 29, 1618
**Also known as:** Sir Walter Raleigh

PRINCIPAL POETRY

*The Poems of Sir Walter Raleigh Now First Collected, with a Biographical and Critical Introduction*, 1813
*The Poems of Sir Walter Raleigh*, 1962 (Agnes Latham, editor)

## OTHER LITERARY FORMS

Almost immediately after his execution in 1618, the reputation of Sir Walter Ralegh (RAWL-ee) as a patriotic and courageous opponent to James I developed, and as opposition to James and Charles I increased, many prose works were attributed to Ralegh from about 1625 through the end of the seventeenth century. Of those certainly written by Ralegh, there are two pamphlets, *A Report of the Fight About the Iles of Açores* (1591) and *The Discoverie of the Large, Rich and Bewtiful Empyre of Guiana* (1596), which express the aggressive buoyancy of Elizabethan imperialist designs on South America and of the control of trade to the New World. Ralegh's major work outside his poetry is the monumental, unfinished *The History of the World* (1614), dedicated to and yet containing scarcely disguised criticism of King James, who had him imprisoned between 1603 and 1616, and who (after Ralegh's hopeless expedition to Guiana to find El Dorado) had him executed. *The History of the World* was part therapy, part histrionic pique and, like most of Ralegh's career, significant far beyond its surface ambiguities and chronological contradictions. Torn between being an account of the "unjointed and scattered frame of our English affairs" and a universal history, it is a tribute as well to the dead Queen Elizabeth, "Her whom I must still honour in the dust," and an indictment of what Ralegh perceived as the corruption of the Jacobean court. For Ralegh, in *The History of the World* as much as in his poetry, the court was his stage, a place of "parts to play," in which survival depended on "fashioning of our selves according to the nature of the time wherein we live," and the power of which dominated his language and, in the most absolute sense, his life. Like his poems, *The History of the World* is a moving and (far beyond his knowledge) revealing document of the power of the court over the men and women who struggled within it.

## ACHIEVEMENTS

Sir Walter Ralegh's importance belies the slimness of his poetic output. The author of perhaps two dozen extant poems and a number of brief verse translations, the latter

*Sir Walter Ralegh*
(Library of Congress)

appearing in his *The History of the World*, Ralegh is nevertheless one of the most important of the Elizabethan courtly makers, articulating with fearful clarity not merely the gaudy surface and fashions of the late Elizabethan age, but also much of the felt pressure of the court, his society's dominant social power, on the lives and sensibilities of those caught in it. Ralegh described himself toward the end of his life as "a seafaring man, a Souldior and a Courtier," and his poetry articulates much of what drove him to those vocations. He knew, deeply and bitterly, that, as he puts it in *The History of the World*, there is nothing more to "becoming a wise man" than "to retire himself from Court." However, the court was his stage, and it was, he wrote, the "token of a worldly wise man, not to warre or contend in vaine against the nature of the times wherein he lived." The achievement of his poetry is that it gives reverberating expression to the struggles of those who lived in and were controlled by the Elizabethan court. Most of his poems look, on the surface, like delicate, even trivial, songs, complaints, and compliments typical of Petrarchanism; but they are rich, if often confused, responses to the complex and powerful set of discourses, symbolic formations, and systems of representation that constituted the Elizabethan court. They offer a unique insight into the interplay between the social text of Elizabethan society (the events that made Ralegh's history) and the literary text (the poems that he made of those events). He is, in many ways, the quintessential court poet of the Elizabethan period inasmuch as his poems are haunted by, determined by, and finally silenced by, the power of the court.

## BIOGRAPHY

Although Ralegh is often spelled Raleigh, Walter Ralegh signed his name once as Rawleyghe, in 1587, then signed it Rauley until 1583, and more or less spelled it consistently as Ralegh from 1584 until his death in 1618. He was the quintessential *arriviste*: Born in Devon, educated at Oxford, he rapidly became a court favorite and was knighted in 1584, but fell into disgrace when, after a bitter rivalry with the up-and-coming younger earl of Essex, he was imprisoned for seducing one of the queen's maids-of-honor, Elizabeth Throckmorton, whom he later married. He was increasingly unpopular for, among other things, his flamboyant lifestyle. When James came to the throne, Ralegh was sentenced to death for treason, although the sentence was reduced to imprisonment in the Tower of London. During his imprisonment, between 1603 and 1616, Ralegh became a close friend of the prince of Wales, wrote extensively, and became a center of influence and even of counterestablishment power. He was released by James in 1616 and sent on an ill-fated expedition to Guiana, and on his return, executed—his death bewailed by as many people in 1618 as had desired it fourteen years earlier.

## ANALYSIS

If readers take him at his face value (or at the value of one of his many faces), Sir Walter Ralegh epitomized, accepted, and chose to live out the daring expansiveness and buoyancy of the Elizabethan court. He conceived of his own life as a poem, as a flamboyant epic gesture, and his poems were the manifestations of his public role and his political ambitions. However disguised in the garment of Petrarchan plaint, mournful song, lament for lost love, carpe diem or *ubi sunt* motif, Ralegh's poems are the articulation of the ruthless and sometimes blatant struggle for power that created and held together the court of Elizabeth. "Then must I needes advaunce my self by skyll,/ And lyve to serve, in hope of your goodwyll" he (possibly) wrote—and advancing himself with skill meant using the court as an arena of self-assertion, or (in another of the metaphors that disseminate contradictions throughout his work) as a new world to be conquered.

Ralegh's career as a poet and a courtier (the two are almost inseparable, literary and social text repeatedly writing and rewriting each other throughout his life) should not be simply seen as the daring, willful assertion of the gentleman adventurer who strode into the queen's favor with a graceful and opportune sweep of his cloak. That would be to take too much for granted at least some of his poems and the power in which, through them, Ralegh hoped to participate. Ralegh's poetry is put into play both by and in power; it demonstrates, probably more clearly than that of any other Elizabethan poet, the unconscious workings of power on discourse, specifically on the language which it controlled, selected, organized, and distributed through approved and determined procedures, delimiting as far as possible the emergence of opposition forces and experiences. The Elizabethan court used poetry and poets alike as the means of stabilizing and controlling its members. To confirm its residual values, it tried to restrict poet and poem as far as possible to the dominant discourses of a colorful, adventurous world, but only at the cost of a frustrating and, in Ralegh's case, despairing powerlessness.

## PETRARCHAN LYRICS

Much of Ralegh's poetry looks like typical Petrarchan love poetry—it can be, and no doubt was, to many members of its original audience, read as such. The surface of his verse presents the typical paraphernalia of the Petrarchan lyric—hope and despair, pleasure and fortune, fake love, frail beauty, fond shepherds, coy mistresses, and deceitful time. The magnificent "As you came from the holy land," which is possibly by Ralegh, can be read as a superbly melancholy affirmation of love, one of the most moving love lyrics of the language. "Nature that washt her hands in milke" takes the reader through a witty blazon of the perfect mistress's charms, her outside made of "snow and silke," her "inside . . . only of wantonesse and witt." Like all Petrarchan mistresses, she has "a heart of stone" and so the lover is poised, in frustration, before his ideal. Then in the second half of the poem, Ralegh ruthlessly tears down all the ideals he has built. What gives the poem its power is the unusually savage use of the Elizabethan commonplace of Time the destroyer, the thief—ravaging, lying, rusting, and annihilating. Time "turnes snow, and silke, and milke, to dust." What was to the lover the "food of joyes" is ceaselessly fed into the maw of death by time and remorselessly turned into excreta; the moistness of the mistress's wantonness rendered dry and repulsive. Likewise, the reply to Christopher Marlowe's "The Passionate Shepherd" is an impressively terse expression of the carpe diem principle, creating an impassioned stoical voice through the stylistic conventions of the plain Elizabethan voice. Typically, Ralegh has superb control of mood, movement, voice modulation, and an appropriately direct rhetoric.

## GIFTED AMATEUR

Ralegh's poems are those of the gifted amateur—seemingly casual compliment, occasional verse typically dropped, as the manuscript title of another poem has it, "into my Lady Laiton's pocket." Such a poem looks like one of the many erotic lyrics of the Renaissance which, as Michel Foucault has written, allowed men to overhear and will another to "speak the truth of" their sexuality. Ralegh's poetry, however, does more than introduce sexuality into discourse: Inevitably the language of erotic compliment and complaint is inseparable from the language of power. Despite their seemingly trivial, light, or occasional nature—epitaphs on Sir Philip Sidney's death, "A farewell to false love," dedicatory poems to works by George Gascoigne or Edmund Spenser, or poems directly or indirectly written to the queen—their significance reverberates far beyond their apparently replete surface configuration of stock metaphor and gracefully logical structure.

### RALEGH'S PUBLIC ROLES

Ralegh's predominant public roles were those of a man who consciously identified entirely with what he perceived as the dominant forces of his society—and, like his poetry, Ralegh's life is like a palimpsest, requiring not only reading but also interpretation and demystification in depth. As Stephen Greenblatt has suggestively argued, "Ralegh" is in a way a curiously hollow creation, the production of many roles in the theater of the court. Greenblatt has argued that Ralegh saw his life as a work of art, and the court as a "great theater" in which the boldest author would be the most successful. His career from the late 1570's might suggest that his multiplicity reflects an inner hollowness as he shifts back and forth among the roles of courtier, politician, explorer, freethinker, poet, philosopher, lover, and husband.

In Ralegh's public career, two dominant discourses clash and contradict—one seeing all human activity as an assertion of the adaptability of the actor, the other a pessimistic view of life as an empty, futile, and unreal theater. While Ralegh adapted to different roles as his ambitions shifted, his very restlessness bespeaks the power of the court. Unlike Sidney, who was a courtier by birth and privilege, Ralegh became one because his identity and survival depended on it. His place in a world that was dangerous and unpredictable was never stable, and even its apparently fixed center, the queen, was unpredictable and arbitrary.

### PROBLEMS OF ATTRIBUTION

Introducing Ralegh's role as a poet, it must be noted how the term "possibly" must be continually used to qualify assertions about the authorship of many of the poems attributed to him. Despite the confident assertions of some modern editors, Michael Rudick has shown that scholars do not in fact know whether many of the poems attributed to Ralegh in the manuscripts and miscellanies in which Elizabethan court poetry habitually circulated are in fact his; despite possessing more holograph material for Ralegh than for any other Elizabethan poets except Sir Thomas Wyatt and Robert Sidney, scholars can only speculate about the authorship of many of the best poems attributed to him. Even modern editors and biographers attribute poems to him on primarily sentimental grounds, but in one important sense, the lack of definitive attribution does not matter: Elizabethan court poetry often speaks with the voice of a collectivity, its authors *scriptors* or spokesmen for the values of a dominant class and its ideology. In short, the author's relationship to the languages that traverse him is much more complex than is allowed for by the sentimental nineteenth century biographical criticism that has held sway in Ralegh scholarship until very recently. In any court lyric, there is an illimitable series of pretexts, subtexts, and post-texts that call into question any concept of its "author" as a free, autonomous person. Ralegh's poems, like those of Sir Philip Sidney or Spenser, are sites of struggle, attempts by Ralegh (or whatever court poet may have "written" them) to write himself into the world. Hence there is a sense in which we should speak of "Ralegh" as the symptomatic court poet, rather than Ralegh the poet— or, perhaps, of "Ralegh" and "his" poems alike as texts, requiring always to be read against what they seem to articulate, often speaking out in their silences, in what they cannot or dare not say but nevertheless manage to express.

## COURT IDEOLOGY

Some of the poems are, however, very explicit about their ideological source, even verging on propagandist art. "Praisd be Dianas faire and harmles light" is a poem (again possibly by Ralegh) which reifies the ideals of the court in a hymn of celebration, demanding in ways that other Elizabethan lyrics rarely do, allegiance to the magical, timeless world of the Elizabethan court, in which no challenge to the replete atmosphere can be admitted and in which the readers are permitted to share only so long as they acknowledge the beauty of the goddess whom the poem celebrates. The poem's atmosphere is incantatory, its movement designed like court music to inculcate unquestioning reverence and subordination. Only the subhuman (presumably any reader foolish, or treasonous, enough to dissent from its vision) are excluded from the charm and power that it celebrates: "A knowledge pure it is hir worth to kno,/ With Circes let them dwell that thinke not so."

George Puttenham mentions Ralegh's poetry approvingly as "most lofty, insolent and passionate," and by the mid-1580's, when he expressed his view, Ralegh already had the reputation of being a fine craftsperson among the "crew of courtly makers, noblemen and gentlemen" of Elizabeth's court. In what another of Ralegh's contemporaries called the *"Terra infirma* of the Court," Ralegh used his verse as one of the many means of scrambling for position. His verse, in C. S. Lewis's words, is that of the quintessential adaptable courtly amateur, "blown this way and that (and sometimes lifted into real poetry)." He is the lover, poor in words but rich in affection; passions are likened to "floudes and streames"; the lover prays "in vayne" to "blinde fortune" but nevertheless resolves: "But love, farewell, thoughe fortune conquer thee,/ No fortune base nor frayle shall alter mee" ("In vayne my Eyes, in vayne yee waste your tears"). However apparently depoliticized these poems are, they are the product of the allurement and dominance of the court, their confidence less that of the poet himself than of the power of the structures in which he struggles to locate himself. His characteristic pose is that of the worshiper, devoted to the unapproachable mistress or, as the idealizing devotee with the queen as the unwavering star, the chaste goddess, the imperial embodiment of justice, the timeless principle around which the universe turns. In the way that Ben Jonson's masques were later to embody the ideology of the Jacobean court, so Ralegh's poems evoke the collective fantasy of the Elizabethan—a world that is harmonious and static, from which all change has been exorcized.

## HATFIELD POEMS

Aside from this miscellany (sometimes startlingly evocative, invariably competent and provoking), there are four closely connected and important poems, all undoubtedly Ralegh's, which were found in his own handwriting among the Cecil Papers in Hatfield House, north of London, the family home of Ralegh's great enemy Robert Cecil. They are "If Synthia be a Queene, a princes, and supreame," "My boddy in the walls captivated," "Sufficeth it to yow, my joyes interred"— which is headed "The 21th: and last booke of the Ocean to Scinthia"—and "The end of the bookes, of the Oceans love to Scinthia, and the beginninge of the 22 Boock, entreatinge of Sorrow." The existence of a poem, or poems, directly written to the queen and titled *Cynthia* seems to be mentioned by Spenser in *The Faerie Queene* (1590, 1596) and it is usually characterized as being parts of or related to the Hatfield poems. It is probably, however, that the third and fourth poems were written, or at least revised, during Ralegh's imprisonment in 1592.

## "THE 21TH: AND LAST BOOKE OF THE OCEAN TO SCINTHIA"

"The 21th: and last booke of the Ocean to Scinthia," the most important of the group, appears to be a scarcely revised draft of an appeal, if not to the queen herself, at least to that part of Ralegh's mind occupied by her power. It lacks narrative links; its four-line stanzas are often imperfect, with repetitions and gaps that presumably would have been revised later. Its unfinished state, however, makes it not only a fascinating revelation of Ralegh's personal and poetic anguish, but also perhaps the clearest example in Elizabethan court poetry of the way the dynamics and contradictions of power speak through a text. "The 21th: and last booke of the Ocean to Scinthia" repeatedly deconstructs the philosophy to which it gives allegiance: Its incoherences, gaps, uncertainties, and repetitions both affirm and negate Elizabethan mythology. What in Ralegh's other poems is expressed as complete ideological closure is undermined by the fractures and symptomatic maladjustments of the text. Nowhere in Elizabethan poetry is a poem as obviously constitutive of ideological struggle.

The poem is addressed to a patently transparent Cynthia who has withdrawn her favor from the faithful lover. Ralegh projects himself as a despairing lover fearfully aware that his service has been swept into oblivion, simultaneously acknowledging that honors inevitably corrupt and that he cannot keep from pursuing them. The "love" that he has seemingly won includes favors that open doors not only to glory but also to ruin and death. However, even knowing this, it is as if he cannot help himself "seeke new worlds, for golde, for prayse, for glory," with the tragic result that "Twelve yeares intire I wasted in this warr." The result of his "twelve yeares" dedication has been imprisonment and disgrace, yet he is helpless before his own inability to abandon the glories of office. "Trew reason" shows power to be worthless, but even while he knows that "all droopes, all dyes, all troden under dust," he knows also that the only stability in the world of power is the necessity of instability and emulation.

The Petrarchan motifs with which the successful courtier has played so effectively, almost on demand—the helpless lover wooing the unapproachable mistress who is the unattainable goal of desire—have suddenly and savagely been literalized. The role that Ralegh has played has exploded his habitual adaptability. He cannot protest that the game of the despairing lover is only a game; it has now become real. In 1592, he wrote to Cecil: "My heart was never broken till this day, that I hear the queen goes away so far off—whom I have followed so many years with so great love and desire, in so many journeys, and am now left behind her in a great prison alone." The letter is an obvious echo of the lines from Ralegh's adaption of the Walsingham ballad, "As you came from the holy land." The contradictions of Ralegh's life which the poem now voices had been repressed and silenced during his imprisonment, but now they are revealed as terrifyingly real. By marrying, Ralegh himself has ceased to play Elizabeth's game; he has thus found that the role of masochistic victim in which he cast himself for political advantage has been taken literally and he has become an outcast. "The 21th: and last booke of the Ocean to Scinthia" expresses the agony of a man whose choices and commitments have been built on the myth of a changeless past in an ever-moving power struggle. The very unfinished quality of Ralegh's fragment is the perfect formal expression of the disruptiveness that has overwhelmed him.

### "THE LIE"

It is fortunate that another key poem in this period is among the Hatfield manuscripts. "The Lie" is a release of explicit rage, a struggle to find form for deep frustration and venom, finding no alternative to renunciation and repulsion. It is a statement of deeply felt impotence, probably written after Ralegh's release from prison in 1592, but before he was restored to favor. Ralegh's poem is seemingly total in its rejection of the ideology by which he has lived: Natural law, universal harmony, love, and court artifice are all rejected in a mood of total condemnation. However, Ralegh's poem is neither philosophically nihilistic nor politically radical: The force of his revulsion from the court does not allow for any alternative to it. What dies is the "I" of the poem, as he gives the lie to the world, and takes refuge in a savage *contemptus mundi*. "The Lie" is at once an explosion of frustration and beneath ideological confidence. In such poems, the ideology is betrayed by writing itself; the poem constantly releases an anxiety for realities that challenge the surface harmonies and struggle unsuccessfully to be heard against the dominant language of the court poetic mode. What readers start to recognize as Ralegh's characteristic melancholic formulation of the persistence of "woe" or pain as the very mark of human self-consciousness is the special telltale sign of his texts as sites of struggle and repression. "The life expires, the woe remaines" is a refrain echoed by "Of all which past, the sorrow, only stays" ("Like truthless dreams") and by phrases in *The History of the World* such as "Of all our vain passions and affections past, the sorrow only abideth." Such recurring motifs impart more than a characteristic tone to Ralegh's verse. They point to the frustrated insurrection of subjugated experience struggling to find expression, knowing that there are no words permitted for it.

## LEGACY

Ralegh's poems, then, are haunted by what they try to exorcise: a fragility that arises from the repressed political uncertainties of court life in the 1580's and 1590's and that undermines his chosen role as the spokesperson of a replete court ideology. Despite its confident surface, all his verse is less a celebration of the queen's power than a conspiracy to remain within its protection. The Petrarchan clichés of "Like truthless dreams, so are my joys expired" and the Neoplatonic commonplaces of the "Walsingham" ballad become desperate pleas for favor, projections into lyric poems of political machinations. "Concept begotten by the eyes" also starts out as a stereotypical contrast between "desire" and "woe" and emerges as a poignant cry of radical insecurity and a powerless acknowledgment that the personality of the court poet and of Ralegh himself is a creation of the discourses he has uneasily inhabited and from which he now feels expelled. The Hatfield poems illustrate with wonderful clarity what all Elizabethan court poetry tries to repress: that however the poet asserts his autonomy, he is constituted through ideology, having no existence outside the social formation and the signifying practice legitimized by the power of the court. Ralegh, like every other poet who wrestled within the court, does not speak so much as he is spoken.

More than twenty years later, after a revival of fortunes under Elizabeth, arrest, imprisonment, release, and rearrest under James, Ralegh prematurely brought his history to an end. The work, written to justify God's providential control of time, articulates a view of history that radically undercuts its author's intentions. For Ralegh, history has no final eschatological goal, no ultimate consummation. It consists only of the continual vengeance of an angry God until "the long day of mankinde is drawing fast towards an evening, and the world's Tragedie and time neare at an end." A few years later, on the eve of his execution, Ralegh took up the last lines of the lyric written twenty-five years before on the ravages of time that he had felt all his life:

> Even such is tyme which takes in trust
> Our yowth, our Joyes, and all we have,
> And payes us butt with age and dust:
> When we have wandred all our wayes,
> Shutts up the storye of our dayes.

He appended to it, in two new lines, the only hope of which he could conceive, a deus ex machina to rescue him, in a way that neither queen nor king had, from the grip of time's power: "And from which earth and grave and dust/ The Lord shall raise me up I trust." It is a cry of desperation, not a transformation of "the consuming disease of time" as he puts it in *The History of the World.* What is finally triumphant over Ralegh is the power of the world in which he courageously yet blindly struggled and of which his handful of poems are an extraordinarily moving acknowledgment and testament.

OTHER MAJOR WORKS

NONFICTION: *A Report of the Fight About the Iles of Açores*, 1591; *The Discoverie of the Large, Rich, and Bewtiful Empyre of Guiana*, 1596; *The History of the World*, 1614.

MISCELLANEOUS: *Works of Sir Walter Ralegh*, 1829 (8 volumes; Thomas Birch and William Oldys, editors); *Selected Prose and Poetry*, 1965 (Agnes Latham, editor).

BIBLIOGRAPHY

Beer, Anna. *Bess: The Life of Lady Ralegh, Wife to Sir Walter.* London: Constable, 2004. Beer tells the story of Elizabeth Throckmorton, whose marriage to Ralegh provoked the queen.

Greenblatt, Stephen J. *Sir Walter Ralegh: The Renaissance Man and His Roles.* New Haven, Conn.: Yale University Press, 1973. Greenblatt discusses Ralegh's role-playing and theatrical nature as demonstrated in his court poetry and in *The History of the World*, both of which receive chapter-length treatments. He also provides the context for *The Discoverie of the Large, Rich, and Bewtiful Empyre of Guiana*, which he regards as reflecting Ralegh's personal sorrow and the national myths of his age.

Lacey, Robert. *Sir Walter Ralegh.* 1974. Reprint. London: Phoenix Press, 2000. Lacey's account reflects the multifaceted nature of his subject in the book's structure. There are some fifty chapters, divided into seven sections, each charting the ups and downs of Ralegh's checkered career. From country upstart to royal favorite, from privateer to traitor in the Tower, his life was never still.

Lyons, Mathew. *The Favourite: Ambition, Politics and Love—Sir Walter Ralegh in Elizabeth I's Court.* London: Constable, 2009. Examines Ralegh's relationship with Queen Elizabeth and how he fell out of favor.

Ralegh, Walter. *The Letters of Sir Walter Ralegh.* Edited by Agnes Latham and Joyce Youings. Exeter, England: University of Exeter Press, 1999. Brings together all that is known of Ralegh's correspondence, uncollected since 1868 and much expanded and refined. Students of history and literature will grasp at this book as it throws a beam across the life of one of the more attractive personalities of the late Tudor and early Jacobean periods.

Waller, Gary. *English Poetry of the Sixteenth Century.* 2d ed. New York: Longman,

1993. Waller deconstructs Ralegh's poetry, which he claims demonstrates how power works on language. For Waller, Ralegh's poetry simultaneously pays homage to and criticizes the courtly arena where he must play different roles. "As You Come from the Holy Land" and one of the "Scinthia" poems, thus, become poems of tension and value.

*Gary F. Waller*

# WILLIAM SHAKESPEARE

**Born:** Stratford-upon-Avon, Warwickshire, England; April 23, 1564
**Died:** Stratford-upon-Avon, Warwickshire, England; April 23, 1616

Principal poetry

*Venus and Adonis*, 1593
*The Rape of Lucrece*, 1594
*The Passionate Pilgrim*, 1599 (miscellany with poems by Shakespeare and others)
*The Phoenix and the Turtle*, 1601
*A Lover's Complaint*, 1609
*Sonnets*, 1609

## Other literary forms

William Shakespeare is perhaps the world's greatest dramatist—certainly, at the very least, the greatest to write in English. Of his thirty-seven plays, written over a career in the theater that spanned, roughly, 1588 to 1613, the most important are *Romeo and Juliet* (pr. c. 1595-1596); *Henry IV, Parts I* and *II* (pr. c. 1597-1598; 1598); *Hamlet, Prince of Denmark* (pr. c. 1600-1601); *Othello, The Moor of Venice* (pr. 1604); *Measure for Measure* (pr. 1604); *King Lear* (pr. c. 1605-1606); *Macbeth* (pr. 1606); *Antony and Cleopatra* (pr. c. 1606-1607); *The Winter's Tale* (pr. c. 1610-1611); and *The Tempest* (pr. 1611).

## Achievements

William Shakespeare also wrote some of the greatest love poems in English. His short erotic narratives, *Venus and Adonis* and *The Rape of Lucrece*, were typical examples of fashionable literary genres. Other minor poems include contributions to the miscellany *The Passionate Pilgrim* and *The Phoenix and the Turtle*, written for a collection of poems appended to *Love's Martyr* (1601), an allegorical treatment of love by Robert Chester. All these pale alongside the sonnets, which, in an age of outstanding love poetry, attain a depth, suggestiveness, and power rarely duplicated in the history of humankind's passionate struggle to match desire with words.

## Biography

William Shakespeare was born in the provincial town of Stratford-upon-Avon in 1564 and died there in 1616. He spent most of his adult life in the London theaters and quickly attained a reputation as a dramatist, actor, and poet. Shakespeare's company prospered under the reign of James I, and by the time of his retirement from playwriting about 1612, Shakespeare had acquired a respectable fortune. His career as a poet,

*William Shakespeare*
(Library of Congress)

distinct from his more public career as a dramatist, was probably confined to perhaps a decade, between 1591 and 1601, although the sonnets were later collected and published (perhaps without his permission) in 1609. Because of the absurd controversies that grew, mainly in the nineteenth century, about whether Shakespeare actually existed, it is worthwhile pointing out that there are many official records (christening record, marriage license, legal documents, correspondence, and so on) which may be consulted by the skeptical.

ANALYSIS

One of William Shakespeare's great advantages as a writer was that, as a dramatist working in the public theater, he was afforded a degree of autonomy from the cultural dominance of the court, his age's most powerful institution. All over Europe, even if belatedly in England, the courts of the Renaissance nation-states conducted an intense campaign to use the arts to further their power. The theater, despite its partial dependency on court favor, achieved through its material products (the script and the performance) a relative autonomy in comparison with the central court arts of poetry, prose fiction, and the propagandistic masque. When Shakespeare briefly turned to Ovidian romance in the 1590's and, belatedly, probably also in the 1590's, to the fashion for sonnets, he moved closer to the cultural and literary dominance of the court's taste—to the fashionable modes of Ovid, Petrarch, and Neoplatonism—and to the need for patronage. Although the power of the sonnets goes far beyond their sociocultural roots, Shakespeare nevertheless adopts the culturally inferior role of the petitioner for favor, and there is an undercurrent of social and economic powerlessness in the sonnets, especially when a rival poet seems likely to supplant the poet. In short, Shakespeare's nondramatic poems grow out of and articulate the strains of the 1590's, when, like many ambitious writers and intellectuals on the fringe of the court, Shakespeare clearly needed to find a language in which to speak—and that was, necessarily, given to him by the court. What he achieved within this shared framework, however, goes far beyond any other collection of poems in the age. Shakespeare's occasional poems are unquestionably minor, interesting primarily because he wrote them; his sonnets, on the other hand, constitute perhaps the language's greatest collection of lyrics. They are love lyrics, and clearly grow from the social, erotic, and literary contexts of his age. Part of their greatness, however, lies in their power to be read again and again in later ages, and to raise compellingly, even unanswerably, more than merely literary questions.

## VENUS AND ADONIS

In his first venture into public poetry, Shakespeare chose to work within the generic constraints of the fashionable Ovidian verse romance. *Venus and Adonis* appealed to the taste of young aristocrats such as the earl of Southampton to whom it was dedicated. It is a narrative poem in six-line stanzas, mixing classical mythology with surprisingly (and incongruously) detailed descriptions of country life, designed to illustrate the story of the seduction of the beautiful youth Adonis by the comically desperate aging goddess Venus. It is relatively static, with too much argument to make it inherently pleasurable reading. Its treatment of love relies on Neoplatonic and Ovidian commonplaces, and it verges (unlike Christopher Marlowe's *Hero and Leander*, 1598, to which Shakespeare's poem is a fair but decidedly inferior fellow) on moralizing allegory, with Venus as flesh, Adonis as spiritual longing. The poem's articulation of the nature of the love that separates them is abstract and often unintentionally comic—although Shakespeare's characterization of Venus as a garrulous plump matron brings something of his theatrical power to enliven the poem. The poem was certainly popular at the time, going through ten editions in as many years, possibly because its early readers thought it fashionably sensual.

## THE RAPE OF LUCRECE

*The Rape of Lucrece* is the "graver labor" that Shakespeare promised to Southampton in the preface to *Venus and Adonis*. Again, he combines a current poetical fashion—the complaint—with a number of moral commonplaces, and writes a novelette in verse: a melodrama celebrating the prototype of matronly chastity, the Roman lady Lucrece, and her suicide after she was raped. The central moral issue—that of honor—at times almost becomes a serious treatment of the psychology of self-revulsion; but the decorative and moralistic conventions of the complaint certainly do not afford Shakespeare the scope of a stage play. There are some fine local atmospheric effects that, in their declamatory power, occasionally bring the directness and power of the stage into the verse.

### THE PHOENIX AND THE TURTLE

*The Phoenix and the Turtle* is an allegorical, highly technical celebration of an ideal love union: It consists of a funeral procession of mourners, a funeral anthem, and a final lament for the dead. It is strangely evocative, dignified, abstract, and solemn. Readers have fretted, without success, over the exact identifications of its characters. Its power lies in its mysterious, eerie evocation of the mystery of unity in love.

### SONNETS

Probably more human ingenuity has been spent on Shakespeare's sonnets than on any other work of English literature. In *Shakespeare's Sonnets* (1978), Stephen Booth briefly summarizes the few facts that have led to a plethora of speculation on such matters as text, authenticity, date, arrangement, and, especially, biographical implications. The sonnets were first published in 1609, although numbers 138 and 144 had appeared in *The Passionate Pilgrim* a decade before. Attempts to reorder the sonnets have been both varied and creative, but none represents the "correct" order. Such attempts simply fulfill an understandable anxiety on the part of some readers to see narrative continuity rather than variations and repetition in the sonnets. The "story behind" the sonnets has, as Booth puts it, "evoked some notoriously creative scholarship": speculation on the identity of the young man mentioned in many of the first 126 sonnets, of Mr. W. H., to whom the sequence is dedicated by the printer, of the "Dark Lady" of sonnets 127-152, and of the rival poet of some of the earlier sonnets—all these matters have filled many library shelves.

Such speculations—which reached their peak in critics and readers wedded to the sentimental Romantic insistence on an intimate tie between literary and historical "events"—are in one sense a tribute to the power of the sonnets. They are arguably the greatest collection of love poems in the language, and they provide a crucial test for the adequacy of both the love of poetry and the sense of the fascinating confusion that makes up human love. In a sense, the sonnets are as "dramatic" as any of Shakespeare's plays inasmuch as their art is that of meditations on love, beauty, time, betrayal, insecurity, and joy. Each sonnet is like a little script, with (often powerful) directions for reading and enactment, with textual meanings that are not given but made anew in every performance, by different readers within their individual and social lives. What Sonnet 87 terms "misprision" may stand as the necessary process by which each sonnet is produced by each reader.

It is conventional to divide the sonnets into two groups—1-126, purportedly addressed or related to a young man, and 127-152, to the "Dark Lady." Such a division is arbitrary at best—within each group there are detachable subgroups, and without the weight of the conventional arrangement, many sonnets would not seem to have a natural place in either group. Sonnets 1-17 (and perhaps 18) are ostensibly concerned with a plea for a young man to marry; but even in this group, which many readers have seen to be the most conventional and unified, there are disruptive suggestions that go far beyond the commonplace context.

What may strike contemporary readers, and not merely after an initial acquaintance with the sonnets, is the apparently unjustified level of idealization voiced by many of the sonnets—an adulatory treatment of noble love that, to a post-Freudian world, might seem archaic, no matter how comforting. The continual self-effacement of the anguished lover, the worship of the "God in love, to whom I am confined" (110), the poet's claim to immortalizing "his beautie . . . in these blacke lines" (63), are all idealizations born out of a world of serene affirmation. Some of the most celebrated sonnets, such as "Shall I compare thee to a summer's day" (18) or "Let me not to the marriage of true minds" (116), may even seem cloyingly affirmative, their texts seemingly replete, rejecting any subtextual challenges to their idealism.

In the two hundred years since Petrarch, the sonnet had developed into an instrument of logic and rhetoric. The Shakespearian sonnet, on the other hand, with its three quatrains and a concluding couplet, allows especially for the concentration on a single mood; it is held together less by the apparent logic of many of the sonnets (for example, the "when . . . then" pattern) than by the invitation to enter into the dramatization of a brooding, sensitive mind. The focus is on emotional richness, on evoking the immediacy of felt experience. Shakespeare uses many deliberately generalized epithets, indeterminate signifiers and floating referents that provoke meaning from their readers rather than providing it. Each line contains contradictions, echoes, and suggestions that require an extraordinary degree of emotional activity on the part of the reader. The couplets frequently offer a reader indeterminate statements, inevitably breaking down any attempt at a limited formalist reading. The greatest of the sonnets—60, 64, 129, as well as many others—have such an extraordinary combination of general, even abstract, words and unspecified emotional power that the reader may take it as the major rhetorical characteristic of the collection.

In particular lines, too, these poems achieve amazing power by their lack of logical specificity and emotional open-endedness. As Booth points out, many lines show "a constructive vagueness" by which a word or phrase is made to do multiple duty—by placing it "in a context to which it pertains but which it does not quite fit idiomatically" or by using phrases that are simultaneously illogical and amazingly charged with meaning. He instances "separable spite" in Sonnet 36 as a phrase rich with suggestion; another example is the way in which the bewilderingly ordinary yet suggestive epithets sit uneasily in the opening lines of Sonnet 64. Often a reader is swept on through the poem by a syntactical movement that is modified or contradicted by associations set up by words and phrases. There is usually a syntactical or logical framework in the sonnet, but so powerful are the contradictory, random, and disruptive effects occurring incidentally as the syntax unfolds that to reduce the sonnet to its seemingly replete logical framework is to miss the most amazing effects of these extraordinary poems.

Shakespeare is writing at the end of a very long tradition of using lyric poems to examine the nature of human love, and there is a weight of insight as well as of rhetorical power behind his collection. Nowhere in the Petrarchan tradition are the extremes of erotic revelation offered in such rawness and complexity. Northrop Frye once characterized the sonnets as a kind of "creative yoga," an imaginative discipline meant to articulate the feelings that swirl around sexuality. Most of the conventional topoi of traditional poetry are the starting points for the sonnets—the unity of lovers (36-40), the power of poetry to immortalize the beloved (18, 19, 55), contests between eye and heart, beauty and virtue (46, 141), and shadow and substance (53, 98, 101). As with Petrarch's *Rerum vulgarium fragmenta* (1470, also known as *Canzoniere*; *Rhymes*, 1976) or Sir Philip Sidney's *Astrophel and Stella* (1591), it would be possible to create a schematic account of commonplace Renaissance thinking about love from the sonnets. To do so, however, would be to nullify their extraordinary power of creation, the way they force ejaculations of recognition, horror, or joy from their readers.

After half a century of existentialism, readers in the late twentieth century understood that one of the most urgent subjects of the sonnets is not the commonplaces of Renaissance thinking about love, nor even the powerful concern with the power of art, but what Sonnet 16 calls people's "war upon this bloody tyrant Time." It is no accident that the "discovery" of the sonnets' concern with time and mutability dates from the 1930's, when the impact of Søren Kierkegaard, Friedrich Nietzsche, and the existentialists, including Martin Heidegger, was starting to be widely felt in England and the United States. The sonnets' invitation to see humans' temporality not merely as an abstract problem but as part of their inherent nature—what Heidegger terms humans' "thrownness," their sense of being thrown into the world—seems central to a perception of the sonnets' power. Unpredictability and change are at the heart of the sonnets—but it is a continually shifting heart, and one that conceives of human love as definable only in terms of such change and finitude. The sonnets avoid the transcendentalism of Geoffrey Chaucer beseeching his young lovers to turn from the world, or of Edmund Spenser rejecting change for the reassurance of God's eternity and his providential guidance of time to a foreknown, if mysterious, end. Shakespeare's sonnets rather overwhelm readers with questions and contradictions. In Sonnet 60, for example, time is not an impartial or abstract background. Even where it is glanced at as a pattern observable in nature or humanity, it is evoked as a disruptive, disturbing experience that cannot be dealt with as a philosophical problem. Some sonnets portray time as a sinister impersonal determinant; some thrust time at the reader as an equally unmanageable force of unforeseeable chances and changes, what Sonnet 115 calls humanity's "million'd accidents."

In Sonnet 15, it may be possible to enter into an understandable protest against time destroying its own creations (a commonplace enough Renaissance sentiment), and to accede to a sense of helplessness before a malignant force greater than the individual human being. When the sonnet tries, however, by virtue of its formally structured argument, to create a consciousness that seeks to understand and so to control this awareness, the reader encounters lines or individual words that may undermine even the temporary satisfaction of the aesthetic form. Such, for example is the force of the appalling awareness that "everything that grows/ Holds in perfection but a little moment." What is the application of "everything" or the emotional effect of the way the second line builds to a seemingly replete climax in "perfection" and then tumbles into oblivion in "but a little moment"? The sonnet does not and need not answer such questions. In a very real sense, it cannot answer them, for readers can only acknowledge time's power in their own contingent lives. What is shocking is not merely the commonplace that "never-resting time leads summer on/ To hideous winter, and confounds him there" (5) but that each reading fights against and so disrupts the logical and aesthetic coherence of the reader's own sense of change and betrayal.

To attempt criticism of the sonnets is, to an unusual extent, to be challenged to make oneself vulnerable, to undergo a kind of creative therapy, as one goes back and forth from such textual gaps and indeterminacies to the shifting, vulnerable self, making the reader aware of the inadequacy and betrayal of words, as well as of their amazing seductiveness. Consider, for example, Sonnet 138. When one falls in love with a much younger person, does one inevitably feel the insecurity of a generation gap? What is more important in such a reading of the sonnets is the insistence that age or youthfulness are not important in themselves: It is the insistence itself that is important, not the mere fact of age—just as it is the anxiety with which a man or woman watches the wrinkles beneath the eyes that is important, not the wrinkles themselves. The note of insistence, in other words, is not attached merely to the speaker's age: It stands for an invitation to participate in some wider psychological revelation, to confess the vulnerability that people encounter in themselves in any relationship that is real and growing, and therefore necessarily unpredictable and risky.

Without vulnerability and contingency, without the sense of being thrown into the world, there can be no growth. Hence the poet invites the reader to accept ruefully what the fact of his age evokes—an openness to ridicule or rejection. The sonnet's insistence on being open to the insecurity represented by the narrator's age points not merely to a contrast between the speaker and his two lovers but rather to a radical self-division. This is especially so in the Dark Lady sonnets, where there is a savage laceration of self, particularly in the fearful exhaustion of Sonnet 129, in which vulnerability is evoked as paralysis. At once logically relentless and emotionally centrifugal, Sonnet 129 generates fears or vulnerability and self-disgust. Nothing is specified: The strategies of the poem work to make the reader reveal or recognize his or her own compulsions and revulsions. The poem's physical, psychological, and cultural basis forces the reader to become aware of his or her awful drive to repress words because they are potentially so destructive.

Even in the seemingly most serene sonnets, there are inevitably dark shadows of insecurity and anxiety. In Sonnet 116, for example, the argument is that a love that alters with time and circumstance is not a true, but a self-regarding love.

The poem purports to define true love by negatives, but if those negatives are deliberately negated, the poem that emerges may be seen as the dark, repressed underside of the apparently unassailable affirmation of a mature, self-giving, other-directed love. If lovers admit impediments, and play with the idea that love is indeed love which "alters when it alteration finds," that it is an "ever-fixed mark" and, most especially, that love is indeed "time's fool," then the poem connects strikingly and powerfully with the strain of insecurity about the nature of change in human love that echoes throughout the whole collection. Such apparent affirmations may be acts of repression, an attempt to regiment the unrelenting unexpectedness and challenge of love. There are poems in the collection that, although less assertive, show a willingness to be vulnerable, to reevaluate constantly, to swear permanence within, not despite, transience—to be, in the words of Saint Paul, deceivers yet true. Elsewhere, part of the torture of the Dark Lady sonnets is that such a consolation does not emerge through the pain.

In short, what Sonnet 116 represses is the acknowledgment that the only fulfillment worth having is one that is struggled for and that is independent of law or compulsion. The kind of creative fragility that it tries to marginalize is that evoked in the conclusion to Sonnet 49 when the poet admits his vulnerability: "To leave poor me thou hast the strength of laws,/ Since, why to love, I can allege no cause." This is an affirmation of a different order—or rather an acknowledgment that love must not be defined by repression and exclusion. Lovers can affirm the authenticity of the erotic only by admitting the possibility that it is not absolute. Love has no absolute legal, moral, or causal claims; nor, in the final analysis, can love acknowledge the bonds of law, family, or state—or if finally they are acknowledged, it is because they grow from love itself. Love moves by its own internal dynamic; it is not motivated by a series of external compulsions. Ultimately it asks from the lover the *nolo contendere* of commitment: Do with me what you will. A real, that is to say, an altering, bending, never fixed and unpredictable love is always surrounded by, and at times seems to live by, battles, plots, subterfuges, quarrels, and irony. At the root is the acknowledgment that any affirmation is made because of, not despite, time and human mortality. As Sonnet 12 puts it, having surveyed the fearful unpredictability of all life, lovers must realize that it is even "thy beauty" that must be questioned. At times this thought "is as a death" (64), a "fearful meditation" (65)—that even the most precious of all human creations will age, wrinkle, fade, and die. Just how can one affirm in the face of that degree of reality?

Under the pressure of such questioning, the affirmation of Sonnet 116 can therefore be seen as a kind of bad faith, a false dread—false, because it freezes lovers in inactivity when they should, on the contrary, accept their finitude as possibility. Frozen in the fear of contingency, which Sonnet 116 so ruthlessly represses in its insistent negatives, readers may miss Shakespeare's essential insight that it is in fact the very fragility of beauty, love, poetry, fair youth, and dark lady alike that enhances their desirability. Paradoxically, it is precisely because they are indeed among the wastes of time that they are beautiful; they are not desirable because they are immortal but because they are irrevocably time-bound. One of the most profound truths is expressed in Sonnet 64: "Ruin hath taught me thus to ruminate/ That Time will come and take my love away./ This thought is as a death, which cannot choose/ But weep to have that which it fears to lose." The power of such lines goes far beyond the serene platitudes of Sonnet 116. At their most courageous, humans do not merely affirm, despite the forces of change and unpredictability that provide the ever-shifting centers of their lives; on the contrary, they discover their greatest strengths because of and within their own contingency. To accept rather than to deny time is to prove that humanity's deepest life ultimately does not recognize stasis but always craves growth, and that fulfillment is built not on the need for finality, for being "ever fixed," but on the need to violate apparent limits, to push forward or die.

Against a sonnet such as 116, some sonnets depict love not as a serene continuation of life but rather as a radical reorientation. Readers are asked not to dismiss, but to affirm fears of limitation. It is in the midst of contingency, when meditations are overwhelmed by the betrayals of the past, while "I sigh the lack of many a thing I sought,/ And with old woes new wail my dear Time's waste" (Sonnet 30), that love may open up the future as possibility, not as completion—so long as one accepts that it is time itself that offers such possibility, not any attempt to escape from it.

The typical Renaissance attitude to time and mutability was one of fear or resignation unless, as in Spenser, the traditional Christian context could be evoked as compensation; but for Shakespeare the enormous energies released by the Renaissance are wasted in trying to escape the burden of temporality. The drive to stasis, to repress experiences and meanings, is a desire to escape the burden of realizing that there are some transformations which love cannot effect. Ultimately, it is impossible to get inside a lover's soul no matter how much the flesh is seized and penetrated. The drive to possess and so to annihilate is a desire derived from the old Platonic ideal of original oneness, which only Shakespeare among the Renaissance poets seems to have seen as a clear and fearful perversion—it certainly haunts the lover of the Dark Lady sonnets and readers are invited to stand and shudder at the speaker's Augustinian self-lacerations. In Sonnet 144, the two loves "of comfort and despair,/ Which like two spirits do suggest me still" are not just a "man right fair" and a "woman, colour'd ill": They are also aspects of each lover's self, the two loves that a dualistic mind cannot affirm and by which people may be paralyzed.

Throughout this discussion of the sonnets, what has been stressed is that their power rests on the seemingly fragile basis not of Shakespeare's but of their readers' shifting and unpredictable experiences. They are offered not in certainty, but in hope. They invite affirmation while insisting that pain is the dark visceral element in which humans must live and struggle. Many of the Dark Lady sonnets are grim precisely because the lover can see no way to break through such pain. What they lack, fundamentally, is hope. By accepting that, for a time, "my grief lies onward and my joy behind" (Sonnet 50), the lover may be able, however temporarily, to make some commitment. Sonnet 124 is particularly suggestive, categorizing love as "dear," costly, not only because it is "fond," beloved, but also because it is affirmed in the knowledge of the world. Moreover, while it "fears not Policy" it is nevertheless "hugely politic." It is as if love must be adaptable, cunning, even deceptive, aware of the untrustworthiness of the world from which it can never be abstracted: "it nor grows with heat, nor drowns with showers." Finally, the poet affirms with a strong and yet strangely ironic twist: "To this I witness call the fools of Time,/ Which die for goodness, who have liv'd for crime."

As Stephen Booth notes, Sonnet 124 "is the most extreme example of Shakespeare's constructive vagueness," its key the word "it," which, "like all pronouns, is specific, hard, concrete, and yet imprecise and general—able to include anything or nothing." "It" occurs five times, each time becoming more indeterminate, surrounded by subjectives and negatives: In this sonnet "composed of precisely evocative words in apparently communicative syntaxes which come to nothing and give a sense of summing up everything, the word *it* stands sure, constant, forthright, simple and blank." The blankness to which Booth points has been filled very specifically by generations of readers to force the poem into a repressive argument like that of Sonnet 116. For example, the key phrase "the fools of time" is usually glossed as local, historical examples of political or religious timeservers—but the phrase contains mysterious reverberations back upon the lovers themselves. There is a sense in which men are all fools of time. When Sonnet 116 affirms that "Love's not Time's fool," it betrays a deliberate and fearful repression; an unwillingness to acknowledge that Love is not able to overcome Time; time is something that can be fulfilled only as it presents opportunity and possibility to humans. People rightly become fools—jesters, dancers in attendance on Time, holy fools before the creative challenge of humanity's finitude—and people die, are fulfilled sexually, existentially, only if they submit themselves, "hugely politic," to the inevitable compromises, violence, and disruption which is life. People "die for goodness" because in a sense they have all "lived for crime." People are deceivers yet true; the truest acts, like the truest poetry, are the most feigning.

The twelve-line Sonnet 126 is conventionally regarded as the culmination of the first part of the sequence. Its serenity is very unlike that of 116. It acknowledges that, even if the fair youth is indeed Nature's "minion," even he must eventually be "rendered." Such realism does not detract from the Youth's beauty or desirability; it in fact constitutes its power.

Whether one considers the Fair Youth or the Dark Lady sonnets, or whether one attempts to see a "hidden" order in the sonnets, or even if one wishes to see a story or some kind of biographical origin "within" them, perhaps their greatness rests on their refusal to offer even the possibility of "solutions" to the "problems" they raise. They disturb, provoke, and ask more than merely "aesthetic" questions; read singly or together, they make readers face (or hide from) and question the most fundamental elements of poetry, love, time, and death.

OTHER MAJOR WORKS

PLAYS: *Edward III*, pr. c. 1589-1595 (attributed to Shakespeare); *Henry VI, Part II*, pr. c. 1590-1591; *Henry VI, Part III*, pr. c. 1590-1591; *Henry VI, Part I*, pr. 1592 (wr. 1589-1590); *Richard III*, pr. c. 1592-1593 (revised 1623); *The Comedy of Errors*, pr. c. 1592-1594; *The Taming of the Shrew*, pr. c. 1593-1594; *Titus Andronicus*, pr., pb. 1594; *Love's Labour's Lost*, pr. c. 1594-1595 (revised 1597 for court performance); *The Two Gentlemen of Verona*, pr. c. 1594-1595; *A Midsummer Night's Dream*, pr. c. 1595-1596; *Richard II*, pr. c. 1595-1596; *Romeo and Juliet*, pr. c. 1595-1596; *King John*, pr. c. 1596-1597; *The Merchant of Venice*, pr. c. 1596-1597; *The Merry Wives of Windsor*, pr. 1597 (revised c. 1600-1601); *Henry IV, Part I*, pr. c. 1597-1598; *Henry IV, Part II*, pr. 1598; *Henry V*, pr. c. 1598-1599; *Much Ado About Nothing*, pr. c. 1598-1599; *As You Like It*, pr. c. 1599-1600; *Julius Caesar*, pr. c. 1599-1600; *Hamlet, Prince of Denmark*, pr. c. 1600-1601; *Twelfth Night: Or, What You Will*, pr. c. 1600-1602; *Troilus and Cressida*, pr. c. 1601-1602; *All's Well That Ends Well*, pr. c. 1602-1603; *Measure for Measure*, pr. 1604; *Othello, the Moor of Venice*, pr. 1604 (revised 1623); *King Lear*, pr. c. 1605-1606; *Macbeth*, pr. 1606; *Antony and Cleopatra*, pr. c. 1606-1607; *Coriolanus*, pr. c. 1607-1608; *Pericles, Prince of Tyre*, pr. c. 1607-1608; *Timon of Athens*, pr. c. 1607-1608; *Cymbeline*, pr. c. 1609-1610; *The Winter's Tale*, pr. c. 1610-1611; *The Tempest*, pr. 1611; *The Two Noble Kinsmen*, pr. c. 1612-1613 (with John Fletcher); *Henry VIII*, pr. 1613 (with Fletcher).

BIBLIOGRAPHY

Ackroyd, Peter. *Shakespeare: The Biography.* New York: Nan A. Talese, 2005. An examination of the life and works of Shakespeare, including his poetry.

Bate, Jonathan. *Soul of the Age: A Biography of the Mind of William Shakespeare.* New York: Random House, 2009. A biography of Shakespeare that attempts to look at his life and writings as they relate to the times in which he lived.

Bloom, Harold, ed. *The Sonnets.* New York: Bloom's Literary Criticism, 2008. A collection of essays that examine Shakespeare's sonnets, perhaps his best poetry.

Cheney, Patrick. *The Cambridge Companion to Shakespeare's Poetry.* New York: Cambridge University Press, 2007. A collection of essays offering literary, historical, and cultural information on Shakespeare's poetry. Bibliographies and suggestions for further reading make this an invaluable source for those interested in Shakespeare.

De Grazia, Margreta, and Stanley Wells, eds. *The Cambridge Companion to Shakespeare.* New York: Cambridge University Press, 2001. This work provides an extensive guide to Shakespeare's life and works.

Dobson, Michael, and Stanley Wells, eds. *The Oxford Companion to Shakespeare.* New York: Oxford University Press, 2001. An encyclopedic treatment of the life and works of Shakespeare.

Hart, Jonathan. *Shakespeare: Poetry, Culture, and History.* New York: Palgrave Macmillan, 2009. Hart looks at the poetry of Shakespeare and examines how culture and history influenced it and were influenced by it.

Heylin, Clinton. *So Long as Men Can Breathe: The Untold Story of Shakespeare's Sonnets.* Philadelphia: Da Capo Press, 2009. Heylin examines the history of the sonnets' publication and researches the possibility that Shakespeare never intended them to be published.

Hope, Warren, and Kim Holston. *The Shakespeare Controversy: An Analysis of the Authorship Theories.* 2d ed. Jefferson, N.C.: McFarland, 2009. The authors examines the various authorship controversies and theories surrounding Shakespeare's work. Although much of the discussion involves plays, it sheds light on the author himself.

Matz, Robert. *The World of Shakespeare's Sonnets: An Introduction.* Jefferson, N.C.: McFarland, 2008. Matz examines the sonnets in terms of the customs and beliefs that shaped them and with reference to Shakespeare's world.

*Gary F. Waller*

# SIR PHILIP SIDNEY

**Born:** Penshurst, Kent, England; November 30, 1554
**Died:** Arnhem, the Netherlands; October 17, 1586

<small>PRINCIPAL POETRY</small>

*Astrophel and Stella*, 1591 (pirated edition printed by Thomas Newman; 1598, first
   authorized edition)
*Certaine Sonnets*, 1598
*The Psalmes of David, Translated into Divers and Sundry Kindes of Verse*, 1823
   (with Mary Sidney Herbert, Countess of Pembroke)
*The Complete Poems of Sir Philip Sidney*, 1873 (2 volumes)
*The Poems of Sir Philip Sidney*, 1962 (William A. Ringler, Jr., editor)
*The Psalms of Sir Philip Sidney and the Countess of Pembroke*, 1963 (J. C. A.
   Rathmell, editor)

<small>OTHER LITERARY FORMS</small>

Although Sir Philip Sidney's best-known work is *Astrophel and Stella*, his major
work and the one to which he devoted most of his literary energy and much of his political frustration was *Arcadia* (originally titled *The Countess of Pembroke's Arcadia*). This
long, much-revised epic prose romance was written and revised between 1578 and
1586; it was first published in an unfinished version in 1590, then in 1593 in a revised
and imperfect version, again in 1598, and repeatedly in many editions for more than a
century. The equivalent in prose of Edmund Spenser's *The Faerie Queene* (1590,
1596), it is an encyclopedic romance of love, politics, and adventure, incorporating
many stories and discussions of philosophical, theological, erotic, and psychological issues. Almost as important is Sidney's critical treatise, *Defence of Poesie* (1595; published in another edition as *An Apologie for Poetry*), written about 1580, and setting
forth in a seductive, if never quite logically coherent argument, a celebration of the nature and power of poetry, along with some prescriptive (and perceptive) comments on
the current malaise of English poetry, drama, and the literary scene generally. Other
works Sidney wrote include *The Lady of May* (pr. 1578), a pastoral entertainment; the
first forty-four poems in a translation of the Psalms, later revised and completed by his
sister Mary; and a number of other miscellaneous poems, prose treatises, and translations, mainly designed to further the cause of the Protestant faction in Elizabeth's court.

<small>ACHIEVEMENTS</small>

"Our English *Petrarke Sir Philip Sidney* . . . often comforteth him selfe in his sonnets
of Stella, though dispairing to attaine his desire. . . ." Thus Sir John Harington in 1591,

*Sir Philip Sidney*
(Library of Congress)

and generations of readers have similarly sighed and sympathized with Astrophel's tragicomic enactment of "poore Petrarch's long deceased woes." In literary history, *Astrophel and Stella* marks a poetical revolution no less than William Wordsworth's *Lyrical Ballads* (1798) or T. S. Eliot's *The Waste Land* (1922); the poem is the product of a young, ambitious poet, acting on his impatience with the poetry he criticized in his manifesto, *Defence of Poesie.* "Poetry almost have we none," he wrote, "but that lyrical kind of songs and sonets," which "if I were a mistresse would never persuade mee they were in love." Sir Philip Sidney has also had a special place in England's broader cultural history. Part of his fascination has been the ways succeeding ages have appropriated him: as a lost leader of the golden Elizabethan age, Victorian gentleman, anguished Edwardian, committed existentialist, apolitical quietist, even a member of the Moral Majority. Like all great writers, Sidney and his works have been continually reinterpreted by successive ages, his poems and his life alike inscribed into different literary, political, and cultural discourses. As contemporary scholars have become more attuned to both the linguistic and ideological complexity of Renaissance literature generally and to the new possibilities of contemporary critical methods, Sidney's writing has been seen, both in its seemingly replete presence and its symptomatic gaps and absences, as central to an understanding of Elizabethan poetry and culture.

None of Sidney's poetry was published in his lifetime, and yet along with his other writings it circulated among a small coterie of family and court acquaintances during the 1580's. Sidney's vocations were those of courtier, statesman, Protestant aristocrat, and patriot before that of a poet, and his poetry encourages the piecing together of a more problematic Sidney than that afforded by conventional hagiography. Sidney's writings often served, as A. C. Hamilton argues, "as a kind of outlet for political interests, compensating for the frustrations and failures" of his life: "problems that prove insurmountable in his career" were transposed and wrestled with in his fictions.

Sidney's major poetic work, *Astrophel and Stella*, in particular marks the triumphant maturity of Elizabethan court poetry, the belated but spectacular adaption of Petrarchanism to English aristocratic culture. It remains one of the most moving, delightful, and provocative collections of love poems in the language, all the more powerful in its impact because of the variety of needs that strain within it for expression— erotic, poetic, political, religious, cultural. One may read it, as Harington did, as the expression of thwarted, obsessive love, but it opens itself, like its author, to much richer readings, which reinforce Sidney's position as the central literary and cultural figure in the English Renaissance before William Shakespeare.

## BIOGRAPHY

Sir Philip Sidney was born into one of England's leading aristocratic families. His father was one of Elizabeth I's most loyal civil servants, serving as Lord President of Wales and Lord Deputy of Ireland. On his mother's side, Sidney was related to the influential Leicester family, one of the major Protestant powers in the country. He was educated under the stern Calvinist Thomas Ashton at Shrewsbury School, along with his lifetime friend and biographer Fulke Greville; in 1568, he went to Oxford, but he left without a degree in 1571. In 1572, he went on a Grand Tour through Europe, where he was introduced to and widely admired by major European scholars and statesmen, especially by leading Huguenot and German Protestants. In 1575, he returned to England and joined Elizabeth's court. He contributed a masque, *The Lady of May*, to one of the royal entertainments in 1578 and was employed by the queen in a number of minor matters. Unfortunately, he alienated Elizabeth, partly because he was so forthright in his support of European and English Protestant ideals and partly because of his own personal charisma. In a stormy career at court, he alternated between periods of willing service and periods of retirement to his sister's house at Wilton, near Salisbury, where an increasing number of Elizabethan poets, intellectuals, and thinkers were gathering—almost as an alternative to the queen's court. In 1580, he quarreled with the earl of Oxford over whether the queen should consider marrying the French Catholic duke of Anjou. His advice on the matter was ignored, or played down, and he contemplated going illegally to the New World. Elizabeth's attitude to the man the English court so much admired (almost as much as many Europeans) was an ambivalent one: Sidney was probably too much a man of outspoken principle to be of use to her in her devious political dealings.

Sidney's literary career therefore developed in part out of the frustrations of his political career. Most of his works were written in his periods of chosen, or enforced, retirement to Wilton, and often grew out of discussions with friends such as Fulke Greville and Edward Dyer and his sister, Mary. He looked at the poetry being written in England, contrasted it most unfavorably with that of European courts, and so set out deliberately, by precept and example, to improve it. The result was an outburst of writing that marked a literary revolution: *Defence of Poesie*, probably started by 1578, was a sophisticated, chatty, and persuasive theoretical treatment. *Astrophel and Stella*, written in 1581-1582, is the first major Petrarchan sonnet collection written in English; the continually revised romance *Arcadia*, dedicated to his sister, was started in 1578, and was still being revised shortly before his tragic death in the Battle of Zutphen in 1586. Sidney was given a hero's funeral in London. Monarchs, statesmen, soldiers, and poets from all over Europe sent condolences, wrote memorials, and for the next sixty years or so, Sidney's person, prestige, and power hung over the English court and culture as a reminder of how the Renaissance ideal of the courtier could be combined with Protestant piety.

### ANALYSIS

Sir Philip Sidney was educated to embrace an unusual degree of political, religious, and cultural responsibility, yet it is clear from his comments in *Defence of Poesie* that he took his literary role as seriously. Both this critical treatise and *Astrophel and Stella* are manifestos—not only of poetic but also of broader cultural practice. Both look forward to a long-needed renaissance of poetry and culture generally. For Sidney, poetry and its broader social uses were inseparable. Indeed, it is only with distortion that one can separate a "literary" from a "social" text, even with a Petrarchan love sequence such as *Astrophel and Stella*. Like other Elizabethan court poets, Sidney wrote his poetry within a structure of power and tried to carve out a discursive space under ideological pressures that attempted to control and direct the languages by which the court operated.

### THE ELIZABETHAN COURT

The court was more than a visible institution for Sidney and his contemporaries: It was a felt pressure that attempted to fix and determine all that came within its reach. Sidney's life and poetry are especially interesting examples of how the Elizabethan court's power operated on poetry. The court poets—for example, Sir Walter Ralegh and the earl of Oxford—acted as spokespeople for the court's values, yet inevitably the strains and tensions of their roles show through in their poetry. Poetry was both an expression of the power of the court and a means of participating in that power. Where a poem like

Ralegh's "Praised be Diana's Fair and Harmles Light" shows the court contemplating its own idealized image, Sidney's poetry has a more uneasy relation to the court's power. Although on the surface his writing appears to embody, in Terry Eagleton's words, a "moment of ideological buoyancy, an achieved synthesis" of courtly values, Sidney's own position in the court makes his poetry an especially revealing instance of the struggles and tensions beneath the seemingly replete surface of the court and court poetry alike.

More than any of his contemporaries before John Donne and Shakespeare, Sidney in his poetry evokes a felt world of bustling activity, psychosocial pressure, cultural demand—in short, the workings of power on literary and historical discourse. The institutions that shape the poetry—the court, its household arrangements, its religious and political controversies—are evoked in the tournaments (41), the gossip of "curious wits" (23) and "courtly nymphs" (54), and make up an atmosphere of energetic worldliness. What distinguishes Sidney's poetry is the forceful way that something more than the glittering surface of the court energizes it. Despite his posthumous reputation as the perfect Renaissance courtier, Sidney's public career was one of political disappointment and humiliation; he seems to have been increasingly torn between public duty and private desire, much in the way the hero of his sonnet sequence is.

All of Sidney's works are permeated with the problem of authority and submission. Like himself, all of his heroes (including Astrophel) are young, noble, well educated, and well intentioned, but as they become aware of the complexities and ambiguities of the world, they become diverted or confused, and Sidney finds himself caught between compassion and condemnation of their activities. In *Arcadia*, Sidney attempted to solve in fiction many of the tensions that beset his life, and *Astrophel and Stella* similarly served as an outlet for political and social frustration. In the prose romance, Sidney's narrative irresolution and (in an early version) premature and repressive closure reveal deep and unsettling doubts; similarly, the ambivalences and hesitations, the shifting distance between poet and character, and the divided responses to intellectual and emotional demands in *Astrophel and Stella* articulate Sidney's ambivalent roles within the court.

## PROTESTANTISM

One of the fundamental influences giving Sidney's life and poetry their particular cast is Protestantism. Indeed, perhaps the most potent factor disrupting the repleteness of the court poetic was Sidney's piety and his struggle with creating a Protestant poetic. In A. C. Hamilton's phrase, Sidney was "a Protestant English Petrarch." Unlike his close friend Fulke Greville, for whom a radical Augustinian suspicion of metaphor and writing itself consistently undermined poetry's value, Sidney tried to hold together what in *Defence of Poesie* he terms humanity's "erected wit" and its "infected will." Indeed, what Sidney perhaps uniquely brought to the Petrarchan lyric was a self-conscious anxiety about the tension between courtly celebration and Protestant inwardness, between the persuasiveness and rhetoric and the self-doubt of sinful humankind, between the insecurity of people's word and the absolute claims of God's.

The tension in Sidney's writing between the courtly and the pious, John Calvin and Baldassare Castiglione, disrupts *Astrophel and Stella* most interestingly. Sidney's own theory sees poetry focusing on the reformation of will and behavior, and it is possible to read his own sequence as an exemplum of the perils of erotic love, or, in Alan Sinfield's words, "the errors of unregulated passion." Sidney displays Astrophel deliberately rejecting virtue, treating Stella as a deity in a "direct challenge to Christianity" and to right reason. His cleverness is displayed in trying to avoid or repel the claims of reason and virtue, and the outcome of the sequence is the inevitable end of self-deception. The inwardness of *Astrophel and Stella*—not necessarily, it should be noted, its supposed autobiographical dimension, but its concern with the persona's self-consciousness, even self-centeredness, as lover, poet, courtier—is thus a fascinating blend of Petrarchan convention and Protestant self-concentration, and one that points to a distinctive late sixteenth century strain within the inherited vocabulary and rhetoric of the poet in his role in the court.

## THE COURT POET

When Sidney returned from his Grand Tour, he looked back across the Channel to the sophisticated academies and court circles that were encouraging writers, scholars, and musicians, and that were united by a synthesis of Christian, usually Protestant, piety and high Neoplatonism. The French academies, in particular, displayed a self-consciousness that distinguished them very strongly from the medieval courts. Shortly after Sidney's return, his sister Mary became the countess of Pembroke and established at Wilton what one of her followers was to term a "little Court," dedicated, both before and after his death, to continuing the renaissance of English courtly culture. Sidney's whole literary career became a frustrated attempt to realize a new role for the court poet, one based on the integrity and responsibility of values that he was unable to embody in his public life, and that more and more he poured into his writing. His remark to the earl of Leicester that he was kept "from the courte since my only service is speeche and that is stopped" has wider application than to its occasion, the French marriage crisis. It articulates a frustration toward the traditional subservience of a poet to the court, a stubborn insistence on forging a distinctive role for the poet.

Part of the fascination Sidney has traditionally evoked is what is often perceived as his ability to balance opposite ideological, rhetorical, or vocational demands on him. Certainly in *Defence of Poesie* and *Astrophel and Stella*, the elements of such a dialectic can be found. The promise of divinity that Astrophel perceives in Stella's eyes is, in Sidney's sympathetic comedy, wittily undermined by his self-consciousness, bashfulness, physical overeagerness, and human imperfection. In *Defence of Poesie*, Sidney describes poetry as a fervent reaching for the sublime, veiling truth to draw its reader toward it, and asserts that the power to move and so to bring about an enactment of poetry's transforming powers certainly lies within humankind's godlike nature. Yet for Sidney there was the seemingly inseparable problem of humanity's "infected will," and the reformed emphasis on human depravity and the untrustworthiness of the mind seems to have posed crucial problems for him and for the possibility of creating a Protestant poetic. Although elements of an opposition between rhetoric and truth, humanism and piety, Calvin and Castiglione, can be isolated, despite his most anxious intentions, Sidney does not manage to hold them together satisfactorily. In fact, his very fascination for later ages and his centrality for understanding sixteenth century poetry are grounded in such contradictions. "Unresolved and continuing conflict," in Stephen Greenblatt's phrase, is a distinctive mark of Renaissance culture, and Sidney's is a central place in that culture.

## The Psalmes of David

The versification of the Psalms, started by Sidney about 1579 and revised and completed by his sister, the countess of Pembroke, after his death, comprises the first post-Reformation religious lyrics that combine the rich emotional and spiritual life of Protestantism with the new rhetorical riches of the secular lyric. There are distinctive Protestant notes—a strong stress on election in Psalm 43, echoing Théodore Bèze's and Calvin's glosses rather than the original text, for example—and other psalms, where a strain of courtly Neoplatonism is highlighted, notably in Psalm 8, which (like Pico della Mirandola rather than Calvin) presents humanity as a privileged, glorious creation "attended" by God, an "owner" of regal and "crowning honour." Humans emerges as free and wondrous beings, like their creator, "freely raunging within the Zodiack of his owne wit," as Sidney put it in *Defence of Poesie*. Here Sidney juxtaposes, without integrating them, the great contraries of his age.

It is now generally believed that the psalms were originally drafted by Sidney early in his career, perhaps about 1579. Also written in this early period are a number of miscellaneous poems, including the so-called Certain Sonnets and many of the poems inserted into *Arcadia*. These are mainly of interest for showing Sidney's eager experimentation—with quantitative verse, pastoral dialogue, song, metrical and stanzaic patterns, and above all the appeal to the feelings of the reader, notably in "Leave me ô Love, which reachest but to dust" and the magnificent double sestina from *Arcadia*, "Yee Gote-heard Gods."

## Astrophel and Stella

Sidney's most sustained and most celebrated work is his sonnet sequence *Astrophel and Stella*, probably written in 1582, which dramatizes a frustrated love affair between a courtier and an admired lady. As Germaine Warkentin has shown, Sidney may have been tinkering with his "Certain Sonnets" during 1581-1582, abandoning them the next summer "to compose one of the three most distinguished sonnet sequences of the English Renaissance." Certainly *Astrophel and Stella* conveys an intensity that suggests a short burst of concentrated writing.

This sequence of 108 sonnets and eleven songs anatomizes the love of a young, restless, self-conscious courtier, Astrophel, for a lady, Stella, his star. His purpose is set out in the opening sonnet, in which he claims, "I sought fit words to paint the blackest face of woe/ Studying inventions fine, her wits to entertain." The reader is taken into the familiar world of Petrarchan convention and cliché: Astrophel the doubting, self-conscious, aggressive lover; Stella, the golden-haired, black-eyed, chaste and (usually) distant and (finally) unobtainable lady. The figures are equally familiar—debates between Hope and Absence, denials of loving at first sight, the frustrated desire alleviated by writing, the beautiful woman with the icy heart who pitilessly resists siege, and the final misery of the lover who ends his plaints in anguish, swearing in the end by all he has left, her "absent presence." Like the best *Petrarchisti*, Sidney makes the traditional motifs intensely dramatic. For the first time in English poetry since Geoffrey Chaucer, C. S. Lewis suggests, "a situation is not merely written about: it is created, presented, so as to compel our imaginations." Earlier Petrarchan poets such as Sir Thomas Wyatt had conveyed urgency and conversational informality, but, read as a whole, English poetry had not, since Chaucer, been distinguished by such continual, even restless, conflict and energy.

## USES OF RHETORIC

Modern critics, reacting against earlier impressionistic, Romantic criticism, have shown how the energy and variety of Sidney's poetry rests on a thorough exploitation of the riches of Renaissance rhetoric—through his use of apostrophe, dialogue, irony, shifts in decorum, and modulations of voice. As Ringler points out, perhaps "the most valuable product of his studies and disputations in Oxford was the thorough training he received in logic and formal classical rhetoric"; to these he added intense study and practice in ways of loosening the rhythmic movement of English line and working within the formal demands of stanzaic and metrical form. By a thorough familiarity with the conventional techniques of Renaissance love verse—which he parodies in 6, 9, and 15, for example—Sidney works within the eloquent courtly poetic, mocking and adapting it where necessary. Sidney uses his poems as workshops, experimenting with a great variety of stanzaic patterns and with devices such as inversion and feminine rhyme. Above all, he tries continually to juxtapose the movement of formal verse with an immediacy of idiom and logical development to involve his reader in the often tortuous movements of his character's broodings, arguments, and self-deceptions. Especially notable is the lightness and wit with which even Astrophel's most tortured self-examination is presented. Parody, the exaggerated use of erotic or literary clichés and puns, are all obvious enough, but the whole sequence is characterized by a sophisticated playfulness—the outrageous puns on "touch" in 9 leading to the self-pity (Astrophel's, not Sidney's) of the last line, the tongue-in-cheek anguish of the sonnets on Cupid, and the uproariousness of some of the erotic sonnets. Above all, the humor of the poet, indulging in his own mastery of language and able to dramatize his character, invites his readers to share his enjoyment at the varied follies and complexities of human love.

## PETRARCHANISM

If the Petrarchan tradition and the resources of Elizabethan rhetoric afforded Sidney a wonderfully flexible and rich poetic vehicle, there is nevertheless something limiting, even disturbing, about the literary mode in which he is working. Petrarchanism purports to be about love, and specifically about the obsession of a lover for a lady before whom he feels inferior, humble, and yet ennobled. Paradoxically, the sonnets become a weapon in an attempted mastery of the woman and their focus is exclusively on the anguish and achievements of the male lover. The conventions of Petrarchanism are those of a male-dominated society and its rhetorical strategies serve to elevate the woman only to subjugate her.

As Ann Jones and Peter Stallybrass have argued, "to Stella, Astrophel may speak of love as service," but outside his devotion to friends, "he can suggest a sub-text of masculine domination." Within the struggle for mastery, rhetoric and erotic convention alike become means of domination. Stella herself is, like other Petrarchan mistresses, reduced to a disconnected set of characteristics, acknowledged only as they are manipulable or impinge on her lover's consciousness. She is entirely the product of her poet-lover's desires. *Astrophel and Stella* is a theater of desire in which the man has all the active roles, and in which she is silent or merely iconic, most present when she refuses him or is absent. Astrophel does not want—although it is arguable that Sidney might—to call into question the power of his anguish or the centrality of his struggles of conscience, yet it seems legitimate to ask what Stella might reply to Astrophel's earnest self-regarding pleas for favor. Even if her replies are not "in" most of the poems (and where they are, as in Song 8, they are reported through Astrophel), what might she say? Is her silence the repression of the character or of Sidney? Does her silence reflect a whole cultural blindness that fixes women as objects of gaze and analysis within a society they did not invent and could not control? When one considers in these ways how the dynamics of Sidney's text function, once again one finds "literary" and "cultural" texts interacting.

## BIOGRAPHICAL ELEMENTS

An older criticism faced (or perhaps avoided) these issues by focusing on the biographical "origins" of the sequence. In part an outcome of the Romantic valorization of poetry as the overflow of sincerity or genuine experience, criticism sentimentalized the obvious connections between Sidney's life and the fiction of Astrophel and Stella into a poetic roman à clef. Undoubtedly, Sidney plays with his reader's curiosity about some kind of identification between himself and Astrophel and between Stella and Lady Penelope Rich (née Devereux), to whom as a youth Sidney's family nearly arranged a betrothal and in whom he may possibly (though there is no firm evidence either way) have had more than a literary interest. Sidney certainly builds into his sequence references to his career, to his father, to contemporary politics, to his friends, and—of most interest to the curious—to Lady Rich's name in two sonnets (24, 37) that were omitted from the first publication of the collection, perhaps for fear of embarrassing repercussions. Even so, the relationship between Sidney and his characters and between the events of his life and those seemingly within his poems should not be simplified. Just as Sidney manages simultaneously to have much in common with Astrophel, be sympathetic with him, and yet to criticize or laugh at him, so the gap between Stella and the historical Lady Rich is even wider—at best one can regard some of the references to Stella as sly or wistful fantasies. As to whether Sidney and Lady Rich were sexually involved, *Astrophel and Stella* gives no firm evidence.

### LOVE AND COURTLY BEHAVIOR

A more rewarding approach is to try to trace the way the poems are traversed by a variety of overlapping and in many cases contradictory influences, including court politics, the psychology of love, poetry, rhetoric, and Christianity. Within its confusions, tensions, and contradictions, *Astrophel and Stella* highlights the diverse and often contradictory pressures and possibilities that constitute the situation of an Elizabethan poet and lover. One of the distinctive possibilities of Petrarchanism was to set the traditional medieval debate on the nature of love in terms of the lover's psychology and within the demands of the codes of courtly behavior. Part of the fascination Petrarch had for English poets in the late sixteenth century was their puzzlement about how the Petrarchist conventions might fit their experiences. The prestige and suggestiveness of Petrarchanism allowed poets to examine not only the relationship between love and poetry, but also the way its worldview, its rich schematization of human experience, and their own changing social and individual realities intersected.

### EROTIC LOVE

One of the dominant concerns of the sequence is undoubtedly that of the problems and difficulties of erotic experience—although depicted entirely from the male viewpoint. *Astrophel and Stella* typically focuses on the "thrownness" of love—on the lover finding himself within a preexisting structuring of experience, a "race" that "hath neither stop nor start" (23), but which continually disrupts his sense of a preexistent self. Sexuality becomes an object to be examined, supervised, confessed, and transformed into poetry. It should be noted, however, that the "self" that is put into question in

*Astrophel and Stella* is not, or not primarily, that of Sidney. The poet offers his poems to an audience of sympathetic listeners as a mirror less of his experiences than of theirs. The intellectual tensions observable in *Astrophel and Stella* are dramatized as paradigms, the effect of which is to highlight the readers' or hearers' awareness of their own experiences. Sidney's poems work on their readers, suggesting and manipulating although never compelling into meaning. At times he refers to quite specific members of his audience—to other lover-poets in 6, in which Astrophel distinguishes his own "trembling voice" and the sincerity of his love from those of other lovers and so provokes them to respond by praising their own mistresses or talents. At times his suffering hero will ostensibly address a rather special audience—"I Stella's ears assayl, invade her ears," he says in Sonnet 61; or he (or Sidney) will address a friend (as in Sonnet 14), and even occasionally himself (as in 30). Yet the most important audience is unnamed: the readers who, through the poem's history, will read them, meditate on, and act out their drama.

## CRITICAL RESPONSE

Surveying the history of Sidney criticism, especially that of the modern era, one discovers a curious anxiety to find a coherent, sequential organization not merely made possible by the poems, but as a required means of reading them. *Astrophel and Stella* is thus often read as if it were a poetic novel. C. S. Lewis cautions against treating the Petrarchan sequence as if it were "a way of telling a story"; *Astrophel and Stella* is, he says, "not a love story but an anatomy of love," while Max Putzel speaks of the poems' "careful disorder." On the other hand, A. C. Hamilton argues that "the sonnets are organized into a sequence with a unifying structure," and other critics have written of what they see as careful structure and sequence. In Hamilton's scheme, sonnets 1-12 form an introduction, 13-30 concentrate on Astrophel's isolation, with 41-68 concerned with his moral rebellion, 71-85 with his attempt at seduction, and the remainder with his failure. Such divisions differ radically among the proponents of a narrative structure; in short, if a reader wishes to find a narrative development and final irresolution rather than an exercise in love's variety, then *Astrophel and Stella* is open to such a reading. Perhaps the most satisfying sequential reading of the collection is that by Ann Rosalind Jones, who stresses that although it is possible (and peculiarly satisfying) to see Astrophel as undergoing a gradual disintegration and loss of control, Sidney's sequence does not use the linking devices of other poets, such as Dante or Maurice Scève, which might strongly encourage a reading of the sequence as a growth in self-knowledge. Even when one constructs a sequence, it is primarily characterized by an unstable, eddying movement, "dramatically *dis*ordered," as Jones argues. "Even at the end of his experience," Astrophel can "predict the course of his writing no better than the course of his love" and so each sonnet becomes a new starting place. In short, while *Astrophel and Stella* allows for a linear development, it does not force one on a reader, encouraging the reader just as readily to view Astrophel's experience as unpredictable, random, and even as an exemplum of failure.

One recurring pattern is a tension between the demands of the public world of politics and responsibility and the private world of erotic desire. In many sonnets, Astrophel presents love in terms of a debate between traditional abstractions such as desire and reason, love and duty. Part of the reader's enjoyment lies in watching him, through Sidney's fond but penetrating perspective, indulging himself in false logic (52) or in seeing his dutifully constructed arguments against love undermined by the simple appearance of his beloved, as in 5, 10, or in the amusing self-contradictions of 47. Astrophel tries in vain to keep his two worlds and their demands separate. He claims that love gives him a private place, a sense of self from which the demands of courtly responsibility are shown to be trivial, but caught between conflicting worlds of self-indulgence and political responsibility, he ends by succeeding in neither. The reader watches him corrupting his avowedly pure love into sensuality by the deviousness of political rhetoric. In Sonnet 23, he appears to reject the world, but in Sonnet 69, he expresses Stella's conditional encouragement of his advances in terms of the court's own language. Since, he argues, she has "of her high heart giv'n" him "the monarchie," as a king, he too can take some advantage from that power.

At the root of Astrophel's self-deception is the structure of Petrarchanism itself, which, as John Stevens and others have pointed out, was at once a literary convention and a very serious courtly game, one "in which three powerful discourses meet and join hands: love, religion, and politics." *Astrophel and Stella* is based on a formula by which the man is subjected to his lady while, at the same time, the situation enables him to pour fourth his eloquence in an attempt to influence her. The relationship is parallel to the relationship between courtier and monarch—built on absolute loyalty and subjection, frustration and rejection—interlaced with devious manipulation for the favors of the capricious, distant beloved. Thus while Astrophel speaks of the "joy" inspired by Stella and of his own "noble fire," he is attempting to manipulate Stella's vulnerability, seeking power over her in the way the devious courtier seeks hidden but real power over the monarch. In terms of sexual politics of the Renaissance court, Astrophel's world is one shared primarily by other male courtiers, using language as a means of domination and treating women as subject to their desire, much in the way courtiers themselves were at the mercy of the monarch.

Thus the reader watches Astrophel indulging himself in small subtle ways—playing on grammar in 63, twisting Stella's words, speaking openly to her in a kind of "manic playfulness," and allowing (or being unable to prevent) the emergence of the underlying physicality of his desires in a series of fantasies of seduction (71, 72, 74, 79, 80, 81). The songs serve especially well to highlight the wish-fulfillment of Astrophel's frustrations—especially the dramatization in Song 5 of Astrophel's self-involvement, and the graceful fantasy of Song 8, viewed wistfully by the narrator from a distance and culminating in Sidney's clever and moving breaking down of the distance between narrator and character in the final line, where he confesses that "my" song is broken.

As the sequence draws to its inevitably inconclusive end, Astrophel's fantasies become less and less realizable. He indulges in self-pity and then more realistically accepts the end of the relationship, vacillating between joy and grief, optimism and despair, dedication and unfaithfulness. As Hamilton points out, the mutability of human love which haunts so many Elizabethan sonnet sequences, especially Shakespeare's, enters Sidney's only indirectly, but where he immerses himself in the intensity of the living moment, as the sequence ends, he realizes he is "forever subject to love's tyranny, a victim of *chronos* forever caught in time's endless linear succession."

Readings of *Astrophel and Stella* inevitably point to it as a quintessential ideological and literary struggle, where a variety of impulses struggle for mastery. Like the best love poems, it asks its readers to look at themselves. Stella herself, the guiding metaphor of the sequence, is distinguished by her nature, behavior, influence, and power, always requiring, like a text, interpretation. Astrophel, like the reader of his creator's sequence, is an exegete of love. "What blushing notes doest thou in margin see," he asks, and goes on, as all readers do with the whole sequence, to choose his own convenient misunderstanding of Stella. Astrophel may state that all his "deed" is to "copy" what in Stella "Nature writes" (3) or assert that "Stella" is, literally, the principle of love in the cosmos (28), and that the words he utters "do well set forth my mind" (44), but Sidney knows, as his readers do, that love and its significance and its expression in language are far more complex matters.

*Astrophel and Stella* is what Roland Barthes terms a "playful" text, one that depends strongly on its audience, inviting participation both to reproduce the process, intellectual and emotional, by which the poem's struggles came to be verbalized and to go beyond them, adding one's own preoccupations. *Astrophel and Stella* has a capacity to invade its readers, to direct and inform their responses, but as well, to open them to an awareness that it functions only through a process of deliberate reciprocity. It is this joyful welcome to its readers that makes it such a landmark in English poetry.

OTHER MAJOR WORKS

LONG FICTION: *Arcadia*, 1590, 1593, 1598 (originally entitled *The Countess of Pembroke's Arcadia*).

PLAYS: *The Lady of May*, pr. 1578 (masque); *Fortress of Perfect Beauty*, pr. 1581 (with Fulke Greville, Lord Brooke; Phillip Howard, the earl of Arundel; and Baron Windsor of Stanwell).

NONFICTION: *Defence of Poesie*, 1595 (also as *An Apologie for Poetry*).

MISCELLANEOUS: *Miscellaneous Prose of Sir Philip Sidney*, 1973.

BIBLIOGRAPHY

Alexander, Gavin. *Writing After Sidney: The Literary Response to Sir Philip Sidney, 1586-1640.* New York: Oxford University Press, 2006. Alexander looks at the legacy of one of the most important Elizabethan writers by examining first his sister Mary Sidney, his brother Robert Sidney, his friend Fulke Greville, and his niece Mary Wroth, then examining poets and writers who were influenced by him.

Berry, Edward I. *The Making of Sir Philip Sidney.* Toronto, Ont.: University of Toronto Press, 1998. Explores how Sidney created himself as a poet by making representations of himself in the roles of some of his most literary creations, including *Astrophel and Stella* and the intrusive persona of *Defence of Poesie.*

Connell, Dorothy. *Sir Philip Sidney: The Maker's Mind.* Oxford, England: Clarendon Press, 1977. Considers Sidney's life and art in a biographical and historical context. Connell discusses in detail important historical influences on Sidney. Includes maps, a bibliography, and an index.

Duncan-Jones, Katherine. *Sir Philip Sidney: Courtier Poet.* New Haven, Conn.: Yale University Press, 1991. This useful biography links the details of Sidney's life at court to his poetic works.

Garrett, Martin, ed. *Sidney: The Critical Heritage.* New York: Routledge, 1996. A collection of essays that gather a large body of critical sources on Sidney. Includes bibliographical references and index.

Hamilton, A. C. *Sir Philip Sidney: A Study of His Life and Works.* New York: Cambridge University Press, 1977. A study of Sidney's life, poetics, and selected works. General survey places his work in a biographical context. Includes an appendix, notes, a bibliography, and an index.

Kay, Dennis, ed. *Sir Philip Sidney: An Anthology of Modern Criticism.* Oxford, England: Clarendon Press, 1987. Kay's introduction places Sidney in a cultural heritage and surveys the changes that have occurred in the critical approaches to Sidney's work. Includes a chronology, a bibliography, an index, and a list of early editions.

Kinney, Arthur F., ed. *Essential Articles for the Study of Sir Philip Sidney.* Hamden, Conn.: Archon Books, 1986. A collection of twenty-five articles with a wide range of critical approaches. Topics include Sidney's biography, *The Lady of May*, *Defence of Poesie*, *Astrophel and Stella*, and *Arcadia*. Includes bibliography.

Sidney, Philip, Sir. *Sir Philip Sidney: Selected Prose and Poetry.* Edited by Robert Kimbrough. Madison: University of Wisconsin Press, 1983. Kimbrough gives detailed attention to *Defence of Poesie*, *Astrophel and Stella*, and *Arcadia*. Also surveys the critical approaches to Sidney. Contains a chronology and a select bibliography.

Stillman, Robert E. *Philip Sidney and the Poetics of Renaissance Cosmopolitanism.* Burlington, Vt.: Ashgate, 2008. Stillman examines the poetry of Sidney, looking at topics such as the influence of his political views and the general culture.

*Gary F. Waller*

# ROBERT SOUTHWELL

**Born:** Horsham St. Faith, Norfolk, England; 1561
**Died:** London, England; March 4, 1595

PRINCIPAL POETRY

*Moeoniae: Or, Certaine Excellent Poems and Spirituall Hymnes*, 1595
*Saint Peter's Complaint, with Other Poems*, 1595
*A Foure-Fould Meditation of the Foure Last Things*, 1605
*The Complete Poems of Robert Southwell*, 1872 (Alexander B. Grosart, editor)
*The Poems of Robert Southwell*, 1967 (James H. McDonald and Nancy Pollard
    Brown, editors)
*Collected Poems*, 2007 (Peter Davidson and Anne Sweeney, editors)

## OTHER LITERARY FORMS

Besides writing poetry Robert Southwell wrote many religious tracts, including *Mary Magdalens Funerall Teares* (1591).

## ACHIEVEMENTS

Robert Southwell's reputation as a poet in his own time is difficult to determine, since he was a priest in hiding and a martyr for his Roman Catholic faith. It is natural that the five manuscript compilations of his verses do not name the author, and that the two printed volumes, both published in the year of his execution, likewise do not name the author; one of them, however, gives his initials. The publishers may have thought that readers would associate the poems with Southwell, who was of much interest at the time, although the government tried to keep his trial secret. Early references to his verse, however, with a single exception, do not indicate knowledge of authorship. Southwell's name did not appear in an edition until 1620.

The musical quality of his verse is remarkable, considering that he almost forgot his native English during his long education abroad and had to relearn it when he returned to England as a priest in hiding. He has been described by Pierre Janelle as the "leading Catholic writer of the Elizabethan age," and one who might have developed into one of the greatest English writers if it were not for his death at the age of thirty-four. His best-known poem is "The Burning Babe," and Ben Jonson is reputed to have said that if he had written that poem, he would have been content to destroy many of his.

## BIOGRAPHY

Robert Southwell was born toward the end of 1561, according to evidence gathered from his admittance to the Society of Jesus and from his trial. His family was prosper-ous, and he spent his boyhood at Horsham St. Faith, Norfolk.

In 1576, when he was about fifteen, he entered the English College of the Jesuit school at Douai; like many young Catholics of that period, he was sent to the Continent for his later education. He studied at the Jesuit College of Clermont in Paris for a short time for his greater safety, returning to Douai in 1577, the year in which he applied to enter the Jesuit novitiate at Tournai. He was at first rejected but was accepted into the novitiate in Rome in 1578, where he was a student at the Roman College and tutor and precept of studies at the English College. Forbidden to speak English, he spoke Latin and Italian, becoming very fluent in the latter and reading a great deal of Italian literature. He wrote Latin poetry, including religious epics, elegies, and epigrams.

His poetry in English was written during his mission to England, from his return in July, 1586, to his arrest in June, 1592. He was stationed in London, working under a superior, the Reverend Henry Garnet. Southwell occupied a house in London and provided lodgings for priests, meeting those coming into the country. He corresponded with the Reverend Claudius Aquaviva, general of the Society of Jesus, giving him reports of the persecution. He received much help from the countess of Arundel, and his prose works were printed secretly. He met at intervals with his superior and other priests; one such meeting was raided, but those at the meeting managed to escape.

He was betrayed by a fellow Jesuit who had been arrested after arriving in England and who described the appearance of Southwell, and by the sister of a Catholic friend with whom he was staying in Uxenden, north of London. This Anne Bellamy, of a loyal Catholic family, had been imprisoned and become pregnant while in prison, probably having been assaulted by the priest-hunter Topcliffe; she married Topcliffe's assistant and betrayed Southwell on the condition that her family would not be molested, a promise that was not kept. Southwell was arrested on June 25, 1592. Topcliffe wrote an exultant letter to the queen about the importance of his prisoner and his intentions. Southwell was brought to Topcliffe's house and tortured many times. One of the tortures was being hung by the hands against a wall. He refused to identify himself or admit that he was a priest; in the absence of such identification, the family that had sheltered him could not be implicated. On Queen Elizabeth's instructions, he was moved to the Gatehouse Prison, where he was tortured and questioned by the Privy Council, but he always kept his silence. After he heard that there was other evidence against the Bellamys (they had been imprisoned on Anne's evidence), he wrote to Sir Robert Cecil, a member of the Council, that he was a priest and a Jesuit. He did not want his silence to be misinterpreted as fear or shame. Imprisoned in the Tower of London, he was arraigned under the Act of 1585 for the treason of returning to England as an ordained Catholic priest and of administering sacraments. Weak as he was, he had to conduct his own defense, but he was constantly interrupted. He was convicted, dragged through the streets, and hanged, drawn, and quartered at Tyburn Tree on March 4, 1595, after praying for his queen, his country, and himself. He was beatified by the Roman Catholic Church in 1929 and canonized as a saint in 1970.

ANALYSIS

Robert Southwell wrote religious poetry with a didactic purpose. In the prose preface to a manuscript, addressed to his cousin, he says that poets who write of the "follies and fayninges" of love have discredited poetry to the point that "a Poet, a Lover, and a Liar, are by many reckoned but three words of one signification." Poetry, however, was used for parts of Scripture, and may be used for hymns and spiritual sonnets. He has written his poetry to give others an example of subject matter, he says, and he hopes that other more skillful poets will follow his example. He flies from "prophane conceits and fayning fits" and applies verse to virtue, as David did. Perhaps his distaste for the stylized love poetry of his time explains the absence of sonnets in his writing. Although Southwell's purpose in writing was didactic, he was often more emotional than purely intellectual. His poems are seldom tranquil. They tend to startle through his use of the unexpected, the fantastic, and the grotesque, and may thus be described as baroque. Southwell is also linked to the baroque movement in his use of Italian models and such themes as weeping, anticipating the seventeenth century Roman Catholic poet Richard Crashaw.

As might be expected, death is a recurring theme in his poetry, yet he makes the theme universal rather than personal, for his purpose was instructive and oral rather than merely self-expressive. In "Upon the Image of Death," for example, he speaks of what is apparently a memento mori kind of picture that he often looks at, but he still does not really believe that he must die; historical personages and people he has known have all died, and yet it is difficult to think that he will die. There are personal touches, such as references to his gown, his knife, and his chair, but all are reminders to him and to all of inevitable death, "And yet my life amend not I." The poem's simplicity and universality give it a proverbial quality.

His most inspired poems were about birth rather than death, the birth of the Christ child. In part 6 of "The Sequence on the Virgin Mary and Christ," "The Nativitie of Christ," he uses the image of the bird that built the nest being hatched in it, and ends with the image of the Christ child as hay, the food for the beasts that human beings have become through sin. His image of Christ is often that of a child, as in "A Child My Choice," where he stresses the superior subject he praises in the poem, compared with the foolish praise of what "fancie" loves. While he loves the Child, he lives in him, and cannot live wrongly. In the middle two stanzas of this four-stanza poem, he uses a great deal of alliteration, parallelism, and antithesis to convey the astonishing nature of this Child, who is young, yet wise; small, yet strong; and man, yet God. At the end of the poem, he sees Christ weeping, sighing, and panting while his angels sing. Out of his tears, sighs, and throbs buds a joyful spring. At the end of the poem, he prays that this Child will help him in correcting his faults and will direct his death. The prayer was of course meant to be didactic, but it assumes a very personal meaning because of Southwell's manner of death. The themes of the Nativity and of death are thus artistically linked.

## "A VALE OF TEARES"

As Vincent Barry Leitch has stated, the Incarnation serves as a paradigm of God's love for human beings and signifies God's sanctification of human life. There is thus a strong sense of the divine in human life in most of Southwell's poems, yet some of the poems are referred to as "desolation poems" because this sense of God in human life is absent. Sin is prevalent, and the sinner feels remorse. In "A vale of teares," for example, God seems to be absent, leaving people alone to work things out for themselves. The poem is heavily descriptive, describing a valley of the Alps and painting a picture of a dreary scene that is in keeping with a sense of loneliness and desolation. It is wild, mountainous, windy, and thunderous, and although the green of the pines and moss suggests hope, hope quails when one looks at the cliffs. The poem ends with an apostrophe to Deep Remorse to possess his breast, and bidding Delights adieu. The poem has been linked to the conventional love lyric in which the lover, in despair, isolates himself from the world, but it has also been linked to the Ignatian Exercises of the Jesuits.

## SAINT PETER'S COMPLAINT

Another poem on the theme of isolation and remorse is the long dramatic poem *Saint Peter's Complaint*, comprising 132 stanzas of six lines each, based on an Italian work by Luigi Tansillo (1510-1568), *Le Lagrime di San Pietro* (the tears of Saint Peter). Southwell wrote a translation of part of Tansillo's poem, titling it, "Peeter Playnt," and two other poems, "S. Peters complaint," a poem of eleven stanzas, and "Saint Peters Complaynte," a poem of twelve stanzas. These three apparently represent stages in the composition of the long poem. In the translation, there is an objective rather than a first-person point of view, and Peter's denying Christ was an action in the immediate past in the courtyard, while reference is made to the suffering Peter will experience in the future. In each of the three original versions, Peter is the speaker and the time and place are indefinite. Much of the material in "Saint Peters Complaynte" is incorporated in the long poem. The uneven quality of the long poem has caused Janelle to assign it to an early period of experimentation, but McDonald and Brown see it as an unpolished work left unfinished when Southwell was arrested.

In the long poem, Saint Peter indulges in an extended nautical conceit, appropriate for this speaker, of sailing with torn sails, using sighs for wind, remorse as the pilot, torment as the haven, and shipwreck as the best reward. He hopes his complaints will be heard so that others will know that there is a more sorrowful one than they, and he lists all the unfortunate things he is, one to a line for a whole stanza, including "An excrement of earth. . . ." He says that others may fill volumes in praise of "your forged Goddesse," a reference to the literary fashion of praising some supposed love, who might not be real at all. Saint Peter's griefs will be his text and his theme. Several times in his works, Southwell makes this distinction between the falseness of stylized love poetry and the reality of religious themes. Saint Peter says that he must weep, and here Southwell employs hyperbole, for a sea will hardly rinse Peter's sin; he speaks of high tides, and says that all those who weep should give him their tears. The poem is heavily rhetorical, with many exclamations, parallelisms, repetitions, questions, and comparisons. Saint Peter had not thought that he would ever deny Christ. In lines 673-677, Southwell characteristically begins a line with a word that had already appeared toward the end of the preceding line, thus patterning Peter's "circkling griefes." Peter compares himself to a leper with sores and asks Christ's forgiveness. The taunts that Peter levels at the woman in the courtyard in the poem have been taken to suggest a parallel between the woman's actions and those of Queen Elizabeth. Alice Mary Lubin, in a study of Southwell's religious complaint lyrics, says that this poem differs from the traditional complaint poem in that the complaining figure is separated from Christ rather than from a figure such as a lover and that it differs from medieval religious complaint poems because it constitutes a statement of remorse rather than being simply a lament. A description of Peter's isolation occupies much of the pom. Lubin does not see the work as an ordered meditative poem; rather, it resembles an Italian "weeper" poem in subject, though not in treatment. She suggests analogues in *A Mirror for Magistrates* (1555) and in the Old Testament Lamentations.

### "THE BURNING BABE"

Southwell's most famous work, "The Burning Babe," combines several of his favorite themes, including the Nativity, isolation, guilt, and purification, into a vision poem that becomes a lament. He presents the material as a mystical vision. The occasion is presented dramatically, for it was a "hoary winter's night" and he was shivering in the snow when he felt the sudden heat that made him look up to see the fire. The dramatic contrasts continue, as he speaks of seeing a pretty baby; but it is in the air, not where a baby would be, and it is "burning bright," like a fire. The image is deliberately odd, ambiguous, and out of place. The next image, that the baby is "scorched" with great heat, turns the odd image into a horrible one, conveying the idea that the baby's body is no longer white but discolored from a fire that is not a mere metaphor. The fire is not from the air, but from inside the body, which means that there is no escape for the baby. The next image is ironic, for the baby cries copiously, as if the "floods" of tears could quench the flames, which they cannot do.

When the baby speaks, it is to lament that he fries in this heat although he has just been born, and yet no one seeks to warm the heart at this fire, and no one but the baby feels this fire. Here the Christ child is very much alone. It is not until the next line, however, that the baby is clearly identified as Christ, when he says that the furnace (the place where the fire is) is his breast, and the fuel is "wounding thorns." The ironic crown of thorns of the Crucifixion becomes fuel for the fire. His breast is kept burning because people wound him with thorns and hurt him through their mocking actions. The Crucifixion was a specific event, but the fire is a continuing torment, so the "wounding thorns" must be not only the crown of thorns but also the sins that people are continuing to commit.

Vision poems have often had a guide figure, someone who leads the viewer and explains the allegorical significance of the vision. Here the baby is both the vision and the guide, resulting in a kind of ironic horror. The image throughout this section of the poem is that of a furnace, a piece of technology used for creating and working things. The baby explains that the fire is love, a rather complicated idea, for it is the "wounding thorns" that keep the fire (the love) alive. Christ's love feeds on the wrongs of human beings. He loves human beings despite their sins, and indeed because of their sins. The smoke is sighs, his emotional dissatisfaction with what is happening and how people are acting. The ashes are the residue, the residual shame and scorn. The shame is Christ's embarrassment at being crucified and the equal embarrassment of the constant crucifixion He suffers because of continuing sin. The scorn is the rejection of his reality and the mission that he came into the world as a baby to accomplish, the taking of sins onto himself. Thus the residue of the fire is the shame and scorn, not entirely consumed in the fire but left over and ever present. Two personifications now enter the allegory. Justice puts the fuel on the fire, for it is not only that the sins and injustices of human beings be burnt, consumed, transformed in this way, but it is also Mercy that "blows the coals," that keeps the fire of love going strong by blowing air onto it. The imagery has changed from the "wounding thorns" causing the baby to be on fire, to the necessity and justice of burning up and burning away the wrongs of humans in the heat of God's love, which is kept going by his mercy.

The metals that are worked in this furnace are the souls of human beings, which have been defiled, but which are to be changed in the fire, thus representing another change in the imagery. Christ is now on fire to change them into something better, and he says that he will "melt into a bath to wash them in my blood." A bath is a cleansing, a purification, and after feeling the love of God, they will be purified by a cooling liquid, ironically not water, but Christ's blood, another touch of horror but also of love and glory. Saying that he would melt, a term meaning depart or disappear, but having special imagistic significance here because of the burning, the Christ child vanishes. The reader is conscious that the baby will become the crucified Christ, and the poet realizes that it is Christmas. Southwell here makes the Christ child the isolated one, most ironically, and develops the symbolism to make the reader feel remorse for his sins. The poem's startlingly grotesque subject clearly links it to the baroque movement.

## JOY AND ALIENATION

Southwell's main themes were the opposing ones of the joyous Incarnation, with its joining of God and human beings, and the tragic desolation of feeling the alienation of self from God through sin. Striking images with strong emotion achieve a religious purpose of affecting the reader. In his short life, Southwell wrote many fine poems in a language he had once forgotten. He referred very little in his poetry to the persecution that overshadowed his life, choosing to write instead of religious experiences that transcended time and place.

OTHER MAJOR WORKS

NONFICTION: *Epistle of a Religious Priest unto to His Father, Exhorting Him to the Perfect Forsaking of the World*, 1589; *Mary Magdalens Funerall Teares*, 1591; *Letter to Sir Robert Cecil*, 1593; *An Humble Supplication to Her Majestie*, pb. 1595 (wr. 1591); *A Short Rule of Good Life: To Direct the Devout Christian in a Regular and Orderly Course*, 1596; *The Triumphs over Death: Or, A Consolatory Epistle for Afflicted Minds, in the Affects of Dying Friends*, pb. 1596 (wr. 1591); *An Epistle of Comfort*, pb. 1605 (wr. 1591); *A Hundred Meditations on the Love of God*, pb. 1873 (wr. c. 1585); *Two Letters and Short Rules of a Good Life*, 1973 (Nancy Pollard Brown, editor).

BIBLIOGRAPHY

Brownlow, F. W. *Robert Southwell*. New York: Twayne, 1996. An introductory biography and critical study of selected works by Southwell. Includes bibliographic references and an index.

Caraman, Philip. *A Study in Friendship: Saint Robert Southwell and Henry Garnet*. St. Louis, Mo.: Institute of Jesuit Sources, 1995. This slim volume from religion scholar Caraman contains a bibliography and an index.

Deane, John F. *From the Marrow-Bone: The Religion of Poetry—The Poetry of Religion*. Blackrock, Ireland: Columba Press, 2008. Part 1 contains essays by the author on a variety of aspects of religion and poetry, and part 2 contains essays on various poets, including Southwell.

Janelle, Pierre. *Robert Southwell the Writer: A Study in Religious Inspiration*. 1935. Reprint. Mamaroneck, N.Y.: Paul J. Appel, 1971. Janelle's biography—the first three chapters of the book—remains the standard account of the life of Southwell. The other chapters concerning Jesuit influence, Petrarchan origins, and Southwell's place among his contemporaries have stood the test of time. Contains an extensive bibliography.

Moseley, D. H. *Blessed Robert Southwell*. New York: Sheed & Ward, 1957. A sympathetic biography drawn from late sixteenth century writings and records, which provides an understanding of the cultural, religious, and political climate in which Southwell lived and wrote. Supplemented by a chronological select bibliography of Southwell criticism.

Pilarz, Scott R. *Robert Southwell and the Mission of Literature, 1561-1595: Writing Reconciliation*. Burlington, Vt.: Ashgate, 2003. Pilarz examines Southwell as a Catholic writer and from the standpoint of his religious mission.

Scallon, Joseph D. *The Poetry of Robert Southwell, S. J.* Salzburg: Institute for English

Language and Literature, 1975. Scallon's monograph provides chapters on Southwell's biography, his short poems (particularly those concerning Christ and the Virgin Mary), and the poems on repentance. *Saint Peter's Complaint*, Southwell's best poem, receives extensive analysis. Contains a substantial bibliography.

Sweeney, Anne R. *Robert Southwell: Snow in Arcadia—Redrawing the English Lyric Landscape, 1586-1595*. New York: Manchester University Press, 2006. Sweeney, the coeditor of a collection of Southwell's poetry, examines Southwell in his role as a lyric poet.

*Rosemary Ascherl*

# EDMUND SPENSER

**Born:** London, England; c. 1552
**Died:** London, England; January 13, 1599

### OTHER LITERARY FORMS

Like most Renaissance writers, Edmund Spenser usually prefaced his poems with dedicatory letters that complimented the recipients and also provided helpful interpretations for other readers. Further indications of Spenser's theories about "English versifying" appear in his correspondence with Gabriel Harvey: *Three Proper, and Wittie, Familiar Letters* (1580) and *Foure Letters and Certaine Sonnets* (1586). Although *A View of the Present State of Ireland* was written in 1596, it was not published until 1633, thirty-four years after the author's death. In this treatise, Spenser presented a clear picture of Elizabethan Ireland and its political, economic, and social evils. The serious tone of this work deepens the significance of the Irish allusions and imagery throughout Spenser's poetry.

### ACHIEVEMENTS

The inscription on Edmund Spenser's monument hails him as "the Prince of Poets in his time," but his reputation as "poet's poet" continued among his Romantic peers three centuries later. What was praised and imitated changed with time, but the changes themselves suggest the extent of Spenser's achievements. His popularity among his contemporaries was documented not only in commentaries written during his lifetime but also in William Camden's account of Spenser's funeral, during which mourning poets threw into his tomb their elegies and the pens with which they had written these tributes.

*Edmund Spenser*
(Library of Congress)

Among his fellow Elizabethans, Spenser first gained renown as a love poet, a pastoral writer, and a restorer of the native language—all three of these roles already enacted in his early work, *The Shepheardes Calender*, in which he demonstrated the expansiveness of rural dialect and English unadulterated with continental vocabulary. Later, in a more courtly work, *The Faerie Queene*, Spenser still sought variety in language more through native archaisms than through foreign idiom. Despite its simplicity of diction, *The Shepheardes Calender* contained an elaborate academic apparatus that demanded recognition for its author as a serious poet. The fact that Spenser took his work seriously was also manifested in various levels of satire and in metrical experimentation that strengthened what Sir Philip Sidney described as his "poetical sinews."

Seventeenth century imitators echoed Spenser's allegorical and pastoral elements, his sensuous description, and his archaic phrasing. These early Spenserians, however, did not fully comprehend their model. Their servile imitations of surface themes and complex metrical forms temporarily diminished Spenser's reputation and probably stimulated later eighteenth century parodies. The serious side of Spenser, however, gradually received more notice. In *Areopagitica* (1644), for example, John Milton extolled him as "a better teacher than Scotus or Aquinas," and when the neoclassicists praised him, it was primarily for allegorical didacticism. In the nineteenth century, admiration of Spenser's moral allegory yielded to delight in his metrical virtuosity and the beauties of his word-pictures. When such great Romantics as Sir Walter Scott, Lord Byron, and John Keats imitated the Spenserian or "Faerie Queene" stanza form, they demonstrated anew the strength and flexibility of Spenser's metrical inventiveness. Modern holistic criticism continues to find deeper levels of Spenserian inventiveness in structural intricacy, allegorical ingenuity, and both narrative and descriptive aptness.

### BIOGRAPHY

If allusions in his own poetry can be read autobiographically, Edmund Spenser was born in London around 1552, apparently into a mercantile family of moderate income. In 1561, the Merchant Taylors' School opened with Richard Mulcaster as its first headmaster, and in that same year or shortly afterward, Spenser was enrolled, probably as a scholarship student. From Mulcaster, Spenser learned traditional Latin and Greek and also an awareness of the intricacies and beauties of the English language unusual among both schoolboys and schoolmasters of that time. Later, Spenser as "Colin Clout" paid tribute to Mulcaser as the "olde Shephearde" who had made him "by art more cunning" in the "song and musicks mirth" that fascinated him in his "looser yeares." Even before Spenser went to Cambridge, fourteen of his schoolboy verse translations had been incorporated into the English version of Jan van der Noot's *Theatre for Worldlings* (1569).

At Pembroke College, Cambridge, Spenser took his B.A. degree in 1573 and his M.A. in 1576; little else is known about his activities during that period except that he made several lifelong friends, among them Gabriel Harvey and Edward Kirke. Both Harvey and Kirke were later among Spenser's prepublication readers and critics, and Kirke today remains the most likely candidate for the role of "E. K.," the commentator whose glosses and arguments interpret enigmatic passages in *The Shepheardes Calender*. The Spenser-Harvey letters reveal young Spenser's theories on poetry and also his hopes for the patronage of Philip Sidney and Sidney's uncle, the earl of Leicester, Queen Elizabeth's favored courtier. Harvey's greetings to a woman, whom he addresses as "Mistress Immerito" and "Lady Colin Clout," also suggest that Spenser was married about 1580; nothing more is known of the first wife, but there are records of a son and a daughter at the time of Spenser's second marriage to Elizabeth Boyle in 1594.

When Spenser found himself unable to gain an appointment as a fellow at Cambridge, he accepted the post of secretary to John Young, bishop of Rochester. In 1580, he went to Ireland as secretary for Arthur Lord Grey, the newly appointed Lord Governor. When Grey was recalled from Ireland two years later because his policies did not control the Irish rebellion as the English court desired, Spenser remained behind. For several years, he moved into minor offices in different sections of the country; about 1589, he became "undertaker" of Kilcolman, an estate in Cork. As an "undertaker,"

Spenser received a grant of land previously confiscated from an Irish rebel, agreeing to see to the restoration of the estate and to establish tenant farmers on it. Love for Kilcolman is reflected in his poetry even though his days there were shadowed by litigation with an Irish neighbor who claimed the property and by a new outbreak of rebellion that eventually destroyed the estate and forced him to leave Ireland about a month before his death in 1599.

With the exception of *The Shepheardes Calender*, all of Spenser's major poetry was written in Ireland. The landscape and the people of his adopted country are reflected in imagery and allusions; political and economic conditions appear in various guises, perhaps nowhere so strongly and pervasively as in book 5 of *The Faerie Queene*, the Book of Justice. Although Spenser lived most of his adult life far from the court of Elizabeth, he maintained constant contact with events and friends there. His strongest bid for court recognition came in *The Faerie Queene*, with its creation of Gloriana, the Fairyland reflection of the living Queen of Britain, who rewarded him for his portrait of her by granting him an annual pension. Two of Queen Elizabeth's favorites played major roles in Spenser's later years: Sir Walter Ralegh and Robert, earl of Essex. Ralegh, who owned an estate neighboring Spenser's Kilcolman, frequently encouraged the poet's work in a general way and, if there is any validity in Spenser's famous prefatory letter, influenced specific changes in the structure of *The Faerie Queene*. Essex financed the poet's funeral and his burial in the Poet's Corner of Westminster Abbey in 1599.

## ANALYSIS

By an eclectic mingling of old traditions, Edmund Spenser created new poetry—new in verse forms, in language, and in genre. From the Middle Ages, Spenser had inherited complex allegorical traditions and a habit of interlacing narrative strands; these traditions were fused with classical myth and generic conventions, some of them transformed by continental imitators before they reached Spenser. This fusion of medievalism and classicism was in turn modified by currents of thought prevalent in Tudor England, especially by the intense nationalism that manifested itself in religion, language, politics, and international affairs.

To some extent, Spenser's poetic development evolved naturally from his deliberate selection of Vergil as his model. Like Vergil, he started his published career with pastoral eclogues; like him, too, he turned, in his last major work, from shepherds to great heroes. Before Spenser evoked classical muses in his epic, however, the tradition of Vergil had picked up romantic coloring and allegorical overtones from continental epics, especially Ludovico Ariosto's highly allegorized *Orlando Furioso* (1516, 1521, 1532; English translation, 1591). Spenser himself announced the three-way pattern adopted for *The Faerie Queene*: "Fierce wars and faithful loves shall moralize my song." Long after Spenser's death, his admirers continued to compare him with Vergil, often to Spenser's advantage. Vergil provided stimulus not only for the pastoral and epic genres in which Spenser wrote his two major works but also for the mythical allusions that permeate most of his work and for the serious use of poetry, especially in political and religious satire and in the reflection of nationalistic pride. Vergil's exaltation of Augustus and the Roman Empire accorded well with the nationalism of Elizabethan England, a nationalism poetically at its zenith in *The Faerie Queene.*

Vergil's sobriquet "Tityrus" became for Spenser a means of double praise when he hailed his fourteenth century predecessor Geoffrey Chaucer as an English Tityrus, the "God of shepheards." Rustic language, interlocked narratives, and experiments in vernacular quantitative verse forms in *The Shepheardes Calender* all reflect Chaucerian influence; in a less direct way, the vogue of courtly love in medieval and Renaissance literature was also channeled partly through Chaucer. During the two centuries between Chaucer and Spenser, love poetry became permeated with a blend of Petrarchan and Neoplatonic elements. Petrarchan lovers taught Spenser's shepherds to lament over their ladies' cruelty, to extol their beauty, and to describe their own pains, anxieties, and ecstasies with conventional images. The more sensuous aspects of love remained central to many of the *Amoretti* sonnets and to several set pieces in *The Faerie Queene*, such as Acrasia's Bower of Bliss and Busiranes' Mask of Cupid, but idealistic Neoplatonic concepts also emerged here. Such Neoplatonic concepts undergird the *Fowre Hymnes.* The first two hymns praise erotic human love and the inspirational force of feminine beauty; the other two deprecate these more earthly powers, elevating in their place the heavenly love and beauty of Christ, the source of all true human love and beauty.

In *The Faerie Queene*, too, idealistic Neoplatonic elements assume more pervasive significance than do Petrarchan motifs. The Platonic identification of the good and the beautiful, for example, is often manifest, especially in Gloriana, Una, and Belphoebe; and the true and false Florimels of books 3 to 5 exemplify true and false beauty, the former inspiring virtuous love and marriage and the second inciting sensuous lust. Although books 3 and 4 are called the Books of Chastity and Friendship, their linked story dramatically demonstrates variant forms of love. The concept of love as either debilitating or inspiring reflects one of the mythical traditions transmitted from antiquity through the Middle Ages: the double significance of Venus as good and evil love. As the goddess of good, fruitful love, Venus herself frequents the Garden of Adonis, where nature is untouched by deceptive art, where spring and harvest meet, and where love flourishes joyfully. In her own temple, Venus listens to the sound of "lovers piteously complaining" rather than rejoicing.

Renaissance pageantry and Tudor emblem books contributed to the pictorial quality with which Spenser brought myths to life—classical tales, rustic folklore, and his own mythic creations. One of the most picturesque of Spenser's new myths describes the "spousals" of the Thames and Medway rivers, a ceremony attended by such "wat'ry gods" as Neptune and his son Albion; by other rivers, remote ones such as the Nile and the Ganges, Irish neighbors such as the Liffey and the Mulla, and streams that paid tribute to one of the betrothed rivers; and by Arion, accompanied by his dolphin and carrying the harp with which he provided wedding music. Scenes like these exemplify the artistry with which Spenser created new poetry out of old traditions.

## THE SHEPHEARDES CALENDER AND COLIN CLOUTS COME HOME AGAINE

Classic and contemporary models, rural and courtly milieu, universal and occasional topics—from such a mixture Spenser formed his first major work, the "little booke," which he dedicated to Sidney and which he signed "Immerito," the Unworthy One. *The Shepheardes Calender* went through five editions between 1579 and 1597, none of them bearing Spenser's name. Such anonymity fits common Renaissance practice, but it may also have had additional motivation from Spenser's awareness of sensitive topical allusions with too thin an allegorical veil. Contemporary praise of Spenser indicates that by 1586 the anonymity was technical rather than real. In his twelve eclogues, one for each month of the year, Spenser imitated conventions that Renaissance writers attributed to Vergil and to his Greek predecessors: debates between rustic speakers in a rural setting, varied by a singing match between shepherds, a lament for the death of a beloved companion, praise of the current sovereign, alternating exultation and despair over one's mistress, and veiled references to contemporary situations. A fifteenth century French work, translated as *The Kalender and Compost of Shepherds*, probably suggested to Spenser not only his title but also the technique of emblematic illustration, the application of zodiacal signs to everyday life and to the seasons, and the arrangement of instructional commentary according to the months. Barbabe Googe's *The Zodiake of Life* (1565) strengthened the satirical and philosophical undertone of the calendar theme.

Despite the surface simplicity connoted by its nominal concern with shepherds, Spenser's book is a complex work. Not the least of its complexities are the paraphernalia added by "E. K.": the dedicatory epistle, the introductory arguments (for the whole book and for each eclogue), and the glosses. Although the initials themselves make Spenser's Cambridge friend Edward Kirke the most likely person to designate as the mysterious commentator, the Renaissance love for name-games does not exclude other possible solutions of the identity puzzle. Even Spenser himself has been suggested as a candidate for the enigmatic role. Many of E. K.'s annotations supply information essential to an understanding of the poet's cryptic allusions, to the identification of real-life counterparts for the characters, and occasionally to a modernization of archaic diction. Some annotations, however, are either accidentally erroneous or pedantically misleading: for example, several source references and the etymology for "aeglogues." E. K. derives the term "eclogues" from "Goteheardes tales" rather than from "conversations of shepherds," the more usual Renaissance understanding of the term; in actuality, "eclogues" are etymologically short selections that convention came to associate with pastoral settings.

The twelve separate selections could have produced a sense of fragmentation, but instead they create a highly unified whole. The most obvious unifying device is the calendar framework, which gives to the individual poems their titles and their moods. Another source of unity lies in the shepherd characters who appear repeatedly, especially Colin Clout, a character borrowed from the Tudor satirist John Skelton and used by Spenser as his own persona. Colin appears in four of the eclogues and is the topic of conversation in three others; his friendship for Hobbinol (identified by E. K. as Harvey), and his love for Rosalind (unidentified) provide a thread of plot throughout the twelve poems. Moreover, the figure of Colin represents the whole life of "everyman"—or at least every poet—as he passes from the role of "shepherd boy" in "January" to that of the mature "gentle shepherd" in "December."

In his general argument, E. K. establishes three categories for the topics of the eclogues: plaintive, recreative, and moral. The four selections that E. K. classifies as plaintive are those in which Colin's is the main voice. "January" and "June" are laments about his futile love for Rosalind; "December," too, is a conventional love plaint, although it adds the dimension of Colin's approaching death. "November," one of the most highly structured eclogues, is a pastoral elegy for Dido, the daughter of one "greate shephearde" and the beloved of another "greate shepheard Lobbin." E. K. pleads ignorance of the identity of both shepherds, but most critics identify "Lobbin" as a typical anagram for Robin (Robert Dudley) plus Leicester, thus suggesting a covert allusion to a love interest of Elizabeth's favorite, the earl of Leicester.

The first of the three recreative selections, "March," is a sprightly, occasionally bawdy, discussion of love by two shepherd boys. "April" starts out with a description of Colin's lovesickness but then moves on to an encomium on "fayre Elissa, Queene of shepheardes all," a transparent allusion to Queen Elizabeth. The singing contest in "August" gives Spenser an opportunity to exploit shifting moods and an intricate variety of metrical patterns.

It is sometimes difficult to interpret the satire in the eclogues that E. K. classes as "moral" because of the ambivalence of the dialogue structure itself and because of the uncertain implications of the fables included in four of the five moral selections. Besides, misperception on the part of the characters or the commentator can be part of the comedy. In "May," "July," and "September," different pairs of shepherds discuss religious "shepherds," making clear allusions to contemporary churchmen. In contrast to the sometimes vehement satire in these religious eclogues, the debate on youth and age in "February" has a light, bantering tone. As a statement of Spenser's views on poetry, "October" is perhaps the most significant "moral" eclogue. When the disillusioned young poet Cuddie complains that his oaten reeds are "rent and wore" without having brought him any reward, the idealistic Piers tries to convince him that glory is better than gain. He encourages Cuddie to leave rustic life, to lift himself "out of the lowly dust," but Cuddie complains that the great worthies that "matter made for Poets on to play" are long dead. The ambivalence of the pastoral debate is particularly evident here because the two voices apparently represent a conflict within Spenser himself. The inner Piers has an almost Platonic vision of poetry and sees potential inspiration in the active life of the court; but the inner Cuddie, fearing the frustrations of the poet's role, resigns himself to the less conspicuous, less stimulating rural life.

In a sequel to the eclogues, *Colin Clouts Come Home Againe*, Colin describes to his friends a trip to London, apparently a reflection of Spenser's trip to make arrangements for the publication of *The Faerie Queene*. The question-and-answer format allows Colin to touch on varied topics: the level of poetic artistry in London, conventional satire of life at court, topographical poetry about the "marriage" of two Irish rivers, and Platonic deification of love. Although this more mature Colin is less critical of court life than the earlier one had been, Ireland rather than England is still "home" to him.

## THE FAERIE QUEENE

Any study of *The Faerie Queene* must take into account the explanatory letter to Ralegh printed in all early editions under the heading "A Letter of the Author's, Expounding his Whole Intention in the course of this Work. . . ." The fact that the letter was printed at the end rather than the beginning of the first edition (books 1-3 only) suggests that Spenser was writing with a retrospective glance at what was already in the printer's press, even though he was also looking toward the overall structure of what had not yet been assembled. Ralegh had apparently requested such an explanation, and Spenser here clarified elements that he considered essential to understanding his "continued Allegory of dark conceit." These elements can be summarized as purpose, genre, narrative structure, and allegorical significance.

In carrying out his purpose "to fashion a gentleman or noble person in vertuous and gentle discipline," Spenser imitated other Renaissance conduct books that set out to form representatives of different levels of polite society, such as those peopled by princes, schoolmasters, governors, and courtiers. By coloring his teaching with "historical fiction," Spenser obeyed Horace's precept to make poetry both useful and pleasing; he also followed the example of classic and Renaissance writers of epic by selecting for the center of that fiction a hero whose historicity was overlaid by legend: Arthur. Theoretically, an epic treats a major action of a single great man, while a romance recounts great deeds of many men. Kaleidoscopic visions of the deeds of many great knights and ladies within the separate books superimpose a coloring of romance, but the overall generic designation of *The Faerie Queene* as "epic" is possible because Arthur appears in the six books as a unifying hero. Through Arthur, the poet also paid tribute to his sovereign, whose family, according to the currently popular Tudor myth, claimed descent from Arthur's heirs.

Although the complexity of the poem stems partly from the blending of epic and romance traditions, Spenser's political concern added an even greater complication to his narrative structure. He wanted to create a major role by which he could pay tribute to a female sovereign in a genre that demanded a male hero. From this desire came two inter-locked plot lines with Gloriana, the Faerie Queene, as the motivating force of both: The young Arthur "before he was king" was seeking as his bride the beautiful Queen of Fairyland whom he had seen in a vision; meanwhile, this same queen had sent out on quests twelve different knights, one for each book of the epic. At strategic points within these separate books Arthur would interrupt his quest to aid the currently central figure. Since Spenser completed only six of the proposed twelve books, the climatic wedding of Arthur and Gloriana never took place and the dramatic dispersion and reassembling of Gloriana's knights occurred only in the poet's explanation, not in his poem.

Patterns of allegory, like patterns of narrative, intertwine throughout the poem. By describing his allegory as "continued," Spenser did not imply that particular meanings were continuously retained but rather that central allegories recurred. In the letter to Ralegh, for example, Spenser explains that in his "general intention," Gloriana means glory, but in a more "particular" way, she is "the glorious person" of Elizabeth. Spenser is not satisfied to "shadow" Elizabeth only as Gloriana. In the letter and in the introduction to book 3, he invites Elizabeth to see herself as both Gloriana and Belphoebe, "In th'one her rule, in th'other her rare chastity." Less pointedly, she is also "shadowed" in Una, the image of true religion (book 1); in Britomart, the beautiful Amazonian warrior (books 3-5); and in Mercilla, the just queen (book 5). The glories of Elizabeth thus appear as a pervasive aspect of the "continued allegory," even though they are represented by different characters. Allegorical continuity also comes from Spenser's plan to have his twelve knights as "patrons" of the "twelve private moral virtues" devised by Aristotle, with Arthur standing forth as the virtue of magnificence, "the perfection of all the rest." The titles of the six completed books indicate the central virtues of their heroes: holiness, temperance, chastity, friendship, justice, and courtesy.

Historical and topical allusions appear frequently. Only when such allusions link references to Arthur and Gloriana, however, do they form a continuous thread of allegory. In the Proem to book 2, "The Legend of Sir Guyon, or of Temperance," Spenser encourages Elizabeth to see her face in the "fair mirror" of Gloriana, her kingdom in the "land of faery," and her "great ancestry" in his poem. In canto 10, he inserts a patch of "historical fiction" in which Arthur and Guyon examine the chronicles of Briton kings and elfin emperors, the first ending with the father of Arthur, Uther Pendagron, and the second with Tanaquil, called "Glorian . . . that glorious flower." Spenser prefaces his lengthy account of British history (stanzas 5-69) with a tribute to his own "sovereign queen" whose "realm and race" had been derived from Prince Arthur; he thus identifies the realm of the "renowned prince" of this story as the England of history. The second chronicle describes an idealized land where succession to the crown is peaceful, where the elfin inhabitants can trace their race back to Prometheus, creator of Elf (Adam) and Fay (Eve), and where Elizabeth-Gloriana can find her father and grandfather figured in

Oberon and Elficleos. The "continued" historical allegory looks to the wedding of Arthur and Gloriana as blending real and ideal aspects within England itself.

Topical political allegory is most sustained in book 5, "The Legend of Artegall, or of Justice." In this book Elizabeth appears as Queen Mercilla and as Britomart; Mary Stuart as Duessa (sentenced by Mercilla) and as Radigund (defeated in battle by Britomart); Arthur Lord Grey as the titular hero, Artegall; and the earl of Leicester as Prince Arthur himself in one segment of the narrative. Several European rulers whom Elizabeth had either opposed or aided also appear in varied forms. Contemporary political problems are reflected in the story of Artegall's rescue of Irena (Ireland) from the giant Grantorto (literally translated as "Great Wrong"), usually allegorically identified as the Pope. Spenser's personal defense of Lord Grey shows through the naïve allegory of canto 12, where Artegall, on the way back to Faery Court, is attacked by two hags, Envy and Detraction, and by the Blatant Beast (Calumny). Spenser thus suggests the cause of the misunderstandings that led to Elizabeth's recalling Grey from Ireland. Elizabeth's controversy with Mary Stuart, doubly reflected in book 5, also provides a significant level of meaning in book 1, "The Legende of the Knight of the Red Crosse, or of Holinesse."

A closer look at the tightly structured development of book 1 shows more clearly Spenser's approach to heroic and allegorical poetry in the epic as a whole. On the literal level of romantic epic, Gloriana assigns to an untrained knight the quest he seeks: the rescue of the parents of a beautiful woman from a dreaded dragon. The plot traces the separation of Red Cross and Una, Red Cross's travels with the deceptive Duessa (duplicity), Una's search for Red Cross, the reunion of Una and her knight, the fulfillment of the quest, and the betrothal of hero and heroine. Vivid epic battles pit Red Cross against the serpentine Error and her swarming brood of lesser monsters, against a trio of evil brothers (Sansfoy, Sansjoy, and Sansloy), against the giant Orgoglio (from whose dungeon he must be rescued by Prince Arthur), and eventually against one of the fiercest, best-described dragons in literature. In canto 10, Red Cross learns his identity as Saint George, changeling descendant of human Saxon kings rather than rustic elfin warrior. Red Cross's dragon-fight clearly reflects pictorial representations of Saint George as dragon-slayer.

All three levels of allegory recognized by medieval exegetes are fully developed in book 1: typical, anagogical, and moral. Typically, Una is the true Church of England, and Elizabeth is the protector of this Church; Duessa is the Church of Rome and Mary Stuart, its supporter. Red Cross is both abstract holiness defending truth and a figure of Christ himself. Arthur, too, is a figure of Christ or of grace in his rescue of Red Cross— here a kind of Everyman—from Orgoglio, the forces of Antichrist.

Anagogical or apocalyptic elements appear primarily in sections treating Duessa and the dragon and in Red Cross's vision of heaven. Duessa, at her first appearance, reflects the description of the scarlet woman in the Revelation of St. John, and the mount given her later by Orgoglio is modeled on the apocalyptic seven-headed beast. The mouth of the great dragon of canto 11 belches forth flames like those often pictured erupting from the jaws of hell in medieval mystery plays. Red Cross is saved from the dragon by his contacts with the Well of Life and the Tree of Life, both borrowed from Revelation. Before Red Cross confronts the dragon, he has an apocalyptic vision of the New Jerusalem, a city rivaling in beauty even the capital of Fairyland, Cleopolis.

The moral level provides the most "continued" allegory in book 1. Red Cross-Everyman must develop within himself the virtue of holiness if he is eventually to conquer sin and attain the heavenly vision. When holiness is accompanied by truth, Error can be readily conquered. However, when holiness is deceived by hypocrisy (Archimago), it is easily separated from truth and is further deceived by duplicity (Duessa) masquerading as fidelity (Fidessa). Tempted to spiritual sloth, Red Cross removes his armor of faith and falls to pride (Orgoglio). He must then be rescued from the chains of this sin by grace (Prince Arthur), must be rescued from Despair by truth, and must be spiritually strengthened in the House of Holiness, conducted by Dame Caelia (heaven) and her daughters Fidelia, Speranza, and Charissa (faith, hope, and charity). Only then can he repent of his own sins and become holy enough to conquer sin embodied in the dragon.

If book 1 best exemplifies self-contained, carefully structured allegorical narrative, books 3 and 4 exemplify the interweaving common in medieval and early Renaissance narrative poetry. Characters pursue one another throughout the two books; several stories are not completed until book 5. In fact, Braggadochio, the cowardly braggart associated with false Florimell in this section, steals Guyon's horse in book 2 and is judged for the crime in book 5. Belphoebe, too, introduced in a comic interlude with Braggadochio in book 2, becomes a central figure in the Book of Chastity. Belphoebe blends the beauty of Venus (Bel) with the chastity of Diana (Phoebe); her twin sister, Amoret, is a more earthly representation of Venus, destined to generate beauty and human love. Britomart, the nominal heroine of book 3, embodies the chastity of Belphoebe in her youth but the generative love of Amoret in maturity. Despite complex and not always consistent allegorical equations applicable to these central characters, Spenser moves them through their adventures with a delicate interlacing of narrative and allegorical threads typical of the romantic epic at its most entertaining level.

## AMORETTI AND EPITHALAMION

The sonnet sequence *Amoretti* (little love poems) and the *Epithalamion* (songs on the marriage bed) together provide a poetic account of courtship and marriage, an account that tradition links to actualities in Spenser's relationship with Elizabeth Boyle, whom he married in 1594. References to seasons suggest that the "plot" of the sonnet sequence extends from New Year's Day in one year (Sonnet 4) through a second New Year's Day (Sonnet 62) to the beginning of a third winter in the closing sonnet (Sonnet 89), a time frame of about two years. Several sonnets contain references that tempt readers to autobiographical interpretations. In Sonnet 60, "one year is spent" since the planet of "the winged god" began to move in the poet; even more significantly, the poet refers to the "sphere of Cupid" as containing the forty years "wasted" before this year. By simple arithmetical calculations, biographers of Spenser have deduced from his assumed age in 1593 his birth in 1552. Two sonnets refer directly to his work on *The Faerie Queene*: Sonnet 33 blames on his "troublous" love his inability to complete the "Queen of Faery" for his "sacred empress," and Sonnet 80 rejoices that having run through six books on Fairyland he can now write praises "low and mean,/ Fit for the handmaid of the Faery Queen."

Collectively and individually the *Amoretti* follow a popular Renaissance tradition established by Petrarch and imitated by numerous English sonneteers. In metrical structure, Spenser's sonnets blended Italian and English forms. The five-rhyme restriction in the Italian octave-plus-sestet pattern (*abbaabba cdecde*) was adapted to fit the English pattern of three quatrains plus couplet; instead of the seven rhymes used in most English sonnets, the interlocked rhymes of the Spenserian quatrains created a more intricate, as well as more restricted, form (*abab bcbc cdcd ee*).

Although Spenser's metrical pattern was innovative, most of his conceits and images were conventional; for example, love is related to a judicial court (Sonnet 10) and to religious worship (Sonnets 22 and 68); the beloved is a cruel causer and observer of his pain (Sonnets 20, 31, 41, 42, and 54) and the Neoplatonic ideal of beauty (Sonnets 3, 9, 45, 61, 79, and 88); love is warfare (Sonnets 11, 12, 14, and 57), a storm (Sonnet 46), sickness (Sonnet 50), and a sea journey (Sonnet 63). The poet at times promises the immortality of fame through his praise (Sonnets 27, 29, 69, 75, and 82); at other times he simply rejoices in the skill that enables him as poet to offer his gift of words (Sonnets 1 and 84). Even the kind of praise offered to his beloved is traditional. In Sonnet 40, "An hundred Graces" sit "on each eyelid" and the lover's "storm-beaten heart" is cheered "when cloudy looks are cleared." Elsewhere, eyes are weapons (Sonnets 7, 16, and 49) and a means of entanglement (Sonnet 37). The beloved is a "gentle deer" (Sonnet 67) and a "gentle bee" caught in a sweet prison woven by the spider-poet (Sonnet 71); but she is also a cruel panther (Sonnet 53) and a tiger (Sonnet 56). Physical beauties are compared to precious metals and gems (Sonnet 15), to sources of light (Sonnet 9), and to the sweet odors of flowers (Sonnet 64). Classical myths color several sonnets, identifying the beloved with Penelope, Pandora, Daphne, and the Golden Apples of Hercules (Sonnets 23, 24, 28, and 77) and the poet-lover with Narcissus, Arion, and Orpheus (Sonnets 35, 38, and 44).

In typical Petrarchan fashion, the lyrical moments in the *Amoretti* fluctuate between joy and pain, between exultation over love returned and anxiety over possible rejection. The sequence ends on a note of anxiety not in keeping with a set of poems conceived as a prelude for the glowing joy of the *Epithalamion*. Despite clear references to the 1592-1594 period of Spenser's life, it seems unlikely that all eighty-nine sonnets were written during this period or that all were originally intended for a sequence in praise of Elizabeth Boyle. The *Epithalamion*, however, is clearly Spenser's celebration of his own wedding at Kilcolman on Saint Barnabas' Day (June 11), 1594.

In its basic form and development, this marriage song is as conventional as the sonnets with which it was first published; but it is also original and personal in its variations on tradition. Classical allusions, for example, are countered by the homely invocation to nymphs of the Irish river and lake near Spenser's home (lines 56-66), by the imprecation against the "unpleasant choir of frogs still croaking" in the same lake (line 349), and by some of the attendants: "merchants' daughters," "fresh boys," and childlike angels "peeping in" the face of the bride. Although allusions to classical gods and goddesses heighten the lyric mood, other elements retain a more personal touch.

Structurally, Spenser adapted the *canzone* form. As used by Dante and Petrarch, the *canzone* consisted of a series of long stanzas followed by a short stanza (a *tornata*) responding to the preceding stanzas. Within the stanzas, one or more three-foot lines varied the basic five-foot line; the *tornata*, too, had one short line. A. Kent Hieatt has demonstrated in *Short Time's Endless Monument* (1960) the ingenuity with which Spenser varied the basic *canzone* structure to reflect units of time in general and to relate poetic divisions with night/day divisions on the longest day of the year in southern Ireland. Hieatt points out that variations in verse form correspond to days in the year (365 long lines), hours in the day (24 stanzas), spring and fall equinoxes (parallel diction, imagery, and thought in stanzas 1-12 and 13-24), degrees of the sun's daily movement (359 long lines before the *tornata*, corresponding to 359 degrees of the sun's movement as contrasted with 360 degrees of the stars' movement), and the division between waking and sleeping hours (indicated by a change in the refrain at the end of stanza 17). It is variations within stanza 17 that most personalize the time element to make the "bedding" of the bride occur at the point in the poem representing nightfall on the poet's wedding day, the day of the summer solstice in southern Ireland. At the end of the stanza, the refrain, which had for sixteen stanzas been describing the answering echo of the woods, changes to "The woods no more shall answer, nor your echo ring": All is quiet so that the poet-bridegroom can welcome night and the love of his bride.

## COMPLAINTS

The collection of moralizing, melancholy verse titled *Complaints* reflects an as yet not fully developed artistry in the author. Although published in the aftermath of fame brought by *The Faerie Queene*, most of the nine poems were probably first drafted much earlier. The most significant poem in this volume was probably the satirical beast fable, "Prosopopoia: Or, Mother Hubberd's Tale." Following the tradition of Giovanni Boccaccio and Geoffrey Chaucer, the poet creates a framework of tale-tellers, one of whom is "a good old woman" named Mother Hubberd. In Mother Hubberd's story, a Fox and an Ape gain personal prosperity through the gullibility of farmers, the ignorance and worldliness of clergymen, and the licentiousness of courtiers. About two-thirds of the way through, the satire turns more specifically to the concern of England in 1579 with a possible marriage between the twenty-four-year-old Duc d'Alencon and Queen Elizabeth, then forty-six. The marriage was being engineered by Lord Burleigh (the Fox of the narrative) and by Jean de Simier, whom Elizabeth playfully called her "Ape." This poem, even more than *The Shepheardes Calender*, demonstrates Spenser's artistic simplicity and the Chaucer-like irony of his worldview. Burleigh's later hostility to Spenser gives evidence of the pointedness of the poet's satiric barbs. "Virgil's Gnat" also exemplifies a satiric beast fable, this time with Leicester's marriage as the target, hit so effectively that Spenser himself was wounded by Leicester's lessened patronage. In "Muiopotmos: Or, The Fate of the Butterfly," beast fable is elevated by philosophical overtones, epic machinery, and classical allusions. Some type of personal or political allegory obviously underlies the poem, but critical interpretations vary widely in attempting to identify the chief figures, the Spider and the Butterfly. Despite such uncertainty, however, one message is clear: Life and beauty are mutable.

Mutability permeates *Complaints*; it is even more central to the posthumous fragment known as the "Mutabilitie Cantos." The publisher Matthew Lownes printed these two cantos as "The Legend of Constancy," a fragmentary book 7 of *The Faerie Queene*. Lownes's identification of these two cantos with the unfinished epic was apparently based on similar poetic form, an allusion to the poet's softening his stern style in singing of hills and woods "mongst warres and knights," and a reference to the records of Fairyland as registering mutability's genealogy. There are, however, no knights, human or elf, in these cantos. Instead, Jove and Nature represent allegorically the cosmic principle of Constancy, the permanence that underlies all change. Despite the philosophical victory of Nature, one of the most effective extended passages in the cantos represents change through a processional pageant of the seasons, the months, day and night, the hours, and life and death.

The principle of underlying permanence applies to Spenser's works as well as to the world of which he wrote. In his shepherds and shepherdesses, his knights and ladies, his own personae, and even in the animal figures of his fables, images of Everyman and Everywoman still live. Time has thickened some of the allegorical veils that conceal as well as reveal, language then new has become archaic, and poetic conventions have become freer since Spenser's poetry first charmed his contemporaries. Despite such changes, however, the evocative and creative power that made Spenser "the Prince of Poets in his time" remains constant.

OTHER MAJOR WORKS

NONFICTION: *Three Proper, and Wittie, Familiar Letters*, 1580; *Foure Letters and Certaine Sonnets*, 1586; *A View of the Present State of Ireland*, pb. 1633 (wr. 1596).

MISCELLANEOUS: *The Works of Edmund Spenser: A Variorum Edition*, 1932-1949 (Edwin Greenlaw, et al., editors).

BIBLIOGRAPHY

Burlinson, Christopher. *Allegory, Space, and the Material World in the Writings of Edmund Spenser.* Rochester, N.Y.: D. S. Brewer, 2006. An analysis of the poetry of Spenser that concentrates on the symbolism and allegory in his work.

Grogan, Jane. *Exemplary Spenser: Visual and Poetic Pedagogy in "The Faerie Queene."* Burlington, Vt.: Ashgate, 2009. Grogan examines Spenser's poetry through an analysis of *The Faerie Queene.*

Hamilton, A. C., et al., eds. *The Spenser Encyclopedia.* Toronto, Ont.: University of Toronto Press, 1990. This 858-page volume represents the cooperative efforts of Spenserian scholars to compile a series of articles on every aspect of Spenser's life and work. With index.

Heale, Elizabeth. *"The Faerie Queene": A Reader's Guide.* New York: Cambridge University Press, 1987. Offers an updated guide to Spenser's *The Faerie Queene,* the first great epic poem in English. Emphasizes the religious and political context for each episode. One chapter is devoted to each book of *The Faerie Queene.* Contains an index for characters and episodes.

Heninger, S. K., Jr. *Sidney and Spenser: The Poet as Maker.* University Park: Pennsylvania State University Press, 1989. In this study of mimesis, or imitation, S. K. Heninger considers the transmutation of allegory to fiction. Examines the aesthetic elements in art, music, and literature, analyzes the forms of Spenser's major works and considers the relationship between form and content. This 646-page study of Renaissance aesthetics offers an essential background for understanding Spenser's art.

Lethbridge, J. B., ed. *Edmund Spenser: New and Renewed Directions.* Madison, N.J.: Fairleigh Dickinson University Press, 2006. This collection of essays covers most of Spenser's works, including those written in later life. It also examines Spenser's friendships with Sir Walter Ralegh and Queen Elizabeth through *The Faerie Queene.*

Morrison, Jennifer Klein, and Matthew Greenfield Aldershot, eds. *Edmund Spenser: Essays on Culture and Allegory.* Burlington, Vt.: Ashgate, 2000. A collection of critical essays dealing with the works of Spenser. Includes bibliographical references and an index.

Oram, William A. *Edmund Spenser.* New York: Twayne, 1997. An introductory biography and critical study of selected works by Spencer. Includes bibliographic references and an index.

Van Es, Bart, ed. *A Critical Companion to Spenser Studies.* New York: Palgrave Macmillan, 2006. Comprising thirteen chapters, this useful resource surveys issues of gender, religion, texts, and critical analyses.

Zurcher, Andrew. *Spenser's Legal Language: Law and Poetry in Early Modern England.* Rochester, N.Y.: D. S. Brewer, 2007. Zurcher provides a look at Spenser's works in terms of what they reveal about law in early modern England.

*Marie Michelle Walsh*

# HENRY HOWARD, EARL OF SURREY

**Born:** Hunsdon, Hertfordshire, England; 1517
**Died:** London, England; January 19, 1547

PRINCIPAL POETRY
*An Excellent Epitaffe of Syr Thomas Wyat*, 1542
*Songes and Sonettes*, 1557 (also known as *Tottel's Miscellany*)
*The Poems of Henry Howard, Earl of Surrey*, 1920, 1928 (Frederick Morgan
  Padelford, editor)

### OTHER LITERARY FORMS

Henry Howard, earl of Surrey, did not contribute to English literature with any other form besides poetry. His poetic innovations, however, helped to refine and stabilize English poetry.

### ACHIEVEMENTS

As a translator and original poet, Henry Howard, earl of Surrey, prepared the way for a number of important developments in English poetry. His translations and paraphrases are not slavishly literal; they are re-creations of classical and continental works in terms meaningful to Englishmen. He naturalized several literary forms—the sonnet, elegy, epigram, and satire—and showed English poets what could be done with various stanzas, metrical patterns, and rhyme schemes, including terza rima, ottava rima, and poulter's measure. He invented the English or Shakespearean sonnet (three quatrains and a couplet) and set another precedent by using the form for subjects other than love. His poems exerted considerable influence, for they circulated in manuscript for some time before they were printed. Forty of them appear in *Songes and Sonettes* (better known as *Tottel's Miscellany*), a collection of more than 270 works which saw nine editions by 1587 and did much to establish iambic meter in English poetry. Surrey shares with Sir Thomas Wyatt the distinction of having introduced the Petrarchan mode of amatory verse in England.

His innovations in poetic diction and prosody have had more lasting significance. Surrey refined English poetry of aureate diction, the archaic and ornate language cultivated by fifteenth century writers. His elegant diction formed the basis of poetic expression until well into the eighteenth century.

His greatest achievement is his demonstration of the versatility and naturalness in English of the iambic pentameter line. Surrey invented blank verse, which later poets brought to maturity. The metrical regularity of much of his rhymed verse (a regularity perhaps enhanced by Tottel's editor) had a stabilizing effect on English prosody, which had long been in a chaotic state. In *The Arte of English Poesie* (1589), George Puttenham hailed Wyatt and Surrey as "the first reformers of our English meetre and stile," for they "pollished our rude & homely maner of vulgar poesie." Until the present century Surrey's smoothness was generally preferred to Wyatt's rougher versification.

Surrey's essential quality, a concern with style, informed his poetry, his life, and the Tudor court of which he was a brilliant representative. Consistently as a poet and frequently as a courtier, he epitomized learning and grace; for his countrymen, he was an exemplar of culture.

### BIOGRAPHY

Henry Howard, earl of Surrey from 1524, was the eldest son of Thomas Howard, third duke of Norfolk. The elder Howard, one of the most powerful leaders of the old nobility, saw to it that his heir received an excellent education. At the age of twelve, Surrey was translating Latin, French, Italian, and Spanish and practicing martial skills. He was selected as the companion of Henry Fitzroy, Henry VIII's illegitimate son who had been created duke of Richmond. The youths, both proud, impetuous, and insecure, were settled at Windsor in the spring of 1530. Surrey was married in 1532 to Lady Frances de Vere; the couple began living together a few years later, and he was evidently devoted to her for the rest of his life.

Surrey and Richmond accompanied the king to France in the autumn of 1532. The young men resided with the French court, then dominated by Italian culture, for most of the following year. Surrey acquired courtly graces and probably became acquainted with the work of Luigi Alamanni, a Florentine writer of unrhymed verse. Shortly after Surrey and Richmond returned to the English court, the king's son married Surrey's sister Mary.

In 1540, Surrey was appointed steward of the University of Cambridge in recognition of his scholarship. Having also distinguished himself in martial games, in 1541 he was made Knight of the Garter. His military education was completed when he was sent to observe the King's continental wars. The first English artistocrat to be a man of letters, statesman, and soldier, the handsome and spirited earl was esteemed as a model courtier. During his final seven years, he was occupied with courtly, military, and domestic matters, finding time to write only when he was out of favor with Henry VIII or otherwise in trouble.

Early in 1543, Surrey, Thomas Clere, Thomas Wyatt the Younger, and another young man indulged in disorderly behavior that led to the earl's brief imprisonment in the Fleet. Still in the king's good graces, he spent most of the next three years serving in France and building an elegant, costly house in the classical style. As marshal of the field and commander of Boulogne, he proved to be a competent officer who did not hesitate to risk his own life. He was wounded while leading a courageous assault on Montreuil. After a defeat in a minor skirmish, he was recalled in the spring of 1546.

By that time, he had made enemies who were intent on destroying him. He was imprisoned for threatening a courtier who had called Norfolk morally unfit to be regent during the minority of the king's son, Edward. Making much of Surrey's pride in his Plantagenet ancestry, his enemies built a case that he intended to seize power. His request to be allowed to confront his chief accuser in single combat—characteristic of his effort to live by the chivalric code of a vanishing era—was denied. His sister Mary and certain supposed friends testified against him. Maintaining his innocence, Surrey forcefully defended himself and reviled his enemies during an eight-hour trial for treason; but, like many others whom the Tudors considered dangerous or expendable, he was condemned and beheaded on Tower Hill.

## ANALYSIS

An aristocrat with a humanistic education, Henry Howard, earl of Surrey, considered literature a pleasant diversion. As a member of the Tudor court, he was encouraged to display his learning, wit, and eloquence by writing love poems and translating continental and classical works. The poet who cultivated an elegant style was admired and imitated by his peers. Poetry was not considered a medium for self-expression. In the production of literature, as in other polite activities, there were conventions to be observed. Even the works that seem to have grown out of Surrey's personal experience also have roots in classical, Christian, Italian, or native traditions. Surrey is classical in his concern for balance, decorum, fluency, and restraint. These attributes are evident throughout his work—the amatory lyrics, elegies, didactic verses, translations, and biblical paraphrases.

## LOVE POEMS

Surrey produced more than two dozen amatory poems. A number of these owe something to Petrarch and other continental poets. The Petrarchan qualities of his work, as well as those of his successors, should not be exaggerated, however, for Tudor and Elizabethan poets were also influenced by native tradition and by rhetorical treatises which encouraged the equating of elegance and excellence. Contemporaries admired the fluency and eloquence which made Surrey, like Petrarch, a worthy model. His sonnet beginning "From Tuscan cam my ladies worthi race," recognized in his own time as polite verse, engendered the romantic legend that he served the Fair Geraldine (Elizabeth Fitzgerald, b. 1528?), but his love poems are now recognized as literary exercises of a type common in Renaissance poetry.

Surrey's courtly lovers complain of wounds; they freeze and burn, sigh, weep, and despair—yet continue to serve Love. Representative of this mode is "Love that doth raine and live within my thought," one of his five translations or adaptations of sonnets by Petrarch. The poem develops from a military conceit: The speaker's mind and heart are held captive by Love, whose colors are often displayed in his face. When the desired lady frowns, Love retreats to the heart and hides there, leaving the unoffending servant alone, "with shamfast looke," to suffer for his lord's sake. Uninterested in the moral aspects of this situation, Surrey makes nothing of the paradox of Love as conqueror and coward. He does not suggest the lover's ambivalence or explore the lady's motives. Wyatt, whose translation of the same sonnet begins "The longe love, that in my thought doeth harbor," indicates (as Petrarch does) that the lady asks her admirer to become a better man. Surrey's speaker, taught only to "love and suffre paine," gallantly concludes, "Sweet is the death that taketh end by love."

The point is not that Surrey's sonnet should be more like Wyatt's but that in this poem and in many of his lyrics, Surrey seems less concerned with the complexity of an experience than with his manner of presenting it. Most of the lines are smooth and regularly iambic, although there are five initial trochees. The poem's matter is carefully accommodated to its form. The first quatrain deals with Love, the second with the lady, and the third with the lover's plight. His resolve is summarized in the couplet: Despite his undeserved suffering, he will be loyal. The sonnet is balanced and graceful, pleasing by virtue of its musical qualities and intellectual conceit.

Some of the longer poems do portray the emotions of courtly lovers. The speaker in "When sommer toke in hand the winter to assail" observes (as several of Surrey's lovers do) that nature is renewed in spring, while he alone continues to be weak and hopeless. Casting off his despondency, he curses and defies Love. Then, realizing the gravity of his offense, he asks forgiveness and is told by the god that he can atone only by greater suffering. Now "undone for ever more," he offers himself as a "miror" for all lovers: "Strive not with love, for if ye do, it will ye thus befall." Lacking the discipline of the sonnet form, this poem in poulter's measure seems to sprawl. Surrey's amatory verse is generally most successful when he focuses on a relatively simple situation or emotion. "When sommer toke in hand the winter to assail," not his best work, is representative in showing his familiarity with native poetry: It echoes Geoffrey Chaucer's *Troilus and Criseyde* (1382) and describes nature in a manner characteristic of English poets. In seven other love poems, Surrey describes nature in sympathy with or in contrast to the lover's condition.

## A WOMAN'S PERSPECTIVE

At a time when most amatory verse was written from the male perspective, Surrey assumed a woman's voice in three of his lyrics. The speaker in "Gyrtt in my giltlesse gowne" defends herself against a charge of craftiness pressed by a male courtier in a companion poem beginning "Wrapt in my carelesse cloke." Accused of encouraging men she does not care for, the lady compares herself to Susanna, who was slandered by corrupt elders. Remarking that her critic himself practices a crafty strategy—trying to ignite a woman's passion by feigning indifference—she asserts that she, like her prototype, will be protected against lust and lies. This pair of poems, if disappointing because

Surrey has chosen not to probe more deeply into the behavior and emotions generated by the game of courtly love, demonstrates the poet's skill in presenting a speaker in a clearly defined setting or situation. His finest lyrics may fairly be called dramatic.

Two other monologues, "O happy dames, that may embrace" and "Good ladies, ye that have your pleasure in exyle," are spoken by women lamenting the absence of their beloved lords. They may have been written for Surrey's wife while he was directing the siege of Boulogne. Long separations troubled him, but his requests to the Privy Council for permission to bring his family to France were denied. After an exordium urging her female audience to "mourne with [her] awhyle," the narrator of "Good ladies" describes tormenting dreams of her "sweete lorde" in danger and at play with "his lytle sonne" (Thomas Howard, oldest of the Surreys' five children, was born in 1536). The immediate occasion for this poem, however personal, is consciously literary: The lady, a sorrowful "wight," burns like a courtly lover when her lord is absent, comforted only by the expectation of his return and reflection that "I feele by sower, how sweete is felt the more" (the sweet-sour antithesis was a favorite with courtly poets). Despite the insistent iambic meter characteristic of poulter's measure, one can almost hear a voice delivering these lines. In the best of his love poetry, Surrey makes new wholes of traditional elements.

## ELEGIAC POEMS

Surrey's elegiac poems reflect his background in rhetoric. Paying tribute to individuals, he would persuade his readers to become more virtuous men and women. "Wyatt resteth here, that quick could never rest," the first of his works to be published, devotes more attention to praise of Wyatt than to lament and consolation. Using the figure of *partitio* (division into parts), Surrey anatomizes the physique of this complete man in order to display his virtues—prudence, integrity, eloquence, justice, courage. Having devoted eight quatrains to praise, Surrey proceeds to the lament—the dead man is "lost" to those he might have inspired—with a consolation at the thought that his spirit is now in heaven. He implies that God has removed "this jewel" in order to punish a nation blind to his worth. In so coupling praise and dispraise, Surrey follows a precedent set by classical rhetoricians. He again eulogized Wyatt in two sonnets, "Dyvers thy death do dyversely bemoan" and "In the rude age," both attacking Wyatt's enemies. The former devotes a quatrain to each of two kinds of mourners, hypocrites who only seem to grieve and malefactors who "Weape envyous teares heer [his] fame so good." In the sestet, he sets himself apart: He feels the loss of so admirable a man. Here, as in a number of his sonnets, Surrey achieves a harmony of form and content. There is no evidence that he knew Wyatt personally. His tributes to the older courtier are essentially public performances, but they convey admiration and regret and offer a stinging rebuke to courtiers who do not come up to Wyatt's standard.

Many sixteenth century poets wrote elegies for public figures; more than twenty appear in *Tottel's Miscellany*. Surrey, as indicated above, was familiar with the literary tribute. In "Norfolk sprang thee," an epitaph for his squire Thomas Clere (d. 1545), he uses some of the conventions of epideictic poetry to express esteem, as well as grief, for the dead. Developed according to the biographical method of praise (seen also in "From Tuscan cam my ladies worthi race"), the sonnet specifies Clere's origins and personal relationships; it traces his career from his birth in Norfolk to his mortal wound at Montreuil—incurred while saving Surrey's life—to his burial in the Howards' chapel at Lambeth. By "placing" Clere geographically and within the contexts of chivalric and human relationships, Surrey immortalizes a brave and noble person. He has succeeded in writing a fresh, even personal poem while observing literary and rhetorical conventions.

Personal feeling and experience certainly went into "So crewell prison," a lament for Richmond (d. 1536) and the poet's youthful fellowship with him at Windsor—ironically, the place of his confinement as a penalty for having struck Edward Seymour. Subtly alluding to the *ubi sunt* tradition, he mentions remembered places, events, and activities—green and graveled courts, dewy meadows, woods, brightly dressed ladies, dances, games, chivalric competition, shared laughter and confidences, promises made and kept—as he does so, conveying his sense of loss. He praises, and longs for, not only his friend but also the irrecoverable past. Of Richmond's soul he says nothing. His consolation, if so it may be called, is that the loss of his companion lessens the pain of his loss of freedom. "So crewell prison," perhaps Surrey's best poem, is at once conventional and personal.

## DIDACTIC POEMS

Taught to regard the courtier as a counselor, Surrey wrote a few explicitly didactic pieces. His sonnet about Sardanapalus, "Th' Assyryans king, in peas with fowle desyre," portrays a lustful, cowardly ruler. Such depravity, Surrey implies, endangers virtue itself. The poem may allude to King Henry VIII, who had executed two Howard queens. (Surrey witnessed Anne Boleyn's trial and Catherine Howard's execution.) The degenerate monarch in Surrey's sonnet, however, bears few resemblances to Henry VIII, who had often shown his regard for Norfolk's heir and Richmond's closest friend. John Gower, John Lydgate, and other poets had also told the story of Sardanapulus as a "mirror" for princes. Surrey's "Laid in my quyett bedd" draws upon Horace's *Ars poetica* (c. 17 B.C.E.; *The Art of Poetry*) and the first of his *Satires* (35 B.C.E., 30 B.C.E.; English translation, 1567). The aged narrator, after surveying the ages of man, remarks that people young and old always wish to change their estate; he concludes that boyhood is the happiest time, though youths will not realize this truth before they become decrepit. Like certain of the love poems, "Laid in my quyett bedd" illustrates Surrey's dramatic ability.

## "LONDON, HAS THOU ACCUSED ME"

The mock-heroic "London, has thou accused me" was probably written while Surrey was imprisoned for harassing and brawling with some citizens and breaking windows with a stonebow. As C. W. Jentoft points out, the satirist, presenting himself as a God-sent "scourge for synn," seems to be delivering an oration. "Thy wyndowes had don me no spight," he explains; his purpose was to awaken Londoners secretly engaged in deadly sins to their peril. Appropriating the structure of the classical oration, he becomes, in effect, not the defendant but the prosecutor of a modern Babylon. The peroration, fortified with scriptural phrasings, warns of divine judgment.

## POETRY TRANSLATIONS

Surrey's translations also reflect the young aristocrat's classical and humanistic education. He translated two poems advocating the golden mean—a Horatian ode and an epigram by Martial. In the former ("Of thy lyfe, Thomas") he imitates the terseness of the original. "Marshall, the thinges for to attayne," the first English translation of that work, is also remarkably concise. His intention to re-create in English the style of a Latin poet is evident in his translations of the second and fourth books of the *Aeneid* (c. 29-19 B.C.E.; English translation, 1553). He did not attempt to reproduce Vergil's unrhymed hexameters in English Alexandrines (as Richard Stanyhurst was to do) or to translate them into rhymed couplets (as the Scottish poet Gawin Douglas had done). Familiar with the decasyllabic line of Chaucer and other native poets and the *verso sciolto* (unrhymed verse) of sixteenth century Italy, he devised blank verse, the form that was to be refined by Christopher Marlowe, William Shakespeare, and John Milton.

Textual scholars have encountered several problems in studying Surrey's translation of the *Aeneid*. His manuscripts are not extant, and all printed versions appeared after his death. The work may have been undertaken as early as 1538 or as late as 1544; in the light of his service at court and in France, it seems likely that the translation was done intermittently. Modern scholars now favor an early period of composition, which would make this translation earlier than many of Surrey's other works and help to account for their refined, decorous style.

Another issue is the relationship of Surrey's work to the *Eneados* of Gawin Douglas (1474?-1522), whose translation had circulated widely in manuscript during Surrey's youth. Scholar Florence Ridley found evidence of Douglas's influence in more than 40 percent of Surrey's lines. In book 4, perhaps completed later than book 2, Surrey borrowed from Douglas less frequently. There is other evidence that his style was maturing and becoming more flexible: more frequent run-ons, feminine endings, pauses within the line, and metrical variations.

The distinctive qualities of Surrey's translation are largely owing to his imitation of Vergil's style. A young humanist working in an immature language and using a new form, Surrey was trying, as Italian translators had done, to re-create in the vernacular his

Latin master's compactness, restraint, and stateliness. He did not always succeed. Generally avoiding both prosaic and aureate vocabulary, he uses relatively formal diction. To a modern reader accustomed to the blank verse developed by later poets, the iambic meter is so regular as to be somewhat monotonous. By means of patterned assonance, consonance, and internal rhyme, as well as the placement of caesuras, he has achieved a flowing movement that approximates Vergilian verse paragraphs. Phonetic effects often pleasing in themselves heighten emotional intensity and help to establish the phrase, not the line, as the poetic unit. It is not surprising, then, that Thomas Warton called Surrey England's first classical poet. Imitation led to innovation, the creation of a form for English heroic poetry. Even though blank verse did not come into general use until late in the sixteenth century, Surrey's achievement remains monumental.

## BIBLICAL PARAPHRASES

The paraphrases of Ecclesiastes 1-5 and Psalms 55, 73, and 88, Surrey's most nearly autobiographical works, portray the "slipper state" of life in the Tudor court. Probably written during his final imprisonment in late 1546, they speak of vanity and vexation of spirit and cry out against vicious enemies, treacherous friends, and a tyrant who drinks the blood of innocents. Like Wyatt, whose penitential psalms he admired, he used Joannes Campensis's Latin paraphrases which had been published in 1532. Surrey's translations are free, amplifying and at times departing from the Vulgate and Campensis, as in this line from his version of Ecclesiastes 2: "By princely acts [such as the pursuit of pleasure and building of fine houses] strave I still to make my fame indure." Although his background was Catholic, these poems express Protestant sentiments.

In his versions of Psalms 73 and 88, he speaks of God's "elect" and "chosen," apparently placing himself in that company. While praying for forgiveness in Psalm 73, he notes that his foes are going unscathed and asks why he is "scourged still, that no offence have doon." Psalm 55 calls for divine help as he faces death and exulting enemies; at the end of this unpolished, perhaps unfinished poem, Surrey completely departs from his printed sources to inveigh against wolfish adversaries. The time to live was almost past, but it was not yet the time to keep silence. Like the other biblical paraphrases, this work has chiefly biographical interest. Expecting imminent execution, Surrey was still experimenting with prosody: Psalm 55 is the one poem in this group to be written in unrhymed hexameters rather than poulter's measure. Even in his last works, the poet is generally detached and self-effacing. Surrey's greatest legacy to English poets is a concern for fluent, graceful expression.

## OTHER MAJOR WORKS

TRANSLATIONS: *The Fourth Boke of Virgill*, 1554; *Certain Bokes of Virgiles Aenaeis*, 1557.

BIBLIOGRAPHY

Childs, Jessie. *Henry VIII's Last Victim: The Life and Times of Henry Howard, Earl of Surrey*. New York: Thomas Dunne Books/St. Martin's Press, 2007. Discusses the poet's life in detail, in particular his relationship with Henry VIII.

Heale, Elizabeth. *Wyatt, Surrey, and Early Tudor Poetry*. New York: Longman, 1998. An indispensable resource that brings together critical analysis of the early Tudor poets. Those who would study Edmund Spenser and William Shakespeare's sonnets will benefit from the reading of these wonderful authors.

Lines, Candace. "The Erotic Politics of Grief in Surrey's 'So crewell prison.'" *Studies in English Literature, 1500-1900* 46, no. 1 (2006): 1-26. Provides a close examination of Surrey's well-known poem, focusing on his expression of grief.

Sessions, William A. *Henry Howard, the Poet Earl of Surrey: A Life*. 1999. Reprint. New York: Oxford University Press, 2003. Sessions's narrative combines historical scholarship with close readings of poetic texts and Tudor paintings to reveal the unique life of the first Renaissance courtier and a poet who wrote and created radically new forms.

Spearing, A. C. *Medieval to Renaissance in English Poetry*. New York: Cambridge University Press, 1985. After discussing Renaissance classicism in Surrey's poetry, Spearing proceeds to extended analyses of three poems: two epitaphs on Sir Thomas Wyatt and "So crewell prison," the poem about Surrey's imprisonment at Windsor.

Thomson, Patricia. "Wyatt and Surrey." In *English Poetry and Prose, 1540-1674*, edited by Christopher Ricks. 1970. Reprint. London: Penguin Books, 1993. Thomson first compares Surrey and Sir Thomas Wyatt to John Skelton, whose poetry was primarily late medieval, then discusses Surrey and particularly Wyatt as inheritors of the Petrarchan tradition.

Walker, Greg. *Writing Under Tyranny: English Literature and the Henrician Reformation*. New York: Oxford University Press, 2005. Contains a chapter on Surrey and Sir Thomas Wyatt that examines their experiences writing under Henry VIII and the innovative forms that Surrey produced.

*Mary De Jong*

# HENRY VAUGHAN

**Born:** Newton-on-Usk, Wales; April 17, 1622
**Died:** Llansantffraed, Wales; April 23, 1695

*Poems*, 1646
*Silex Scintillans*, parts 1 and 2, 1650, 1655
*Olor Iscanus*, 1651
*Thalia Rediviva*, 1678
*The Secular Poems of Henry Vaughan*, 1958 (E. L. Marilla, editor)
*The Complete Poetry of Henry Vaughan*, 1964 (French Fogle, editor)

## OTHER LITERARY FORMS

Henry Vaughan (vawn, also von), whose religious poetry reflects the influence of John Donne and George Herbert, published translations of several religious and medical treatises.

## ACHIEVEMENTS

Henry Vaughan is usually grouped with the Metaphysical poets, anthologized particularly with Donne, Herbert, Richard Crashaw, and Andrew Marvell. While there is some justification for this association, in Vaughan's instance it has resulted in a somewhat too narrow estimation of his work and its historical context. In the Metaphysical collections, to be sure, Vaughan has been represented by some of his best poems, such as "Regeneration," "The World," or "Affliction," drawn from *Silex Scintillans*. These works, however, have often been grouped in contrast with the lyrics from Herbert's *The Temple* (1633). Invariably Vaughan has been admired only as a lesser foil to his great predecessor; while admittedly Vaughan had his great moments, he lacked the sustained intensity of Herbert. Moreover, Vaughan's gracious preface to the 1655 edition of *Silex Scintillans* shows much regard for the creator of *The Temple*. Given such authority, it is not surprising that Vaughan's modern reputation, emerging in the Metaphysical revival of the twentieth century, has been overshadowed by the accomplishments of Herbert.

Fortunately, recent scholarship has begun to redress the imbalances concerning Vaughan with thorough study of his work and his milieu. By his own admission, Vaughan lived "when religious controversy had split the English people into factions: I lived among the furious conflicts of Church and State" ("Ad Posteros" in *Olor Iscanus*). His was the time that saw a people indict, condemn, and execute its monarch in the name of religious fervor and political expedience. His was the time that saw the final vestiges of ancient families' power supplanted by parliamentary prerogatives of a potent middle class. Vaughan defined his place outside the struggle in order to take part in it as conservator of the Anglican-Royalist cause, a defender of the British Church in poetry and prose tied closely to the attitudes and values of pagan and Christian pastoral literature. Moreover, in his own Welsh countryside and lineage, Vaughan found the touchstone for his conservatorship, an analogue of the self-imposed exiles of early church fathers who took refuge from the conflicts and hazards of the world.

## BIOGRAPHY

Henry Vaughan was one of twins born to Thomas Vaughan and Denise Vaughan in 1622, ten years after a union that brought the elder Vaughan into possession of house and lands at Trenewydd (Newton-on-Usk). The father of the poet apparently had no calling except that of a gentleman, and in later life, he seems to have been fond of suing and being sued by his relatives. The Vaughan family had resided in the Brecknock region of Wales for generations and traced their line back to David ap Llwellen, known as Davey Gam, who was knighted and slain at the Battle of Agincourt in 1415. The poet's twin, also named Thomas, obtained a greater measure of fame in his own lifetime than Henry did. He was a philosopher of the occult sciences who at one point engaged in a pamphlet war with Henry More, the noted Cambridge Platonist writer. He settled near Oxford and died in 1666. Contemporary scholars have suggested that the elaborate pastoral eclogue, *Daphnis*, appearing in *Thalia Rediviva*, was the poet's farewell to his twin.

As befit the heirs of a minor country gentleman, the twins began their formal studies about 1632 with the rector of Llangatock, Matthew Herbert, continuing until 1638. The poet recalls that Herbert, "Though one man . . . gave me double treasure: learning and love." Following this tutelage, the twins were sent off to Jesus College, Oxford. They were seventeen; they had grown up steeped in Welsh language and culture. While the record of Thomas Vaughan's matriculation at Jesus College survives, no similar record exists for the poet. He apparently remained in Oxford until 1640, when he set forth to London with the intention of studying law. Shortly after his arrival, the king's favorite, the earl of Stafford, and Archbishop Laud were indicted. Stafford was executed by a reluctant monarch in the following May. Perhaps at this time Vaughan began translating Juvenal's tenth satire on the vanity of human wishes. While at London, Vaughan began his poetic "apprenticeship," steeping himself in the writings of Ben Jonson and his Cavalier followers such as Thomas Randolph. These efforts were published in the *Poems* of 1646. One imagines the young Vaughan's brief tenure in London as preparation for a respectable civic life, perhaps dividing his time between the city and the Welsh countryside. It was not to be.

In the summer of 1642, the first civil war erupted; Vaughan hastened to Wales. There he accepted the post of secretary to the chief justice of the Great Sessions, Sir Marmaduke Lloyd, probably retaining it until 1645. At the same time, Vaughan courted

Catherine Wise, the daughter of a Warwickshire family. The "Amoret" poems in the 1646 volume were probably written and arranged in honor of his courtship and subsequent marriage to her. With the outbreak of the second civil war, Vaughan left the service of the law to join the Royalist army.

The appearance of the first part of *Silex Scintillans* in 1650, arguably the finest volume of poetry published by anyone in the years of the Interregnum, was unspectacular. Not until 1655, when he added several poems and a revealing preface, did Vaughan provide posterity with the ill-conceived notion of his religious "conversion." Of all the facts concerning Vaughan's life, no nonevent is as important as the "conversion." It was invented in the nineteenth century by the Reverend H. F. Lyte, who edited the first publication of Vaughan's work since the poet's lifetime. Lyte took remarks in the 1655 preface concerning Vaughan's illness as a metaphor for a spiritual malaise cured by a heavy dose of Protestant piety. As a result of Lyte's homily, Vaughan's secular poetry suffered absolute neglect until the mid-twentieth century. *Silex Scintillans* was considered artistic proof of a conversion because it is Vaughan's best, most sustained work. A more accurate reading of what happened to Vaughan was that he matured, as a man and as an artist. He found his unique voice in the urgency of the moment, in the defeat of his religious and political party, in the example of Herbert's poetry, in the pastoralism of passages in the Bible, in the whole tradition of finding the virtuous life in rural surroundings.

One senses, throughout his mature work, Vaughan's urgent defense of the values of simplicity and rural piety tempered from within by resolve. Vaughan included translations of Boethius and Maciej Kazimierz Sarbiewski (Mathias Casimirus Sarbievius) in *Olor Iscanus*. They offer a pattern of stoic acceptance of this world's reversals by seeking virtue in retirement. Retirement, as Vaughan sees it, is not passive, however. It is a conscious choice. Thus, his allusions to illness in his preface to *Silex Scintillans* must be regarded within the larger context of his discovery of Herbert's poems and his condemnation of trifling, uncommitted poetry. Vaughan was always an Anglican and a Royalist. He did not convert: He simply found his way to fight back. From the remove of the country, Vaughan discovered a role for himself in a strife-torn society more potent than that of soldier or solicitor: as a poetic defender of God and king.

No doubt other events contributed to Vaughan's recognition of his poetic mission, including the death of a younger brother, William, in 1648, and of his first wife, Catherine, five years later. He married her sister Elizabeth in 1655, the same year that his translation of Heinrich Nolle's *Hermetical Physick* appeared. By then Vaughan had elected medicine as a new career. That he continued to write verse is evidenced by the dates of poems in Vaughan's final collection, *Thalia Rediviva*. Thalia is the Muse of pastoral poetry. Vaughan continued to see himself in terms of the rural tradition of poetry because he found there a synthesis of images, metaphors, and implied or explicit values that harmonized with his religious and political beliefs. He continued to practice medicine, according to one contemporary account, as late as autumn, 1694. When he died the following spring, he was buried overlooking the countryside he so long celebrated, in the churchyard of the faith he so vehemently defended, his stone reciting his link to the Silures, the ancient Welsh tribe from which he took his epithet, "The Silurist," by which he was often known.

## ANALYSIS

Henry Vaughan's first collection, *Poems*, is very derivative; in it can be found borrowings from Donne, Jonson, William Hobington, William Cartwright, and others. It contains only thirteen poems in addition to the translation of Juvenal. Seven poems are written to Amoret, believed to idealize the poet's courtship of Catherine Wise, ranging from standard situations of thwarted and indifferent love to this sanguine couplet in "To Amoret Weeping": "Yet whilst Content, and Love we joyntly vye,/ We have a blessing which no gold can buye." Perhaps in "Upon the Priorie Grove, His Usuall Retirement," Vaughan best captures the promise of love accepted and courtship rewarded even by eternal love:

> So there again, thou 'It see us move
> In our first Innocence, and Love:
> And in thy shades, as now, so then
> Wee'le kisse, and smile, and walke again.

The lines move with the easy assurance of one who has studied the verses of the urbane Tribe of Ben. That other favorite sport of the Tribe—after wooing—was drink, and in "*A Rhapsodie*, Occasionally written upon a meeting with some friends at the Globe Taverne, . . ." one sees the poet best known for his devout poems celebrating with youthful fervor all the pleasures of the grape and rendering a graphic slice of London street life. Though imitative, this little volume possesses its own charm. Perhaps it points to the urbane legal career that Vaughan might have pursued had not the conflicts of church and state driven him elsewhere.

## OLOR ISCANUS

The poet of *Olor Iscanus* is a different man, one who has returned from the city to the country, one who has seen the face of war and defeat. Nowhere in his writing does Vaughan reject the materials of his poetic apprenticeship in London: He favors, even in his religious lyrics, smooth and graceful couplets where they are appropriate. This volume contains various occasional poems and elegies expressing Vaughan's disgust with the defeat of the Royalists by Oliver Cromwell's armies and the new order of Puritan piety. The leading poem, "To the River *Isca*," ends with a plea for freedom and safety, the river's banks "redeem'd from all disorders!" The real current pulling this river—underscoring the quality of *Olor Iscanus* which prompted its author to delay publication—is a growing resolve to sustain one's friends and one's sanity by choosing rural simplicity.

The idea of this country fortitude is expressed in many ways. For example, the Cavalier invitation poem, "To my worthy friend, *Master T. Lewes*," opens with an evocation of nature "Opprest with snow," its rivers "All bound up in an *Icie Coat.*" The speaker in the poem asks his friend to pass the harsh time away and, like nature itself, preserve the old pattern for reorder:

> Let us meet then! and while this world
> In wild *Excentricks* now is hurld,
> Keep wee, like nature, the same *Key*,
> And walk in our forefathers way.

In the elegy for Lady Elizabeth, daughter of the late Charles I, Vaughan offers this metaphor: "Thou seem'st a Rose-bud born in *Snow*,/ A flowre of purpose sprung to bow/ To headless tempests, and the rage/ Of an Incensed, stormie Age." Then, too, in *Olor Iscanus*, Vaughan includes his own translations from Boethius's *De consolatione philosophiae* (523; *The Consolation of Philosophy*, late ninth century) and the Horatian odes of the seventeenth century Polish writer Sarbiewski. In these, the "country shades" are the seat of refuge in an uncertain world, the residence of virtue, and the best route to blessedness. Moreover, affixed to the volume are three prose adaptations and translations by Vaughan: *Of the Benefit Wee may get by our Enemies*, after Plutarch; *Of the Diseases of the Mind and the Body*, after Maximum Tirius; and *The Praise and Happiness of the Countrie-Life*, after Antonio de Guevera. In this last, Vaughan renders one passage: "*Pietie and Religion* may be better Cherish'd and preserved in the Country than any where else."

The themes of humility, patience, and Christian stoicism abound in *Olor Iscanus* in many ways, frequently enveloped in singular works praising life in the country. The literary landscape of pastoral melds with Vaughan's Welsh countryside. For Vaughan, the enforced move back to the country ultimately became a boon; his retirement from a "world gone mad" (his words) was no capitulation, but a pattern for endurance. It would especially preserve and sustain the Anglican faith that two civil wars had challenged. In Vaughan's greatest work, *Silex Scintillans*, the choices that Vaughan made for himself are expressed, defended, and celebrated in varied, often brilliant ways.

## SILEX SCINTILLANS

New readers of *Silex Scintillans* owe it to themselves and to Vaughan to consider it a whole book containing engaging individual lyrics; in this way its thematic, emotional, and Imagistic patterns and cross references will become apparent. The first part contains seventy-seven lyrics; it was entered in the Stationers' Register on March 28, 1650, and includes the anonymous engraving dramatizing the title. Fifty-seven lyrics were added for the 1655 edition, including a preface. The first part appears to be the more intense, many of the poems finding Vaughan reconstructing the moment of spiritual illumination. The second part finds Vaughan extending the implications of the first. Above all, though, the whole of *Silex Scintillans* promotes the active life of the spirit, the contemplative life of natural, rural solitude.

Some of the primary characteristics of Vaughan's poetry are prominently displayed in *Silex Scintillans*. First, there is the influence of the Welsh language and Welsh verse. Welsh is highly assonant; consider these lines from the opening poem, "Regeneration": "Yet *i*t was frost w*i*th*i*n/ And surly w*i*nds/ Blasted my *i*nfant buds, and s*i*nne/ L*i*ke clouds eccl*i*ps'd my m*i*nd." The *dyfalu*, or layering of comparison upon comparison, is a technique of Welsh verse that Vaughan brings to his English verse. A second characteristic is Vaughan's use of Scripture. For example, the idea of spiritual espousal that informs the Song of Solomon is brought forward to the poet's own time and place. "Hark! how his *winds* have chang'd their *note*,/ And with warm *whispers call* thee out" ("The Revival") recalls the Song of Solomon 2:11-12. In "The Dawning," Vaughan imagines the last day of humankind and incorporates the language of the biblical Last Judgment into the cycle of a natural day. Will man's judge come at night, asks the poet, or "shal these early, fragrant hours/ Unlock thy bowres? . . ./ That with thy glory doth best chime,/ All now are stirring, ev'ry field/ Ful hymns doth yield."

Vaughan adapts and extends scriptural symbols and situations to his own particular spiritual crisis and resolution less doctrinally than poetically. In this practice, Vaughan follows Herbert, surely another important influence, especially in *Silex Scintillans*. Nearly sixty poems use a word or phrase important to *The Temple*; some borrowings are direct responses, as in the concluding lines of "The Proffer," recalling Herbert's "The Size." Sometimes the response is direct; Vaughan's "The Match" responds to Herbert's "The Proffer." Herbert provided Vaughan with an example of what the best poetry does, both instructing the reader and communicating one's own particular vision. This is Vaughan's greatest debt to Herbert, and it prompts his praise for the author of *The Temple* in the preface to *Silex Scintillans*. Further, Vaughan emulates Herbert's book of unified lyrics, but the overall structure of *The Temple*—governed by church architecture and by the church calendar—is transformed in Vaughan to the Temple of Nature, with its own rhythms and purposes.

The Temple of Nature, God's "second" book, is alive with divinity. The Welsh have traditionally imagined themselves to be in communication with the elements, with flora and fauna; in Vaughan, the tradition is enhanced by Hermetic philosophy, which maintained that the sensible world was made by God to see God in it. The poet no doubt knew the work of his brother Thomas, one of the leading Hermetic voices of the time. Henry Vaughan adapts concepts from Hermeticism (as in the lyric based on Romans 8:19), and also borrows from its vocabulary: Beam, balsam, commerce, essence, exhalations, keys, ties, sympathies occur throughout *Silex Scintillans*, lending force to a poetic vision already imbued with natural energy. "Observe God in his works," Vaughan writes in "Rules and Lessons," noting that one cannot miss "his Praise; Each *tree, herb, flowre*/

Are shadows of his wisedome, and his *Pow'r*."

Vaughan is no pre-Romantic nature lover, however, as some early commentators have suggested. Rather, *Silex Scintillans* often relies on metaphors of active husbandry and rural contemplation drawn from the twin streams of pagan and biblical pastoral. Many of the lyrics mourn the loss of simplicity and primitive holiness; others confirm the validity of retirement; still others extend the notion of husbandry to cultivating a paradise within as a means of recovering the lost past. Drawing on the Cavalier poets' technique of suggesting pastoral values and perspective by including certain details or references to pastoral poems, such as sheep, cots, or cells, Vaughan intensifies and varies these themes. Moreover, he crosses from secular traditions of rural poetry to sacred ones. "The Shepheards"—a nativity poem—is one fine example of Vaughan's ability to conflate biblical pastoralism asserting the birth of Christ with "literary" conventions regarding shepherds.

Several poems illuminating these important themes in *Silex Scintillans*, are "Religion," "The Brittish Church," "Isaac's Marriage," and "The Retreate" (loss of simplicity associated with the primitive church); "Corruption," "Vanity of Spirit," "Misery," "Content," and "Jesus Weeping" (the validity of retirement); "The Resolve," "Love, and Discipline," "The Seed Growing Secretly," "Righteousness," and "Retirement" (cultivating one's own paradise within). These are, of course, not the only lyrics articulating these themes, nor are these themes "keys" to all the poems of *Silex Scintillans*, but Vaughan's treatment of them suggests a reaffirmation of the self-sufficiency celebrated in his secular work and devotional prose. In his finest volume of poems, however, this strategy for prevailing against unfortunate turns of religion and politics rests on a heartfelt knowledge that even the best human efforts must be tempered by divine love.

## THALIA REDIVIVA

Vaughan's last collection of poems, *Thalia Rediviva*, was subtitled *The Pass-times and Diversions of a Countrey-Muse*, as if to reiterate his regional link with the Welsh countryside. The John Williams who wrote the dedicatory epistle for the collection was probably Prebendary of Saint David's, who within two years became archdeacon of Cardigan. He was probably responsible for soliciting the commendatory poems printed at the front of the volume. That Vaughan gave his endorsement to this Restoration issue of new lyrics is borne out by the fact that he takes pains to mention it to his cousin John Aubrey, author of *Brief Lives* (1898) in an autobiographical letter written June 15, 1673. Moreover, when it finally appeared, the poet probably was already planning to republish *Olor Iscanus*. Thus, though his great volume of verse was public reading for more than two decades, Vaughan had not repudiated his other work.

Nor would he have much to apologize for, since many of the finest lyrics in this miscellany are religious, extending pastoral and retirement motifs from *Silex Scintillans*: "Retirement," "The Nativity," "The True Christmas," "The Bee," and "To the pious memorie of C. W. . . . ." Moreover, *Thalia Rediviva* contains numerous topical poems and translations, many presumably written after *Silex Scintillans*. The most elaborate of these pieces is a formal pastoral eclogue, an elegy presumably written to honor the poet's twin, Thomas. It is Vaughan's most overt treatment of literary pastoral; it closes on a note that ties its matter to the diurnal rhythms of the world, but one can recognize in it the spirit of *Silex Scintillans*: "While feral birds send forth unpleasant notes,/ And night (the Nurse of thoughts,) sad thoughts promotes./ But Joy will yet come with the morning-light,/ Though sadly now we bid good night!" Though not moving in the dramatic fashion of *Silex Scintillans* through a reconstruction of the moment and impact of divine illumination, the poems of *Thalia Rediviva* nevertheless offer further confirmation of Vaughan's self-appointed place in the literature of his age.

OTHER MAJOR WORKS

NONFICTION: *The Mount of Olives: Or, Solitary Devotions*, 1652.

TRANSLATIONS: *Hermetical Physick*, 1655 (of Heinrich Nolle); *The Chymists Key to Open and to Shut*, 1657 (of Nolle).

MISCELLANEOUS: *The Works of Henry Vaughan*, 1914, 1957 (L. C. Martin, editor).

BIBLIOGRAPHY

Davies, Stevie. *Henry Vaughan*. Chester Springs, Pa.: Dufour Editions, 1995. A concise historical narrative of the life and works of Vaughan. Includes an index and a bibliography.

Dickson, Donald R., and Holly Faith Nelson, eds. *Of Paradise and Light: Essays on Henry Vaughan and John Milton in Honor of Alan Rudrum*. Newark: University of Delaware Press, 2004. A collection of essays on Vaughan and Milton; topics include *Silex Scintillans*, nature, and religion.

Manning, John. *The Swan of Usk: The Poetry of Henry Vaughan*. Lampeter: Trivium, University of Wales, Lampeter, 2008. Part of the Tucker Lecture series, this work examines the poetry of Vaughan in detail.

Nelson, Holly Faith. "Historical Consciousness and the Politics of Translation in the Psalms of Henry Vaughan." In *John Donne and the Metaphysical Poets*, edited by Harold Bloom. New York: Bloom's Literary Criticism, 2010. Examines Vaughan's psalms and treats Vaughan as a Metaphysical poet.

Post, Jonathan F. S. *Henry Vaughan: The Unfolding Vision*. Princeton, N.J.: Princeton University Press, 1982. Post, who divides his emphasis between Vaughan's secular and religious poems, declares the heart of his study is *Silex Scintillans*. Although he covers many of Vaughan's poems, some—among them "The Night" and "Regeneration"—receive lengthy analysis. Contains a general index, as well as an index to Vaughan's poems.

Shawcross, John T. "Kidnapping the Poets: The Romantics and Henry Vaughan." In

*Milton, the Metaphysicals, and Romanticism*, edited by Lisa Low and Anthony John Harding. New York: Cambridge University Press, 2009. Looks at the influence of Vaughan and other Metaphysicals on Romanticism.

Sullivan, Ceri. *The Rhetoric of the Conscience in Donne, Herbert, and Vaughan*. New York: Oxford University Press, 2009. Notes that these poets—Vaughan, John Donne, and George Herbert—see the conscience as only partly under their own control. Finds similarities in the ways these poets seek their authentic nature in relation to the divine.

Young, R. V. *Doctrine and Devotion in Seventeenth-Century Poetry: Studies in Donne, Herbert, Crashaw, and Vaughan*. Rochester, N.Y.: D. S. Brewer, 2000. Young provides a critical interpretation of English early modern and Christian poetry. Includes bibliographical references and index.

*Kenneth Friedenreich*

# CHECKLIST FOR EXPLICATING A POEM

## I. The Initial Readings

A. Before reading the poem, the reader should:
1. Notice its form and length.
2. Consider the title, determining, if possible, whether it might function as an allusion, symbol, or poetic image.
3. Notice the date of composition or publication, and identify the general era of the poet.

B. The poem should be read intuitively and emotionally and be allowed to "happen" as much as possible.

C. In order to establish the rhythmic flow, the poem should be reread. A note should be made as to where the irregular spots (if any) are located.

## II. Explicating the Poem

A. *Dramatic situation.* Studying the poem line by line helps the reader discover the dramatic situation. All elements of the dramatic situation are interrelated and should be viewed as reflecting and affecting one another. The dramatic situation serves a particular function in the poem, adding realism, surrealism, or absurdity; drawing attention to certain parts of the poem; and changing to reinforce other aspects of the poem. All points should be considered. The following questions are particularly helpful to ask in determining dramatic situation:
1. What, if any, is the narrative action in the poem?
2. How many personae appear in the poem? What part do they take in the action?
3. What is the relationship between characters?
4. What is the setting (time and location) of the poem?

B. *Point of view.* An understanding of the poem's point of view is a major step toward comprehending the poet's intended meaning. The reader should ask:
1. Who is the speaker? Is he or she addressing someone else or the reader?
2. Is the narrator able to understand or see everything happening to him or her, or does the reader know things that the narrator does not?
3. Is the narrator reliable?
4. Do point of view and dramatic situation seem consistent? If not, the inconsistencies may provide clues to the poem's meaning.

C. *Images and metaphors.* Images and metaphors are often the most intricately crafted vehicles of the poem for relaying the poet's message. Realizing that the images and metaphors work in harmony with the dramatic situation and point of view will help the reader to see the poem as a whole, rather than as disassociated elements.

1. The reader should identify the concrete images (that is, those that are formed from objects that can be touched, smelled, seen, felt, or tasted). Is the image projected by the poet consistent with the physical object?
2. If the image is abstract, or so different from natural imagery that it cannot be associated with a real object, then what are the properties of the image?
3. To what extent is the reader asked to form his or her own images?
4. Is any image repeated in the poem? If so, how has it been changed? Is there a controlling image?
5. Are any images compared to each other? Do they reinforce one another?
6. Is there any difference between the way the reader perceives the image and the way the narrator sees it?
7. What seems to be the narrator's or persona's attitude toward the image?

D. *Words.* Every substantial word in a poem may have more than one intended meaning, as used by the author. Because of this, the reader should look up many of these words in the dictionary and:

1. Note all definitions that have the slightest connection with the poem.
2. Note any changes in syntactical patterns in the poem.
3. In particular, note those words that could possibly function as symbols or allusions, and refer to any appropriate sources for further information.

E. *Meter, rhyme, structure, and tone.* In scanning the poem, all elements of prosody should be noted by the reader. These elements are often used by a poet to manipulate the reader's emotions, and therefore they should be examined closely to arrive at the poet's specific intention.

1. Does the basic meter follow a traditional pattern such as those found in nursery rhymes or folk songs?
2. Are there any variations in the base meter? Such changes or substitutions are important thematically and should be identified.
3. Are the rhyme schemes traditional or innovative, and what might their form mean to the poem?
4. What devices has the poet used to create sound patterns (such as assonance and alliteration)?
5. Is the stanza form a traditional or innovative one?
6. If the poem is composed of verse paragraphs rather than stanzas, how do they affect the progression of the poem?

7. After examining the above elements, is the resultant tone of the poem casual or formal, pleasant, harsh, emotional, authoritative?

F. *Historical context.* The reader should attempt to place the poem into historical context, checking on events at the time of composition. Archaic language, expressions, images, or symbols should also be looked up.

G. *Themes and motifs.* By seeing the poem as a composite of emotion, intellect, craftsmanship, and tradition, the reader should be able to determine the themes and motifs (smaller recurring ideas) presented in the work. He or she should ask the following questions to help pinpoint these main ideas:
   1. Is the poet trying to advocate social, moral, or religious change?
   2. Does the poet seem sure of his or her position?
   3. Does the poem appeal primarily to the emotions, to the intellect, or to both?
   4. Is the poem relying on any particular devices for effect (such as imagery, allusion, paradox, hyperbole, or irony)?

# BIBLIOGRAPHY

GENERAL REFERENCE SOURCES

**CRITICISM**

Brooks, Cleanth, and Robert Penn Warren. *Understanding Poetry*. 4th ed. Reprint. Fort Worth, Tex.: Heinle & Heinle, 2003.

Cline, Gloria Stark, and Jeffrey A. Baker. *An Index to Criticism of British and American Poetry*. Metuchen, N.J.: Scarecrow Press, 1973.

Day, Gary. *Literary Criticism: A New History*. Edinburgh, Scotland: Edinburgh University Press, 2008.

Donow, Herbert S., comp. *The Sonnet in England and America: A Bibliography of Criticism*. Westport, Conn.: Greenwood Press, 1982.

Draper, James P., ed. *World Literature Criticism 1500 to the Present: A Selection of Major Authors from Gale's Literary Criticism Series*. 6 vols. Detroit: Gale Research, 1992.

Habib, M. A. R. *A History of Literary Criticism: From Plato to the Present*. Malden, Mass.: Wiley-Blackwell, 2005.

Jason, Philip K., ed. *Masterplots II: Poetry Series, Revised Edition*. 8 vols. Pasadena, Calif.: Salem Press, 2002.

*Literature Criticism from 1400 to 1800*. Detroit: Gale Research, 1984-    .

Magill, Frank N., ed. *Magill's Bibliography of Literary Criticism*. 4 vols. Englewood Cliffs, N.J.: Salem Press, 1979.

*MLA International Bibliography*. New York: Modern Language Association of America, 1922-    .

Vedder, Polly, ed. *World Literature Criticism Supplement: A Selection of Major Authors from Gale's Literary Criticism Series*. 2 vols. Detroit: Gale Research, 1997.

_____. *Traditional Poetry: Medieval to Late Victorian*. Vol. 2 in *The Explicator Cyclopedia*. Chicago: Quadrangle Books, 1968.

*The Year's Work in English Studies*. 1921-    .

Young, Robyn V., ed. *Poetry Criticism: Excerpts from Criticism of the Works of the Most Significant and Widely Studied Poets of World Literature*. 29 vols. Detroit: Gale Research, 1991.


**DICTIONARIES, HISTORIES, AND HANDBOOKS**

Deutsch, Babette. *Poetry Handbook: A Dictionary of Terms*. 4th ed. New York: Funk & Wagnalls, 1974.

Drury, John. *The Poetry Dictionary*. Cincinnati, Ohio: Story Press, 1995.

Kinzie, Mary. *A Poet's Guide to Poetry*. Chicago: University of Chicago Press, 1999.

Lennard, John. *The Poetry Handbook: A Guide to Reading Poetry for Pleasure and Practical Criticism.* New York: Oxford University Press, 1996.

Matterson, Stephen, and Darryl Jones. *Studying Poetry.* New York: Oxford University Press, 2000.

Packard, William. *The Poet's Dictionary: A Handbook of Prosody and Poetic Devices.* New York: Harper & Row, 1989.

Preminger, Alex, et al., eds. *The New Princeton Encyclopedia of Poetry and Poetics.* 3d rev. ed. Princeton, N.J.: Princeton University Press, 1993.

Shipley, Joseph Twadell, ed. *Dictionary of World Literary Terms, Forms, Technique, Criticism.* Rev. ed. Boston: Writer, 1970.

### INDEXES OF PRIMARY WORKS

Frankovich, Nicholas, ed. *The Columbia Granger's Index to Poetry in Anthologies.* 11th ed. New York: Columbia University Press, 1997.

_____. *The Columbia Granger's Index to Poetry in Collected and Selected Works.* New York: Columbia University Press, 1997.

Hazen, Edith P., ed. *Columbia Granger's Index to Poetry.* 10th ed. New York: Columbia University Press, 1994.

Kline, Victoria. *Last Lines: An Index to the Last Lines of Poetry.* 2 vols. Vol. 1, *Last Line Index, Title Index*; Vol. 2, *Author Index, Keyword Index.* New York: Facts On File, 1991.

### POETICS, POETIC FORMS, AND GENRES

Attridge, Derek. *Poetic Rhythm: An Introduction.* New York: Cambridge University Press, 1995.

Brogan, T. V. F. *English Versification, 1570-1980: A Reference Guide with a Global Appendix.* Baltimore: Johns Hopkins University Press, 1981.

_____. *Verseform: A Comparative Bibliography.* Baltimore: Johns Hopkins University Press, 1989.

Fussell, Paul. *Poetic Meter and Poetic Form.* Rev. ed. New York: McGraw-Hill, 1979.

Hollander, John. *Rhyme's Reason.* 3d ed. New Haven, Conn.: Yale University Press, 2001.

Malof, Joseph. *A Manual of English Meters.* Bloomington: Indiana University Press, 1970.

Padgett, Ron, ed. *The Teachers and Writers Handbook of Poetic Forms.* 2d ed. New York: Teachers & Writers Collaborative, 2000.

Pinsky, Robert. *The Sounds of Poetry: A Brief Guide.* New York: Farrar, Straus and Giroux, 1998.

Preminger, Alex, and T. V. F. Brogan, eds. *New Princeton Encyclopedia of Poetry and Poetics.* 3d ed. Princeton, N.J.: Princeton University Press, 1993.

Shapiro, Karl, and Robert Beum. *A Prosody Handbook*. New York: Harper, 1965.

Spiller, Michael R. G. *The Sonnet Sequence: A Study of Its Strategies*. Studies in Literary Themes and Genres 13. New York: Twayne, 1997.

Turco, Lewis. *The New Book of Forms: A Handbook of Poetics*. Hanover: University Press of New England, 1986.

Williams, Miller. *Patterns of Poetry: An Encyclopedia of Forms*. Baton Rouge: Louisiana State University Press, 1986.


BRITISH RENAISSANCE POETRY

Frank, Joseph. *Hobbled Pegasus: A Descriptive Bibliography of Minor English Poetry, 1641-1660*. Albuquerque: University of New Mexico Press, 1968.

Gutierrez, Nancy A. *English Historical Poetry, 1476-1603: A Bibliography*. Garland Reference Library of the Humanities 410. New York: Garland, 1983.

Martinez, Nancy C., and Joseph G. R. Martinez. *Renaissance*. Vol. 2 in *Guide to British Poetry Explication*. Boston: G. K. Hall, 1991.

Ringler, William A., Jr. *Bibliography and Index of English Verse Printed 1476-1558*. New York: Mansell, 1988.

Ringler, William A., Michael Rudick, and Susan J. Ringler. *Bibliography and Index of English Verse in Manuscript, 1501-1558*. New York: Mansell, 1992.

Rivers, Isabel. *Classical and Christian Ideas in English Renaissance Poetry: A Student's Guide*. 2d ed. New York: Routledge, 1994.

# GUIDE TO ONLINE RESOURCES

## WEB SITES

*The following sites were visited by the editors of Salem Press in 2010. Because URLs frequently change, the accuracy of these addresses cannot be guaranteed; however, long-standing sites, such as those of colleges and universities, national organizations, and government agencies, generally maintain links when their sites are moved.*

### The Cambridge History of English and American Literature
http://www.bartleby.com/cambridge

This site provides an exhaustive examination of the development of all forms of literature in Great Britain and the United States. The multivolume set on which this site is based was published in 1907-1921 but remains a relevant, classic work. It offers "a wide selection of writing on orators, humorists, poets, newspaper columnists, religious leaders, economists, Native Americans, song writers, and even non-English writing, such as Yiddish and Creole."

### LiteraryHistory.com
http://www.literaryhistory.com

This site is an excellent source of academic, scholarly, and critical literature about eighteenth, nineteenth, and twentieth century American and English writers. It provides numerous pages about specific eras and genres, including individual pages for eighteenth, nineteenth, and twentieth century literature and for African American and postcolonial literatures. These pages contain alphabetical lists of authors that link to articles, reviews, overviews, excerpts of works, teaching guides, podcasts, and other materials.

### Literary Resources on the Net
http://andromeda.rutgers.edu/~jlynch/Lit

Jack Lynch of Rutgers University maintains this extensive collection of links to Web sites that are useful to researchers, including numerous sites about American and English literature. This collection is a good place to begin online research about poetry, as it links to other sites with broad ranges of literary topics. The site is organized chronologically, with separate pages about the Middle Ages, the Renaissance, the eighteenth century, the Romantic and Victorian eras, and twentieth century British and Irish literature. It also has separate pages providing links to Web sites about American literature and to women's literature and feminism.

## LitWeb

http://litweb.net

LitWeb provides biographies of hundreds of world authors throughout history that can be accessed through an alphabetical listing. The pages about each writer contain a list of his or her works, suggestions for further reading, and illustrations. The site also offers information about past and present winners of major literary prizes.

## Poet's Corner

http://theotherpages.org/poems

The Poet's Corner, one of the oldest text resources on the Web, provides access to about seven thousand works of poetry by several hundred different poets from around the world. Indexes are arranged and searchable by title, name of poet, or subject. The site also offers its own resources, including Faces of the Poets—a gallery of portraits— and Lives of the Poets—a growing collection of biographies.

## Representative Poetry Online

http://rpo.library.utoronto.ca

This award-winning resource site, maintained by Ian Lancashire of the Department of English at the University of Toronto in Canada, has several thousand English- language poems by hundreds of poets. The collection is searchable by poet's name, title of work, first line of a poem, and keyword. The site also includes a time line, a glossary, essays, an extensive bibliography, and countless links organized by country and by subject.

## Western European Studies

http://wess.lib.byu.edu

The Western European Studies Section of the Association of College and Research Libraries maintains this collection of resources useful to students of Western European history and culture. It also is a good place to find information about non-English- language literature. The site includes separate pages about the literatures and languages of the Netherlands, France, Germany, Iberia, Italy, and Scandinavia, in which users can find links to electronic texts, association Web sites, journals, and other materials, the majority of which are written in the languages of the respective countries.

## ELECTRONIC DATABASES

*Electronic databases usually do not have their own URLs. Instead, public, college, and university libraries subscribe to these databases, provide links to them on their Web sites, and make them available to library card holders or other specified patrons. Readers can visit library Web sites or ask reference librarians to check on availability.*

### Canadian Literary Centre

Produced by EBSCO, the Canadian Literary Centre database contains full-text content from ECW Press, a Toronto-based publisher, including the titles in the publisher's Canadian fiction studies, Canadian biography, and Canadian writers and their works series, *ECW's Biographical Guide to Canadian Novelists*, and *George Woodcock's Introduction to Canadian Fiction*. Author biographies, essays and literary criticism, and book reviews are among the database's offerings.

### Literary Reference Center

EBSCO's Literary Reference Center (LRC) is a comprehensive full-text database designed primarily to help high school and undergraduate students in English and the humanities with homework and research assignments about literature. The database contains massive amounts of information from reference works, books, literary journals, and other materials, including more than 31,000 plot summaries, synopses, and overviews of literary works; almost 100,000 essays and articles of literary criticism; about 140,000 author biographies; more than 605,000 book reviews; and more than 5,200 author interviews. It also contains the entire contents of Salem Press's MagillOnLiterature Plus. Users can retrieve information by browsing a list of authors' names or titles of literary works; they can also use an advanced search engine to access information by numerous categories, including author name, gender, cultural identity, national identity, and the years in which he or she lived, or by literary title, character, locale, genre, and publication date. The Literary Reference Center also features a literary-historical time line, an encyclopedia of literature, and a glossary of literary terms.

### MagillOnLiterature Plus

MagillOnLiterature Plus is a comprehensive, integrated literature database produced by Salem Press and available on the EBSCOhost platform. The database contains the full text of essays in Salem's many literature-related reference works, including *Masterplots*, *Cyclopedia of World Authors*, *Cyclopedia of Literary Characters*, *Cyclopedia of Literary Places*, *Critical Survey of Poetry*, *Critical Survey of Long Fiction*, *Critical Survey of Short Fiction*, *World Philosophers and Their Works*, *Magill's Literary Annual*, and *Magill's Book Reviews*. Among its contents are articles on more than 35,000 literary works and more than 8,500 poets, writers, dramatists, essayists, and philosophers; more than 1,000 images; and a glossary of more than 1,300 literary terms. The biographical essays include lists of authors' works and secondary bibliographies, and hundreds of overview essays examine and discuss literary genres, time periods, and national literatures.

*Rebecca Kuzins; updated by Desiree Dreeuws*

# CATEGORY INDEX

# SUBJECT INDEX

*Subject Index*